The Modern Vulkan Cookbook

A practical guide to 3D graphics and advanced real-time rendering techniques in Vulkan

Preetish Kakkar

Mauricio Maurer

<packt>

The Modern Vulkan Cookbook

Copyright © 2024 Packt Publishing

All rights reserved. No part of this book may be reproduced, stored in a retrieval system, or transmitted in any form or by any means, without the prior written permission of the publisher, except in the case of brief quotations embedded in critical articles or reviews.

Every effort has been made in the preparation of this book to ensure the accuracy of the information presented. However, the information contained in this book is sold without warranty, either express or implied. Neither the authors, nor Packt Publishing or its dealers and distributors, will be held liable for any damages caused or alleged to have been caused directly or indirectly by this book.

Packt Publishing has endeavored to provide trademark information about all of the companies and products mentioned in this book by the appropriate use of capitals. However, Packt Publishing cannot guarantee the accuracy of this information.

Group Product Manager: Rohit Rajkumar

Publishing Product Manager: Kaustubh Manglurkar

Book Project Manager: Sonam Pandey

Senior Editor: Nathanya Dias

Technical Editor: Reenish Kulshrestha

Copy Editor: Safis Editing

Indexer: Pratik Shirodkar

Production Designer: Prafulla Nikalje

DevRel Marketing Coordinators: Anamika Singh and Nivedita Pandey

First published: April 2024

Production reference: 1150324

Published by Packt Publishing Ltd.
Grosvenor House
11 St Paul's Square
Birmingham
B3 1RB, UK

ISBN 978-1-80323-998-9

www.packtpub.com

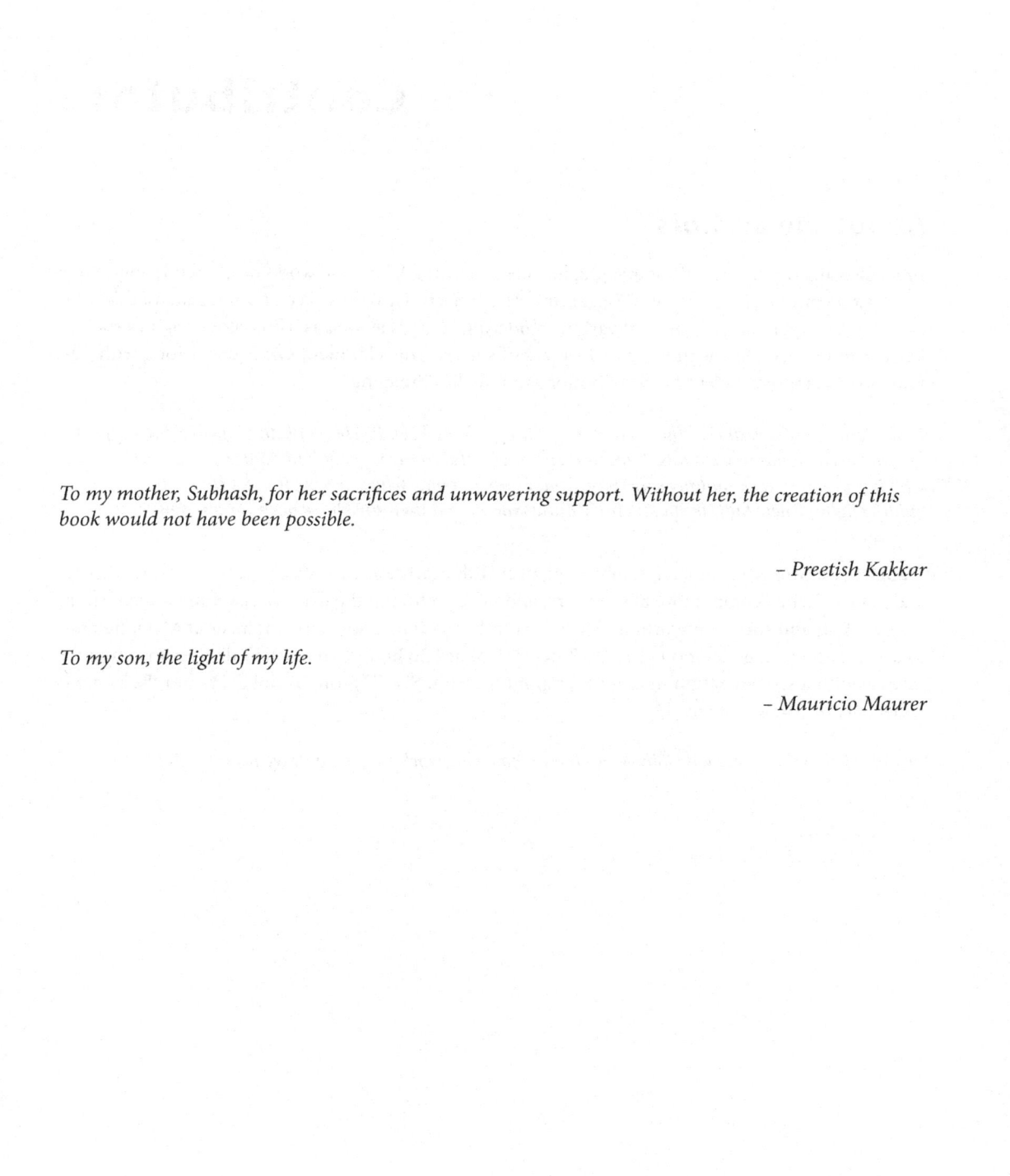

To my mother, Subhash, for her sacrifices and unwavering support. Without her, the creation of this book would not have been possible.

– *Preetish Kakkar*

To my son, the light of my life.

– *Mauricio Maurer*

Contributors

About the authors

Preetish Kakkar is a senior computer graphics engineer with Adobe and works on the rendering engine that powers products such as Aero, Stager, and After Effects. He has worked at Microsoft, MathWorks, and Stryker, where he co-authored various rendering engines as well as using other engines such as Unreal and Unity. He has more than 15 years of software development experience along with 10+ years in 3D graphics, scientific visualization, and medical imaging.

In the journey of life, and in the path of my writing, I have been blessed with the unwavering support of some exceptional individuals. I am immensely grateful to my wife, Saloni, and my son, Aarush, who has been my rock and my sanctuary, and to my parents, who were my first teachers and my guiding lights. Their faith in me, their encouragement, and their love have been my strength and my inspiration.

Mauricio Maurer is a computer graphics engineer with nearly 20 years of experience working with 2D and 3D rendering, computational geometry, and rasterization in the fields of scientific visualization, CAD/CAM, and social networking. He is currently a graphics software engineer at Meta, helping to develop the next generation of AR/VR devices. Mauricio holds two master's degrees in computer science with a specialization in computer graphics from SUNY Stony Brook, NY, and the Federal University of Parana, Brazil.

I would like to thank my wife, Silvye, without whom this work would not have been possible.

About the reviewers

Kevin Nappoly is a software engineer at Enduring Games, specializing in graphics/rendering, where he also leads engineering project efforts. He has shipped six games across multiple current and previous generations of consoles and PC. During his tenure, he has worked with Vulkan, DirectX 12, DirectX 11, OpenGL, and other proprietary graphics APIs, and is very much interested in the low-level optimizations that go into game engine architecture and design.

Mausam Yadav is a distinguished graduate of the **National Institute of Technology (NITP)** Patna, with a passion for technological innovation. As a **Graphics Processing Unit (GPU)** software engineer at Qualcomm, Mausam's expertise and experience have established him as a leader in his field. His professional journey includes valuable contributions to prominent hardware and software companies such as Balize and Embinsys Technologies.

Mausam's dedication to cutting-edge research in accelerator architecture and systems, coupled with his extensive work on GPUs and **Graph Streaming Processor (GSP)**, has solidified his reputation as a trailblazer in the realm of technology.

Table of Contents

Preface — xv

1

Vulkan Core Concepts — 23

Technical requirements	24	Enumerating available instance extensions	36
Getting to know the Vulkan API	25	Getting ready	36
Calling API functions	26	How to do it…	36
Getting ready	26	Initializing the Vulkan instance	38
How to do it…	27	Getting ready	38
Learning about Vulkan objects	28	How to do it…	38
Getting ready	29	Creating a surface	39
How to do it…	29	Getting ready	39
Using Volk to load Vulkan functions and extensions	30	How to do it…	39
Getting ready	30	Enumerating Vulkan physical devices	40
How to do it…	31	Getting ready	40
Using Vulkan extensions correctly	31	How to do it…	41
Getting ready	32	Caching the properties of queue families	41
How to do it…	32	Getting ready	42
Using the Validation Layer for error checking	33	How to do it…	42
Getting ready	33	Enumerating physical device extensions	43
How to do it…	33	Getting ready	43
Enumerating available instance layers	34	How to do it…	43
Getting ready	34	Reserving queue families	44
How to do it…	35		

Getting ready	44
How to do it…	44

Creating a Vulkan logical device 46
Getting ready	46
How to do it…	46

Retrieving the queue object handle 47
Getting ready	48
How to do it…	48

Creating a command pool 48
Getting ready	48
How to do it…	49

Allocating, recording, and submitting commands 49
Getting ready	49
How to do it…	50

Reusing command buffers 51
Getting ready	52
How to do it…	52

Creating render passes 53
Getting ready	55
How to do it…	55

Creating framebuffers 59
Getting ready	59
How to do it…	59

Creating image views 60
Getting ready	60
How to do it…	60

The Vulkan graphics pipeline 61
How to do it...	63

Compiling shaders to SPIR-V 63
Getting ready	63
How to do it…	64

Dynamic states 66
Getting ready	67
How to do it…	67

Creating a graphics pipeline 68
Getting ready	68
How to do it…	68

Swapchain 69
Getting ready	69
How to do it…	69

Understanding synchronization in the swapchain – fences and semaphores 70
Getting ready	70
How to do it…	70

Populating submission information for presentation 73
Getting ready	73
How to do it…	73

Presenting images 74
Getting ready	74
How to do it…	74

Rendering a triangle 74
Getting ready	74
How to do it…	75

2
Working with Modern Vulkan 81

Technical requirements	82	Getting ready	99
Understanding Vulkan's memory model	82	How to do it…	99
		Providing shader data	**100**
Getting ready	82	Getting ready	100
How to do it…	84	How to do it…	100
Instantiating the VMA library	**84**	Specifying descriptor sets with descriptor set layouts	101
How to do it…	85	Getting ready	101
Creating buffers	**85**	How to do it…	102
Getting ready	86	Passing data to shaders using push constants	104
How to do it…	86	Getting ready	104
Uploading data to buffers	**87**	How to do it…	104
		Creating a pipeline layout	105
Getting ready	87	Getting ready	105
How to do it…	88	How to do it…	105
Creating a staging buffer	**89**	Creating a descriptor pool	106
Getting ready	89	Getting ready	106
How to do it…	89	How to do it…	106
How to avoid data races using ring buffers	**90**	Allocating descriptor sets	107
		Getting ready	107
Getting ready	91	How to do it…	107
How to do it…	91	Updating descriptor sets during rendering	108
Setting up pipeline barriers	**92**	Getting ready	108
Getting ready	93	How to do it…	108
How to do it…	94	Passing resources to shaders (binding descriptor sets)	111
Creating images (textures)	**95**	Getting ready	111
Getting ready	96	How to do it…	111
How to do it…	96	Updating push constants during rendering	111
Creating an image view	**97**	Getting ready	111
Getting ready	97	How to do it…	111
How to do it…	98	**Customizing shader behavior with specialization constants**	**112**
Creating a sampler	**99**	Getting ready	112
		How to do it…	112

Implementing MDI and PVP	113	Getting ready	117
Implementing MDI	113	How to do it...	117
Getting ready	114	**Transferring resources between**	
How to do it...	115	**queue families**	**118**
Using PVP	115	Getting ready	118
Getting ready	116	How to do it...	119
How to do it...	116		
Adding flexibility to the rendering pipeline using dynamic rendering	**117**		

3

Implementing GPU-Driven Rendering   125

Technical requirements	126	Drawing text using SDF	139
Implementing GPU-driven line rendering	**126**	Getting ready	141
		How to do it...	141
Getting ready	126	See also	147
How to do it...	126	**Frustum culling using compute shaders**	**147**
Expanding line-drawing techniques to render textual values from shaders	**133**	Getting ready	148
Getting ready	133	How to do it...	148
How to do it...	133	How it works...	150

4

Exploring Techniques for Lighting, Shading, and Shadows   155

Technical requirements	155	Getting ready	160
Implementing G-buffer for deferred rendering	**156**	How to do it...	160
		See also	164
Getting ready	156	**Implementing shadow maps for real-time shadows**	**164**
How to do it...	157		
Implementing screen space reflections	**159**	Getting ready	165
		How to do it...	165

There's more…	171	See also	177
See also	171	**Implementing a lighting pass for illuminating the scene**	**177**
Implementing screen space ambient occlusion	**172**	Getting ready	177
Getting ready	172	How to do it…	178
How to do it…	173		

5

Deciphering Order-Independent Transparency   185

Technical requirements	186	How to do it…	201
Implementing Depth-Peeling	186	There's more…	208
Getting ready	186	See also	208
How to do it…	187	**Implementing Weighted Order-Independent Transparency**	**208**
Implementing Dual Depth-Peeling	192	Getting ready	209
Getting ready	192	How to do it…	209
How to do it…	193	There's more…	213
Implementing Linked-List Order-Independent Transparency	201	See also	213
Getting ready	201		

6

Anti-Aliasing Techniques   215

Technical requirements	215	**Utilizing TAA**	**229**
Enabling and using Vulkan's MSAA	216	Getting ready	231
Getting ready	216	How to do it…	232
How to do it…	217	**Applying DLSS**	**237**
Applying FXAA	**219**	Getting ready	237
Getting ready	219	How to do it…	238
How to do it…	220	See also	241

7

Ray Tracing and Hybrid Rendering 243

Technical requirements	244	See also	265
Implementing a GPU ray tracer	244	Implementing hybrid rendering	265
Monte Carlo method	247	Getting ready	266
Getting ready	248	How to do it…	266
How to do it…	250		

8

Extended Reality with OpenXR 269

Technical requirements	270	Retrieving eye gaze information from OpenXR in your app	287
Getting started with OpenXR	270	Getting ready	287
Getting ready	271	How to do it…	288
How to do it…	273		
See also	281	Implementing dynamic foveated rendering using Qualcomm's fragment density map Offset extension	294
How to implement single pass multiview rendering	281	Getting ready	295
Getting ready	282	How to do it…	295
How to do it…	282		
Implementing static foveated rendering with a fragment density map	283	Using half floats to reduce memory load	298
Getting ready	283	Getting ready	299
How to do it…	283	How to do it…	299
See also	287		

9
Debugging and Performance Measurement Techniques 301

Technical requirements	301	Intercepting validation	
Frame debugging	302	layer messages	313
Getting ready	302	Getting ready	313
How to do it…	303	How to do it…	313
See also	307	Retrieving debug information	
Naming Vulkan objects for		from shaders	315
easy debugging	308	Getting ready	316
Getting ready	308	How to do it…	316
How to do it…	309	Measuring performance in	
Printing values from shaders		Vulkan with timestamp queries	318
in Vulkan	310	Getting ready	318
Getting ready	311	How to do it…	319
How to do it…	311		

Index 323

Other Books You May Enjoy 330

Preface

This book is designed for experienced computer graphics software engineers who might be well versed in older graphics APIs such as OpenGL and DirectX 10 but are relatively new to modern graphics APIs. Like you, we found ourselves needing to learn Vulkan but struggling to implement practical solutions because we didn't understand the basic concepts of Vulkan, which is, in itself, a complicated and vast API. The goal of this book is to introduce you to the essential concepts of the API and then walk you through hand-picked, tried-and-true algorithms that show you the new and nuanced aspects of Vulkan in each recipe.

This book is divided into five parts and covers, in this order, the following:

- Basic Vulkan concepts, how and why to use them, and how they fit into the bigger picture of writing an application using the Vulkan API
- General graphics algorithms implemented using Vulkan, including their features and how they can be used to achieve all sorts of tasks relevant to graphics applications
- Using Vulkan to build a GPU ray tracer and a hybrid renderer
- How to use Vulkan and OpenXR to write applications for the incredible new world of VR, MR, and AR
- Ways to debug and profile your Vulkan implementation

There are many resources that cover the first part of what this book explores, but in this book, we offer a two-part story that progressively helps you understand the basic Vulkan concepts by providing easy and practical examples. The subsequent parts present implementations that work and can be used as a reference for the implementation of your own graphics engine.

The main goal of the repository provided with this book was not to achieve the highest performance, find clever ways to implement things, or even implement the shiniest new algorithm shown at last year's GDC or SIGGRAPH. It was simplicity and completeness. We offer tips and tricks on how some Vulkan features can and/or must be used, and most recipes have been tested and debugged and provide you with a self-contained working solution that you can improve and use in your own code base. Each recipe is its own executable and can be inspected independently from the others, making them easy to read. That also makes it easy to understand all the details of each algorithm from beginning to end.

Vulkan is the future de-facto graphics API for all devices and types of applications. It's a mature, feature-rich, and maintained API, supported by all GPU vendors, operating systems, frameworks, and languages. If you intend to write graphics applications or write one that uses only the compute facilities of Vulkan, getting to know the API is a must, and you need to learn it right now!

Who this book is for

This book has been written for experienced graphics software engineers who would like to learn more about Vulkan. Knowing at least one other graphics API, such as OpenGL, and one of its variants, such as WebGL, OpenGL ES, or DirectX (up to version 9 or 10), is suggested but not strictly necessary. It is important to know graphics principles, such as transformations, graphics pipelines, shaders, lighting, the basics of ray tracing, and depth and stencil buffers, to name a few. More advanced topics, such as PBR and all its concepts, aren't necessary but may be helpful.

Finally, the code has been written entirely in C++, as it is the most widely used programming language for writing graphics applications. Even though some C++20 features are used in the book because they help reduce Vulkan's verbosity, you are not expected to have intimate knowledge of the newest C++ features.

What this book covers

Chapter 1, Vulkan Core Concepts, provides a walk-through of the most basic Vulkan concepts and objects and how to create and use them. The chapter covers how Vulkan can be used and initialized and how its objects interplay and are managed from the application. At the end of the chapter, we present a recipe for how those concepts can be used to create the simplest graphics application in Vulkan.

Chapter 2, Working with Modern Vulkan, presents more advanced Vulkan concepts and objects, such as barriers, descriptors, and pipelines, that allow you to start using resources other than just data provided directly in the shader code. This chapter also offers a brief overview of modern rendering techniques, such as **Programmable Vertex Pulling** (**PVP**) and **Multidraw Indirect** (**MDI**).

Chapter 3, Implementing GPU-Driven Rendering, has recipes that implement what is called GPU-driven rendering: techniques that generate data directly from shaders with little or no input from the CPU. The generated data remains in the GPU after being generated and can be used to direct how to render a scene; or, the data can be presented directly on screen as debug information.

Chapter 4, Exploring Techniques for Lighting, Shading, and Shadows, explores known graphics techniques but from a Vulkan perspective. Recipes include implementations of deferred rendering, screen-space reflections, shadow maps, and screen-space ambient occlusion, demonstrating how to achieve practical results while navigating the complexity of Vulkan.

Chapter 5, Deciphering Order-Independent Transparency, contains recipes for implementing transparency using Vulkan, all the way from simpler algorithms, such as depth-peeling and dual depth-peeling, to more advanced and physically correct implementations, such as order-independent transparency, that run exclusively on the GPU. While some of those recipes may seem old, they really show the power of the Vulkan API.

Chapter 6, Anti-Aliasing Techniques, provides a comprehensive list of anti-aliasing techniques that can be used with Vulkan. The first recipe uses the multisample anti-aliasing feature provided by Vulkan, while the others offer alternate ways to provide antialiasing without using the facilities provided by the API.

Chapter 7, Ray Tracing and Hybrid Rendering, is an introduction to ray tracing with Vulkan and uses the new Vulkan ray tracing extensions. Most of the chapter will walk you through how to implement a path tracer in your application and use it to render a ray-traced scene and display it on screen. The chapter spends the last few pages demonstrating how to use a hybrid approach in your existing rasterization engine to make it pop with a few ray-traced features.

Chapter 8, Extended Reality with OpenXR, introduces you to the realm of extended reality, which encompasses virtual, mixed, and augmented reality. The chapter introduces OpenXR, including its main features and how to use it. The chapter then explains how to improve your rendering engine's performance using Vulkan and OpenXR features, such as multiview rendering and dynamic foveation.

Chapter 9, Debugging and Performance Measurement Techniques, concludes the book by guiding you through some ways to debug your Vulkan application and how to measure its performance.

To get the most out of this book

You will need a computer with a recent graphics card (to use some of the newer extensions, such as ray tracing, for example, you will need a card equivalent to NVIDIA's 3050). The code in the repository and in this book has been compiled and tested with Visual Studio 2022 and the Vulkan SDK 1.3.268.

Software/hardware covered in the book	Operating system requirements
Vulkan SDK	Windows; Android for Quest devices
CMake and Visual Studio 2022	Windows
Android Studio Hedgehog 2023.1.1	Windows
RenderDoc	Windows
Tracy Profiler 0.9.1	Windows

We advise you to clone the code from the book's GitHub repository (a link is available in the next section). Doing so will help you avoid any potential errors related to copying and pasting of code.

> Important note:
> This book contains many horizontally long screenshots. These have been captured to provide you with an overview of the execution plans for various Vulkan concepts. As a result, the text in these images may appear small at 100% zoom.

Download the example code files

You can clone the example code files for this book from GitHub at `https://github.com/PacktPublishing/The-Modern-Vulkan-Cookbook`. If there's an update to the code, it will be updated in the GitHub repository.

We also have other code bundles from our rich catalog of books and videos available at https://github.com/PacktPublishing/. Check them out!

Conventions used

There are a number of text conventions used throughout this book.

`Code in text`: Indicates code words in text, database table names, folder names, filenames, file extensions, pathnames, dummy URLs, user input, and Twitter handles. Here is an example: "For host-visible memory, it's enough to retrieve a pointer to the destination using `vmaMapMemory` and copy the data using `memcpy`."

A block of code is set as follows:

```
const VmaAllocationCreateInfo allocCreateInfo = {
    .flags = VMA_ALLOCATION_CREATE_DEDICATED_MEMORY_BIT,
    .usage = VMA_MEMORY_USAGE_AUTO_PREFER_DEVICE,
    .priority = 1.0f,
};
```

When we wish to draw your attention to a particular part of a code block, the relevant lines or items are set in bold:

```
samplerShadowMap_ = context.createSampler(
    VK_FILTER_NEAREST, VK_FILTER_NEAREST,
    VK_SAMPLER_ADDRESS_MODE_CLAMP_TO_EDGE,
    VK_SAMPLER_ADDRESS_MODE_CLAMP_TO_EDGE,
    VK_SAMPLER_ADDRESS_MODE_CLAMP_TO_EDGE, 1.0f,
    true, VK_COMPARE_OP_LESS_OR_EQUAL,
    "lighting pass shadow");
```

Bold: Indicates a new term, an important word, or words that you see onscreen. For instance, words in menus or dialog boxes appear in **bold**. Here is an example: "To guarantee that partial updates work, we need to copy the last active buffer, **Buffer 0**, into **Buffer 1** first, and then update **viewport matrix**."

> **Tips or important notes**
> Appear like this.

Sections

In this book, you will find several headings that appear frequently (*Getting ready*, *How to do it...*, *How it works...*, *There's more...*, and *See also*).

To give clear instructions on how to complete a recipe, use these sections as follows:

Getting ready

This section tells you what to expect in the recipe and describes how to set up any software or any preliminary settings required for the recipe.

How to do it...

This section contains the steps required to follow the recipe.

How it works...

This section usually consists of a detailed explanation of what happened in the previous section.

There's more...

This section consists of additional information about the recipe in order to make you more knowledgeable about the recipe.

See also

This section provides helpful links to other useful information for the recipe.

Get in touch

Feedback from our readers is always welcome.

General feedback: If you have questions about any aspect of this book, mention the book title in the subject of your message and email us at `customercare@packtpub.com`.

Errata: Although we have taken every care to ensure the accuracy of our content, mistakes do happen. If you have found a mistake in this book, we would be grateful if you would report this to us. Please visit `www.packtpub.com/support/errata`, selecting your book, clicking on the Errata Submission Form link, and entering the details.

Piracy: If you come across any illegal copies of our works in any form on the Internet, we would be grateful if you would provide us with the location address or website name. Please contact us at `copyright@packt.com` with a link to the material.

If you are interested in becoming an author: If there is a topic that you have expertise in and you are interested in either writing or contributing to a book, please visit `authors.packtpub.com`.

Reviews

Please leave a review. Once you have read and used this book, why not leave a review on the site that you purchased it from? Potential readers can then see and use your unbiased opinion to make purchase decisions, we at Packt can understand what you think about our products, and our authors can see your feedback on their book. Thank you!

For more information about Packt, please visit `packtpub.com`.

Share Your Thoughts

Once you've read *The Modern Vulkan Cookbook*, we'd love to hear your thoughts! Scan the QR code below to go straight to the Amazon review page for this book and share your feedback.

`https://packt.link/r/1-803-23998-0`

Your review is important to us and the tech community and will help us make sure we're delivering excellent quality content.

Download a free PDF copy of this book

Thanks for purchasing this book!

Do you like to read on the go but are unable to carry your print books everywhere?

Is your e-book purchase not compatible with the device of your choice?

Don't worry!, Now with every Packt book, you get a DRM-free PDF version of that book at no cost.

Read anywhere, any place, on any device. Search, copy, and paste code from your favorite technical books directly into your application.

The perks don't stop there, you can get exclusive access to discounts, newsletters, and great free content in your inbox daily

Follow these simple steps to get the benefits:

1. Scan the QR code or visit the following link:

    `https://packt.link/free-ebook/9781803239989`

2. Submit your proof of purchase.
3. That's it! We'll send your free PDF and other benefits to your email directly.

1
Vulkan Core Concepts

Our goal for this chapter is to implement a simple program that displays a shaded triangle on screen, with the triangle's vertices and attributes being sourced directly from the shaders. In the process of implementing the code to render this triangle, we will cover most of Vulkan's fundamental objects, the ones you need to create a very simple application. Although the code required for this minimal example is extensive, the majority of it can be reused and tweaked for other applications. By the end of the chapter, you will know how to bootstrap communication with the driver, how to create and manage basic Vulkan objects, and how to issue rendering commands to the GPU.

In this chapter, following a brief introduction to the Vulkan API, we will cover the following recipes:

- Calling API functions
- Learning about Vulkan objects
- Using Volk to load Vulkan functions and extensions
- Using Vulkan extensions correctly
- Using the Validation Layer for error checking
- Enumerating available instance layers
- Enumerating available instance extensions
- Initializing the Vulkan instance
- Creating a surface
- Enumerating Vulkan physical devices
- Caching the properties of queue families
- Enumerating physical device extensions
- Reserving queue families
- Creating a Vulkan logical device

- Retrieving the queue object handle
- Creating a command pool
- Allocating, recording, and submitting commands
- Reusing command buffers
- Creating render passes
- Creating framebuffers
- Creating image views
- The Vulkan graphics pipeline
- Compiling shaders to SPIR-V
- Dynamic states
- Creating a graphics pipeline
- Swapchain
- Understanding synchronization in the swapchain – fences and semaphores
- Populating submission information for presentation
- Presenting images
- Rendering a triangle

Technical requirements

To successfully run the code featured in this and rest of chapters, your system must meet the following requirements:

A Windows computer equipped with a GPU that supports Vulkan 1.3. We recommend having a machine with at least 16 GB of RAM and a modern graphics card. The code for various chapters was tested with GTX 1080, GTX 1060, RTX 3050, and RTX 4060. Please note that *Chapter 7, Ray Tracing and Hybrid Rendering*, requires RTX 3050/4060 series card since it demonstrates use of ray tracing.

To get started, follow these steps:

1. Download and Install Vulkan SDK 1.3.268: Visit the LunarG website at `https://sdk.lunarg.com/sdk/download/1.3.268.0/windows/VulkanSDK-1.3.268.0-Installer.exe` and download the Vulkan SDK 1.3.268 installer. Run the installer to complete the installation process.
2. Install Python 3.12: Download the latest version of Python 3.12 from the official Python website and follow the installation instructions provided.

3. Clone the Repository: Ensure you have Git installed on your computer. If not, download and install Git from `https://git-scm.com/downloads`. Once Git is installed, open a command prompt or terminal and execute git clone `https://github.com/PacktPublishing/The-Modern-Vulkan-Cookbook` to clone the repository.
4. Open the Project in Visual Studio 2022: Launch Visual Studio 2022. Navigate to **File** | **Open** | **Folder** and select the folder where you cloned the repository. This action will load the project into Visual Studio.
5. Build the Project: Within Visual Studio, you can choose to build the project for debugging or release. For learning purposes and when making changes to the code, it's recommended to use the **Debug** build configuration. This allows you to step through the code and understand its execution flow. For simply running the executables, you can use the **Release** build configuration.

The project is structured to facilitate easy navigation and understanding of the code examples provided in each chapter. Here's a detailed guide on how to locate and work with the code:

The project is organized into several key directories, each serving a specific purpose:

- `source/chapterX`: This directory contains the main source code for each chapter. Replace X with the chapter number you are working on. For example, the source code for this chapter is located in `source/chapter1`.
- `source/vulkancore`: This directory is dedicated to the Vulkan specific code and components. It includes utilities, wrappers, and other Vulkan related functionalities that are used throughout the project.
- `source/enginecore`: This directory houses the core engine components that are shared across multiple chapters. These components provide foundational functionality that is reused in various parts of the project.

The recipe for this chapter can be run by launching `Chapter01_Traingle.exe` executable.

Getting to know the Vulkan API

The Vulkan API, introduced in 2016 by the Khronos Group, is a low-overhead, cross-platform computing API that is the successor to OpenGL and its variants (WebGL and OpenGL ES). In fact, Vulkan was called **Next Generation OpenGL** (or **glNext**) before it was officially named Vulkan. OpenGL has been around since 1992 and it was the de facto introductory graphics API everyone learned (and learns still today). Allied with its simplicity, OpenGL is ubiquitous even today.

So, how is Vulkan different from OpenGL? It starts with its complexity. Vulkan is intended to provide application authors more control over the graphics hardware so that they can implement a solution that caters to their needs. Applications can implement solutions as simple as they want or as complex as they need. In practice, this means that the application is now responsible for controlling the hardware, making it more complex. The drivers, on the other hand, became simpler. For instance, if an application is really concerned about resource management, it can implement its own resource management algorithms and not rely on the driver's implementation.

In short, Vulkan offers more fine-grained control over the GPU compared to OpenGL due to its *lower-level* nature. It empowers applications to handle tasks that were traditionally managed by graphics drivers, such as initiating communication between the application and the hardware. However, this increased control comes with added complexity. Vulkan abstracts a large part of the GPU-specific implementation, allowing the same code to run on a wide range of GPUs. While it is possible to use device-specific extensions to maximize the computation potential of a particular GPU, these are not necessities but optional choices to optimize performance. In both desktop and mobile environments, managing this complexity to make optimal use of the GPU can be challenging due to the vast array of possibilities.

Calling API functions

Due to the many knobs Vulkan provides to control every little thing that the hardware can do, Vulkan tends to be more verbose than OpenGL. Since the control of every single aspect of the rendering process is now exposed to the application, there is simply more information that needs to be communicated with the graphics driver (mind you, the graphics driver still exists; it's just simpler than it used to be).

The most prominent pattern used by the Vulkan API is structure-as-parameter. It is used for creating and allocating objects, querying their capabilities and information, describing layouts, and much more. In this pattern, instead of passing all possible values for the creation of an object as parameters of a function, you must stick all that information in a structure provided by the Vulkan SDK and then pass that structure as a parameter to the function.

In this recipe, you will learn how Vulkan functions are expected to be called and how to check their return value.

Getting ready

Creating objects in Vulkan requires you to fill an instance of a special structure (there's one for each object you would like to create) and pass it to the creation function, which takes a pointer to a variable that will store the object's handle upon return. Most functions in the API return a result that can be used to detect errors, and it's usually a very good idea to do so to catch errors as soon as possible.

How to do it...

This recipe will show how to create a Vulkan sampler (VkSampler) by calling the vkCreateSampler function and how you can create a macro that can be used to check the return value of Vulkan function calls without repeating the same code over and over again.

1. The following code demonstrates how to create a VkSampler sampler, a Vulkan object that dictates how a texture is sampled in a shader.

2. Before calling the vkCreateSampler function that creates the sampler, you need to fill a structure called VkSamplerCreateInfo with all the parameters you'd like the new sampler to have.

   In the example, we are setting its minification and magnification filter types, how the texture coordinates are treated before sampling the texture, and everything else that Vulkan allows to be controlled in an object of this type:

   ```
   VkDevice device;
   const VkSamplerCreateInfo samplerInfo = {
         .sType = VK_STRUCTURE_TYPE_SAMPLER_CREATE_INFO,
         .magFilter = VK_FILTER_LINEAR,
         .minFilter = VK_FILTER_LINEAR,
         .addressModeU = VK_SAMPLER_ADDRESS_MODE_REPEAT,
         .addressModeV = VK_SAMPLER_ADDRESS_MODE_REPEAT,
         .addressModeW = VK_SAMPLER_ADDRESS_MODE_REPEAT,
         .mipLodBias = 0,
         .anisotropyEnable = VK_FALSE,
         .minLod = 0,
         .maxLod = maxLod,
     };
   VkSampler sampler = VK_NULL_HANDLE;
   const VkResult result = vkCreateSampler(device, &samplerInfo,
   nullptr, &sampler);
   assert(result == VK_SUCCESS);
   ```

   Another interesting thing about this pattern is that besides instantiating the right type of structure (VkSamplerCreateInfo in this example), we also need to set the sType member to the correct value that matches the type of structure being used (VK_STRUCTURE_TYPE_ SAMPLER_CREATE_INFO in the snippet). This property is of type VkStructureType declared by the Vulkan SDK. If you use the wrong value for sType, you won't get a compilation error, and maybe not even a runtime error. Maybe not even an error at all! Well, at least not while running it on your development machine. As soon as someone else tries your code on their device, then it could crash. Luckily, there is a mechanism that helps us detect this kind of mistake at runtime. It's called the Validation Layer, and we're going to talk more about it in this chapter.

The last thing to notice about the listing is that while creating objects in Vulkan, the handle to the object is not returned from the function but is stored in a pointer passed to the function. In our preceding example, the handle to the new sampler will be stored in the variable sampler (the last parameter to the `vkCreateSampler` function). That's why we're passing the address of the local variable to the function.

The reason for that is that most functions in the API return a result denoting whether the operation was successful or not. In most cases, checking the return value, of type `VkResult`, against `VK_SUCCESS` is fine (and displaying a message on screen or terminating), but in a few cases, the result may not represent an irrecoverable error but a situation that needs to be rectified before we can continue.

3. This pattern is so common that we use a simple utility macro that checks the return value. If the result is anything different than `VK_SUCCESS`, it prints a message, along with the stringified error code, and asserts. Check it out:

```
#define VK_CHECK(func)                                       \
{                                                            \
    const VkResult result = func;                            \
    if (result != VK_SUCCESS) {                              \
        std::cerr << "Error calling function " << #func      \
                  << " at " << __FILE__ << ":"               \
                  << __LINE__ << ". Result is "              \
                  << string_VkResult(result)                 \
                  << std::endl;                              \
        assert(false);                                       \
    }                                                        \
}
```

Vulkan objects are created almost always the same way: by providing their attributes in a structure, calling a `create` function, and providing a pointer to store the handle to the newly created object. Most functions return a `VkResult` value that can be used to check whether the function succeeded or not.

Learning about Vulkan objects

The Vulkan API is extensive and many times larger than OpenGL (in any way you'd like to measure). Nonetheless, only a handful of very important objects are necessary to write many types of applications. As mentioned at the beginning of this chapter, the Vulkan API was leveled against the most demanding applications, those that need to control every single minute detail of the hardware to extract the maximum performance. But most applications don't need all that flexibility and can get by with just the *basics*.

In this recipe, you will learn what Vulkan objects are and how they relate to each other.

Getting ready

Objects in Vulkan are opaque handles, and their types begin with the letters `Vk`. A Vulkan instance is called `VkInstance`, a Vulkan device is called `VkDevice`, and so on. Some objects need an instance of other objects to be created or allocated from. This dependency creates an implicit logical sequence as to object creation. A Vulkan physical device, `VkPhysicalDevice`, which represents a GPU on the system, can only be created if a Vulkan instance, `VkInstance`, already exists. The next section will present a diagram that may be helpful in understanding Vulkan's capabilities and *when* objects may be created.

How to do it...

Figure 1.1 is a summary of what we consider the most important objects in Vulkan; the ones that we cover in this book and that will satisfy most graphics applications. They are also the bare minimum for a simple – but flexible – program.

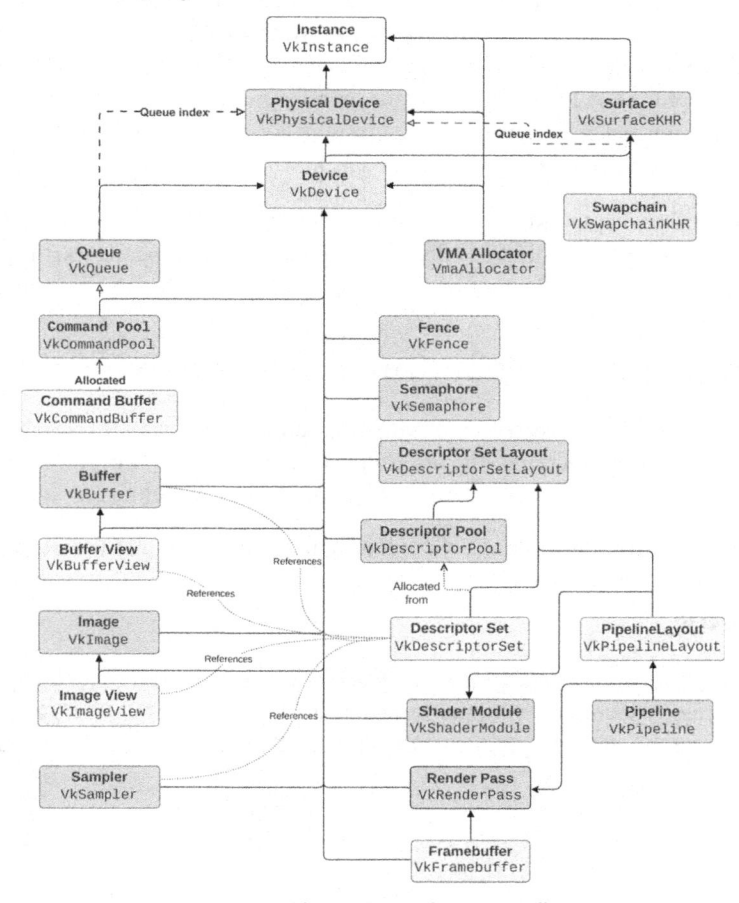

Figure 1.1 – Object dependency in Vulkan

1. In the preceding diagram, each node is a Vulkan object with its name on the top half and its Vulkan type in the bottom half. The diagram also encodes the dependency between the objects, explicit and implicit. The arrows connecting objects denote what an object needs to be created (besides their parameters, which are not depicted there).

2. Solid arrows are explicit dependencies: an object needs a reference to all objects pointed by the arrows leaving its node. For example, a device needs a reference to a physical device to be created; a buffer view needs a reference to a buffer and the device. Dashed arrows indicate implicit dependencies: a queue object needs a reference to a device, but it doesn't explicitly need a reference to a physical device, only a queue index to a family of queues, which is obtained from a physical device. It doesn't need a physical device, but it needs something that is provided by one.

3. Solid lines with an open arrow at the end denote objects that are allocated from others, generally a pool of those types of objects. A command buffer isn't created; it is allocated from a command pool (which in turn needs to be created at some point).

4. This diagram is useful for the beginner because it helps visualize multiple dependencies that aren't exactly obvious. The descriptor set is one of those objects: to obtain one, you need a reference to a descriptor set layout. They are not created by the application; they are allocated from a descriptor pool. Finally, a descriptor set references buffers, image views, and samplers. They are not required, and that's why that type of relation in the diagram represents an optional reference. We'll talk more about descriptor sets in *Chapter 2, Working with Modern Vulkan*.

In the remainder of this chapter and the next chapter, we will cover the creation of all objects in the diagram in the order that they would usually be implemented. That means starting at the top with the Vulkan instance and moving downward, fulfilling the dependencies represented in the diagram.

Using Volk to load Vulkan functions and extensions

Volk is an open source library created by Arseny Kapoulkine that provides simple cross-platform support for loading Vulkan functions. The library provides several key features, the most important ones being automatically loading Vulkan's function pointers and providing cross-platform support.

In this recipe, you will learn how to use Volk to load Vulkan functions and their extensions.

Getting ready

Download Volk from `https://github.com/zeux/volk` and add `volk.c` to your project and enable the preprocessor defines for your platform, `VK_USE_PLATFORM_WIN32_KHR`, `VK_USE_PLATFORM_XLIB_KHR`, `VK_USE_PLATFORM_MACOS_MVK`, and so on, before including `volk.h`.

How to do it...

Volk automatically loads Vulkan's function pointers, so you don't have to manually handle the details of loading them and checking for available extensions. If you use Volk in your application, do not link against the static version of the Vulkan library (`VKstatic.1.lib` on Windows) or load the shared library directly (such as `vulkan-1.dll` on Windows). Volk will do that for you.

1. Call `volkInitialize()` during the application's startup process, before any other Vulkan functions are used.
2. Call `volkLoadInstance` after the creation of the Vulkan instance. It replaces global function pointers with functions retrieved with `vkGetInstanceProcAddr`.
3. Call `volkLoadDevice` after the creation of the Vulkan logical device. It replaces global function pointers with functions retrieved with `vkGetDeviceProcAddr`.

Using Vulkan extensions correctly

Vulkan relies heavily on extensions. Extensions are functions and types that are part of the *Vulkan Specification*; they are provided in addition to the core API but aren't guaranteed to exist for a particular version of the API. Either they are experimental or vendor- and card-specific and are not guaranteed to be present, either at compile time or runtime. Official extensions are registered with the Khronos Group and are part of the spec, so you can find their documentation there.

Extensions may be introduced to a *Vulkan Specification* version and later promoted to the core set of functionalities on a newer version. Or not at all! The functionality to present rendering results to a surface (such as a window on a GUI), for example, is still an extension even in Vulkan 1.3 (the most recent version as of the writing of this book). If you are curious, here's a link to it, the `VK_KHR_surface` device extension: https://registry.khronos.org/vulkan/specs/1.3-extensions/man/html/VK_KHR_surface.html.

Figure 1.2 offers a high-level overview of the process:

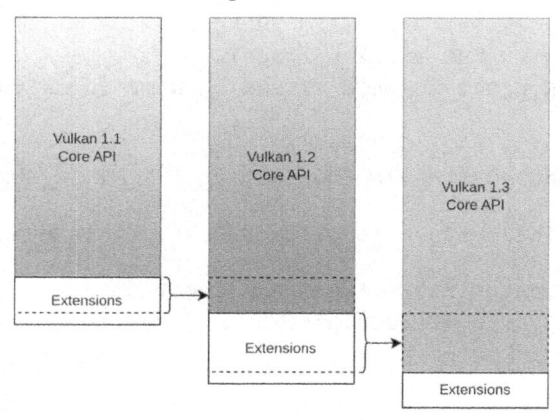

Figure 1.2 – Vulkan extensions

Vulkan version 1.1, for example, contains its core functionality – functions and types present in that version – plus extensions. Some, all, or none of those extensions may be promoted to the core set of functionalities in Vulkan 1.2. Some might be considered deprecated and removed. The same thing happens when the specification is updated to version 1.3: some, all, or none of those extensions may be promoted from version 1.2 to the new version, and some might be deprecated.

In this recipe, we will present the right way to deal with extensions during compile time and during runtime.

Getting ready

There are two types of extensions in Vulkan: instance- and device-level extensions. Before using an extension, you need to check if it is available during compile time and only add code that uses the extension if the extension is available. Generally speaking, you don't need to check extensions at runtime. You also need to request the instance or device to enable the extensions by providing the name of the extension as a string.

How to do it...

In addition to an extension being present at compile time, you need to enable it at the right level (instance or device) and check if it has been enabled just before using it at runtime.

1. The pattern of checking whether a particular extension can be used at compile time and runtime is shown next:

```
bool isEnabledForDevice(VkDevice device,
                        const std::string &extName) {
  // std::unordered_map<std::string> deviceExtensions;
  return deviceExtensions.contains(extName);
}

  VkDevice device;   // Valid Vulkan Device
#if defined(VK_KHR_win32_surface)
  // VK_KHR_WIN32_SURFACE_EXTENSION_NAME is defined as the string
  // "VK_KHR_win32_surface"
  if (isEnabledForDevice(device, VK_KHR_WIN32_SURFACE_EXTENSION_NAME)) {
    // VkWin32SurfaceCreateInfoKHR struct is available, as well as the
    // vkCreateWin32SurfaceKHR() function
    VkWin32SurfaceCreateInfoKHR surfaceInfo;
  }
#endif
```

2. Besides new functions and types, the Vulkan SDK offers macros for each extension. Those macros can be used to check whether they are present, their name, and version. In the preceding listing, a `VK_KHR_win32_surface` macro is defined and set to `1` if the extension is available. The `VK_KHR_WIN32_SURFACE_EXTENSION_NAME` macro defines a `const char *` as the name of the extension (in this case, it is `VK_KHR_win32_surface`) and a `VK_KHR_WIN32_SURFACE_SPEC_VERSION` macro, defined as an integer, that specifies its version number.

3. Before creating an instance of `VkWin32SurfaceCreateInfoKHR`, we check if the `VK_KHR_win32_surface` device extension is present and enabled. The code is guarded by an `+#if+` directive, and if the extension is present, we proceed to check if it's enabled at runtime using the `VK_KHR_WIN32_SURFACE_EXTENSION_NAME` macro.

This check is especially important if you are writing cross-platform code. While it may seem obvious that some extensions should be available, they may not be available for all platforms or graphics cards you are planning to support.

Using the Validation Layer for error checking

In the spirit of a high-performant, low-overhead API, Vulkan does not perform error-checking by default. Doing so would incur a performance penalty, which may be unacceptable for some applications. On the other hand, due to Vulkan's complexity, it is very easy for the application to make mistakes.

To help application authors detect errors, Vulkan provides layers, which can be enabled during development and later disabled for shipping. That combination isn't mandatory, as developers don't have to enable error-detecting layers for testing nor disable them for shipping, although that is the most common scenario.

In this recipe, we will introduce what Vulkan layers are and how their messages are presented, as well as offer tips on how to learn more about the meaning of those messages.

Getting ready

Layers are provided with the Vulkan SDK, so if you are using Vulkan, chances are you also have access to layers by default.

How to do it...

Layers are implementations of Vulkan functions that can be inserted in the call chain, intercepting entry points into the API. Those implementations can then perform error checking, performance measurements, or even detect possible optimizations.

The Vulkan SDK provides a few layers that are **Plug and Play** (**PnP**). The only work you need to do is find which layers are present and enable them for the Vulkan instance. After that, at runtime, layers should start doing their jobs as soon as you start calling Vulkan functions.

1. The most important layer available in the SDK is the Validation Layer. This layer will validate all Vulkan function calls and their parameters. It also maintains an internal state – which Vulkan does not – to ensure that your application is not missing a synchronization step or using the wrong layouts for images.

2. As an example, the following message shows a real message displayed by the Validation Layer. Although somewhat cryptic, the message is very useful: it starts by displaying the error ID (VUID-VkSamplerCreateInfo-sType-sType), which you can use to search for it on the web; it also displays the device associated with the error; and finally, it displays the message ID and text, which informs us, in this example, that the structure we used to create a sampler (VkSamplerCreateInfo) needs to have its sType member equal to VK_STRUCTURE_TYPE_SAMPLER_CREATE_INFO:

```
VUID-VkSamplerCreateInfo-sType-sType(ERROR / SPEC): msgNum:
-129708450 - Validation Error: [ VUID-VkSamplerCreateInfo-
sType-sType ] Object 0: handle = 0x1fbd501b6e0, name = Device,
type = VK_OBJECT_TYPE_DEVICE; | MessageID = 0xf844ce5e |
vkCreateSampler: parameter pCreateInfo->sType must be VK_
STRUCTURE_TYPE_SAMPLER_CREATE_INFO. The Vulkan spec states:
sType must be VK_STRUCTURE_TYPE_SAMPLER_CREATE_INFO (https://
vulkan.lunarg.com/doc/view/1.3.236.0/windows/1.3-extensions/
vkspec.html#VUID-VkSamplerCreateInfo-sType-sType)
    Objects: 1
        [0] 0x1fbd501b6e0, type: 3, name: Device
```

Even the most experienced graphics programmers will face Validation Layer errors. Getting used to how they look and how to figure out what they mean is the first step in writing a Vulkan application that is Validation Layer error-free.

Enumerating available instance layers

Enabling an instance layer is as easy as providing its name as a `const char *` to the instance creation function. Unfortunately, not all layers exist in all implementations, and we need to check the available ones before trying to enable them.

In this recipe, you will learn how to enumerate the available instance layers and how to transform them into strings so that they are easier to manage.

Getting ready

The code snippets shown in this section are part of our `Context` class.. It encapsulates most of the initialization and object creation functions.

How to do it...

Checking the available extensions is easy to do:

1. First, you need to query the number of extensions using the `vkEnumerateInstanceLayerProperties` function, create an array of `VkLayerProperties` big enough to store all extensions, and request their data by issuing a call to the same function again, like this:

   ```
   uint32_t instanceLayerCount{0};
   VK_CHECK(vkEnumerateInstanceLayerProperties(
       &instanceLayerCount, nullptr));
   std::vector<VkLayerProperties> layers(
       instanceLayerCount);
   VK_CHECK(vkEnumerateInstanceLayerProperties(
       &instanceLayerCount, layers.data()));
   ```

   The second call to `vkEnumerateInstanceLayerProperties` will store all available layers in the `layers` vector, which then can be used for querying, diagnostics, and so on.

2. With that information in hand, it's always a good idea to verify whether the layers you are trying to enable are available. Since the instance creation function accepts the name of the layers in `const char *` format, we need to convert the extension names to strings:

   ```
   std::vector<std::string> availableLayers;
   std::transform(
       layers.begin(), layers.end(),
       std::back_inserter(availableLayers),
       [](const VkLayerProperties& properties) {
         return properties.layerName;
       });
   ```

3. Finally, the requested layers need to be filtered according to the available ones. With two vectors of strings, one for the available layers and one for the requested layers, we can use the following utility function to perform filtering:

   ```
   std::unordered_set<std::string> filterExtensions(
       std::vector<std::string> availableExtensions,
       std::vector<std::string> requestedExtensions) {
     std::sort(availableExtensions.begin(),
               availableExtensions.end());
     std::sort(requestedExtensions.begin(),
               requestedExtensions.end());
     std::vector<std::string> result;
     std::set_intersection(
         availableExtensions.begin(),
   ```

```
            availableExtensions.end(),
            requestedExtensions.begin(),
            requestedExtensions.end(),
            std::back_inserter(result));
    return std::unordered_set<std::string>(
            result.begin(), result.end());
}
```

This function is very handy because instance layers and instance and device extensions are all referred to by their names as `const char*`. This function can be applied to filter all layers and extensions you need in Vulkan.

Enumerating available instance extensions

The same process of filtering requested layers against available ones should be repeated for instance extensions.

In this recipe, you will learn how to obtain available instance extensions, how to store them as strings, and how to convert them to pointers to characters so that they can be passed to the Vulkan API.

Getting ready

The process is very similar to the one described in the previous recipe, which also includes a utility function to perform an intersection of the available layers and the requested ones.

How to do it...

Obtaining a list of extensions is as easy as obtaining the available layers.

1. First, call `vkEnumerateInstanceExtensionProperties` twice, once to determine how many extensions are available and then one more time to fetch the extensions:

   ```
   uint32_t extensionsCount{0};
   vkEnumerateInstanceExtensionProperties(
       nullptr, &extensionsCount, nullptr);
   std::vector<VkExtensionProperties>
       extensionProperties(extensionsCount);
   vkEnumerateInstanceExtensionProperties(
       nullptr, &extensionsCount,
       extensionProperties.data());

   std::vector<std::string> availableExtensions;
   std::transform(
       extensionProperties.begin(),
   ```

```
        extensionProperties.end(),
        std::back_inserter(availableExtensions),
        [](const VkExtensionProperties& properties) {
          return properties.extensionName;
        });
```

2. Finally, we can filter the requested layers and extensions using the list of available layers and extensions from the previous steps. Notice that we are requesting the Validation Layer and guarding all extensions with a conditional preprocessor block:

```
const std::vector<std::string>
    requestedInstanceLayers = {
        "VK_LAYER_KHRONOS_validation"};
const std::vector<std::string>
    requestedInstanceExtensions = {
#if defined(VK_KHR_win32_surface)
    VK_KHR_WIN32_SURFACE_EXTENSION_NAME,
#endif
#if defined(VK_EXT_debug_utils),
    VK_EXT_DEBUG_UTILS_EXTENSION_NAME,
#endif
#if defined(VK_KHR_surface)
    VK_KHR_SURFACE_EXTENSION_NAME,
#endif
    };
const auto enabledInstanceLayers =
    filterExtensions(availableLayers,
                     requestedInstanceLayers);
const auto enabledInstanceExtensions =
    filterExtensions(availableExtensions,
                     requestedInstanceExtensions);
```

3. To pass the vectors of strings to the API, we need to convert them to vectors of `const char*` because the API only accepts `const char*` parameters. We also need to perform the same conversion for the vector of instance layers (which is omitted here for brevity):

```
std::vector<const char*> instanceExtensions(
    enabledInstanceExtensions.size());
std::transform(enabledInstanceExtensions.begin(),
               enabledInstanceExtensions.end(),
               instanceExtensions.begin(),
               std::mem_fn(&std::string::c_str));
```

> **Important note**
> The `instanceExtensions` vector must *not* outlive the `enabledInstanceExtensions` vector. As `instanceExtensions` contains pointers to the strings in `enabledInstanceExtensions`, once the latter is destroyed, the pointers in `instanceExtensions` would all be dangling.

Initializing the Vulkan instance

To start using Vulkan, we need to create a Vulkan instance. One can think of a Vulkan instance as a way of initializing the Vulkan library. To create one, you need to provide a set of required and optional information such as application name, engine name, version, and a list of desired layers and extensions.

In this recipe, you will learn how to create a Vulkan instance.

Getting ready

Instantiating the `VkApplicationInfo` structure used to create an instance requires the version of the application and the Vulkan API version. The former can be created using the `VK_MAKE_VERSION` macro, while the latter can be provided as one of the preprocessor definitions available in the SDK.

How to do it...

With all of those in hand, all we need to do is create a Vulkan instance:

1. Create an instance of the `VkApplicationInfo` structure first:

    ```
    const VkApplicationInfo applicationInfo_ = {
        .sType = VK_STRUCTURE_TYPE_APPLICATION_INFO,
        .pApplicationName = "Essential Graphics With Vulkan",
        .applicationVersion = VK_MAKE_VERSION(1, 0, 0),
        .apiVersion = VK_API_VERSION_1_3,
    };
    ```

2. You will also need an instance of the `VkInstanceCreateInfo` structure with the requested instance layers and extensions. Then, call `vkCreateInstance`:

    ```
    const VkInstanceCreateInfo instanceInfo = {
        .sType =
            VK_STRUCTURE_TYPE_INSTANCE_CREATE_INFO,
        .pApplicationInfo = &applicationInfo_,
        .enabledLayerCount = static_cast<uint32_t>(
            requestedLayers.size()),
        .ppEnabledLayerNames = requestedLayers.data(),
        .enabledExtensionCount = static_cast<uint32_t>(
    ```

```
                    instanceExtensions.size()),
    .ppEnabledExtensionNames = instanceExtensions.data(),
};
VkInstance instance_{VK_NULL_HANDLE};
VK_CHECK(vkCreateInstance(&instanceInfo, nullptr,
                          &instance_));
```

Once the Vulkan instance has been created, you should keep it stored safely, as it will need to be destroyed before your application exits.

Creating a surface

Just as in OpenGL, presenting the final render output to the screen needs support from the windowing system and is platform-dependent. For this reason, the Vulkan Core API does not contain functions to render the final image to the screen. Those functions and types are extensions. For this recipe, we'll use the VK_KHR_surface and VK_KHR_swapchain extensions. We will cover only the Windows case here and use the VK_KHR_win32_surface extension.

In this recipe, you will learn how to create a surface for presenting the final output of your rendering.

Getting ready

The first step in the process of rendering an image onto the screen starts with the creation of a VkSurfaceKHR object. Since this object is needed while reserving queues from a physical device, this step is done after the instance has been created but before the physical devices are enumerated and before the device is created, as the device needs information about which queue families we will use.

How to do it...

Creating a VkSurfaceKHR object is simple but needs support from the windowing system.

1. On Windows, you need an instance handle to the executable a (HINSTANCE) and a window handle (HWND) for where to present the image. We're using GLFW, so the window used by the VkWin32SurfaceCreateInfoKHR structure can be obtained with glfwGetWin32Window(GLFWwindow*). The handle to the VkSurfaceKHR object is stored in Context::surface_:

```
const auto window = glfwGetWin32Window(glfwWindow);
#if defined(VK_USE_PLATFORM_WIN32_KHR) && \
    defined(VK_KHR_win32_surface)
    if (enabledInstanceExtensions_.contains(
            VK_KHR_WIN32_SURFACE_EXTENSION_NAME)) {
      if (window != nullptr) {
        const VkWin32SurfaceCreateInfoKHR ci = {
```

```
                    .sType =
                        VK_STRUCTURE_TYPE_WIN32_SURFACE_CREATE_INFO_KHR,
                    .hinstance = GetModuleHandle(NULL),
                    .hwnd = (HWND)window,
                };
                VK_CHECK(vkCreateWin32SurfaceKHR(
                    instance_, &ci, nullptr, &surface_));
            }
        }
#endif
```

The surface creation varies slightly between platforms, but the process is very similar.

Enumerating Vulkan physical devices

Before we can create a device in Vulkan, we need to select a suitable physical device, as a system may have multiple Vulkan-capable GPUs and we want to choose one with the capabilities required by our application. To do this, we need to enumerate all available physical devices on the system. This can be achieved by calling the `vkEnumeratePhysicalDevices` function, which returns a list of all physical devices on the system that support the Vulkan API. Once we have the list of physical devices, we can inspect their properties and features using the `vkGetPhysicalDeviceProperties` and `vkGetPhysicalDeviceFeatures` functions to determine if they have the required capabilities. Finally, we can choose the most suitable physical device and use it to create a logical device through the `vkCreateDevice` function.

In this recipe, you will learn how to enumerate all Vulkan-capable devices present in the system so that you can choose one that best fits your needs.

Getting ready

In our code, we encapsulate a physical device in a class called `VulkanCore::PhysicalDevice`, which retrieves a physical device's properties and stores them for later use.

Also, make sure to check out the `Context::choosePhysicalDevice()` method if you'd like to use a better heuristic to choose one physical device on systems that have multiple devices that support Vulkan.

How to do it...

Enumerating physical devices employs the same pattern used throughout the API, which requires us to first request the number of items available and then fetch and store them into a vector:

1. `vkEnumeratePhysicalDevices` is called twice, first to query how many objects are available, and a second time to fetch the handles to `VkPhysicalDevice` objects:

```cpp
std::vector<PhysicalDevice>
Context::enumeratePhysicalDevices(
    const std::vector<std::string>&
        requestedExtensions) const {
  uint32_t deviceCount{0};
  VK_CHECK(vkEnumeratePhysicalDevices(
      instance_, &deviceCount, nullptr));
  ASSERT(deviceCount > 0,
         "No Vulkan devices found");
  std::vector<VkPhysicalDevice> devices(
      deviceCount);
  VK_CHECK(vkEnumeratePhysicalDevices(
      instance_, &deviceCount, devices.data()));

  std::vector<PhysicalDevice> physicalDevices;
  for (const auto device : devices) {
    physicalDevices.emplace_back(PhysicalDevice(
        device, surface_, requestedExtensions,
        printEnumerations_));
  }
  return physicalDevices;
}
```

This method returns a vector of `PhysicalDevice` objects. In the code, this list is passed to the `Context::choosePhysicalDevice()` helper method, which can be used to select an appropriate physical device based on the requested extensions and other GPU capabilities you may need. For the sake of simplicity, we always choose the first physical device from the list.

Caching the properties of queue families

In Vulkan, a physical device can have one or more queue families, where each queue family represents a set of command queues that share certain properties, such as capabilities or usage. *Figure 1.3* depicts a fictional set of families and their queues:

Vulkan Core Concepts

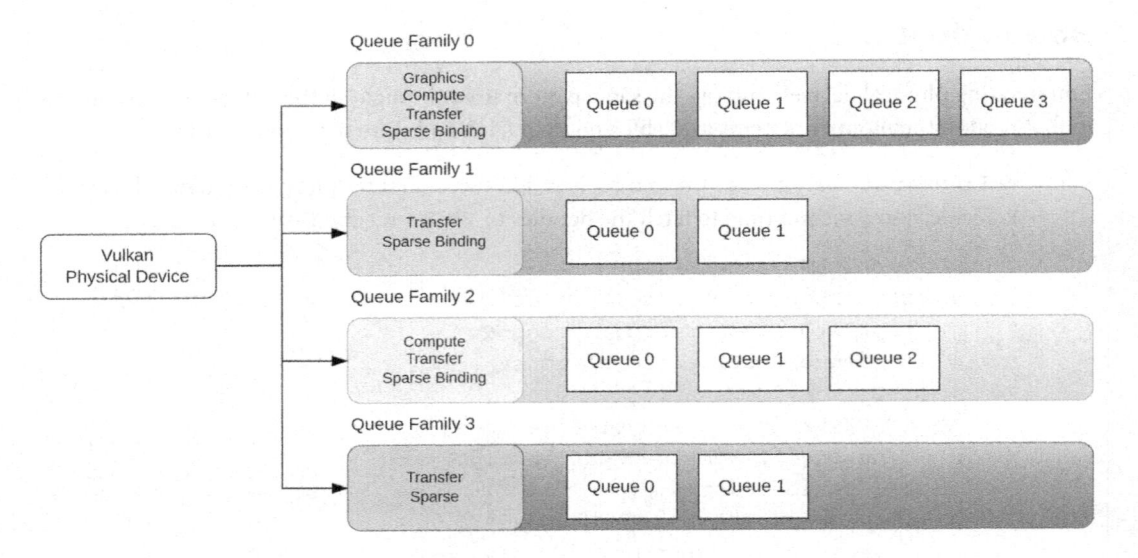

Figure 1.3 – Queue families and their queues

Each queue family supports a specific set of operations and commands that can be executed in parallel. For example, there may be a graphics queue family, a compute queue family, and a transfer queue family, each optimized for different types of operations.

In this recipe, you will learn how to retrieve the properties of a queue family and where they are stored in the code in the repository.

Getting ready

In the repository provided with this book, queue families and their properties are stored and managed by the `VulkanCore::PhysicalDevice` class.

How to do it...

Each queue family has its own set of properties, such as the number of queues, the type of operations it can perform, and the priority of the queues. When creating a logical device, we must specify which queue families and how many queues of each type we want to use.

1. To query the queue families available and their properties, use the `vkGetPhysicalDeviceQueueFamilyProperties` function:

    ```
    uint32_t queueFamilyCount{0};
    vkGetPhysicalDeviceQueueFamilyProperties(
        physicalDevice_, &queueFamilyCount, nullptr);
    queueFamilyProperties_.resize(queueFamilyCount);
    ```

```
vkGetPhysicalDeviceQueueFamilyProperties(
    physicalDevice_, &queueFamilyCount,
    queueFamilyProperties_.data());
```

The properties of the families are stored in `std::vector<VkQueueFamilyProperties> PhysicalDevice::queueFamilyProperties_`.

Enumerating physical device extensions

Physical device extensions must be explicitly enabled by the application and may only be available on specific physical devices or device drivers. It's important to check for the availability of required extensions and to gracefully handle situations where extensions are not supported.

In this recipe, you will learn how to enumerate all physical device extensions and how to convert and store them to strings for later use.

Getting ready

Enumerating physical device extensions is managed by the `VulkanCore::PhysicalDevice` class.

How to do it...

Obtaining all physical device extensions for a physical device is simple. Here, we also provide code to store them as strings so that they are easier to work with.

1. Enumerating all physical device extensions is done by using the `vkEnumerateDeviceExtensionProperties` function. The result is an array of `VkExtensionProperties`. This structure contains information such as the extension name, version, and a brief description of the extension's purpose:

    ```
    uint32_t propertyCount{0};
    VK_CHECK(vkEnumerateDeviceExtensionProperties(
        physicalDevice_, nullptr, &propertyCount,
        nullptr));
    std::vector<VkExtensionProperties> properties(
        propertyCount);
    VK_CHECK(vkEnumerateDeviceExtensionProperties(
        physicalDevice_, nullptr, &propertyCount,
        properties.data()));
    ```

2. Convert the extension's name to `std::string`:

```
std::transform(
    properties.begin(), properties.end(),
    std::back_inserter(extensions_),
    [](const VkExtensionProperties& property) {
      return std::string(property.extensionName);
    });
```

3. This array is processed so that we end up with only the names of the extensions as strings. Further processing filters the requested extensions against the available ones using our `filterExtensions` utility function and stores them in `std::unordered_set<std::string> PhysicalDevice::enabledExtensions_`:

```
enabledExtensions_ = util::filterExtensions(
    extensions_, requestedExtensions);
```

In summary, mastering the enumeration of physical device extensions is an important aspect of Vulkan. It ensures optimal utilization of your device's capabilities.

Reserving queue families

In Vulkan, a queue family is a group of one or more queues that share common properties, such as the type of operations they can perform. When creating a Vulkan device, we must specify which queue families we want to use and how many queues of each family we need.

For rendering and presentation, we typically need at least one graphics queue family, which is responsible for executing graphics commands. Additionally, we may require a compute queue family for executing compute workloads and a transfer queue family for handling data transfers.

In this recipe, you will learn how to find queue families based on their properties and how to select a queue family that supports presentation, which can be used to present the final render output on the screen.

Getting ready

In the repository, reserving queues is encapsulated by the `VulkanCore::PhysicalDevice` class.

How to do it...

One additional step necessary before creating a Vulkan device is to gather the indices to the queue families we'd like to use. For that, we created a `PhysicalDevice::reserveQueues()` method in the `PhysicalDevice` class to handle the process, which takes the type of queues we'd like to reserve as a parameter. It also takes a handle to a Vulkan surface (`VkSurfaceKHR`), which we will use later to verify whether a queue supports presentation, necessary to display the final render on the screen.

1. We iterate over the queue families properties, stored in `queueFamilyProperties_`, and store the index to the queue family index if its type has been requested:

```
uint32_t graphicsFamilyIndex{UINT32_MAX};
uint32_t presentationFamilyIndex{UINT32_MAX};
for (uint32_t queueFamilyIndex = 0;
     queueFamilyIndex <
         queueFamilyProperties_.size() &&
     requestedQueueTypes != 0;
     ++queueFamilyIndex) {
  if (graphicsFamilyIndex == UINT32_MAX &&
      (queueFamilyProperties_[queueFamilyIndex]
           .queueFlags &
       VK_QUEUE_GRAPHICS_BIT)) {
    graphicsFamilyIndex = queueFamilyIndex;
  }
```

2. To detect if a queue family supports presentation, we use the `vkGetPhysicalDeviceSurfaceSupportKHR` function, guarded by the preprocessor macros:

```
#if defined(VK_KHR_surface)
  if (enabledInstanceExtensions_.contains(
          VK_KHR_SURFACE_EXTENSION_NAME)) {
    if (presentationFamilyIndex == UINT32_MAX &&
        surface != VK_NULL_HANDLE) {
      VkBool32 supportsPresent{VK_FALSE};
      vkGetPhysicalDeviceSurfaceSupportKHR(
          physicalDevice_, queueFamilyIndex,
          surface, &supportsPresent);
      if (supportsPresent == VK_TRUE) {
        presentationFamilyIndex = queueFamilyIndex;
      }
    }
  }
#endif
}
```

The indices of other types of queue families may be obtained in a similar manner.

Creating a Vulkan logical device

A Vulkan device is a logical representation of a physical GPU. It's an object that is associated with a selected physical device (an existing GPU in the system) and is used to perform all graphics and compute operations. The device also provides access to physical GPU capabilities through queues. Queues are used to submit commands to the GPU, such as draw calls or memory transfers. The device also provides access to other Vulkan objects, such as pipelines, buffers, and images.

In this recipe, you will learn how to create a Vulkan logical device.

Getting ready

The code in this recipe is available as part of the `VulkanCore::Context` class in the repository. The `Context` class represents a Vulkan logical device.

How to do it...

To create a Vulkan device, we need to provide a physical device and the indices of the queue families we want to use. Using this information, we can create a vector of `VkDeviceQueueCreateInfo` structures, which determines the number of queues we want to use from each family and their respective priorities.

1. The most common use case for creating a device is to use one queue per family and set its priority to 1:

    ```
    auto physicalDevice_ = enumeratePhysicalDevices(
        requestedExtensions)[0];

    // Retrieves a vector of (queue family indices and
    // their number)
    const vector<uint32_t> familyIndices =
        physicalDevice_.reservedFamilies();

    std::vector<VkDeviceQueueCreateInfo>
        queueCreateInfos;
    float priority{1.0f};
    for (const auto& queueFamilyIndex :
            familyIndices) {
      queueCreateInfos.emplace_back(
        VkDeviceQueueCreateInfo{
            .sType =
                VK_STRUCTURE_TYPE_DEVICE_QUEUE_CREATE_INFO,
            .queueFamilyIndex = queueFamilyIndex,
            .queueCount = 1,
    ```

```
                .pQueuePriorities = &priority,
        });
    ++index;
}
```

2. The list of requested device extensions is converted from strings to `const char*`, filtered against the available extensions, and added to the `VkDeviceCreateInfo` structure, along with the index of the families we'd like to use and the layers we'd like to enable:

```
std::vector<const char*> deviceExtensions(
    physicalDevice_.enabledExtensions().size());
std::transform(
    physicalDevice_.enabledExtensions().begin(),
    physicalDevice_.enabledExtensions().end(),
    deviceExtensions.begin(),
    std::mem_fn(&std::string::c_str));

const VkDeviceCreateInfo dci = {
    .sType = VK_STRUCTURE_TYPE_DEVICE_CREATE_INFO,
    .queueCreateInfoCount = static_cast<uint32_t>(
        queueCreateInfos.size()),
    .pQueueCreateInfos = queueCreateInfos.data(),
    .enabledLayerCount = static_cast<uint32_t>(
        requestedLayers.size()),
    .ppEnabledLayerNames = requestedLayers.data(),
    .enabledExtensionCount = static_cast<uint32_t>(
        deviceExtensions.size()),
    .ppEnabledExtensionNames =
        deviceExtensions.data(),
};
VK_CHECK(vkCreateDevice(
    physicalDevice_.vkPhysicalDevice(), &dci,
    nullptr, &device_));
```

A Vulkan device is one of the most important objects you need, as it's needed to create almost every other Vulkan object there is.

Retrieving the queue object handle

Once the logical device has been created, we need to obtain the handle to queues. That is accomplished with the `vkGetDeviceQueue` function. This handle will be used to submit command buffers for processing on the GPU.

In this recipe, you will learn how to obtain the handle to a Vulkan queue.

Getting ready

In the repository, all queues are retrieved and stored by the `VulkanCore::Context` class. That class maintains a list for each type of queue: graphics, compute, transfer, and sparse, along with a special queue for presentation.

How to do it...

To retrieve the handle to a queue, just call the `vkGetDeviceQueue` function with the queue family index and the queue index:

```
VkQueue queue{VK_NULL_HANDLE};
uint32_t queueFamilyIndex; // valid queue family
vkGetDeviceQueue(device, queueFamilyIndex, 0, &queue);
```

Knowing which queue families are available is not enough. Once we determine which queues are available and the queues we need, we request the handle to one of the queues from the family using the API presented in this recipe.

Creating a command pool

Command buffers provide the ability to record graphics and compute commands, while command queues allow those buffers to be submitted to the hardware. Commands recorded in the command buffers are then executed by the GPU.

Each queue is associated with a specific queue family, which defines the capabilities of the queue. For example, a queue family may only support graphics operations, or it may support both graphics and compute operations. The number of families and their capabilities can be retrieved using the `vkGetPhysicalDeviceQueueFamilyProperties` function, discussed in the *Caching the properties of queue families* recipe. A queue family may contain one or more queues.

Command buffers are containers for the actual commands that are executed by the GPU. To record commands, you allocate a command buffer, then use the `vkCmd*` family of functions to record the commands into them. Once the commands have been recorded, the command buffer can be submitted to a command queue for execution.

Command buffers are allocated from a command pool, which in turn is created from a device and is associated with a specific queue family.

In this recipe, you will learn how to create a command pool.

Getting ready

Command pools and allocating and submitting command buffers is managed by the `VulkanCore::CommandQueueManager` class.

How to do it...

Creating a command pool is easy. All you need is the queue family index and a creation flag. The VK_COMMAND_POOL_CREATE_RESET_COMMAND_BUFFER_BIT flag is enough for our purposes.

To create a command pool, use the vkCreateCommandPool function. The VK_COMMAND_POOL_CREATE_RESET_COMMAND_BUFFER_BIT flag means that each command buffer allocated from this pool may be reset individually or implicitly by calling vkCmdBeginCommandBuffer:

```
uint32_t queueFamilyIndex; // Valid queue family index
const VkCommandPoolCreateInfo commandPoolInfo = {
    .sType = VK_STRUCTURE_TYPE_COMMAND_POOL_CREATE_INFO,
    .flags =
      VK_COMMAND_POOL_CREATE_RESET_COMMAND_BUFFER_BIT,
    .queueFamilyIndex = queueFamilyIndex,
};
VkCommandPool commandPool{VK_NULL_HANDLE};
VK_CHECK(
    vkCreateCommandPool(device, &commandPoolInfo,
                        nullptr, &commandPool));
```

With a command pool object, you can start allocating command buffers for recording commands.

Allocating, recording, and submitting commands

Command buffers are allocated from command pools using the vkAllocateCommandBuffers function. Command buffers must be initialized with the vkBeginCommandBuffer function before being recorded into the buffer and prepared for submission with vkEndCommandBuffer. Commands are recorded into the buffer between those function calls and are executed only after the command buffer is submitted to the device with vkQueueSubmit.

In this recipe, you will learn how to allocate command buffers, how to record commands in the command buffer, and how to submit them for execution on the GPU.

Getting ready

Command buffers are allocated from the VulkanCore::CommandQueueManager class and submitted using the same class. VulkanCore::CommandQueueManager provides basic functions to maintain a set of command buffers for processing.

How to do it...

A command buffer's life cycle starts with its allocation from a command pool. Once it has started, commands can be recorded into it. Before submission, you need to explicitly message them that recording has ended. They can then be submitted for execution:

1. To allocate command buffers, you call `vkAllocateCommandBuffers`, passing in the command pool, the number of buffers you want to allocate, and a pointer to a structure that specifies the properties of the command buffers:

   ```
   const VkCommandBufferAllocateInfo commandBufferInfo = {
         .sType =
             VK_STRUCTURE_TYPE_COMMAND_BUFFER_ALLOCATE_INFO,
         .commandPool = commandPool_,
         .level = VK_COMMAND_BUFFER_LEVEL_PRIMARY,
         .commandBufferCount = 1,
   };
   VkCommandBuffer cmdBuffer{VK_NULL_HANDLE};
   VK_CHECK(vkAllocateCommandBuffers(
       device, &commandBufferInfo, &cmdBuffer));
   ```

2. After successfully allocating a command buffer, the recording of Vulkan commands can begin. The recording process is initiated through a call to the `vkBeginCommandBuffer` function, with parameters including the command buffer and a pointer to a structure that defines recording properties. Once recording is completed, the `vkEndCommandBuffer` function is called to finalize the process:

   ```
   const VkCommandBufferBeginInfo info = {
         .sType = VK_STRUCTURE_TYPE_COMMAND_BUFFER_BEGIN_INFO,
         .flags = VK_COMMAND_BUFFER_USAGE_ONE_TIME_SUBMIT_BIT,
   };
   VK_CHECK(vkBeginCommandBuffer(cmdBuffer, &info));
   ```

   Here are some examples of commonly used commands that can be recorded in a Vulkan command buffer:

   - `vkCmdBindPipeline`: Binds a pipeline to the command buffer. This command sets the current pipeline state for subsequent draw calls.

   - `vkCmdBindDescriptorSets`: Binds descriptor sets to the command buffer. Descriptor sets hold references to buffer and image resources that can be used by shaders.

   - `vkCmdBindVertexBuffers`: Binds vertex buffers to the command buffer. Vertex buffers contain the vertex data for a mesh.

   - `vkCmdDraw`: Executes a draw call, which processes vertices and rasterizes the resulting pixels.

- `vkCmdDispatch`: Executes a compute shader.
- `vkCmdCopyBuffer`: Copies data from one buffer to another.
- `vkCmdCopyImage`: Copies data from one image to another.

3. Once you are done recording commands, you must call `vkEndCommandBuffer`:

```
VK_CHECK(vkEndCommandBuffer(cmdBuffer));
```

4. Once a command buffer has been recorded, it still lives in your application and needs to be submitted to the GPU for processing. That is accomplished by the `vkQueueSubmit` function:

```
VkDevice device;  // Valid Vulkan Device
VkQueue queue;   // Valid Vulkan Queue
VkFence fence{VK_NULL_HANDLE};
const VkFenceCreateInfo fenceInfo = {
    .sType = VK_STRUCTURE_TYPE_FENCE_CREATE_INFO,
    .flags = VK_FENCE_CREATE_SIGNALED_BIT,
};
VK_CHECK(vkCreateFence(device, &fenceInfo, nullptr,
                       &fence));
const VkSubmitInfo submitInfo = {
    .sType = VK_STRUCTURE_TYPE_SUBMIT_INFO,
    .commandBufferCount = 1,
    .pCommandBuffers = cmdBuffer,
};
VK_CHECK(
    vkQueueSubmit(queue, 1, submitInfo, fence));
```

In the preceding code, the fence is a specific Vulkan object that facilitates synchronization between the GPU and the CPU. The `vkQueueSubmit` function is an asynchronous operation that does not block the application. Therefore, once a command buffer is submitted, we can only determine whether it has been processed by checking the status of the fence using functions such as `vkGetFenceStatus` or `vkWaitForFences`. See the *Understanding synchronization in the swapchain – fences and semaphores* recipe to understand how fences can be used to synchronize your application and the execution of commands submitted to the GPU.

Reusing command buffers

Command buffers can be recorded once and submitted multiple times. They can also be used once and reset before the next use or just recorded, submitted, and discarded.

In this recipe, you will learn how to reuse a command buffer without creating a race condition between your application and the GPU.

Getting ready

The code provided in `VulkanCore::CommandQueueManager` doesn't synchronize command buffers but provides functions to help you do so, such as `goToNextCmdBuffer`, `waitUntilSubmitIsComplete`, and `waitUntilAllSubmitsAreComplete`.

How to do it...

Using command buffers can be accomplished in two ways:

1. Create a command buffer and reuse it indefinitely. In this case, once the command buffer is submitted, you must wait for it to be processed before starting to record new commands. One way to guarantee that the buffer has finished being processed is by checking the status of the fences associated with it. If the fence is to be reused, you need to reset its state as well:

```
VkDevice device; // Valid Vulkan Device
VK_CHECK(vkWaitForFences(device, 1, &fences, true,
                         UINT32_MAX));
VK_CHECK(vkResetFences(device, 1, &fences));
```

Figure 1.4 shows the case where the command buffer submitted for processing is reused immediately after being submitted for processing on the GPU. Without any form of synchronization, reusing the command buffer will result in a race condition, as it may be still processing in the GPU:

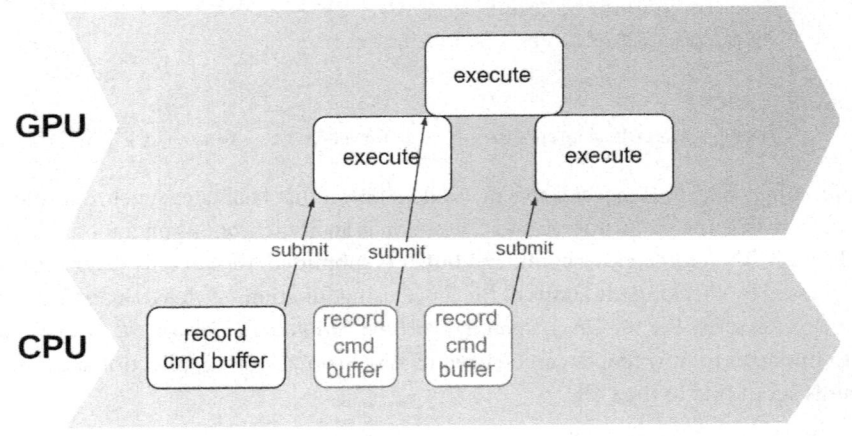

Figure 1.4 – Recording and submitting command buffers without using fences

By using fences, as depicted in *Figure 1.5*, it's possible to prevent a race condition by checking the state of the fence associated with a command buffer before reusing it. If the fence has been signaled, no wait is necessary, but if the fence has not been signaled before reusing a command buffer, the application must wait for it to be signaled before continuing:

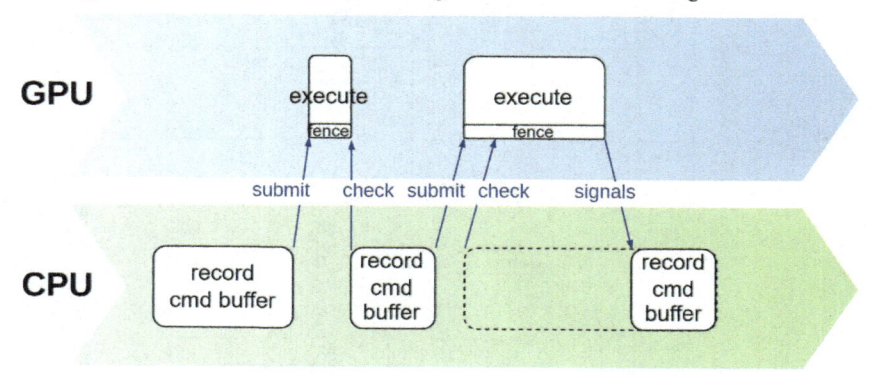

Figure 1.5 – Recording and submitting command buffers using fences

2. Allocate command buffers as needed. This is the easiest approach. Whenever you need to record and submit commands, just allocate a new command buffer from the pool, record commands, submit it, and forget about it. In this case, you need to pass the VK_COMMAND_POOL_CREATE_TRANSIENT_BIT flag when creating the command pool. You might still need a fence associated with the buffer if you need to track the state of resources used by the commands in that buffer.

Limiting the number of command buffers your application uses is a good practice that can help reduce the amount of memory your program needs.

Creating render passes

A render pass object represents a series of rendering operations that read from and write to images. It's a high-level abstraction that helps the GPU optimize the rendering process. An attachment in Vulkan is a reference to an image that is used as a target during a render pass. Attachments can be color attachments (for storing color information) or depth or stencil attachments (for storing depth/stencil information). *Figure 1.6* shows an overview of what a render pass object consists of:

Vulkan Core Concepts

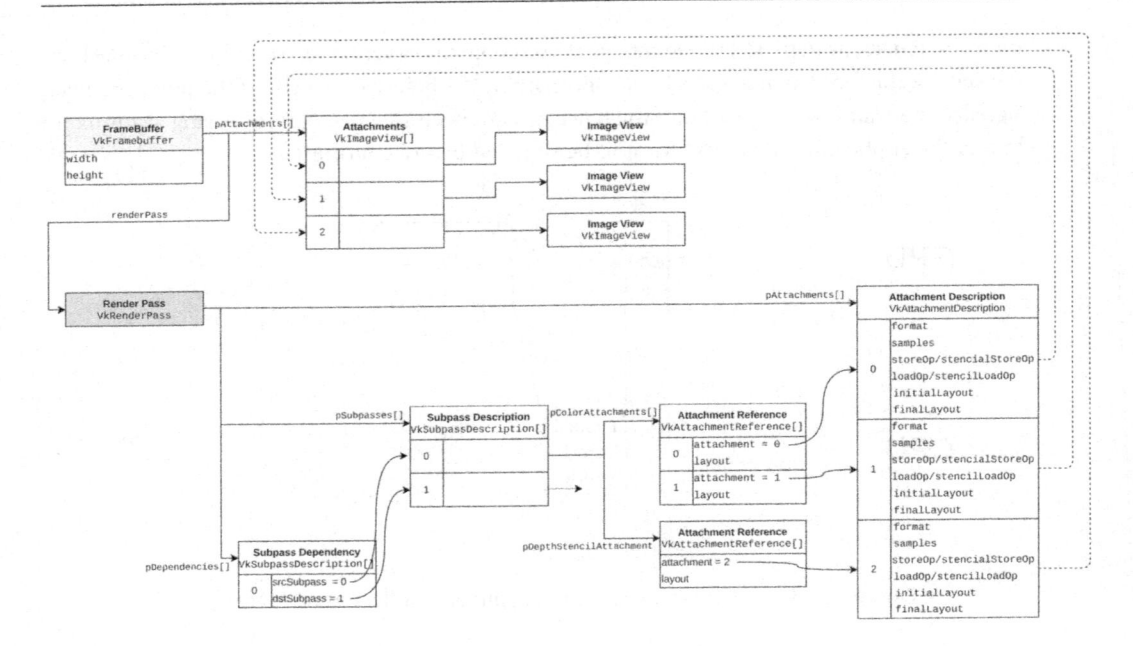

Figure 1.6 – Render pass and framebuffer composition

The `VkAttachmentDescription` structure is used when creating a render pass in Vulkan to define the properties of each attachment. The `initialLayout` and `finalLayout` fields play a crucial role in optimizing the usage of attachments and layout transitions during the render pass execution. By setting the initial and final layouts correctly, you can avoid using additional pipeline barriers to transition image layouts, as these transitions are automatically managed by the render pass execution. For example, if you can have a color attachment that is initially in the `VK_IMAGE_LAYOUT_UNDEFINED` layout and should transition to the `VK_IMAGE_LAYOUT_PRESENT_SRC_KHR` layout at the end of the render pass, you can set the `initialLayout` and `finalLayout` fields accordingly. This eliminates the need for an explicit pipeline barrier to handle the transition, as the render pass will automatically perform the layout transition as part of its execution.

A subpass is a part of a render pass that performs a specific rendering operation. Attachments are loaded for each subpass, read and/or written to, and finally stored at the end of the subpass. Load and store operations define whether an attachment's contents should be loaded, cleared, or not cared about (which means the driver/hardware is free to choose what to do – or what not to do) while being loaded and whether they should be stored or not cared about when stored at the end of the pass. They have a significant impact on performance, especially on mobile GPUs. For mobile GPUs, minimizing the number of load/store operations can lead to significant performance improvements. By using `VK_ATTACHMENT_LOAD_OP_DONT_CARE` and `VK_ATTACHMENT_STORE_OP_DONT_CARE` when possible, we can avoid unnecessary memory bandwidth usage, which is a common bottleneck on mobile devices.

A subpass dependency describes the order in which subpasses should be executed and the synchronization required between them. On mobile GPUs, using multiple subpasses can help reduce memory bandwidth usage by keeping intermediate data in on-chip memory (tile-based rendering). This avoids the need to write and read back data from the main memory, which can be expensive in terms of power consumption and performance.

Vulkan also supports render pass compatibility, which allows a framebuffer created for one render pass to be used with another compatible render pass, enhancing resource utilization and performance. Compatibility requires matching attachment counts, formats, load/store operations, sample counts, and compatible layouts; however, subpass structures can differ.

In this recipe, you will learn how to create render passes.

Getting ready

The creation of a render pass isn't complicated but requires an assortment of information that is easier to manage if encapsulated in its own class. This way, the destructor of the class can take care of destroying the object at the right time, without us having to add code to deal with its destruction.

Render passes are wrapped by the `VulkanCore::RenderPass` class in the code provided with the book.

How to do it...

Creating a render pass needs a list of all attachments that will be used in that pass, along with their load and store operations and the final layout desired for each one of the attachments. A render pass must be associated with a type of pipeline (graphics, compute, and so on), so the constructor also takes a value of type `VkPipelineBindPoint`.

The following code sample shows one of the constructors of the `VulkanCore::RenderPass` class. Be aware that we have not yet introduced Vulkan images (which are encapsulated in the `Texture` class in the code). We will discuss images in more detail in *Chapter 2, Working with Modern Vulkan*, in the *Creating images (textures)* recipe.

1. The constructor iterates over all attachments that will be used in the render pass and creates a `VkAttachmentDescription` structure for each one. This structure contains basic information that is extracted from the attachments themselves (such as format and initial layout), but it also records what to do with each attachment when it is loaded and stored. While iterating over all the attachments used in the render pass, we create two other auxiliary variables: one list with the indices of attachments that are of type color (`colorAttachmentReferences`) and a variable that stores the index of the attachment that is depth and/or stencil (`depthStencilAttachmentReference`), since render passes only support one depth/stencil attachment:

    ```
    RenderPass::RenderPass(
        const Context& context,
    ```

Vulkan Core Concepts

```cpp
    const std::vector<std::shared_ptr<Texture>>
        attachments,
    const std::vector<VkAttachmentLoadOp>& loadOp,
    const std::vector<VkAttachmentStoreOp>& storeOp,
    const std::vector<VkImageLayout>& layout,
    VkPipelineBindPoint bindPoint,
    const std::string& name)
    : device_{context.device()} {
ASSERT(attachments.size() == loadOp.size() &&
           attachments.size() == storeOp.size() &&
           attachments.size() == layout.size(),
       "The sizes of the attachments and their load "
       "and store operations and final layouts "
       "must match");

std::vector<VkAttachmentDescription>
    attachmentDescriptors;
std::vector<VkAttachmentReference>
    colorAttachmentReferences;
std::optional<VkAttachmentReference>
    depthStencilAttachmentReference;
```

2. For each attachment, create a `VkAttachmentDescription` structure and append it to the `attachmentDescriptors` vector:

```cpp
for (uint32_t index = 0; index < attachments.size();
     ++index) {
  attachmentDescriptors.emplace_back(
      VkAttachmentDescription{
          .format = attachments[index]->vkFormat(),
          .samples = VK_SAMPLE_COUNT_1_BIT,
          .loadOp =
              attachments[index]->isStencil()
                  ? VK_ATTACHMENT_LOAD_OP_DONT_CARE
                  : loadOp[index],
          .storeOp =
              attachments[index]->isStencil()
                  ? VK_ATTACHMENT_STORE_OP_DONT_CARE
                  : storeOp[index],
          .stencilLoadOp =
              attachments[index]->isStencil()
                  ? loadOp[index]
                  : VK_ATTACHMENT_LOAD_OP_DONT_CARE,
          .stencilStoreOp =
```

```
                attachments[index]->isStencil()
                    ? storeOp[index]
                    : VK_ATTACHMENT_STORE_OP_DONT_CARE,
            .initialLayout =
                attachments[index]->vkLayout(),
            .finalLayout = layout[index],
        });
```

3. If the attachment is a depth or a stencil texture, create a `VkAttachmentReference` structure for it and store it in the `depthStencilAttachmentReference` auxiliary variable. Otherwise, the attachment is a color attachment, and we create and store a `VkAttachmentReference` structure to the `colorAttachmentReferences` vector:

```
    if (attachments[index]->isStencil() ||
        attachments[index]->isDepth()) {
      depthStencilAttachmentReference =
            VkAttachmentReference{
                .attachment = index,
                .layout =
                    VK_IMAGE_LAYOUT_DEPTH_STENCIL_ATTACHMENT_OPTIMAL,
            };
    } else {
      colorAttachmentReferences.emplace_back(
            VkAttachmentReference{
                .attachment = index,
                .layout =
                    VK_IMAGE_LAYOUT_COLOR_ATTACHMENT_OPTIMAL,
            });
    }
}
```

4. The `RenderPass` class only creates one subpass, which stores the color attachment references and the depth/stencil attachment reference:

```
    const VkSubpassDescription spd = {
        .pipelineBindPoint =
            VK_PIPELINE_BIND_POINT_GRAPHICS,
        .colorAttachmentCount = static_cast<uint32_t>(
            colorAttachmentReferences.size()),
        .pColorAttachments =
            colorAttachmentReferences.data(),
        .pDepthStencilAttachment =
```

```
                depthStencilAttachmentReference.has_value()
                    ? &depthStencilAttachmentReference
                        .value()
                    : nullptr,
};
```

5. The only subpass we use for this recipe depends on an external subpass (since there's only one subpass, it must depend on an external one):

```
const VkSubpassDependency subpassDependency = {
    .srcSubpass = VK_SUBPASS_EXTERNAL,
    .srcStageMask =
        VK_PIPELINE_STAGE_COLOR_ATTACHMENT_OUTPUT_BIT |
        VK_PIPELINE_STAGE_EARLY_FRAGMENT_TESTS_BIT,
    .dstStageMask =
        VK_PIPELINE_STAGE_COLOR_ATTACHMENT_OUTPUT_BIT |
        VK_PIPELINE_STAGE_EARLY_FRAGMENT_TESTS_BIT,
    .dstAccessMask =
        VK_ACCESS_COLOR_ATTACHMENT_WRITE_BIT |
        VK_ACCESS_DEPTH_STENCIL_ATTACHMENT_WRITE_BIT,
};
```

6. Lastly, all this information is stored in a structure of type `VkRenderPassCreateInfo`, which is passed, along with the device, to create a render pass with `vkCreateRenderPass`. The handle is stored in the `RenderPass::renderPass_` member variable:

```
const VkRenderPassCreateInfo rpci = {
    .sType =
        VK_STRUCTURE_TYPE_RENDER_PASS_CREATE_INFO,
    .attachmentCount = static_cast<uint32_t>(
        attachmentDescriptors.size()),
    .pAttachments = attachmentDescriptors.data(),
    .subpassCount = 1,
    .pSubpasses = &spd,
    .dependencyCount = 1,
    .pDependencies = &subpassDependency,
};
VK_CHECK(vkCreateRenderPass(device_, &rpci, nullptr,
                            &renderPass_));
context.setVkObjectname(renderPass_,
                VK_OBJECT_TYPE_RENDER_PASS,
                "Render pass: " + name);
}
```

7. Destroying the render pass happens in the destructor, by calling the `vkDestroyRenderPass` function:

   ```
   RenderPass::~RenderPass() {
     vkDestroyRenderPass(device_, renderPass_, nullptr);
   }
   ```

Render passes store information on *what to do* with attachments (loaded, cleared, stored) and describe subpass dependencies. They also describe which attachments are resolve attachments (see the *Enabling and using Vulkan's MSAA* recipe in *Chapter 6, Anti-Aliasing Techniques*, to know more about resolve attachments and how they are used to implement MSAA in Vulkan).

Creating framebuffers

While the render pass object contains information about what to do with each attachment and their initial and final layouts, a framebuffer contains actual references to the attachments used in the render pass, which are provided in the form of `VkImageViews`.

In this recipe, you will learn how to create a framebuffer object.

Getting ready

In the repository, Vulkan framebuffers are encapsulated by the `VulkanCore::Framebuffer` class.

How to do it...

Framebuffers refer to attachments (it answers the question "Which attachments will we be using for this render pass?").

1. The references are image views and are passed as a list, along with the handle of the render pass, to the `vkCreateFramebuffer` framebuffer creation function:

   ```
   uint32_t width, height; // Width and height of attachments
   VkDevice device; // Valid Vulkan Device
   std::vector<VkImageView> imageViews; // Valid Image Views
   const VkFramebufferCreateInfo framebufferInfo = {
       .sType = VK_STRUCTURE_TYPE_FRAMEBUFFER_CREATE_INFO,
       .renderPass = renderPass,
       .attachmentCount =
           static_cast<uint32_t>(attachments.size()),
       .pAttachments = imageViews.data(),
       .width = attachments[0]->vkExtents().width,
       .height = attachments[0]->vkExtents().height,
       .layers = 1,
   ```

```
    };
    VK_CHECK(
        vkCreateFramebuffer(device_, &framebufferInfo,
                            nullptr, &framebuffer_));
```

Creating framebuffers is straightforward, and they are not strictly necessary anymore if you use dynamic rendering.

Creating image views

In Vulkan, an image view is a way to specify how an image should be interpreted and accessed by the GPU. It provides a view into an image's memory and defines its format, dimensions, and data layout.

An image view can be thought of as a window into an image's memory that describes how the image should be accessed. It allows the image to be used in a variety of ways, such as a source or destination for rendering commands, or as a texture in a shader.

Image views are created by specifying the image they will be associated with, along with a set of parameters that define the image's format, aspect ratio, and range. Once created, an image view can be bound to a pipeline or shader to be used in rendering or other operations. They are represented by the `VkImage` type.

In this recipe, you will learn how to create image views.

Getting ready

In the repository, image views are stored by the `VulkanCore::Texture` class and don't have a dedicated wrapper.

How to do it...

Before creating an image view, you need the handle a Vulkan image object:

1. Creating an image view is simple; all you need is the handle to a Vulkan image object (`VkImage`) and a few parameters that dictate how to access the underlying image:

    ```
    VkImage image; // Valid VkImage
    const VkImageAspectFlags aspectMask =
        isDepth() ? VK_IMAGE_ASPECT_DEPTH_BIT
                  : VK_IMAGE_ASPECT_COLOR_BIT;
    const VkImageViewCreateInfo imageViewInfo = {
        .sType = VK_STRUCTURE_TYPE_IMAGE_VIEW_CREATE_INFO,
        .image = image_,
        .viewType = viewType,
    ```

```
        .format = format,
        .components =
            {
                .r = VK_COMPONENT_SWIZZLE_IDENTITY,
                .g = VK_COMPONENT_SWIZZLE_IDENTITY,
                .b = VK_COMPONENT_SWIZZLE_IDENTITY,
                .a = VK_COMPONENT_SWIZZLE_IDENTITY,
            },
        .subresourceRange = {
            .aspectMask = aspectMask,
            .baseMipLevel = 0,
            .levelCount = numMipLevels,
            .baseArrayLayer = 0,
            .layerCount = layers,
        }};

    VK_CHECK(vkCreateImageView(context_.device(),
                                &imageViewInfo, nullptr,
                                &imageView_));
```

Image views can span an entire image (mip levels and layers), just one element (mip level or layer), or even just a portion of the image.

The Vulkan graphics pipeline

The graphics pipeline is a crucial concept that describes the process of rendering graphics in a Vulkan application. The pipeline consists of a series of stages, each with a specific purpose, that take raw data and transform it into a fully rendered image on the screen. While some stages of the pipeline are more obvious, such as the viewport or rasterization, other stages such as the shader stage, vertex input, and dynamic states are less apparent but equally important. In the following recipes, we will explore some of the less obvious stages of the pipeline and explain their importance in the rendering process. *Figure 1.7* shows an overview of all structures you may need to populate to create a graphics pipeline and their properties:

62   Vulkan Core Concepts

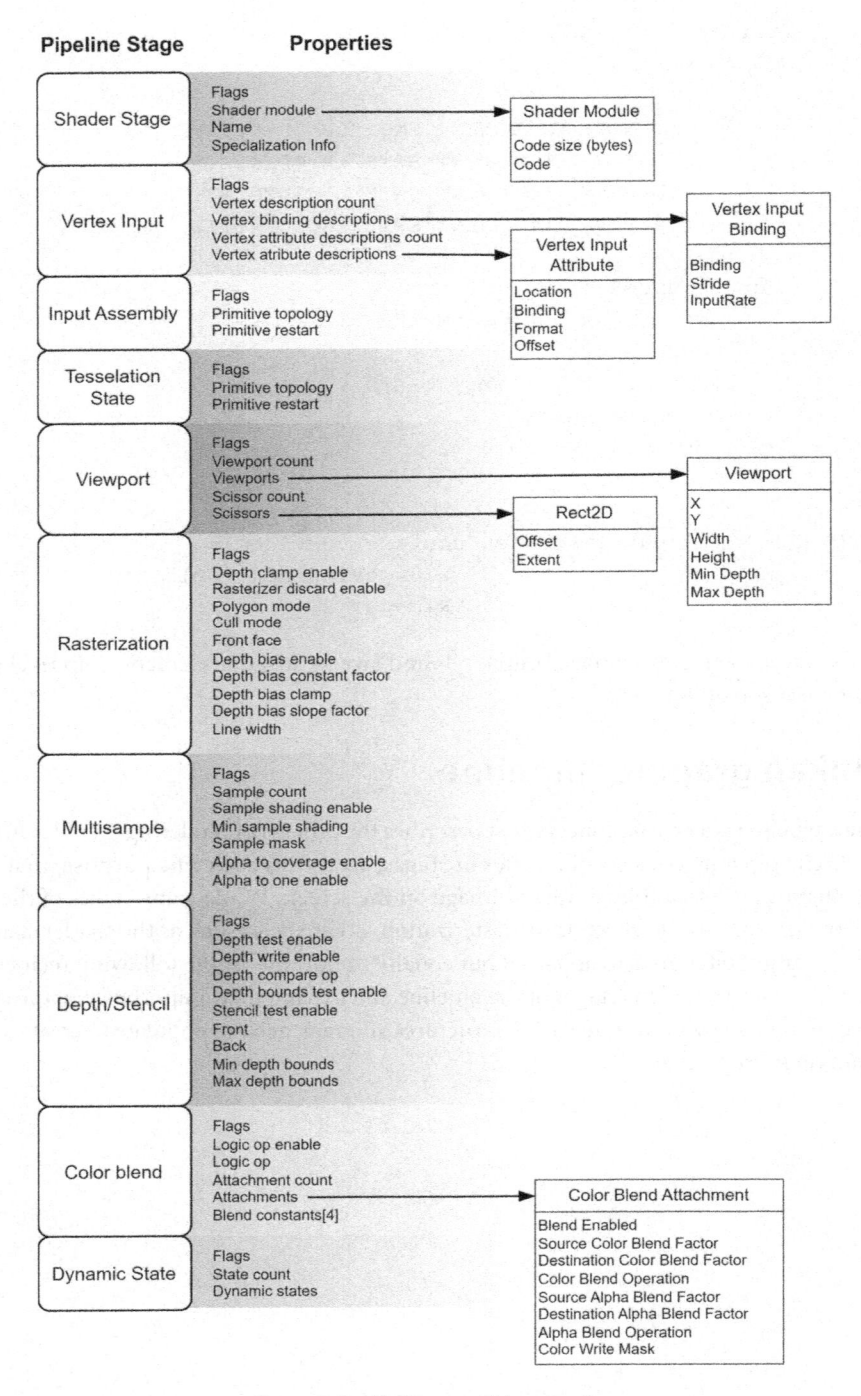

Pipeline Stage	Properties
Shader Stage	Flags / Shader module / Name / Specialization Info
Vertex Input	Flags / Vertex description count / Vertex binding descriptions / Vertex attribute descriptions count / Vertex atribute descriptions
Input Assembly	Flags / Primitive topology / Primitive restart
Tesselation State	Flags / Primitive topology / Primitive restart
Viewport	Flags / Viewport count / Viewports / Scissor count / Scissors
Rasterization	Flags / Depth clamp enable / Rasterizer discard enable / Polygon mode / Cull mode / Front face / Depth bias enable / Depth bias constant factor / Depth bias clamp / Depth bias slope factor / Line width
Multisample	Flags / Sample count / Sample shading enable / Min sample shading / Sample mask / Alpha to coverage enable / Alpha to one enable
Depth/Stencil	Flags / Depth test enable / Depth write enable / Depth compare op / Depth bounds test enable / Stencil test enable / Front / Back / Min depth bounds / Max depth bounds
Color blend	Flags / Logic op enable / Logic op / Attachment count / Attachments / Blend constants[4]
Dynamic State	Flags / State count / Dynamic states

Shader Module: Code size (bytes) / Code

Vertex Input Attribute: Location / Binding / Format / Offset

Vertex Input Binding: Binding / Stride / InputRate

Rect2D: Offset / Extent

Viewport: X / Y / Width / Height / Min Depth / Max Depth

Color Blend Attachment: Blend Enabled / Source Color Blend Factor / Destination Color Blend Factor / Color Blend Operation / Source Alpha Blend Factor / Destination Alpha Blend Factor / Alpha Blend Operation / Color Write Mask

Figure 1.7 – Vulkan graphics pipeline

In this recipe, you will learn a little more about pipelines in Vulkan and their most important characteristics.

How to do it...

Here are the most important characteristics of pipelines in Vulkan:

1. In Vulkan, graphics pipelines are mostly immutable objects, meaning that once they are created, they cannot be modified except in certain instances. This is why it is necessary to create a new pipeline with a different topology if you wish to reuse a pipeline to draw different shapes. However, some pipeline properties can be changed dynamically at runtime, such as the viewport and scissor rectangles, which are referred to as dynamic states.

2. One important exception to the pipeline stages that won't be covered in this book is the vertex input state. Although it is not entirely straightforward to create, we will not discuss it here since we exclusively utilize the **Programmable Vertex Pulling (PVP)** method to access indices and vertices at the vertex shader stage. For additional information about PVP, please refer to the *Implementing Programmable Vertex Pulling and Multi-Draw Indirect* recipe in *Chapter 2, Working with Modern Vulkan*.

3. Similarly, the pipeline layout, a property of the graphics pipeline (and not a stage), is a data structure that outlines the anticipated layout of resources utilized by the shaders, including their location, quantity, and type, as well as pertinent details regarding push constants. Since this chapter does not provide any resources to the shaders, the pipeline layout is initialized with default values. Descriptor sets and push constants will be covered in *Chapter 2, Working with Modern Vulkan*.

Compiling shaders to SPIR-V

In contrast to OpenGL, which typically compiles shaders from high-level languages into binary format during runtime, Vulkan only supports an intermediate representation called SPIR-V. SPIR-V is a cross-platform, low-level intermediate representation that can be produced from various shading languages.

In this recipe, you will learn how to compile GLSL to SPIR-V using the `glslang` library.

Getting ready

In this recipe, we use a third-party library that compiles GLSL code into SPIR-V at runtime called `glslang`. It can be downloaded from `https://github.com/KhronosGroup/glslang.git`.

In our code, we provide the `VulkanCore::ShaderModule` class that encapsulates shaders. It provides the `ShaderModule::glslToSpirv` method (and overloads) that compiles shader source code from GLSL to SPIR-V.

How to do it...

The steps presented here are part of the `ShaderModule::glslToSpirv()` method. Here's how it works:

1. The `glslang` library needs to be initialized once by calling `glslang::InitializeProcess()`, so its initialization is guarded by a static Boolean variable:

    ```
    std::vector<char> ShaderModule::glslToSpirv(
        const std::vector<char>& data,
        EShLanguage shaderStage,
        const std::string& shaderDir,
        const char* entryPoint) {
      static bool glslangInitialized = false;

      if (!glslangInitialized) {
        glslang::InitializeProcess();
        glslangInitialized = true;
      }
    ```

2. The `TShader` object is instantiated by a function to contain shaders and various other parameters that are necessary for generating SPIR-V bytecode. These parameters include the input client and GLSL versions, as well as entry points into the shaders:

    ```
    glslang::TShader tshader(shaderStage);
    const char* glslCStr = data.data();
    tshader.setStrings(&glslCStr, 1);

    glslang::EshTargetClientVersion clientVersion =
        glslang::EShTargetVulkan_1_3;
    glslang::EShTargetLanguageVersion langVersion =
        glslang::EShTargetSpv_1_3;

    tshader.setEnvInput(glslang::EShSourceGlsl,
                        shaderStage,
                        glslang::EShClientVulkan, 460);

    tshader.setEnvClient(glslang::EShClientVulkan,
                         clientVersion);
    tshader.setEnvTarget(glslang::EShTargetSpv,
                         langVersion);

    tshader.setEntryPoint(entryPoint);
    tshader.setSourceEntryPoint(entryPoint);
    ```

3. Afterward, we collect constraints on resources that are typically available for shaders in the system, such as the maximum number of textures or vertex attributes, and establish messages that the compiler should present. Lastly, we compile the shader into SPIR-V and verify the result:

```
const TBuiltInResource* resources =
    GetDefaultResources();
const EShMessages messages =
    static_cast<EShMessages>(
        EShMsgDefault | EShMsgSpvRules |
        EShMsgVulkanRules | EShMsgDebugInfo |
        EShMsgReadHlsl);
CustomIncluder includer(shaderDir);

std::string preprocessedGLSL;
if (!tshader.preprocess(
        resources, 460, ENoProfile, false, false,
        messages, &preprocessedGLSL, includer)) {
    std::cout << "Preprocessing failed for shader: "
              << std::endl;
    printShader(data);
    std::cout << std::endl;
    std::cout << tshader.getInfoLog() << std::endl;
    std::cout << tshader.getInfoDebugLog()
              << std::endl;
    ASSERT(false, "includes are forbidden");
    return std::vector<char>();
}
```

4. In the last phase, linking options are established for both debug and release builds. In debug builds, regular debugging information is enabled while optimizations and debug information stripping are disabled. Conversely, in release builds, the optimizer is enabled, which may result in the removal of unused shader variables, including structure members. However, because discrepancies in structure sizes may cause problems if the same optimizations are not applied to the C++ code, optimizations are also disabled in release builds:

```
    glslang::SpvOptions options;
#ifdef _DEBUG
    tshader.setDebugInfo(true);
    options.generateDebugInfo = true;
    options.disableOptimizer = true;
    options.optimizeSize = false;
    options.stripDebugInfo = false;
    options.emitNonSemanticShaderDebugSource = true;
#else
```

```cpp
    options.disableOptimizer = true;   // Special care!
    options.optimizeSize = true;
    options.stripDebugInfo = true;
#endif

    glslang::TProgram program;
    program.addShader(&tshader);
    if (!program.link(messages)) {
      std::cout << "Parsing failed for shader "
                << std::endl;
      std::cout << program.getInfoLog() << std::endl;
      std::cout << program.getInfoDebugLog()
                << std::endl;
      ASSERT(false, "link failed");
    }

    std::vector<uint32_t> spirvData;
    spv::SpvBuildLogger spvLogger;
    glslang::GlslangToSpv(
        program.getIntermediate(shaderStage), spirvData,
        &spvLogger, &options);

    std::vector<char> byteCode;
    byteCode.resize(spirvData.size() *
                    (sizeof(uint32_t) / sizeof(char)));
    std::memcpy(byteCode.data(), spirvData.data(),
                byteCode.size());

    return byteCode;
}
```

For truly performant applications, shaders are not compiled from GLSL at runtime. They are compiled at build time and loaded from disk in the SPIR-V format when the application starts.

Dynamic states

While **pipeline state objects** (**PSOs**) include immutable states, such as shader programs and vertex input bindings, some properties of a pipeline state can be changed dynamically at draw time using dynamic state objects. This feature provides greater flexibility and can minimize the necessity to recreate pipelines. Dynamic state objects can be used to change properties such as viewport and scissor rectangles, line width, blend constants, and stencil reference values. However, not all properties of a pipeline can be changed dynamically, and the use of dynamic states can have a small performance overhead.

Without using dynamic states, the application has a few alternatives available:

1. Create pipelines during the application startup. If you are aware of which pipelines will be required, they can be created beforehand at the expense of a higher startup cost.
2. Utilize pipeline caches. The graphics driver features a built-in mechanism for pipeline caching that can automatically generate a cache for you.

Several parameters, such as the viewport, line width, and depth bias, can be dynamically modified. While some dynamic states were included in Vulkan 1.0, others were added as extensions or included as part of Vulkan 1.3. If a parameter is marked as dynamic (using the appropriate structure), its value is ignored during pipeline creation.

In this recipe, you will learn about dynamic states, which allow some pipeline parameters to be dynamically set after a pipeline has been created.

Getting ready

Dynamic states are created using the `VkPipelineDynamicStateCreateInfo` structure. An instance of this structure is filled with states you would like to be dynamic and is later plugged into the creation of a pipeline, which we'll cover in the next recipe.

How to do it...

To allow parameters to be dynamically set, we need to create an instance of the `VkPipelineDynamicStateCreateInfo` structure.

1. The next code fragment shows how to enable the dynamic state for the viewport parameter:

    ```
    const std::array<VkDynamicState, 1> dynamicStates = {
        VK_DYNAMIC_STATE_VIEWPORT,
    };

    const VkPipelineDynamicStateCreateInfo dynamicState = {
        .sType =
            VK_STRUCTURE_TYPE_PIPELINE_DYNAMIC_STATE_CREATE_INFO,
        .dynamicStateCount =
            static_cast<uint32_t>(dynamicStates.size()),
        .pDynamicStates = dynamicStates.data(),
    };
    ```

    `VkDynamicState` is an enumeration that contains all possible states that can be dynamically set. In the preceding snippet, the `dynamicStates` array contains only the `VK_DYNAMIC_STATE_VIEWPORT` value, but it may contain a much larger set of values from `VkDynamicState`.

The previously created instance will be used in the next recipe.

Creating a graphics pipeline

Once all the required states and pipeline properties have been gathered and instantiated, creating a graphics pipeline in Vulkan is a straightforward process. This involves populating the `VkGraphicsPipelineCreateInfo` structure and calling `vkCreateGraphicsPipelines`.

In this recipe, you will learn how to create a graphics pipeline object in Vulkan.

Getting ready

For more information, please refer to the constructor of the `VulkanCore::Pipeline` class in the repository.

How to do it...

Populating the structures referenced by `VkGraphicsPipelineCreateInfo` is not complicated, but a tedious task.

1. Once all structures of all states have been instantiated, all we need to do is create an instance of `VkGraphicsPipelineCreateInfo` and call `vkCreateGraphicsPipelines`:

   ```
   const VkGraphicsPipelineCreateInfo pipelineInfo = {
       .sType=VK_STRUCTURE_TYPE_GRAPHICS_PIPELINE_CREATE_INFO,
       .stageCount = uint32_t(shaderStages.size()),
       .pStages = shaderStages.data(),
       .pVertexInputState = &vinfo,
       .pInputAssemblyState = &inputAssembly,
       .pViewportState = &viewportState,
       .pRasterizationState = &rasterizer,
       .pMultisampleState = &multisampling,
       .pDepthStencilState = &depthStencilState, // Optional
       .pColorBlendState = &colorBlending,
       .pDynamicState = &dynamicState,
       .layout = layout,
       .renderPass = renderPass,
       .basePipelineHandle = VK_NULL_HANDLE, // Optional
       .basePipelineIndex = -1,  // Optional
   };

   VkPipeline gfxPipeline = VK_NULL_HANDLE;
   VK_CHECK(vkCreateGraphicsPipelines(
       device_, VK_NULL_HANDLE, 1, &pipelineInfo,
       nullptr, &gfxPipeline));
   ```

Creating a graphics pipeline is an expensive operation. One way to avoid the penalty of creating pipelines is to cache them and reuse them the next time your application runs.

Swapchain

A swapchain in Vulkan mimics the functionality of double and triple buffering from OpenGL but with a more explicit role for the application in managing swapchain buffers. This approach provides better control over the configuration, synchronization, and presentation of images.

A Vulkan swapchain is a collection of images associated with a surface (`VkSurfaceKHR`) that are used to display rendering outputs in a window. Even though it is a key part of the Vulkan API, the functions and types used to create and manage a swapchain are part of the `VK_KHR_swapchain` extension.

The number of images in a swapchain object must be determined during its construction but must fall between the minimum (`minImageCount`) and maximum (`maxImageCount`) possible values provided by the device. Those values can be retrieved from the `VkSurfaceCapabilitiesKHR` structure of the Vulkan physical device.

Swapchain images (`VkImage`) are created and owned by the swapchain object and, as a result, their memory isn't provided or allocated by the application. Image views (`VkImageView`) are not created by the swapchain object and thus must be created separately.

In this recipe, you will learn how to create, manage, and destroy swapchain images.

Getting ready

The swapchain is managed by the `VulkanCore::Swapchain` class in the code.

How to do it...

The swapchain extension provides a set of functions and types to create, manage, and destroy swapchains. Some key functions and types include the following:

1. `vkCreateSwapchainKHR`: This function is used to create a swapchain. You need to provide a `VkSwapchainCreateInfoKHR` structure that contains details about the surface, the number of images, their format, dimensions, usage flags, and other swapchain properties.
2. `vkGetSwapchainImagesKHR`: After creating a swapchain, this function is used to retrieve handles to the images in the swapchain. You can then create image views and framebuffers for rendering and presentation.

3. `vkAcquireNextImageKHR`: This function is used to acquire an available image from the swapchain for rendering. It also requires providing a semaphore or fence to signal when the image is ready for rendering.

4. `vkQueuePresentKHR`: Once rendering is complete, this function is used to submit the swapchain image for presentation on the display device.

5. `vkDestroySwapchainKHR`: This function is responsible for destroying the swapchain and cleaning up resources associated with it.

Understanding synchronization in the swapchain – fences and semaphores

The application and the GPU processes run in parallel; unless specified otherwise, the command buffers and their commands also run in parallel on the GPU. To enforce an order between the CPU and the GPU, and between command buffers being processed in the GPU, Vulkan provides two mechanisms: **fences** and **semaphores**. Fences are used to synchronize work between the GPU and the CPU, while semaphores are used to synchronize workloads executed in the GPU.

In this recipe, you will learn about fences and semaphores: why they are necessary, how they are used (and when), and how to use semaphores with a swapchain.

Getting ready

Examples of semaphores can be found in the `VulkanCore::Swapchain` class, while examples of fences can be found in the `VulkanCore::CommandQueueManager` class.

How to do it...

Fences and semaphores have different uses. Let's explore each one of those elements and how to use semaphores with swapchains.

1. *Figure 1.8* shows how an application, running on the CPU, may submit commands to the GPU and proceed with its work right after submission (without synchronization). This may be intended, but if you wish to wait for commands on the GPU to finish being processed before continuing, you may use a fence to signal when work on the GPU has been completed. Once commands on the GPU are finished processing, the fence is signaled, and the application may proceed:

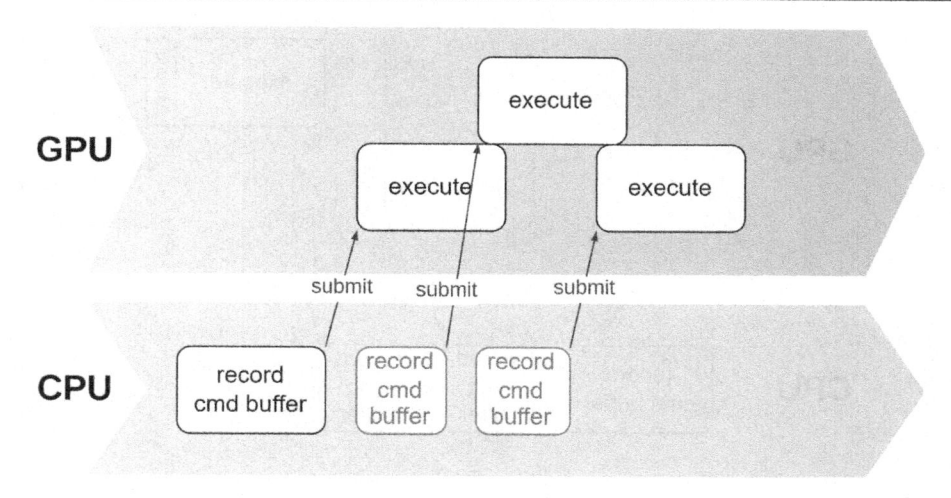

Figure 1.8 – Command buffer recording and execution on the device without synchronization

2. Semaphores work in a similar manner but are used between commands or jobs running on the GPU. *Figure 1.10* illustrates using a semaphore to synchronize commands being processed on the GPU. The application is responsible for creating semaphores and adding dependencies between command buffers and semaphores itself before submitting the buffers for processing. Once a task is processed on the GPU, the semaphore is signaled, and the next task can continue. This enforces an ordering between commands:

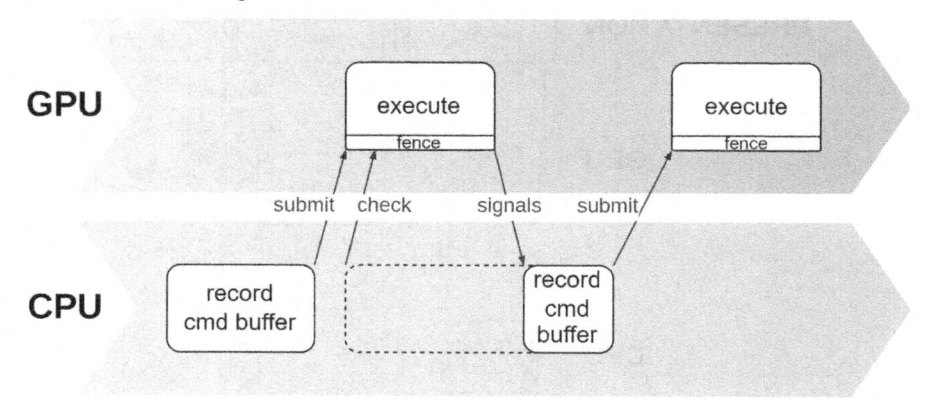

Figure 1.9 – Fences

The process of acquiring an image, rendering, and presenting are all asynchronous and need to be synchronized. In this recipe, we will use two semaphores for the synchronization: `imageAvailable` and `imageRendered`. *Figure 1.10* illustrates how semaphores affect the execution of commands on the device:

72   Vulkan Core Concepts

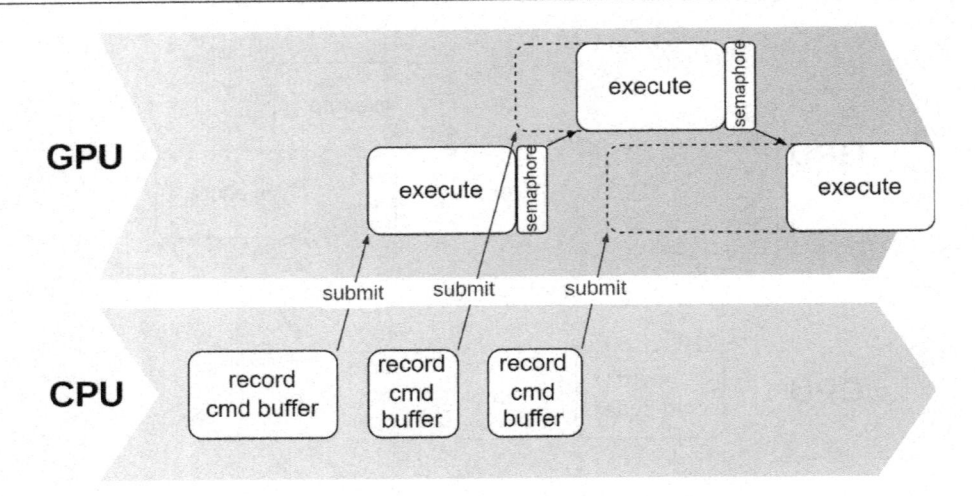

Figure 1.10 – Semaphores

`imageAvailable_` is signaled once the image acquired is available, prompting the command queue that will render into the image to start processing. Once the command buffer finishes, it signals the other semaphore, `imageRendered`, which in turn allows the presentation of that image to start. *Figure 1.11* demonstrates how synchronization is implemented using two semaphores:

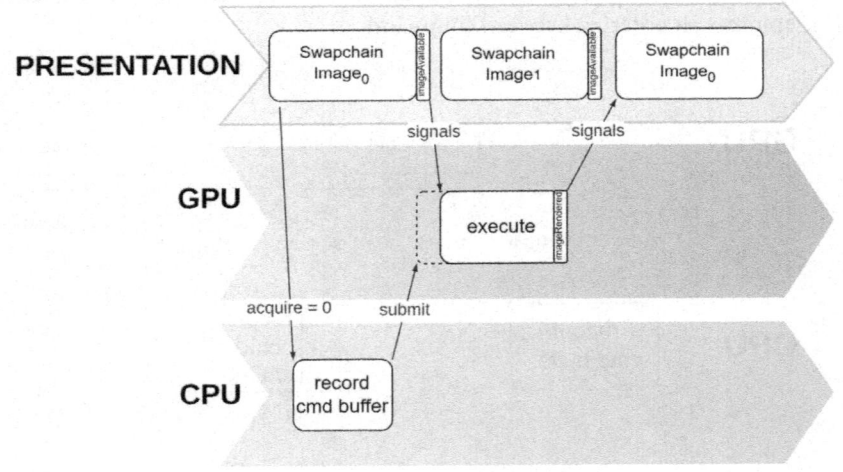

Figure 1.11 – Synchronization of the swapchain

Fences and semaphores aren't difficult to understand, but they are crucial for synchronization in Vulkan. Make sure you understand how they are used before continuing.

Populating submission information for presentation

Submitting a command buffer requires an instance of the `VkSubmitInfo` structure, which allows specifying semaphores for waiting (to start processing) and signaling (once the command buffer finishes executing). Those semaphores are optional and usually not needed. But when submitting a command buffer for presenting images onto the screen, those semaphores allow Vulkan to synchronize the execution of the buffer with the presentation engine.

In this recipe, you will learn how to submit a command buffer for processing by the GPU after it has been recorded.

Getting ready

The `VulkanCore::Swapchain` class in the repository provides a utility function to fill the `VkSubmitInfo` structure for you since the semaphores used to synchronize the execution with the presentation engine are stored in the swapchain. If no semaphores are needed in the structure, the `waitForImageAvailable` and `signalImagePresented` parameters should be set to `false`.

How to do it...

The synchronization information used to submit command buffers that need to be synchronized with the presentation engine is provided by an instance of the `VkSubmitInfo` structure and contains references to the semaphores that will be used for synchronization in the device. It also contains the command buffer that will be submitted.

1. The fence is associated with the command buffer and is not a specific one for synchronizing the swapchain:

   ```
   const VkSubmitInfo submitInfo = {
       .sType = VK_STRUCTURE_TYPE_SUBMIT_INFO,
       .waitSemaphoreCount = 1,
       .pWaitSemaphores = &imageAvailable,
       .pWaitDstStageMask = submitStageMask,
       .commandBufferCount = 1,
       .pCommandBuffers = buffer,
       .signalSemaphoreCount = 1,
       .pSignalSemaphores = &imagePresented,
   };
   VK_CHECK(vkQueueSubmit(queue_, 1, &submitInfo, fence));
   ```

Once a command buffer has been submitted for processing, it's up to the driver and the GPU to execute the commands recorded there. The only way to know whether the command buffer has finished processing is by checking the fence provided to `vkQueueSubmit`.

Presenting images

Presenting an image onto the screen isn't automatic in Vulkan. You need to call the `vkQueuePresentKHR` function along with an instance of the `VkPresentInfoKHR` structure.

In this recipe, you will learn how to queue an image for presentation once it has finished rendering.

Getting ready

The presentation in our code is done in the `VulkanCore::Swapchain::present()` method.

How to do it...

Requesting an acquired image to be presented is done by calling `vkQueuePresentKHR`.

This time, we need to provide the `imageRendered` semaphore, which indicates when the rendering process has finished using the image:

```
const VkPresentInfoKHR presentInfo{
    .sType = VK_STRUCTURE_TYPE_PRESENT_INFO_KHR,
    .waitSemaphoreCount = 1,
    .pWaitSemaphores = &imageRendered_,
    .swapchainCount = 1,
    .pSwapchains = &swapchain_,
    .pImageIndices = &imageIndex_,
};
VK_CHECK(vkQueuePresentKHR(presentQueue_, &presentInfo));
```

The image won't be presented right away once `VkQueuePresentKHR` is called. This call merely sets up the synchronization mechanism so that Vulkan knows when the image can be sent for display.

Rendering a triangle

Now that we've learned about all basic Vulkan objects and how they work, we can finally create a small example application that displays a static shaded triangle on the screen.

In this recipe, we will present a full example that renders a static triangle on the screen. The vertex data and attributes are statically provided in the vertex shader.

Getting ready

The code in this recipe can be found in the repository in `source/chapter1/main.cpp`. The vertex and fragment shaders are located in `source/chapter1/resources/shaders`, in the `triangle.vert` and `triangle.frag` files.

How to do it...

The code presented here is an unabridged version of the code in the repository.

1. For this recipe, we will use two shaders: `triangle.vert` and `triangle.frag`. The vertex shader does not accept any inputs, as all the data it needs is defined right there in the shader itself as two arrays: one for vertex data (`positions`) and the other for color data (`colors`).

   Both sets of data are sent to the output as-is without any transformations, as they are already in their respective output spaces (screen space for the position data and the output color space for the color data). The position is output through the built-in `gl_VertexIndex` variable, while the color is written to the `outColor` variable at location 0:

   ```
   #version 460

   layout(location = 0) out vec4 outColor;

   vec2 positions[3] = vec2[](
       vec2(0.0, -0.5),
       vec2(0.5, 0.5),
       vec2(-0.5, 0.5)
   );

   vec3 colors[3] = vec3[](
       vec3(1.0, 0.0, 0.0),
       vec3(0.0, 1.0, 0.0),
       vec3(0.0, 0.0, 1.0)
   );

   void main() {
       gl_Position = vec4(positions[gl_VertexIndex], 0.0, 1.0);
       outColor = vec4(colors[gl_VertexIndex], 1.0);
   }
   ```

2. The fragment shader accepts the color data from the vertex stage and directly outputs it as the fragment color through the `outColor` variable at location 0:

   ```
   #version 460

   layout(location = 0) in vec4 inColor;
   layout(location = 0) out vec4 outColor;

   void main() {
       outColor = inColor;
   }
   ```

We only need one render pass that will output the render result to a framebuffer with only one attachment, color attachment 0. The color attachment's load operation is *clear* as we will clear it for rendering, whereas the store operation is *store* as we want the output to be recorded into the attachment. The output will go straight into the swapchain, so the acquired swapchain image is the color attachment 0. Since each render pass outputs directly onto the swapchain image, and a framebuffer is associated with an attachment and is immutable, we need the number of framebuffers to match the number of swapchain images. Each framebuffer will be associated with one swapchain image as the color attachment 0. The shaders don't need access to external buffers, such as vertex and index, or textures.

3. The first step is to initialize a window and create a context with the features we will use by default in this book. For more details, please refer to the `VulkanCore::VulkanFeatureChain` class in the repo. The context, which encapsulates the instance and the physical and logical devices, is initialized with a few useful extensions, one graphics queue, and the default features:

```
int main(int argc, char** argv) {
  initWindow(&window_);

  // Create Context
  VulkanCore::VulkanFeatureChain featureChain;
  VulkanCore::Context::createDefaultFeatureChain(
      featureChain);
  VulkanCore::Context context(
      (void*)glfwGetWin32Window(window_),
      {},  // layers
      {
          VK_KHR_WIN32_SURFACE_EXTENSION_NAME,
          VK_KHR_SURFACE_EXTENSION_NAME,
          VK_KHR_GET_PHYSICAL_DEVICE_PROPERTIES_2_EXTENSION_NAME,
      },  // instance extensions
      {VK_KHR_SWAPCHAIN_EXTENSION_NAME},  // device
                                          // extensions
      VK_QUEUE_GRAPHICS_BIT,  // request a graphics
                              // queue only
      featureChain, true);
```

4. The swapchain is initialized with a common format and color space, along with the extensions from the physical device. In this example, we use the **First In First Out** (**FIFO**) presentation mode because it's the only mode that is supported by default:

```
// Create Swapchain
const VkExtent2D extents = context.physicalDevice()
```

```
                            .surfaceCapabilities()
                            .minImageExtent;
context.createSwapchain(
    VK_FORMAT_B8G8R8A8_UNORM,
    VK_COLORSPACE_SRGB_NONLINEAR_KHR,
    VK_PRESENT_MODE_FIFO_KHR, extents);
const VkRect2D renderArea = {
    .offset = {.x = 0, .y = 0}, .extent = extents};
```

5. Both shaders are initialized from the resources in the repo, along with a vector of framebuffers. The number of framebuffers matches the number of swapchain images, as we'll need one framebuffer for each acquired image later:

```
// Create Shader Modules
const auto shadersPath =
    std::filesystem::current_path() /
    "resources/shaders";
const auto vertexShaderPath =
    shadersPath / "triangle.vert";
const auto fragShaderPath =
    shadersPath / "triangle.frag";
const auto vertexShader = context.createShaderModule(
    vertexShaderPath.string(),
    VK_SHADER_STAGE_VERTEX_BIT);
const auto fragShader = context.createShaderModule(
    fragShaderPath.string(),
    VK_SHADER_STAGE_FRAGMENT_BIT);

// Create Framebuffers
std::vector<std::shared_ptr<VulkanCore::Framebuffer>>
    swapchain_framebuffers(
        context.swapchain()->numberImages());
```

6. We only need one render pass with one subpass. A render pass isn't associated with any resources. It only specifies the load and store operations of each framebuffer's color attachment and their use by the subpasses. For this reason, we don't need multiple render passes, like framebuffers do. One is enough, and it is reused for all swapchain images. The final layout of the color attachment 0, the swapchain image, is VK_IMAGE_LAYOUT_PRESENT_SRC_KHR, as it will be presented:

```
// Create Render Pass
std::shared_ptr<VulkanCore::RenderPass> renderPass =
    context.createRenderPass(
        {context.swapchain()->texture(0)},
```

```
            {VK_ATTACHMENT_LOAD_OP_CLEAR},
            {VK_ATTACHMENT_STORE_OP_STORE},
            {VK_IMAGE_LAYOUT_PRESENT_SRC_KHR},
            VK_PIPELINE_BIND_POINT_GRAPHICS);
```

Finally, we create a pipeline that contains mostly the default parameters. Besides the two shaders compiled before, we set the viewport to be the size of the output and disable depth testing. We then create a Command Queue Manager instance to manage the command buffers and their fences:

```
// Create Graphics Pipeline
auto pipeline = context.createGraphicsPipeline(
    VulkanCore::Pipeline::GraphicsPipelineDescriptor{
        .vertexShader_ = vertexShader,
        .fragmentShader_ = fragShader,
        .viewport = context.swapchain()->extent(),
        .depthTestEnable = false,
    },
    renderPass->vkRenderPass());

// Create Command Queue Manager
auto commandMgr = context.createGraphicsCommandQueue(
    context.swapchain()->numberImages(),
    context.swapchain()->numberImages());

// FPS Counter
EngineCore::FPSCounter fps(glfwGetTime());
```

7. The main render loop executes until the `GLFW` window is closed. On each iteration, we first acquire a swapchain image and its index. If a framebuffer for this swapchain image doesn't exist yet, we create one. We then obtain a command buffer for rendering:

```
// Main Render Loop
while (!glfwWindowShouldClose(window_)) {
    fps.update(glfwGetTime());

    const auto texture =
        context.swapchain()->acquireImage();
    const auto swapchainImageIndex =
        context.swapchain()->currentImageIndex();

    // Create the framebuffer the first time we get
    // here, once for each swapchain image
    if (swapchain_framebuffers[swapchainImageIndex] ==
        nullptr) {
```

```
        swapchain_framebuffers[swapchainImageIndex] =
            context.createFramebuffer(
                renderPass->vkRenderPass(), {texture},
                nullptr, nullptr);
    }

    auto commandBuffer =
        commandMgr.getCmdBufferToBegin();
```

8. Before starting rendering, we begin the render pass by providing a clear color (black), and the render pass and framebuffer handles. We then bind the pipeline to the current command buffer, and we are ready to start rendering:

```
    // Begin Render Pass
    constexpr VkClearValue clearColor{0.0f, 0.0f, 0.0f,
                                      0.0f};
    const VkRenderPassBeginInfo renderpassInfo = {
        .sType =
            VK_STRUCTURE_TYPE_RENDER_PASS_BEGIN_INFO,
        .renderPass = renderPass->vkRenderPass(),
        .framebuffer =
            swapchain_framebuffers[swapchainImageIndex]
                ->vkFramebuffer(),
        .renderArea = renderArea,
        .clearValueCount = 1,
        .pClearValues = &clearColor,
    };
    vkCmdBeginRenderPass(commandBuffer,
                         &renderpassInfo,
                         VK_SUBPASS_CONTENTS_INLINE);

    pipeline->bind(commandBuffer);
```

9. Finally, we issue the draw call with three vertices and one instance. This call will invoke the vertex shader three times (one for each vertex), instantiating the `gl_VertexIndex` variable in the shader to 0, 1, and 2. We use this variable to index into the position and color arrays in the shader itself. We then submit the command buffer and present the swapchain image:

```
    vkCmdDraw(commandBuffer, 3, 1, 0, 0);

    vkCmdEndRenderPass(commandBuffer);

    commandMgr.endCmdBuffer(commandBuffer);
    constexpr VkPipelineStageFlags flags =
```

```
            VK_PIPELINE_STAGE_COLOR_ATTACHMENT_OUTPUT_BIT;
    const auto submitInfo =
        context.swapchain()->createSubmitInfo(
            &commandBuffer, &flags);
    commandMgr.submit(&submitInfo);
    commandMgr.goToNextCmdBuffer();

    // Present render output to the screen
    context.swapchain()->present();

    glfwPollEvents();

    // Increment frame number
    fps.incFrame();
}
```

10. After the render loop ends, and before exiting the program, we wait for all queues to finish processing before destroying all Vulkan objects in the opposite order in which they were created:

```
    commandMgr.waitUntilAllSubmitsAreComplete();

    glfwDestroyWindow(window_);
    glfwTerminate();

    return 0;
}
```

The result of this recipe should look like *Figure 1.12*:

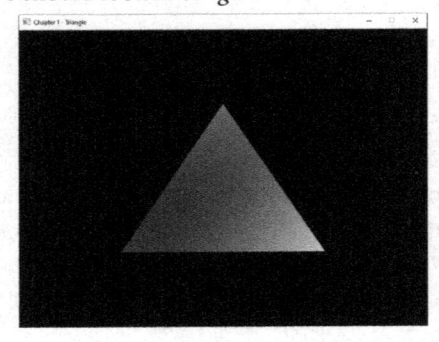

Figure 1.12 – Recipe result

Vulkan is verbose and, as mentioned before, provides many ways to customize your graphics application. A simple example such as this needed around 1,000 lines of code! But there is no reason for panic. Most of that code can be reused (and will be reused) for the remainder of the book to explain all techniques and recipes in the text.

2
Working with Modern Vulkan

The goal of this chapter is to show you how to render a scene that accepts input information, such as textures and uniform data, from the application side. This chapter will cover advanced topics in the Vulkan API that build upon the core concepts discussed in the previous chapter and present all the information you need to render complex scenes, along with newer features of the API. Additionally, the chapter will demonstrate techniques to enhance the rendering speed.

In this chapter, we're going to cover the following recipes:

- Understanding Vulkan's memory model
- Instantiating the VMA library
- Creating buffers
- Uploading data to buffers
- Creating a staging buffer
- How to avoid data races using ring buffers
- Setting up pipeline barriers
- Creating images (textures)
- Creating an image view
- Creating a sampler
- Providing shader data
- Customizing shader behavior with specialization constants
- Implementing MDI and PVP
- Adding flexibility to the rendering pipeline using dynamic rendering
- Transferring resources between queue families

Technical requirements

For this chapter, you will need to make sure you have VS 2022 installed along with the Vulkan SDK. Basic familiarity with the C++ programming language and an understanding of OpenGL or any other graphics API will be useful. Please revisit *Chapter 1, Vulkan Core Concepts*, under the *Technical requirements* section for details on setting up and building executables for this chapter. The recipe for this chapter can be run by launching `Chapter02_MultiDrawIndirect.exe` executable.

Understanding Vulkan's memory model

Memory allocation and management are crucial in Vulkan, as almost none of the details of memory usage are managed by Vulkan. Except for deciding the exact memory address where memory should be allocated, all other details are the responsibility of the application. This means the programmer must manage memory types, their sizes, and alignments, as well as any sub-allocations. This approach gives applications more control over memory management and allows developers to optimize their programs for specific uses. This recipe will provide some fundamental information about the types of memory provided by the API as well as a summary of how to allocate and bind that memory to resources.

Getting ready

Graphics cards come in two variants, integrated and discrete. Integrated graphics cards share the same memory as the CPU, as shown in *Figure 2.1*:

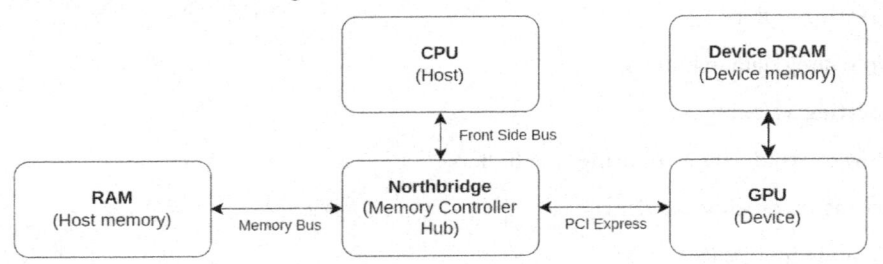

Figure 2.1 – Typical memory architecture for discrete graphics cards

Discrete graphics cards have their own memory (device memory) separate from the main memory (host memory), as shown in *Figure 2.2*:

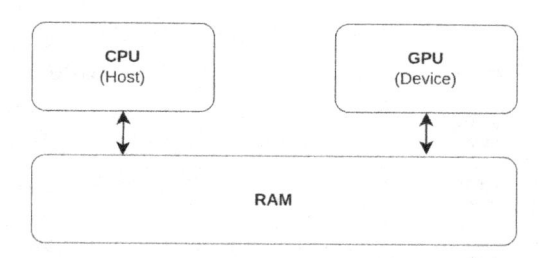

Figure 2.2 – Typical memory architecture for integrated graphics cards

Vulkan provides different types of memory:

- **Device-local memory**: This type of memory is optimized for use by the GPU and is local to the device. It is typically faster than host-visible memory but is not accessible from the CPU. Usually, resources such as render targets, storage images, and buffers are stored in this memory.

- **Host-visible memory**: This type of memory is accessible from both the GPU and the CPU. It is typically slower than device-local memory but allows for efficient data transfer between the GPU and CPU. Reads from GPU to CPU happen across **Peripheral Component Interconnect Express (PCI-E)** lanes in the case of non-integrated GPU. It's typically used to set up staging buffers, where data is stored before being transferred to device-local memory, and uniform buffers, which are constantly updated from the application.

- **Host-coherent memory**: This type of memory is like host-visible memory but provides guaranteed memory consistency between the GPU and CPU. This type of memory is typically slower than both device-local and host-visible memory but is useful for storing data that needs to be frequently updated by both the GPU and CPU.

Figure 2.3 summarizes the three aforementioned types of memory. Device-local memory is not visible from the host, while host-coherent and host-visible are. Copying data from the CPU to the GPU can be done using mapped memory for those two types of memory allocations. For device-local memory, it's necessary to copy the data from the CPU to host-visible memory first using mapped memory (the staging buffer), and then perform a copy of the data from the staging buffer to the destination, the device-local memory, using a Vulkan function:

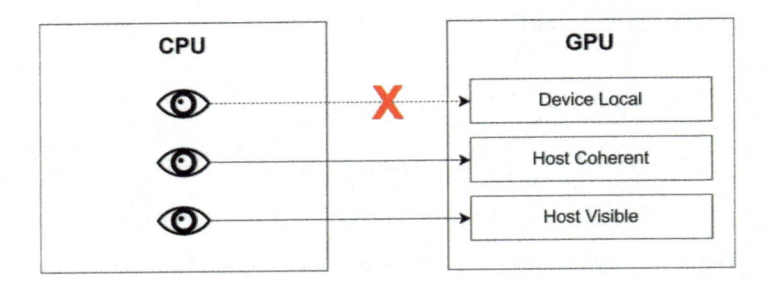

Figure 2.3 – Types of memory and their visibility from the application in Vulkan

Images are usually device-local memory, as they have their own layout that isn't readily interpretable by the application. Buffers can be of any one of the aforementioned types.

How to do it...

A typical workflow for creating and uploading data to a buffer includes the following steps:

1. Create a buffer object of type `VkBuffer` by using the `VkBufferCreateInfo` structure and calling `vkCreateBuffer`.
2. Retrieve the memory requirements based on the buffer's properties by calling `vkGetBufferMemoryRequirements`. The device may require a certain alignment, which could affect the necessary size of the allocation to accommodate the buffer's contents.
3. Create a structure of type `VkMemoryAllocateInfo`, specify the size of the allocation and the type of memory, and call `vkAllocateMemory`.
4. Call `vkBindBufferMemory` to bind the allocation with the buffer object.
5. If the buffer is visible from the host, map a pointer to the destination with `vkMapMemory`, copy the data, and unmap the memory with `vkUnmapMemory`.
6. If the buffer is a device-local buffer, copy the data to a staging buffer first, then perform the final copy from the staging buffer to the device-local memory using the `vkCmdCopyBuffer` function.

As you can see, that's a complex procedure that can be simplified by using the VMA library, an open source library that provides a convenient and efficient way to manage memory in Vulkan. It offers a high-level interface that abstracts the complex details of memory allocation, freeing you from the burden of manual memory management.

Instantiating the VMA library

To use VMA, you first need to create an instance of the library and store a handle in a variable of type `VmaAllocator`. To create one, you need a Vulkan physical device and a device.

How to do it...

Creating a VMA library instance requires instancing two different structures. One stores pointers to API functions that VMA needs to find other function pointers and another structure that provides a physical device, a device, and an instance for creating an allocator:

```
VkPhysicalDevice physicalDevice;  // Valid Physical Device
VkDevice device; // Valid Device
VkInstance instance; // Valid Instance
const uint32_t apiVersion = VK_API_VERSION_1_3;
const VmaVulkanFunctions vulkanFunctions = {
    .vkGetInstanceProcAddr = vkGetInstanceProcAddr,
    .vkGetDeviceProcAddr = vkGetDeviceProcAddr,
#if VMA_VULKAN_VERSION >= 1003000
    .vkGetDeviceBufferMemoryRequirements =
        vkGetDeviceBufferMemoryRequirements,
    .vkGetDeviceImageMemoryRequirements =
        vkGetDeviceImageMemoryRequirements,
#endif
};

VmaAllocator allocator = nullptr;
const VmaAllocatorCreateInfo allocInfo = {
    .physicalDevice = physicalDevice,
    .device = device,
    .pVulkanFunctions = &vulkanFunctions,
    .instance = instance,
    .vulkanApiVersion = apiVersion,
};
vmaCreateAllocator(&allocInfo, &allocator);
```

The allocator needs pointers to a few Vulkan functions so that it can work based on the features you would like to use. In the preceding case, we provide only the bare minimum for allocating and deallocating memory. The allocator needs to be freed once the context is destroyed with `vmaDestroyAllocator`.

Creating buffers

A buffer in Vulkan is simply a contiguous block of memory that holds some data. The data can be vertex, index, uniform, and more. A buffer object is just metadata and does not directly contain data. The memory associated with a buffer is allocated after a buffer has been created.

Table 2.1 summarizes the most important usage types of buffers and their access type:

Buffer Type	Access Type	Uses
Vertex or Index	Read-only	
Uniform	Read-only	Uniform data storage
Storage	Read/write	Generic data storage
Uniform texel	Read/write	Data is interpreted as texels
Storage texel	Read/write	Data is interpreted as texels

Table 2.1 – Buffer types

Creating buffers is easy, but it helps to know what types of buffers exist and what their requirements are before setting out to create them. In this chapter, we will provide a template for creating buffers.

Getting ready

In the repository, Vulkan buffers are managed by the `VulkanCore::Buffer` class, which provides functions to create and upload data to the device, as well as a utility function to use a staging buffer to upload data to device-only heaps.

How to do it...

Creating a buffer using VMA is simple:

1. All you need are buffer creation flags (–a value of 0 for the flags is correct for most cases), the size of the buffer in bytes, its usage (this is how you define how the buffer will be used), and assign those values to an instance of the `VkBufferCreateInfo` structure:

    ```
    VkDeviceSize size;     // The requested size of the buffer
    VmaAllocator allocator;   // valid VMA Allocator
    VkUsageBufferFlags use;   // Transfer src/dst/uniform/SSBO
    VkBuffer buffer;         // The created buffer
    VkBufferCreateInfo createInfo = {
        .sType = VK_STRUCTURE_TYPE_BUFFER_CREATE_INFO,
        .pNext = nullptr,
        .flags = {},
        .size = size,
    ```

```
        .usage = use,
        .sharingMode = VK_SHARING_MODE_EXCLUSIVE,
        .queueFamilyIndexCount = {},
        .pQueueFamilyIndices = {},
    };
```

You will also need a set of VmaAllocationCreateFlagBits values:

```
    const VmaAllocationCreateFlagBits allocCreateInfo = {
        VMA_ALLOCATION_CREATE_MAPPED_BIT,
        VMA_MEMORY_USAGE_CPU_ONLY,
    };
```

2. Then, call `vmaCreateBuffer` to obtain the buffer handle and its allocation:

```
    VmaAllocation allocation;  // Needs to live until the
                               // buffer is destroyed
    VK_CHECK(vmaCreateBuffer(allocator, &createInfo,
                             &allocCreateInfo, &buffer,
                             &allocation, nullptr));
```

3. The next step is optional but useful for debugging and optimization:

```
    VmaAllocationInfo allocationInfo;
    vmaGetAllocationInfo(allocator, allocation,
                         &allocationInfo);
```

Some creation flags affect how the buffer can be used, so you might need to make adjustments to the preceding code depending on how you intend to use the buffers you create in your application.

Uploading data to buffers

Uploading data from the application to the GPU depends on the type of buffer. For host-visible buffers, it's a direct copy using `memcpy`. For device-local buffers, we need a staging buffer, which is a buffer that is visible both by the CPU and the GPU. In this recipe, we will demonstrate how to upload data from your application to the device-visible memory (into a buffer's memory region on the device).

Getting ready

If you haven't already, please refer to the *Understanding Vulkan's memory model* recipe.

How to do it...

The upload process depends on the type of buffer:

1. For host-visible memory, it's enough to retrieve a pointer to the destination using `vmaMapMemory` and copy the data using `memcpy`. The operation is synchronous, so the mapped pointer can be unmapped as soon as `memcpy` returns.

   It's fine to map a host-visible buffer as soon as it is created and leave it mapped until its destruction. That is the recommended approach, as you don't incur the overhead of mapping the memory every time it needs to be updated:

   ```
   VmaAllocator allocator;         // Valid VMA allocator
   VmaAllocation allocation;       // Valid VMA allocation
   void *data;                     // Data to be uploaded
   size_t size;                    // Size of data in bytes
   void *map = nullptr;
   VK_CHECK(vmaMapMemory(allocator, allocation,
                         &map));
   memcpy(map, data, size);
   vmaUnmapMemory(allocator_, allocation_);
   VK_CHECK(vmaFlushAllocation(allocator_,
                               allocation_, offset,
                               size));
   ```

2. Uploading data to a device-local memory needs to be (1) copied to a buffer that is visible from the host first (called a staging buffer) and then (2) copied from the staging buffer to the device-local memory using `vkCmdCopyBuffer`, as depicted in *Figure 2.4*. Note that this requires a command buffer:

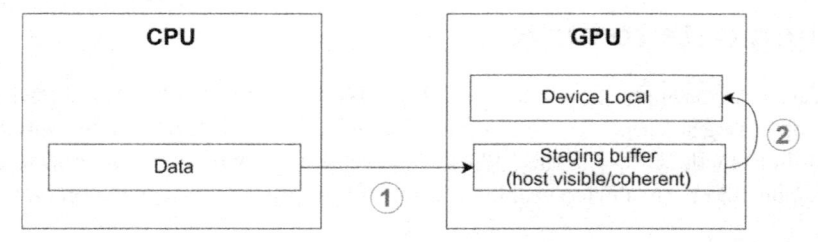

Figure 2.4 – Staging buffers

3. Once the data is residing on the device (on the host-visible buffer), copying it to the device-only buffer is simple:

   ```
   VkDeviceSize srcOffset;
   VkDeviceSize dstOffset;
   VkDeviceSize size;
   VkCommandBuffer commandBuffer; // Valid Command Buffer
   ```

```
VkBuffer stagingBuffer; // Valid host-visible buffer
VkBuffer buffer; // Valid device-local buffer
VkBufferCopy region(srcOffset, dstOffset, size);
vkCmdCopyBuffer(commandBuffer, stagingBuffer, buffer, 1,
&region);
```

Uploading data from your application to a buffer is accomplished either by a direct `memcpy` operation or by means of a staging buffer. We showed how to perform both uploads in this recipe.

Creating a staging buffer

Creating a staging buffer is like creating a regular buffer but requires flags that specify that the buffer is host-visible. In this recipe, we will show how to create a buffer that can be used as a staging buffer – one that can be used as an intermediary destination of the data being uploaded from your application on its way to a device-local memory.

Getting ready

The *Creating buffers* recipe explains how to create buffers in general, while this recipe shows which flags and parameters you need to create a staging buffer.

How to do it...

`VkBufferCreateInfo::usage` needs to contain `VK_BUFFER_USAGE_TRANSFER_SRC_BIT` as it will be the source operation for a `vkCmdCopyBuffer` command:

```
const VkBufferCreateInfo stagingBufferInfo = {
    .sType = VK_STRUCTURE_TYPE_BUFFER_CREATE_INFO,
    .size = size,
    .usage = VK_BUFFER_USAGE_TRANSFER_SRC_BIT,
};

const VmaAllocationCreateInfo
    stagingAllocationCreateInfo = {
        .flags = VMA_ALLOCATION_CREATE_HOST_ACCESS_SEQUENTIAL_WRITE_
BIT |
            VMA_ALLOCATION_CREATE_MAPPED_BIT,
        .usage = VMA_MEMORY_USAGE_CPU_ONLY,
};

const VmaAllocationCreateFlagBits allocCreateInfo = {
    VMA_ALLOCATION_CREATE_MAPPED_BIT,
    VMA_MEMORY_USAGE_CPU_ONLY,
};
```

```
VmaAllocation allocation;  // Needs to live until the
                           // buffer is destroyed
VK_CHECK(vmaCreateBuffer(allocator, &stagingBufferInfo,
                  &allocCreateInfo, &buffer,
                  &allocation, nullptr));
```

A staging buffer may be better implemented using a wrapper in your application. A wrapper can increase or decrease the size of the buffer as needed, for example. One staging buffer may be enough for your application, but you need to watch the requirements imposed by some architectures.

How to avoid data races using ring buffers

When a buffer needs to be updated every frame, we run the risk of creating a data race, as shown in *Figure 2.5*. A data race is a situation where multiple threads within a program concurrently access a shared data point, with at least one thread performing a write operation. This concurrent access can result in unforeseen behavior due to the unpredictable order of operations. Take the example of a uniform buffer that stores the view, model, and viewport matrices and needs to be updated every frame. The buffer is updated while the first command buffer is being recorded, initializing it (version 1). Once the command buffer starts processing on the GPU, the buffer contains the correct data:

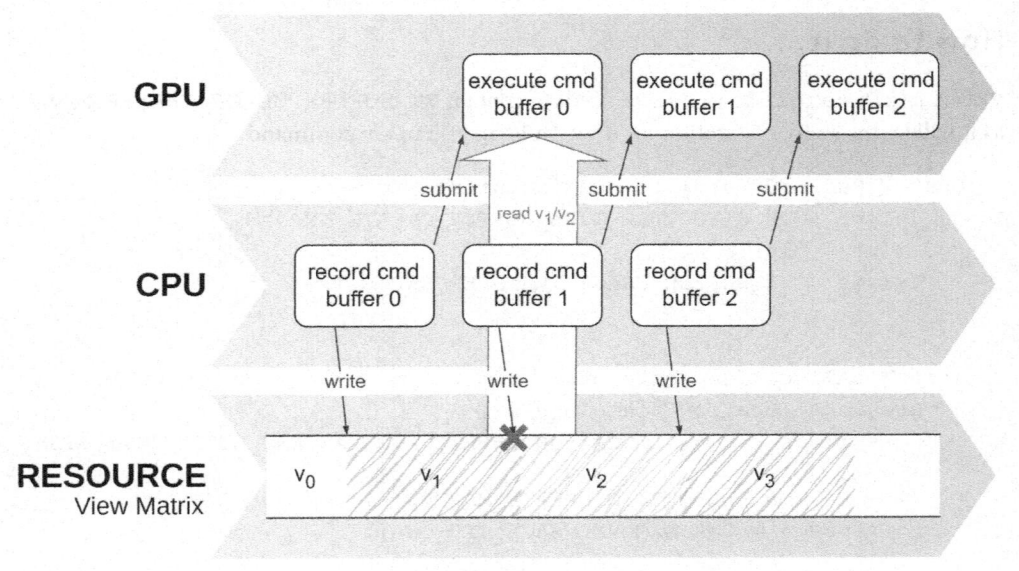

Figure 2.5 – Data race when using one buffer

After the first command buffer starts processing in the GPU, the application may try to update the buffer's contents to version 2 while the GPU is accessing that data for rendering!

Getting ready

Synchronization is by far the hardest aspect of Vulkan. If synchronization elements such as semaphores, fences, and barriers are used too greedily, then your application becomes a series and won't use the full power of the parallelism between the CPU and the GPU.

Make sure you also read the *Understanding synchronization in the swapchain – fences and semaphores* recipe in *Chapter 1, Vulkan Core Concepts*. That recipe and this one only scratch the surface of how to tackle synchronization, but are very good starting points.

A ring-buffer implementation is provided in the `EngineCore::RingBuffer` repository, which has a configurable number of sub-buffers. Its sub-buffers are all host-visible, persistent buffers; that is, they are persistently mapped after creation for ease of access.

How to do it…

There are a few ways to avoid this problem, but the easiest one is to create a ring buffer that contains several buffers (or any other resource) equal to the number of frames in flight. *Figure 2.6* shows events when there are two buffers available. Once the first command buffer is submitted and is being processed in the GPU, the application is free to process copy 1 of the buffer, as it's not being accessed by the device:

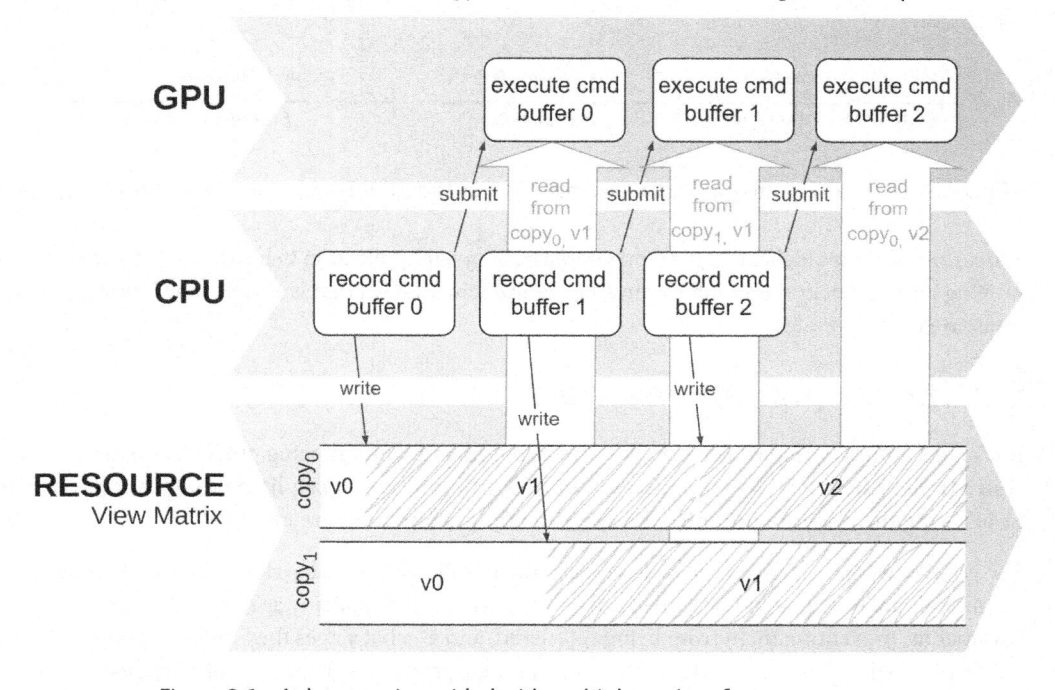

Figure 2.6 – A data race is avoided with multiple copies of a resource

Even though this is a simple solution, it has a caveat: if partial updates are allowed, care must be taken when the buffer is updated. Consider *Figure 2.7*, in which a ring buffer that contains three sub-allocations is partially updated. The buffer stores the view, model, and viewport matrices. During initialization, all three sub-allocations are initialized to three identity matrices. On **Frame 0**, while **Buffer 0** is active, the model matrix is updated and now contains a translation of (10, 10, 0). On the next frame, **Frame 1**, **Buffer 1** becomes active, and the viewport matrix is updated. Because **Buffer 1** was initialized to three identity matrices, updating only the viewport matrix makes buffers **0** and **1** out of sync (as well as **Buffer 3**). To guarantee that partial updates work, we need to copy the last active buffer, **Buffer 0**, into **Buffer 1** first, and then update the viewport matrix:

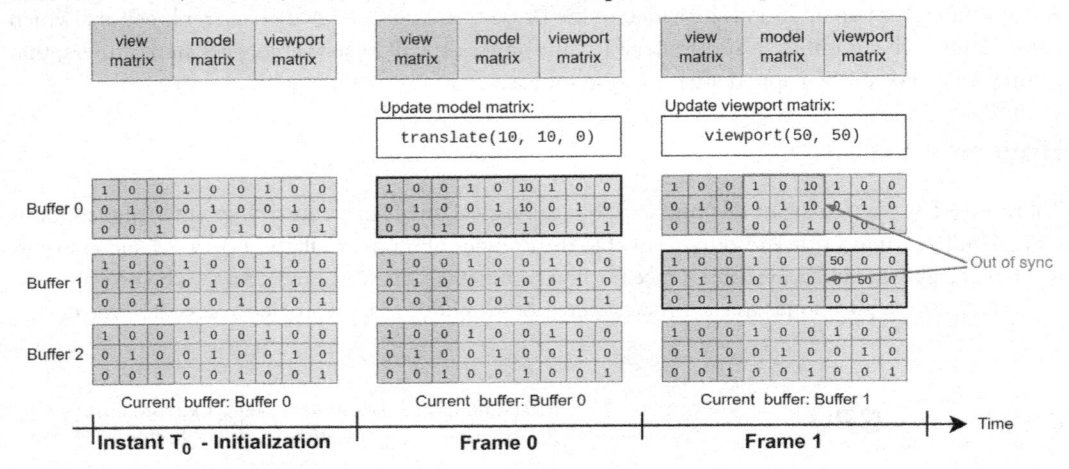

Figure 2.7 – Partial update of a ring buffer makes all sub-allocations out of sync if they are not replicated

Synchronization is a delicate topic, and guaranteeing your application behaves correctly with so many moving parts is tricky. Hopefully, a ring-buffer implementation that is simple may help you focus on other areas of the code.

Setting up pipeline barriers

In Vulkan, commands may be reordered when a command buffer is being processed, subject to certain restrictions. This is known as command buffer reordering, and it can help to improve performance by allowing the driver to optimize the order in which commands are executed.

The good news is that Vulkan provides a mechanism called pipeline barriers to ensure that dependent commands are executed in the correct order. They are used to explicitly specify dependencies between commands, preventing them from being reordered, and at what stages they might overlap. This recipe will explain what pipeline barriers are and what their properties mean. It will also show you how to create and install pipeline barriers.

Getting ready

Consider two draw calls issued in sequence. The first one writes to a color attachment, while the second draw call samples from that attachment in the fragment shader:

```
vkCmdDraw(...); // draws into color attachment 0
vkCmdDraw(...); // reads from color attachment 0
```

Figure 2.8 helps visualize how those two commands may be processed by the device. In the diagram, commands are processed from top to bottom and progress on the pipeline from left to right. Clock cycles are a loose term, because processing may take multiple clock cycles, but are used to indicate that – in general – some tasks must happen after others.

In the example, the second vkCmdDraw call starts executing at **C2**, after the first draw call. This offset is not enough, as the second draw call needs to read the color attachment at the **Fragment Shader** stage, which is not produced by the first draw call until it reaches the **Color Attach Output** stage. Without synchronization, this setup may cause data races:

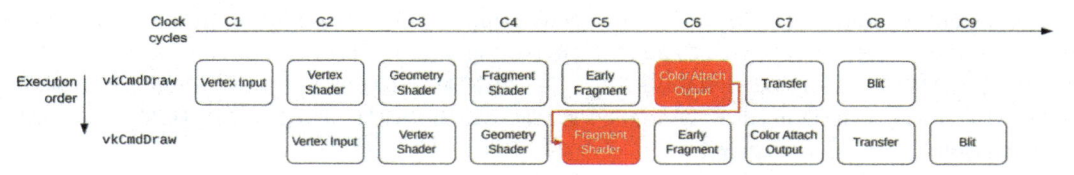

Figure 2.8 – Two consecutive commands recorded on the same command buffer being processed without synchronization

A pipeline barrier is a feature that is recorded into the command buffer and that specifies the pipeline stages that need to have been completed for all commands that appear before the barrier and before the command buffer continues processing. Commands recorded before the barrier are said to be in the *first synchronization scope* or first scope. Commands recorded after the barrier are said to be part of the *second synchronization scope* or second scope.

The barrier also allows fine-grained control to specify at which stage commands after the barrier must wait until commands in the first scope finish processing. That's because commands in the second scope don't need to wait until commands in the first scope are done. They can start processing as soon as possible, as long as the conditions specified in the barrier are met.

In the example in *Figure 2.8*, the first draw call, in the first scope, needs to write to the attachment before the second draw call can access it. The second draw call does not need to wait until the first draw call finishes processing the **Color Attach Output** stage. It can start right away, as long as its fragment stage happens after the first draw call is done with its **Color Attach Output** stage, as shown in *Figure 2.9*:

Figure 2.9 – Two consecutive commands recorded on the same command buffer being processed with synchronization

There are three types of barriers:

1. **Memory barriers** are global barriers and apply to all commands in the first and second scopes.
2. **Buffer memory barriers** are barriers that apply only to commands that access a portion of the buffer, as it's possible to specify to which portion of the buffer the barrier applies (offset + range).
3. **Image memory barriers** are barriers that apply only to commands that access a subresource of an image. It's possible to add barriers based on mip level, sections of the image, or array layers. This is an especially important barrier as it is also used to transition an image from one layout to another. For instance, while generating mipmaps and blitting from one mip level to the next, the levels need to be in the correct layout. The previous level needs to be in the `VK_IMAGE_LAYOUT_TRANSFER_SRC_OPTIMAL` layout, as it will be read from, while the next mip level needs to be in the `VK_IMAGE_LAYOUT_TRANSFER_DST_OPTIMAL` layout, as it will be written to.

How to do it...

Pipeline barriers are recorded with the `vkCmdPipelineBarrier` command, in which you can provide several barriers of multiple types at the same time. The following code snippet shows how to create a barrier used to create a dependency between the two draw calls in *Figure 2.9*:

```
VkCommandBuffer commandBuffer;   // Valid Command Buffer
VkImage image;                   // Valid image

const VkImageSubresourceRange subresource = {
    .aspectMask =.baseMipLevel = 0,
    .levelCount = VK_REMAINING_MIP_LEVELS,
    .baseArrayLayer = 0,
    .layerCount = 1,
};

const VkImageMemoryBarrier imageBarrier = {
    .sType = VK_STRUCTURE_TYPE_IMAGE_MEMORY_BARRIER,
    .srcAccessMask =
        VK_ACCESS_2_COLOR_ATTACHMENT_WRITE_BIT_KHR,
    .dstAccessMask = VK_ACCESS_2_SHADER_READ_BIT_KHR,
```

```
        .oldLayout = VK_IMAGE_LAYOUT_ATTACHMENT_OPTIMAL,
        .newLayout = VK_IMAGE_LAYOUT_READ_ONLY_OPTIMAL,
        .srcQueueFamilyIndex = VK_QUEUE_FAMILY_IGNORED,
        .dstQueueFamilyIndex = VK_QUEUE_FAMILY_IGNORED,
        .image = image,
        .subresourceRange = &subresource,
    };

    vkCmdPipelineBarrier(
        commandBuffer,
        VK_PIPELINE_STAGE_COLOR_ATTACHMENT_OUTPUT_BIT,
        VK_PIPELINE_STAGE_FRAGMENT_SHADER_BIT, 0, 0,
        nullptr, 0, nullptr, 1, &memoryBarrier);
```

The barrier needs to be recorded between the two draw calls:

```
vkCmdDraw(...); // draws into color attachment 0
vkCmdPipelineBarrier(...);
vkCmdDraw(...); // reads from color attachment 0
```

Pipeline barriers are tricky but absolutely fundamental in Vulkan. Make sure you understand what they offer and how they operate before continuing to read the other recipes.

Creating images (textures)

Images are used for storing 1D, 2D, or 3D data, although they are mostly used for 2D data. Different than buffers, images have the advantage of being optimized for locality in memory layout. This is because most GPUs have a fixed-function texture unit or sampler that reads texel data from an image and applies filtering and other operations to produce a final color value. Images can have different formats, such as RGB, RGBA, BGRA, and so on.

An image object is only metadata in Vulkan. Its data is stored separately and is created in a similar manner to buffers (*Figure 2.10*):

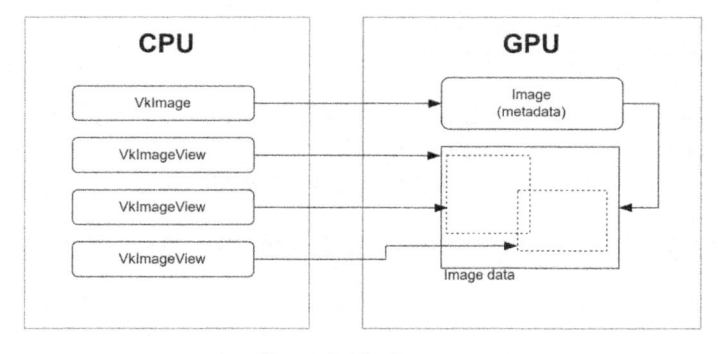

Figure 2.10 – Images

Images in Vulkan cannot be accessed directly and need to be accessed only by means of an image view. An image view is a way to access a subset of the image data by specifying the subresource range, which includes the aspect (such as color or depth), the mip level, and the array layer range.

Another *very important* aspect of images is their layout. It is used to specify the intended usage of an image resource in Vulkan, such as whether it should be used as a source or destination for a transfer operation, a color or depth attachment for rendering, or as a shader read or write resource. The correct image layout is important because it ensures that the GPU can efficiently access and manipulate the image data in accordance with the intended usage. Using the wrong image layout can lead to performance issues or rendering artifacts and can result in undefined behavior. Therefore, it's essential to correctly specify the image layout for each usage of an image in a Vulkan application. Common image layouts are undefined (`VK_IMAGE_LAYOUT_UNDEFINED`) color attachment (`VK_IMAGE_LAYOUT_COLOR_ATTACHMENT_OPTIMAL`), depth/stencil attachment (`VK_IMAGE_LAYOUT_DEPTH_STENCIL_ATTACHMENT_OPTIMAL`), and shader read(`VK_IMAGE_LAYOUT_SHADER_READ_ONLY_OPTIMAL`). Image layout transitions are done as part of the `vkCmdPipelineBarrier` command.

In this recipe, you will learn how to create images on a device.

Getting ready

In the `VulkanCore::Texture` class within our repository, we've encapsulated the intricate management of images and image views, offering a comprehensive solution for handling Vulkan textures. From facilitating efficient data uploads to handling transitions between image layouts and generating mipmaps, the `Texture` class equips us with the means to seamlessly integrate textures in the Vulkan examples.

How to do it...

Creating an image requires some basic information about it, such as type (1D, 2D, 3D), size, format (RGBA, BGRA, and so on), number of mip levels, number of layers (faces for cubemaps), and a few others:

```
VkFormat format;        // Image format
VkExtents extents;      // Image size
uint32_t mipLevels;     // Number of mip levels
uint32_t layerCount;    // Number of layers (sides of cubemap)
const VkImageCreateInfo imageInfo = {
    .sType = VK_STRUCTURE_TYPE_IMAGE_CREATE_INFO,
    .flags = 0, // optional
    .imageType = VK_IMAGE_TYPE_2D,   // 1D, 2D, 3D
    .format = format,
    .extent = extents,
    .mipLevels = mipLevels,
```

```
    .arrayLayers = layerCount,
    .samples = VK_SAMPLE_COUNT_1_BIT,
    .tiling = VK_IMAGE_TILING_OPTIMAL,
    .usage = VK_IMAGE_USAGE_COLOR_ATTACHMENT_BIT,
    .sharingMode = VK_SHARING_MODE_EXCLUSIVE,
    .initialLayout = VK_IMAGE_LAYOUT_UNDEFINED,
};
```

The following structure tells VMA that the image will be a device-only image:

```
const VmaAllocationCreateInfo allocCreateInfo = {
    .flags = VMA_ALLOCATION_CREATE_DEDICATED_MEMORY_BIT,
    .usage = VMA_MEMORY_USAGE_AUTO_PREFER_DEVICE,
    .priority = 1.0f,
};
```

The resulting image's handle will be stored in `image`:

```
VkImage image = VK_NULL_HANDLE;
VK_CHECK(vmaCreateImage(vmaAllocator_, &imageInfo,
                        &allocCreateInfo, &image,
                        &vmaAllocation_, nullptr));
```

The next step is optional but useful for debugging or optimizing the code:

```
VmaAllocationInfo allocationInfo;
vmaGetAllocationInfo(vmaAllocator_, vmaAllocation_,
                     &allocationInfo);
```

This recipe only showed you how to create an image in Vulkan, not how to upload data to it. Uploading data to an image is just like uploading data to a buffer.

Creating an image view

Image views provide a way to interpret images in terms of size, location, and format, except in terms of their layout, which needs to be transformed explicitly and transitioned using image barriers. In this recipe, you will learn how to create an image view object in Vulkan.

Getting ready

Image views are stored and managed by the `VulkanCore::Texture` class in the repository.

How to do it...

Creating an image view is easy; all you need is the handle of the image it is associated with and the region of the image that you would like to represent:

```
VkDevice device;    // Valid Vulkan Device
VkImage image;      // Valid Image object
VkFormat format;
uint32_t numMipLevels;  // Number of mip levels
uint32_t layers;   // Number of layers (cubemap faces)
const VkImageViewCreateInfo imageViewInfo = {
    .sType = VK_STRUCTURE_TYPE_IMAGE_VIEW_CREATE_INFO,
    .image = image,
    .viewType =
        VK_IMAGE_VIEW_TYPE_2D,   // 1D, 2D, 3D, Cubemap
                                 // and arrays
    .format = format,
    .components =
        {
            .r = VK_COMPONENT_SWIZZLE_IDENTITY,
            .g = VK_COMPONENT_SWIZZLE_IDENTITY,
            .b = VK_COMPONENT_SWIZZLE_IDENTITY,
            .a = VK_COMPONENT_SWIZZLE_IDENTITY,
        },
    .subresourceRange = {
        .aspectMask = VK_IMAGE_ASPECT_COLOR_BIT,
        .baseMipLevel = 0,
        .levelCount = numMipLevels,
        .baseArrayLayer = 0,
        .layerCount = layers,
    }};

VkImageView imageView{VK_NULL_HANDLE};
VK_CHECK(vkCreateImageView(device, &imageViewInfo,
                    nullptr, &imageView));
```

Without an image view, a texture cannot be used by shaders. Even when used as color attachments, images need image views.

Creating a sampler

A sampler in Vulkan transcends a simple object; it's a crucial bridge between shader execution and image data. Beyond interpolation, it governs filtering, addressing modes, and mipmapping. Filters dictate interpolation between texels, while addressing modes control how coordinates map to image extents. Anisotropic filtering further enhances sampling fidelity. Mipmapping, a pyramid of downsampled image levels, is another facet managed by samplers. In essence, creating a sampler involves orchestrating these attributes to seamlessly harmonize image data and shader intricacies. In this recipe, you will learn how to create a sampler object in Vulkan.

Getting ready

Samplers are implemented by the `VulkanCore::Sampler` class in the repository.

How to do it...

The properties of a sampler define how an image is interpreted in the pipeline, usually in a shader. The process is simple – instantiate a `VkSamplerCreateInfo` structure and call `vkCreateSampler`:

```
VkDevice device;  // Valid Vulkan Device
VkFilter minFilter;
VkFilter maxFilter;
float maxLod;  // Max mip level
const VkSamplerCreateInfo samplerInfo = {
    .sType = VK_STRUCTURE_TYPE_SAMPLER_CREATE_INFO,
    .magFilter = minFilter,
    .minFilter = magFilter,
    .mipmapMode = maxLod > 0
                  ? VK_SAMPLER_MIPMAP_MODE_LINEAR
                  : VK_SAMPLER_MIPMAP_MODE_NEAREST,
    .addressModeU = VK_SAMPLER_ADDRESS_MODE_REPEAT,
    .addressModeV = VK_SAMPLER_ADDRESS_MODE_REPEAT,
    .addressModeW = VK_SAMPLER_ADDRESS_MODE_REPEAT,
    .mipLodBias = 0,
    .anisotropyEnable = VK_FALSE,
    .minLod = 0,
    .maxLod = maxLod,
};
VkSampler sampler{VK_NULL_HANDLE};
VK_CHECK(vkCreateSampler(device, &samplerInfo, nullptr,
                    &sampler));
```

A sampler is one of the simplest objects to create in Vulkan and one of the easiest to understand, as it describes very common computer graphics concepts.

Providing shader data

Providing data from your application that will be used in shaders is one of the most convoluted aspects of Vulkan and requires several steps that need to be accomplished in the right order (and with the right parameters). In this recipe, with many smaller recipes, you will learn how to provide data used in shaders, such as textures, buffers, and samplers.

Getting ready

Resources consumed by shaders are specified using the `layout` keyword, along with `set` and `binding` qualifiers:

```
layout(set = 0, binding=0) uniform Transforms
{
    mat4 model;
    mat4 view;
    mat4 projection;
} MVP;
```

Each resource is represented by a binding. A set is a collection of bindings. One binding doesn't necessarily represent just one resource; it can also represent an array of resources of the same type.

How to do it...

Providing a resource as input to shaders is a multi-step process that involves the following:

1. Specifying sets and their bindings using descriptor set layouts. This step doesn't associate real resources with sets/bindings. It just specifies the number and types of bindings in a set.
2. Building a pipeline layout, which describes which sets will be used in a pipeline.
3. Creating a descriptor pool that will provide instances of descriptor sets. A descriptor pool contains a list of how many bindings it can provide grouped by binding type (texture, sampler, **shader storage buffer** (**SSBO**), uniform buffers).
4. Allocate descriptor sets from the pool with `vkAllocateDescriptorSets`.
5. Bind resources to bindings using `vkUpdateDescriptorSets`. In this step, we associate a real resource (a buffer, a texture, and so on) with a binding.
6. Bind descriptor sets and their bindings to a pipeline during rendering using `vkCmdBindDescriptorSet`. This step makes resources bound to their set/bindings in the previous step available to shaders in the current pipeline.

The next recipes will show you how to perform each one of those steps.

Specifying descriptor sets with descriptor set layouts

Consider the following GLSL code, which specifies several resources:

```
struct Vertex {
    vec3 pos;
    vec2 uv;
    vec3 normal;
};
layout(set = 0, binding=0) uniform Transforms
{
    mat4 model;
    mat4 view;
    mat4 projection;
} MVP;

layout(set = 1, binding = 0) uniform texture2D textures[];
layout(set = 1, binding = 1) uniform sampler    samplers[];

layout(set = 2, binding = 0) readonly buffer VertexBuffer
{
    Vertex vertices[];
} vertexBuffer;
```

The code requires three sets (0, 1, and 2), so we need to create three descriptor set layouts. In this recipe, you will learn how to create a descriptor set layout for the preceding code.

Getting ready

Descriptor sets and bindings are created, stored, and managed by the `VulkanCore::Pipeline` class in the repository. A descriptor set in Vulkan acts as a container that holds resources, such as buffers, textures, and samplers, for use by shaders. Binding refers to the process of associating these descriptor sets with specific shader stages, enabling seamless interaction between shaders and resources during rendering. These descriptor sets serve as gateways through which resources are seamlessly bound to shader stages, orchestrating harmony between data and shader execution. To facilitate this synergy, the class simplifies descriptor set creation and management, complemented by methods for efficient resource binding within the Vulkan rendering pipeline.

How to do it...

A descriptor set layout states its bindings (number and types) with the `vkDescriptorSetLayout` structure. Each binding is described using an instance of the `vkDescriptorSetLayoutBinding` structure. The relationship between the Vulkan structures needed to create a descriptor set layout for the preceding code is shown in *Figure 2.11*:

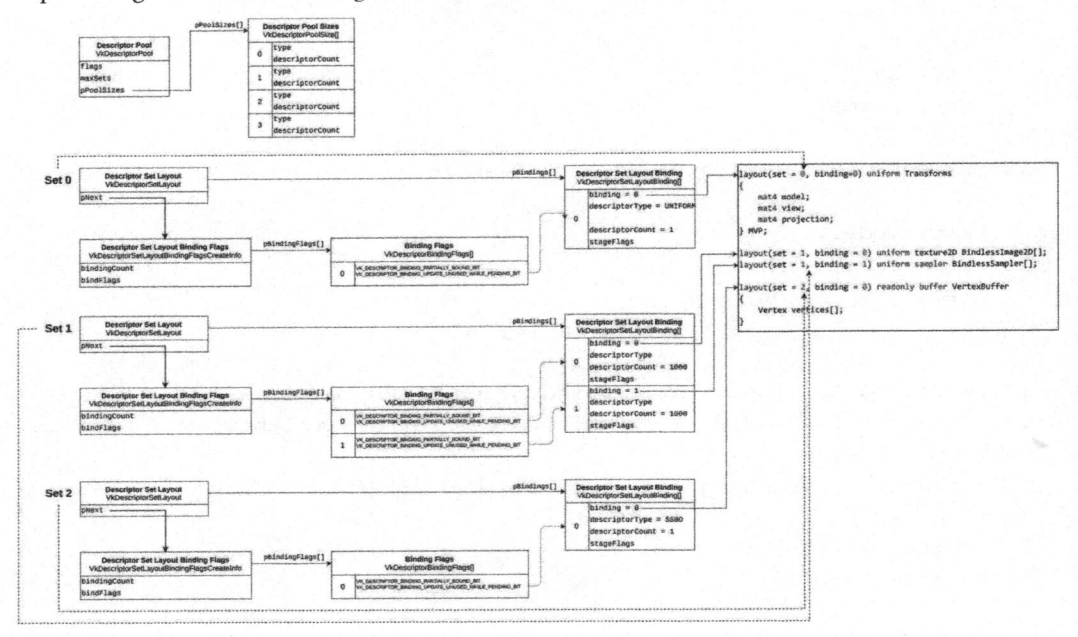

Figure 2.11 – Illustrating the configuration of descriptor set layouts for GLSL shaders

The following code shows how to specify two bindings for set 1, which are stored in a vector of bindings:

```
constexpr uint32_t kMaxBindings = 1000;
const VkDescriptorSetLayoutBinding texBinding = {
    .binding = 0,
    .descriptorType = VK_DESCRIPTOR_TYPE_SAMPLED_IMAGE,
    .descriptorCount = kMaxBindings,
    .stageFlags = VK_SHADER_STAGE_VERTEX_BIT,
};

const VkDescriptorSetLayoutBinding samplerBinding = {
    .binding = 1,
    .descriptorType = VK_DESCRIPTOR_TYPE_SAMPLER,
    .descriptorCount = kMaxBindings,
```

```
    .stageFlags = VK_SHADER_STAGE_VERTEX_BIT,
};

struct SetDescriptor {
  uint32_t set_;
  std::vector<VkDescriptorSetLayoutBinding> bindings_;
};

std::vector<SetDescriptor> sets(1);
sets[0].set_ = 1;
sets[0].bindings_.push_back(texBinding);
sets[0].bindings_.push_back(samplerBinding);
```

Since each binding describes a vector, and the `VkDescriptorSetLayoutBinding` structure requires the number of descriptors, we are using a large number that hopefully will accommodate all elements we need in the array. The vector of bindings is stored in a structure that describes a set with its number and all its bindings. This vector will be used to create a descriptor set layout:

```
constexpr VkDescriptorBindingFlags flagsToEnable =
    VK_DESCRIPTOR_BINDING_PARTIALLY_BOUND_BIT |
    VK_DESCRIPTOR_BINDING_UPDATE_UNUSED_WHILE_PENDING_BIT;

for (size_t setIndex = 0;
     const auto& set : sets) {
  std::vector<VkDescriptorBindingFlags> bindFlags(
      set.bindings_.size(), flagsToEnable);
  const VkDescriptorSetLayoutBindingFlagsCreateInfo
      extendedInfo{
          .sType =
              VK_STRUCTURE_TYPE_DESCRIPTOR_SET_LAYOUT_BINDING_FLAGS_CREATE_INFO,
          .pNext = nullptr,
          .bindingCount = static_cast<uint32_t>(
              set.bindings_.size()),
          .pBindingFlags = bindFlags.data(),
      };

  const VkDescriptorSetLayoutCreateInfo dslci = {
      .sType =
          VK_STRUCTURE_TYPE_DESCRIPTOR_SET_LAYOUT_CREATE_INFO,
      .pNext = &extendedInfo,
      .flags =
          VK_DESCRIPTOR_SET_LAYOUT_CREATE_UPDATE_AFTER_BIND_POOL_BIT_EXT,
```

```
        .bindingCount =
            static_cast<uint32_t>(set.bindings_.size()),
        .pBindings = set.bindings_.data(),
    };

    VkDescriptorSetLayout descSetLayout{VK_NULL_HANDLE};
    VK_CHECK(vkCreateDescriptorSetLayout(
        context_->device(), &dslci, nullptr,
        &descSetLayout));
}
```

Each set requires its own descriptor set layout, and the preceding process needs to be repeated for each one. The descriptor set layout needs to be stored so that it can be referred to in the future.

Passing data to shaders using push constants

Push constants are another way to pass data to shaders. Although a very performant and easy way to do so, push constants are very limited in size, 128 bytes being the only guaranteed amount by the Vulkan specification.

This recipe will show you how to pass a small amount of data from your application to shaders, using push constants for a simple shader.

Getting ready

Push constants are stored and managed by the `VulkanCore::Pipeline` class.

How to do it...

Push constants are recorded directly onto the command buffer and aren't prone to the same synchronization issues that exist with other resources. They are declared in the shader as follows, with one maximum block per shader:

```
layout (push_constant) uniform Transforms {
    mat4 model;
} PushConstants;
```

The pushed data must be split into the shader stages. Parts of it can be assigned to different shader stages or assigned to one single stage. The important part is that the data cannot be greater than the total amount available for push constants. The limit is provided in `VkPhysicalDeviceLimits::maxPushConstantsSize`.

Before using push constants, we need to specify how many bytes we are using in each shader stage:

```
const VkPushConstantRange range = {
    .stageFlags = VK_SHADER_STAGE_VERTEX_BIT,
    .offset = 0,
    .size = 64,
};

std::vector<VkPushConstantRange> pushConsts;
pushConsts.push_back(range);
```

The code states that the first (`offset == 0`) 64 bytes of the push constant data recorded in the command buffer (the size of a 4x4 matrix of floats) will be used by the vertex shader. This structure will be used in the next recipe to create a pipeline layout object.

Creating a pipeline layout

A pipeline layout is an object in Vulkan that needs to be created and destroyed by the application. The layout is specified using structures that define the layout of bindings and sets. In this recipe, you will learn how to create a pipeline layout.

Getting ready

A `VkPipelineLayoutCreateInfo` instance is created automatically by the `VulkanCore::Pipeline` class in the repository based on information provided by the application using a vector of `VulkanCore::Pipeline::SetDescriptor` structures.

How to do it...

With all descriptor set layouts for all sets and the push constant information in hand, the next step consists of creating a pipeline layout:

```
std::vector<VkDescriptoSetLayout> descLayouts;
const VkPipelineLayoutCreateInfo pipelineLayoutInfo = {
    .sType = VK_STRUCTURE_TYPE_PIPELINE_LAYOUT_CREATE_INFO,
    .setLayoutCount = (uint32_t)descLayouts.size(),
    .pSetLayouts = descLayouts.data(),
    .pushConstantRangeCount =
        !pushConsts.empty()
            ? static_cast<uint32_t>(pushConsts.size())
            : 0,
    .pPushConstantRanges = !pushConsts.empty()
                               ? pushConsts.data()
                               : nullptr,
```

```
};

VkPipelineLayout pipelineLayout{VK_NULL_HANDLE};
VK_CHECK(vkCreatePipelineLayout(context_->device(),
                                &pipelineLayoutInfo,
                                nullptr,
                                &pipelineLayout));
```

Once you have the descriptor set layout in hand and know how to use the push constants in your application, creating a pipeline layout is straightforward.

Creating a descriptor pool

A descriptor pool contains a maximum number of descriptors it can provide (be allocated from), grouped by binding type. For instance, if two bindings of the same set require one image each, the descriptor pool would have to provide at least two descriptors. In this recipe, you will learn how to create a descriptor pool.

Getting ready

Descriptor pools are allocated in the `VulkanCore::Pipeline::initDescriptorPool()` method.

How to do it...

Creating a descriptor pool is straightforward. All we need is a list of binding types and the maximum number of resources we'll allocate for each one:

```
constexpr uint32_t swapchainImages = 3;
std::vector<VkDescriptorPoolSize> poolSizes;
poolSizes.emplace_back(VkDescriptorPoolSize{
    VK_DESCRIPTOR_TYPE_SAMPLED_IMAGE,
    swapchainImages* kMaxBindings});
poolSizes.emplace_back(VkDescriptorPoolSize{
    VK_DESCRIPTOR_TYPE_SAMPLER,
    swapchainImages* kMaxBindings});
```

Since we duplicate the resources based on the number of swapchain images to avoid data races between the CPU and the GPU, we multiply the number of bindings we requested before (kMaxBindings = 1000) by the number of swapchain images:

```
const VkDescriptorPoolCreateInfo descriptorPoolInfo = {
    .sType =
        VK_STRUCTURE_TYPE_DESCRIPTOR_POOL_CREATE_INFO,
    .flags =
```

```
                VK_DESCRIPTOR_POOL_CREATE_FREE_DESCRIPTOR_SET_BIT |
                VK_DESCRIPTOR_POOL_CREATE_UPDATE_AFTER_BIND_BIT,
        .maxSets = MAX_DESCRIPTOR_SETS,
        .poolSizeCount =
            static_cast<uint32_t>(poolSizes.size()),
        .pPoolSizes = poolSizes.data(),
};
VkDescriptorPool descriptorPool{VK_NULL_HANDLE};
VK_CHECK(vkCreateDescriptorPool(context_->device(),
                                &descriptorPoolInfo,
                                nullptr,
                                &descriptorPool));
```

Be careful not to create pools that are too large. Achieving a high-performing application means not allocating more resources than you need.

Allocating descriptor sets

Once a descriptor layout and a descriptor pool have been created, before you can use it, you need to allocate a descriptor set, which is an instance of a set with the layout described by the descriptor layout. In this recipe, you will learn how to allocate a descriptor set.

Getting ready

Descriptor set allocations are done in the `VulkanCore::Pipeline::allocateDescriptors()` method. Here, developers define the count of descriptor sets required, coupled with binding counts per set. The subsequent `bindDescriptorSets()` method weaves the descriptors into command buffers, preparing them for shader execution.

How to do it…

Allocating a descriptor set (or a number of them) is easy. You need to fill the `VkDescriptorSetAllocateInfo` structure and call `vkAllocateDescriptorSets`:

```
VkDescriptorSetAllocateInfo allocInfo = {
    .sType =
        VK_STRUCTURE_TYPE_DESCRIPTOR_SET_ALLOCATE_INFO,
    .descriptorPool = descriptorPool,
    .descriptorSetCount = 1,
    .pSetLayouts = &descSetLayout,
};

VkDescriptorSet descriptorSet{VK_NULL_HANDLE};
VK_CHECK(vkAllocateDescriptorSets(context_->device(),
```

```
                             &allocInfo,
                             &descriptorSet));
```

When using multiple copies of a resource to avoid race conditions, there are two approaches:

1. Allocate one descriptor set for each resource. In other words, call the preceding code once for each copy of the resource.
2. Create one descriptor set and update it every time you need to render.

Updating descriptor sets during rendering

Once a descriptor set has been allocated, it is not associated with any resources. This association must happen once (if your descriptor sets are immutable) or every time you need to bind a different resource to a descriptor set. In this recipe, you will learn how to update descriptor sets during rendering and after you have set up the pipeline and its layout.

Getting ready

In the repository, `VulkanCore::Pipeline` provides methods to update different types of resources, as each binding can only be associated with one type of resource (image, sampler, or buffer): `updateSamplersDescriptorSets()`, `updateTexturesDescriptorSets()`, and `updateBuffersDescriptorSets()`.

How to do it...

Associating a resource with a descriptor set is done with the `vkUpdateDescriptorSets` function. Each call to `vkUpdateDescriptorSets` can update one or more bindings of one or more sets. Before updating a descriptor set, let's look at how to update *one* binding.

You can associate either a texture, a texture array, a sampler, a sampler array, a buffer, or a buffer array with one binding. To associate images or samplers, use the `VkDescriptorImageInfo` structure. To associate buffers, use the `VkDescriptorBufferInfo` structure. Once one or more of those structures have been instantiated, use the `VkWriteDescriptorSet` structure to bind them all with a binding. Bindings that represent an array are updated with a vector of `VkDescriptor*Info`.

1. Consider the bindings declared in the shader code presented next:

```
layout(set = 1, binding = 0) uniform texture2D textures[];
layout(set = 1, binding = 1) uniform sampler    samplers[];

layout(set = 2, binding = 0) readonly buffer VertexBuffer
{
  Vertex vertices[];
} vertexBuffer;
```

2. To update the `textures[]` array, we need to create two instances of `VkDescriptorImageInfo` and record them in the first `VkWriteDescriptorSet` structure:

```
VkImageView imageViews[2];   // Valid Image View objects
VkDescriptorImageInfo texInfos[] = {
 VkDescriptorImageInfo{
   .imageView = imageViews[0],
   .imageLayout = VK_IMAGE_LAYOUT_SHADER_READ_ONLY_OPTIMAL,
   },
 VkDescriptorImageInfo{
   .imageView = imageViews[1],
   .imageLayout = VK_IMAGE_LAYOUT_SHADER_READ_ONLY_OPTIMAL,
   },
};

const VkWriteDescriptorSet texWriteDescSet = {
    .sType = VK_STRUCTURE_TYPE_WRITE_DESCRIPTOR_SET,
    .dstSet = 1,
    ee,
    .dstArrayElement = 0,
    .descriptorCount = 2,
    .descriptorType = VK_DESCRIPTOR_TYPE_SAMPLED_IMAGE,
    .pImageInfo = &texInfos,
    .pBufferInfo = nullptr,
};
```

3. The two image views will be bound to set 1 (`.dstSet = 1`) and binding 0 (`.dstBinding = 0`) as elements 0 and 1 of the array. If you need to bind more objects to the array, all you need are more instances of `VkDescriptorImageInfo`. The number of objects bound to the current binding is specified by the `descriptorCount` member of the structure.

The process is similar for sampler objects:

```
VkSampler sampler[2];   // Valid Sampler object
VkDescriptorImageInfo samplerInfos[] = {
    VkDescriptorImageInfo{
        .sampler = sampler[0],
    },
    VkDescriptorImageInfo{
        .sampler = sampler[1],
    },
};
const VkWriteDescriptorSet samplerWriteDescSet = {
    .sType = VK_STRUCTURE_TYPE_WRITE_DESCRIPTOR_SET,
    .dstSet = 1,
```

```
        .dstBinding = 1,
        .dstArrayElement = 0,
        .descriptorCount = 2,
        .descriptorType = VK_DESCRIPTOR_TYPE_SAMPLED_IMAGE,
        .pImageInfo = &samplerInfos,
        .pBufferInfo = nullptr,
};
```

This time, we are binding the sampler objects to set 1, binding 1. Buffers are bound using the `VkDescriptorBufferInfo` structure:

```
VkBuffer buffer;                // Valid Buffer object
VkDeviceSize bufferLength;      // Range of the buffer
const VkDescriptorBufferInfo bufferInfo = {
        .buffer = buffer,
        .offset = 0,
        .range = bufferLength,
};
const VkWriteDescriptorSet bufferWriteDescSet = {
        .sType = VK_STRUCTURE_TYPE_WRITE_DESCRIPTOR_SET,
        .dstSet = 2,
        .dstBinding = 0,
        .dstArrayElement = 0,
        .descriptorCount = 1,
        .descriptorType = VK_DESCRIPTOR_TYPE_SAMPLED_IMAGE,
        .pImageInfo = nullptr,
        .pBufferInfo = &bufferInfo,
};
```

Besides storing the address of the `bufferInfo` variable to the `.pBufferInfo` member of `VkWriteDescriptorSet`, we are binding one buffer (`.descriptorCount = 1`) to set 2 (`.dstSet = 2`) and binding 0 (`.dstBinding = 0`).

4. The last step consists of storing all `VkWriteDescriptorSet` instances in a vector and calling `vkUpdateDescriptorSets`:

```
VkDevice device; // Valid Vulkan Device
std::vector<VkWriteDescriptorSet> writeDescSets;
writeDescSets.push_back(texWriteDescSet);
writeDescSets.push_back(samplerWriteDescSet);
writeDescSets.push_back(bufferWriteDescSet);
vkUpdateDescriptorSets(device, static_cast<uint32_
t>(writeDescSets.size()),
                       writeDescSets.data(), 0, nullptr);
```

Encapsulating this task is the best way to avoid repetition and bugs introduced by forgetting a step in the update procedure.

Passing resources to shaders (binding descriptor sets)

While rendering, we need to bind the descriptor sets we'd like to use during a draw call.

Getting ready

Binding sets is done with the `VulkanCore::Pipeline::bindDescriptorSets()` method.

How to do it...

To bind a descriptor set for rendering, we need to call `vkCmdBindDescriptorSets`:

```
VkCommandBuffer commandBuffer;      // Valid Command Buffer
VkPipelineLayout pipelineLayout;    // Valid Pipeline layout
uint32_t set;                        // Set number
VkDescriptorSet descSet;            // Valid Descriptor Set
vkCmdBindDescriptorSets(
    commandBuffer, VK_PIPELINE_BIND_POINT_GRAPHICS,
    pipelineLayout, set, 1u, &descSet, 0, nullptr);
```

Now that we've successfully bound a descriptor set for rendering, let's turn our attention to another crucial aspect of our graphics pipeline: updating push constants.

Updating push constants during rendering

Push constants are updated during rendering by recording their values directly into the command buffer being recorded.

Getting ready

Updating push constants is done with the `VulkanCore::Pipeline::udpatePushConstants()` method.

How to do it...

Once rendered, updating push constants is straightforward. All you need to do is call `vkCmdPushConstants`:

```
VkCommandBuffer commandBuffer;      // Valid Command Buffer
VkPipelineLayout pipelineLayout;    // Valid Pipeline Layout
glm::vec4 mat;                       // Valid matrix
```

```
vkCmdPushConstants(commandBuffer, pipelineLayout,
                   VK_SHADER_STAGE_FRAGMENT_BIT, 0,
                   sizeof(glm::vec4), &mat);
```

This call records the contents of `mat` into the command buffer, starting at offset 0 and signaling that this data will be used by the vertex shader.

Customizing shader behavior with specialization constants

The process of compiling shader code results in immutability once completed. The compilation procedure carries a substantial time overhead and is generally circumvented during runtime. Even minor adjustments to a shader necessitate recompilation, leading to the creation of a fresh shader module and potentially a new pipeline as well – all entailing significant resource-intensive operations.

In Vulkan, specialization constants allow you to specify constant values for shader parameters at pipeline creation time, instead of having to recompile the shader with new values every time you want to change them. This can be particularly useful when you want to reuse the same shader with different constant values multiple times. In this recipe, we will delve deeper into the practical application of specialization constants in Vulkan to create more efficient and flexible shader programs, allowing you to adjust without the need for resource-intensive recompilations.

Getting ready

Specialization constants are available in the repository through the `VulkanCore::Pipeline::GraphicsPipelineDescriptor` structure. You need to provide a vector of `VkSpecializationMapEntry` structures for each shader type you'd like to apply specialization constants to.

How to do it…

Specialization constants are declared in GLSL using the `constant_id` qualifier along with an integer that specifies the constant's ID:

```
layout (constant_id = 0) const bool useShaderDebug = false;
```

To create a pipeline with specialized constant values, you first need to create a `VkSpecializationInfo` structure that specifies the constant values and their IDs. You then pass this structure to the `VkPipelineShaderStageCreateInfo` structure when creating a pipeline:

```
const bool kUseShaderDebug = false;
const VkSpecializationMapEntry useShaderDebug = {
    .constantID = 0, // matches the constant_id qualifier
```

```
        .offset = 0,
        .size = sizeof(bool),
    };
    const VkSpecializationInfo vertexSpecializationInfo = {
        .mapEntryCount = 1,
        .pMapEntries = &useShaderDebug,
        .dataSize = sizeof(bool),
        .pData = &kUseShaderDebug,
    };
    const VkPipelineShaderStageCreateInfo shaderStageInfo = {
      ...
      .pSpecializationInfo = &vertexSpecializationInfo,
    };
```

Because specialization constants are real constants, branches that depend on them may be entirely removed during the final compilation of the shader. On the other hand, specialization constants should not be used to control parameters such as uniforms, as they are not as flexible and require to be known during the construction of the pipeline.

Implementing MDI and PVP

MDI and PVP are features of modern graphics APIs that allow for greater flexibility and efficiency in vertex processing.

MDI allows issuing multiple draw calls with a single command, each of which derives its parameters from a buffer stored in the device (hence the *indirect* term). This is particularly useful because those parameters can be modified in the GPU itself.

With PVP, each shader instance retrieves its vertex data based on its index and instance IDs instead of being initialized with the vertex's attributes. This allows for flexibility because the vertex attributes and their format are not baked into the pipeline and can be changed solely based on the shader code.

In the first sub-recipe, we will focus on the implementation of **MDI**, demonstrating how this powerful tool can streamline your graphics operations by allowing multiple draw calls to be issued from a single command, with parameters that can be modified directly in the GPU. In the following sub-recipe, we will guide you through the process of setting up **PVP**, highlighting how the flexibility of this feature can enhance your shader code by enabling changes to vertex attributes without modifying the pipeline.

Implementing MDI

For using MDI, we store all mesh data belonging to the scene in one big buffer for all the meshes' vertices and another one for the meshes' indices, with the data for each mesh stored sequentially, as depicted in *Figure 2.12*.

114   Working with Modern Vulkan

The drawing parameters are stored in an extra buffer. They must be stored sequentially, one for each mesh, although they don't have to be provided in the same order as the meshes:

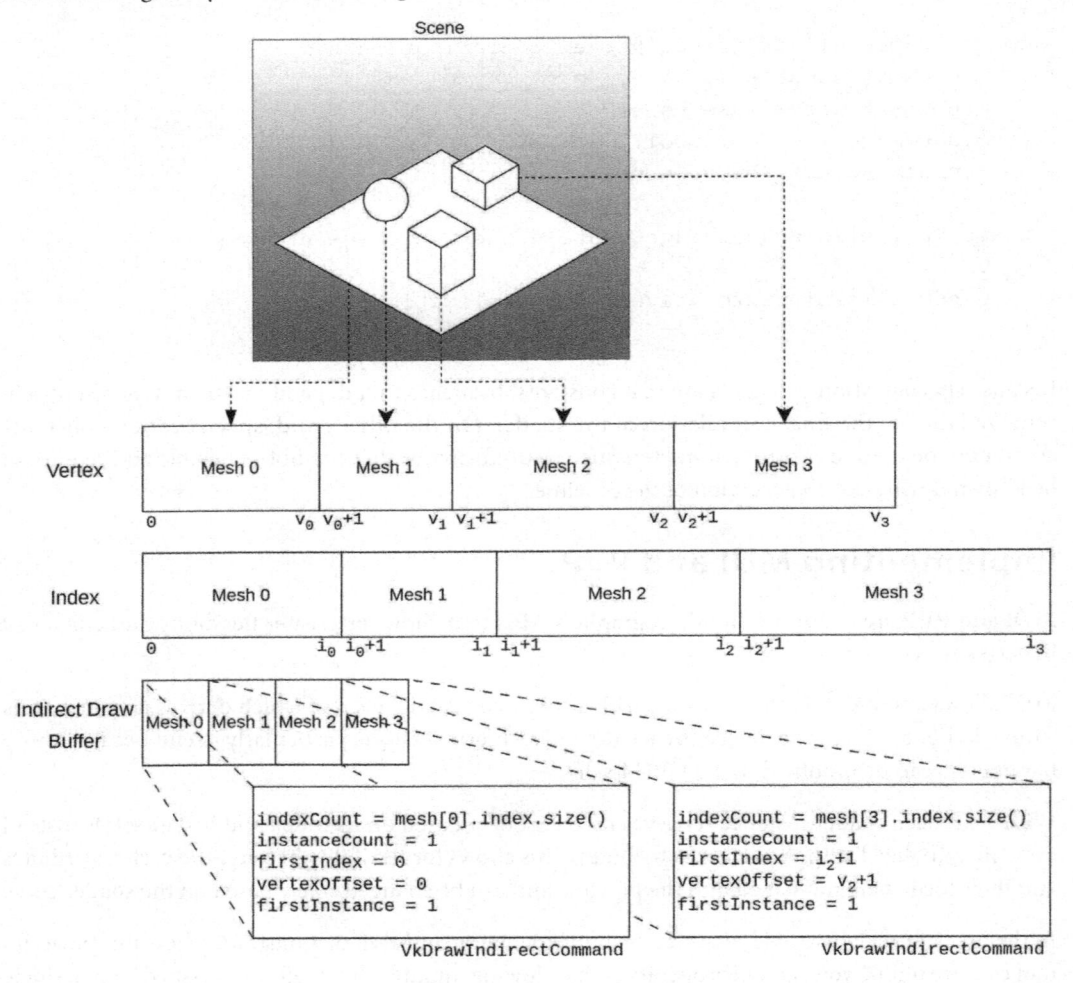

Figure 2.12 – MDI data layout

We will now learn how to implement MDI using the Vulkan API.

Getting ready

In the repository, we provide a utility function to decompose an `EngineCore::Model` object into multiple buffers suitable for an MDI implementation, called `EngineCore::convertModel2OneBuffer()`, located in `GLBLoader.cpp`.

How to do it…

Let's begin by looking at the indirect draw parameters' buffer.

The commands are stored following the same layout as the `VkDrawIndexedIndirectCommand` structure:

```
typedef struct VkDrawIndexedIndirectCommand {
    uint32_t    indexCount;
    uint32_t    instanceCount;
    uint32_t    firstIndex;
    int32_t     vertexOffset;
    uint32_t    firstInstance;
} VkDrawIndexedIndirectCommand;
```

`indexCount` specifies how many indices are part of this command and, in our case, is the number of indices for a mesh. One command reflects one mesh, so its `instanceCount` value is one. The `firstVertex` member is the index of the first index element in the buffer to use for this mesh, while `vertexOffset` points to the first vertex element in the buffer to use. An example with the correct offsets is shown in *Figure 2.12*.

Once the vertex, index, and indirect commands buffers are bound, calling `vkCmdDrawIndexedIndirect` consists of providing the buffer with the indirect commands and an offset into the buffer. The rest is done by the device:

```
VkCommandBuffer commandBuffer;   // Valid Command Bufer
VkBuffer indirectCmdBuffer;      // Valid buffer w/
                                 // indirect commands
uint32_t meshCount;     // Number of indirect commands in
                        // the buffer
uint32_t offset = 0;    // Offset into the indirect commands
                        // buffer
vkCmdDrawIndexedIndirect(
    commandBuffer, indirectCmdBuffer, offset,
    meshCount,
    sizeof(VkDrawIndexedIndirectDrawCommand));
```

In this recipe, we learned how to utilize `vkCmdDrawIndexedIndirect`, a key function in Vulkan that allows for high-efficiency drawing.

Using PVP

The PVP technique allows vertex data and their attributes to be extracted from buffers with custom code instead of relying on the pipeline to provide them to vertex shaders.

Getting ready

We will use the following structures to perform the extraction of vertex data – the `Vertex` structure, which encodes the vertex's position (`pos`), `normal`, UV coordinates (`uv`), and its material index (`material`):

```
struct Vertex {
    vec3 pos;
    vec3 normal;
    vec2 uv;
    int material;
};
```

We will also use a buffer object, referred to in the shader as `VertexBuffer`:

```
layout(set = 2, binding = 0) readonly buffer VertexBuffer
{
    Vertex vertices[];
} vertexBuffer;
```

Next, we will learn how to use the `vertexBuffer` object to access vertex data.

How to do it...

The shader code used to access the vertex data looks like this:

```
void main() {
  Vertex vertex = vertexBuffer.vertices[gl_VertexIndex];
}
```

Note that the vertex and its attributes are not declared as inputs to the shader. `gl_VertexIndex` is automatically computed and provided to the shader based on the draw call and the parameters recorded in the indirect command retrieved from the indirect command buffer.

> **Index and vertex buffers**
>
> Note that both the index and vertex buffers are still provided and bound to the pipeline before the draw call is issued. The index buffer must have the `VK_BUFFER_USAGE_INDEX_BUFFER_BIT` flag enabled for the technique to work.

Adding flexibility to the rendering pipeline using dynamic rendering

In this recipe, we will delve into the practical application of dynamic rendering in Vulkan to enhance the flexibility of the rendering pipeline. We will guide you through the process of creating pipelines without the need for render passes and framebuffers and discuss how to ensure synchronization. By the end of this section, you will have learned how to implement this feature in your projects, thereby simplifying your rendering process by eliminating the need for render passes and framebuffers and giving you more direct control over synchronization.

Getting ready

To enable the feature, we must have access to the `VK_KHR_get_physical_device_properties2` instance extension, instantiate a structure of type `VkPhysicalDeviceDynamicRenderingFeatures`, and set its `dynamicRendering` member to `true`:

```
const VkPhysicalDeviceDynamicRenderingFeatures
dynamicRenderingFeatures = {
    .sType = VK_STRUCTURE_TYPE_PHYSICAL_DEVICE_DYNAMIC_RENDERING_FEATURES,
    .dynamicRendering = VK_TRUE,
};
```

This structure needs to be plugged into the `VkDeviceCreateInfo::pNext` member when creating a Vulkan device:

```
const VkDeviceCreateInfo dci = {
    .sType = VK_STRUCTURE_TYPE_DEVICE_CREATE_INFO,
    .pNext = &dynamicRenderingFeatures,
    ...
};
```

Having grasped the concept of enabling dynamic rendering, we will now move forward and explore its implementation using the Vulkan API.

How to do it...

Instead of creating render passes and framebuffers, we must call the `vkCmdBeginRendering` command and provide the attachments and their load and store operations using the `VkRenderingInfo` structure. Each attachment (colors, depth, and stencil) must be specified with instances of the `VkRenderingAttachmentInfo` structure. *Figure 2.13* presents a diagram of the structure participating in a call to `vkCmdBeginRendering`:

Working with Modern Vulkan

Rendering Info VkRenderingInfo
renderArea
layerCount
viewMask
colorAttachmentCount

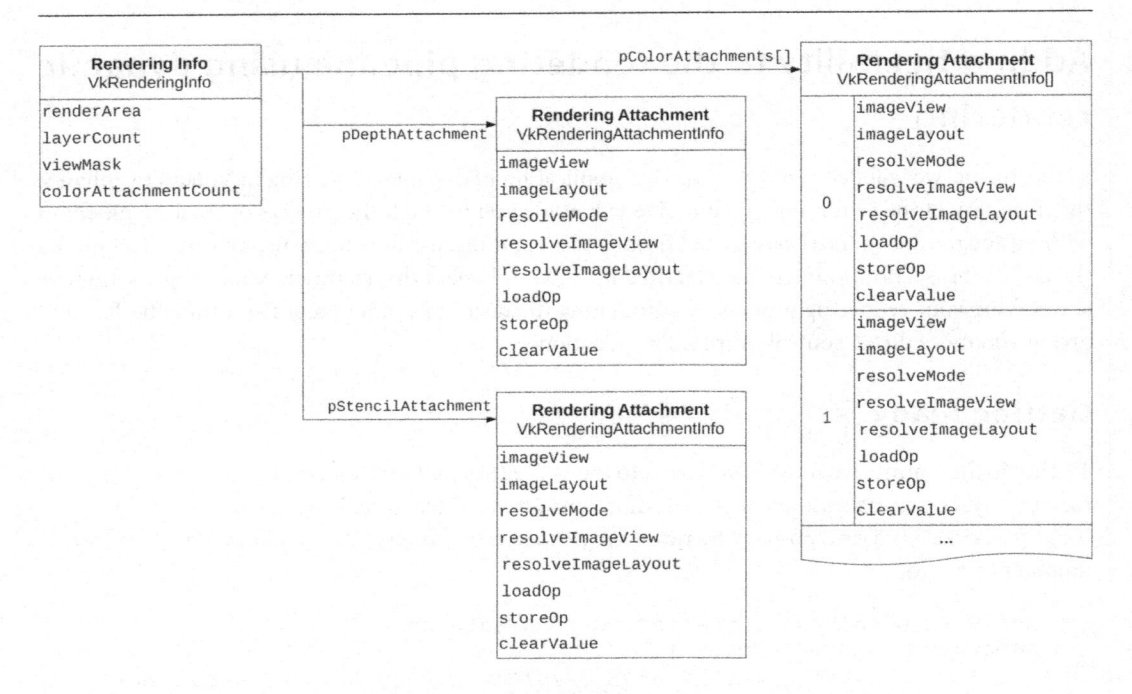

Rendering Attachment VkRenderingAttachmentInfo
imageView
imageLayout
resolveMode
resolveImageView
resolveImageLayout
loadOp
storeOp
clearValue

Rendering Attachment VkRenderingAttachmentInfo
imageView
imageLayout
resolveMode
resolveImageView
resolveImageLayout
loadOp
storeOp
clearValue

Rendering Attachment VkRenderingAttachmentInfo[]	
imageView	0
imageLayout	
resolveMode	
resolveImageView	
resolveImageLayout	
loadOp	
storeOp	
clearValue	
imageView	1
imageLayout	
resolveMode	
resolveImageView	
resolveImageLayout	
loadOp	
storeOp	
clearValue	
...	

Figure 2.13 – Dynamic rendering structure diagram

Any one of the attachments, `pColorAttachments`, `pDepthAttachment`, and `pStencilAttachment`, can be `null`. Shader output written to location x is written to the color attachment at `pColorAttachment[x]`.

Transferring resources between queue families

In this recipe, we will demonstrate how to transfer resources between queue families by uploading textures to a device from the CPU using a transfer queue and generating mip-level data in a graphics queue. Generating mip levels needs a graphics queue because it utilizes `vkCmdBlitImage`, supported only by graphics queues.

Getting ready

An example is provided in the repository in `chapter2/mainMultiDrawIndirect.cpp`, which uses the `EngineCore::AsyncDataUploader` class to perform texture upload and mipmap generation on different queues.

How to do it...

In the following diagram, we illustrate the procedure of uploading texture through a transfer queue, followed by the utilization of a graphics queue for mip generation:

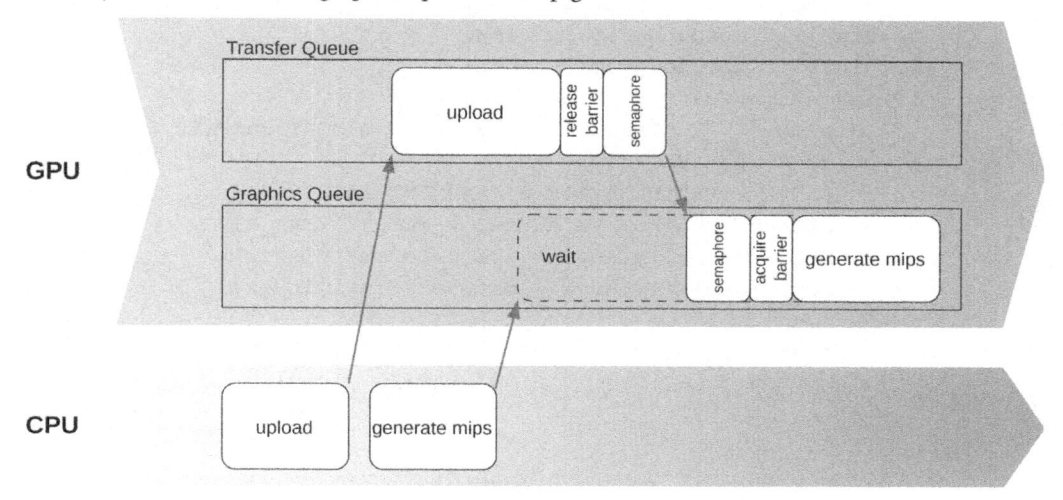

Figure 2.14 – Recoding and submitting commands from different threads and transferring a resource between queues from different families

The process can be summarized as follows:

1. Record the commands to upload the texture to the device and add a barrier to release the texture from the transfer queue using the `VkDependencyInfo` and `VkImageMemoryBarrier2` structures, specifying the source queue family as the family of the transfer queue and the destination queue family as the family of the graphics queue.

2. Create a semaphore and use it to signal when the command buffer finishes, and attach it to the submission of the command buffer.

3. Create a command buffer for generating mip levels and add a barrier to acquire the texture from the transfer queue into the graphics queue using the `VkDependencyInfo` and `VkImageMemoryBarrier2` structures.

4. Attach the semaphore created in *step 2* to the `SubmitInfo` structure when submitting the command buffer for processing. The semaphore will be signaled when the first command buffer has completed, allowing the mip-level-generation command buffer to start.

Two auxiliary methods will help us create acquire and release barriers for a texture. They exist in the `VulkanCore::Texture` class. The first one creates an acquire barrier:

```
void Texture::addAcquireBarrier(
    VkCommandBuffer cmdBuffer,
    uint32_t srcQueueFamilyIndex,
    uint32_t dstQueueFamilyIndex) {
  VkImageMemoryBarrier2 acquireBarrier = {
      .sType = VK_STRUCTURE_TYPE_IMAGE_MEMORY_BARRIER_2,
      .dstStageMask =
          VK_PIPELINE_STAGE_2_FRAGMENT_SHADER_BIT,
      .dstAccessMask = VK_ACCESS_2_MEMORY_READ_BIT,
      .srcQueueFamilyIndex = srcQueueFamilyIndex,
      .dstQueueFamilyIndex = dstQueueFamilyIndex,
      .image = image_,
      .subresourceRange = {VK_IMAGE_ASPECT_COLOR_BIT,
                           0, mipLevels_, 0, 1},
  };

  VkDependencyInfo dependency_info{
      .sType = VK_STRUCTURE_TYPE_DEPENDENCY_INFO,
      .imageMemoryBarrierCount = 1,
      .pImageMemoryBarriers = &acquireBarrier,
  };

  vkCmdPipelineBarrier2(cmdBuffer, &dependency_info);
}
```

Besides the command buffer, this function requires the indices of the source and destination family queues. It also assumes a few things, such as the subresource range spanning the entire image.

5. Another method records the release barrier:

```
void Texture::addReleaseBarrier(
    VkCommandBuffer cmdBuffer,
    uint32_t srcQueueFamilyIndex,
    uint32_t dstQueueFamilyIndex) {
  VkImageMemoryBarrier2 releaseBarrier = {
      .sType = VK_STRUCTURE_TYPE_IMAGE_MEMORY_BARRIER_2,
      .srcStageMask = VK_PIPELINE_STAGE_2_TRANSFER_BIT,
      .srcAccessMask = VK_ACCESS_TRANSFER_WRITE_BIT,
      .dstAccessMask = VK_ACCESS_SHADER_READ_BIT,
      .srcQueueFamilyIndex = srcQueueFamilyIndex,
      .dstQueueFamilyIndex = dstQueueFamilyIndex,
      .image = image_,
```

```
            .subresourceRange = {VK_IMAGE_ASPECT_COLOR_BIT,
                                 0, mipLevels_, 0, 1},
    };

    VkDependencyInfo dependency_info{
        .sType = VK_STRUCTURE_TYPE_DEPENDENCY_INFO,
        .imageMemoryBarrierCount = 1,
        .pImageMemoryBarriers = &releaseBarrier,
    };

    vkCmdPipelineBarrier2(cmdBuffer, &dependency_info);
}
```

This method makes the same assumptions as the previous one. The main differences are the source and destination stages and access masks.

6. To perform the upload and mipmap generation, we create two instances of `VulkanCore::CommandQueueManager`, one for the transfer queue and another for the graphics queue:

    ```
    auto transferQueueMgr =
        context.createTransferCommandQueue(
            1, 1, "transfer queue");
    auto graphicsQueueMgr =
        context.createGraphicsCommandQueue(
            1, 1, "graphics queue");
    ```

7. With valid `VulkanCore::Context` and `VulkanCore::Texture` instances in hand, we can upload the texture by retrieving a command buffer from the transfer family. We also create a staging buffer for transferring the texture data to device-local memory:

    ```
    VulkanCore::Context context;   // Valid Context
    std::shared_ptr<VulkanCore::Texture>
        texture;          // Valid Texture
    void* textureData;    // Valid texture data

    // Upload texture
    auto textureUploadStagingBuffer =
        context.createStagingBuffer(
            texture->vkDeviceSize(),
            VK_BUFFER_USAGE_TRANSFER_SRC_BIT,
            "texture upload staging buffer");

    const auto commandBuffer =
        transferQueueMgr.getCmdBufferToBegin();
    ```

```cpp
texture->uploadOnly(commandBuffer,
                    textureUploadStagingBuffer.get(),
                    textureData);

texture->addReleaseBarrier(
    commandBuffer,
    transferQueueMgr.queueFamilyIndex(),
    graphicsQueueMgr.queueFamilyIndex());

transferQueueMgr.endCmdBuffer(commandBuffer);

transferQueueMgr.disposeWhenSubmitCompletes(
    std::move(textureUploadStagingBuffer));
```

8. For submitting the command buffer for processing, we create a semaphore to synchronize the upload command buffer and the one used for generating mipmaps:

```cpp
VkSemaphore graphicsSemaphore;
const VkSemaphoreCreateInfo semaphoreInfo{
    .sType = VK_STRUCTURE_TYPE_SEMAPHORE_CREATE_INFO,
};
VK_CHECK(vkCreateSemaphore(context.device(),
                           &semaphoreInfo, nullptr,
                           &graphicsSemaphore));

VkPipelineStageFlags flags =
    VK_PIPELINE_STAGE_TRANSFER_BIT;
auto submitInfo =
    context.swapchain()->createSubmitInfo(
        &commandBuffer, &flags, false, false);
submitInfo.signalSemaphoreCount = 1;
submitInfo.pSignalSemaphores = &graphicsSemaphore;
transferQueueMgr.submit(&submitInfo);
```

9. The next step is to acquire a new command buffer from the graphics queue family for generating mipmaps. We also create an acquire barrier and reuse the semaphore from the previous command buffer submission:

```cpp
// Generate mip levels
auto commandBuffer =
    graphicsQueueMgr.getCmdBufferToBegin();

texture->addAcquireBarrier(
```

```
            commandBuffer,
            transferCommandQueueMgr_.queueFamilyIndex(),
            graphicsQueueMgr.queueFamilyIndex());
    texture->generateMips(commandBuffer);

    graphicsQueueMgr.endCmdBuffer(commandBuffer);
    VkPipelineStageFlags flags =
        VK_PIPELINE_STAGE_COLOR_ATTACHMENT_OUTPUT_BIT;
    auto submitInfo =
        context_.swapchain()->createSubmitInfo(
            &commandBuffer, &flags, false, false);
    submitInfo.pWaitSemaphores = &graphicsSemaphore;
    submitInfo.waitSemaphoreCount = 1;
```

In this chapter, we have navigated the complex landscape of advanced Vulkan programming, building upon the foundational concepts introduced earlier. Our journey encompassed a diverse range of topics, each contributing crucial insights to the realm of high-performance graphics applications. From mastering Vulkan's intricate memory model and efficient allocation techniques to harnessing the power of the VMA library, we've equipped ourselves with the tools to optimize memory management. We explored the creation and manipulation of buffers and images, uncovering strategies for seamless data uploads, staging buffers, and ring-buffer implementations that circumvent data races. The utilization of pipeline barriers to synchronize data access was demystified, while techniques for rendering pipelines, shader customization via specialization constants, and cutting-edge rendering methodologies such as PVP and MDI were embraced. Additionally, we ventured into dynamic rendering approaches without relying on render passes and addressed the intricacies of resource handling across multiple threads and queues. With these profound understandings, you are primed to create graphics applications that harmonize technical prowess with artistic vision using the Vulkan API.

3
Implementing GPU-Driven Rendering

In this chapter, we embark on a deep dive into the intricacies of manipulating geometry specifically for GPU rendering. The traditional approach heavily relies on the CPU for various tasks, which can be a bottleneck in many scenarios. Our goal here is to liberate your rendering techniques from such constraints. We aim to put the GPU in the driver's seat, ensuring efficient processing by capitalizing on its parallel processing prowess. We will unravel the technique of generating and drawing lines, not from the traditional space of the CPU but directly from shaders, such as vertex or fragment shaders. This not only enhances efficiency but also opens new realms of creativity. Taking a step further, we'll demonstrate how to extend this novel line-drawing feature to display numbers right from shaders. This capability paves the way for real-time displays and feedback without toggling between GPU and CPU. We then shift our gaze to a more intricate topic – rendering text on the GPU. By employing the **Signed Distance Fields** (**SDF**) approach, we'll guide you in achieving smoother and more versatile text rendering on the GPU.

Lastly, we'll address one of the classic challenges in rendering: frustum culling. **Frustum culling** involves avoiding the rendering of objects that are outside the camera's **field of view** (**FOV**). **Frustum** refers to the volume of space that is visible through the camera. **Culling** means discarding or ignoring objects that fall outside this frustum, thus they are not processed for rendering. Instead of the traditional approach, we'll show you how to implement this directly on the GPU using compute shaders, ensuring objects outside the camera view do not consume valuable GPU resources. By the chapter's close, you'll have a holistic grasp of GPU-driven rendering, enabling you to harness the GPU's capabilities to its fullest and streamline your rendering tasks.

In this chapter, we will cover the following recipes:

- Implementing GPU-driven line rendering
- Expanding line-drawing techniques to render textual values from shaders
- Drawing text using SDF
- Frustum culling using compute shaders

Technical requirements

For this chapter, you will need to make sure you have VS 2022 installed along with the Vulkan SDK. Basic familiarity with the C++ programming language and an understanding of OpenGL or any other graphics API will be useful. Please revisit *Chapter 1, Vulkan Core Concepts*, under the *Technical requirements* section for details on setting up and building executables for this chapter. This chapter has multiple recipes, which can be launched using the following executables:

1. `Chapter03_GPU_Lines.exe`
2. `Chapter03_GPU_Text.exe`
3. `Chapter03_GPU_Text_SDF.exe`
4. `Chapter03_GPU_Culling.exe`

Implementing GPU-driven line rendering

In this recipe, you will learn a technique that allows drawing lines directly from shaders such as vertex or fragment shaders. In many graphics applications, the challenge arises when one wishes to draw lines directly and efficiently using the inherent capabilities of shaders, particularly vertex or fragment shaders. To address this, our recipe delves into a specialized technique tailored for this very purpose. We'll be presenting a recipe that seamlessly integrates with a variety of pipelines and render passes. Through our approach, data, be it vertices or colors, gets stored in a device buffer, ensuring a streamlined process. The culmination of this procedure is the utilization of this accumulated data in a subsequent pass, where these lines are then masterfully rendered onto a framebuffer. By the end, you will have a robust and efficient method to directly render lines using shaders.

Getting ready

Before diving into the recipe, you should make sure you have VS 2022 installed and that you are able to build the repository as per the steps provided in *Chapter 1, Vulkan Core Concepts*.

You should be able to launch the executable named `Chapter03_GPU_Lines.exe` from VS 2022.

The code covered in this recipe can be found in the repository, in `chapter3/mainGPULines.cpp` and `chapter3/resources/shaders`, in the `gpuLines.frag`, `gpuLines.vert`, `gpuLinesDraw.frag`, and `gpuLinesDraw.vert` files.

How to do it…

In this section, we'll guide you through the comprehensive procedure of directly drawing lines from shaders and integrating them into the final rendered frame using GPU-driven techniques. By leveraging a dedicated device buffer and carefully orchestrated render passes, this technique allows for real-time visual feedback and streamlined graphical processes. By the end of this walkthrough, you'll have a robust mechanism in place for efficiently rendering lines directly from the GPU with minimal CPU involvement.

The idea relies on having a device buffer that serves as a repository for lines and parameters for the indirect draw structure used to render those lines. After all render passes are complete, one additional render pass is performed to draw lines in the buffer. Here are the steps to do it:

1. The first step is to create a buffer that will contain not only the line data but also metadata that is used for determining how many lines can fit into the buffer and other parameters used by the final indirect draw call. The following snippet defines the buffer structure in C++, with `GPULineBuffer` being the structure of the buffer used to store/draw lines:

   ```
   constexpr uint32_t kNumLines = 65'536;
   struct Line {
     glm::vec4 v0_;
     glm::vec4 color0_;
     glm::vec4 v1_;
     glm::vec4 color1_;
   };
   struct Header {
     uint32_t maxNumlines_;
     uint32_t padding0 = 0u;
     uint32_t padding1 = 0u;
     uint32_t padding2 = 0u;
     VkDrawIndirectCommand cmd_;
   };
   struct GPULineBuffer {
     Header header_;
     Line lines_[kNumLines];
   };
   ```

   This structure defines the device buffer we'll use to store the GPU-generated lines and can store up to 65,536 lines plus the data in the `Header` section.

   Figure 3.1 shows the buffer's layout as *seen* by the GPU:

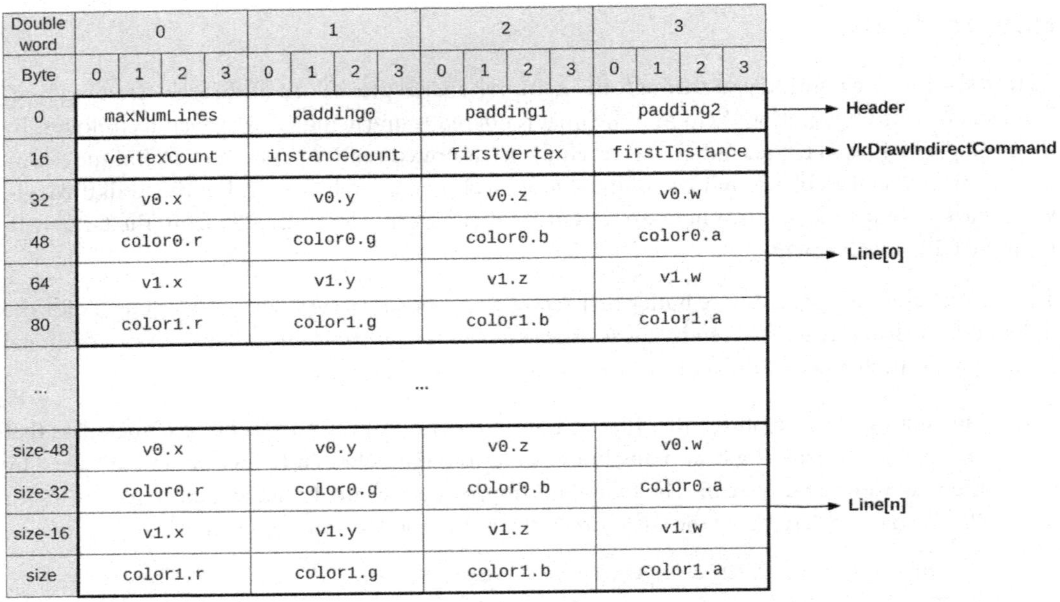

Implementing GPU-Driven Rendering

Double word	0				1				2				3				
Byte	0	1	2	3	0	1	2	3	0	1	2	3	0	1	2	3	
0	maxNumLines				padding0				padding1				padding2				→ Header
16	vertexCount				instanceCount				firstVertex				firstInstance				→ VkDrawIndirectCommand
32	v0.x				v0.y				v0.z				v0.w				
48	color0.r				color0.g				color0.b				color0.a				→ Line[0]
64	v1.x				v1.y				v1.z				v1.w				
80	color1.r				color1.g				color1.b				color1.a				
...	...																
size-48	v0.x				v0.y				v0.z				v0.w				
size-32	color0.r				color0.g				color0.b				color0.a				→ Line[n]
size-16	v1.x				v1.y				v1.z				v1.w				
size	color1.r				color1.g				color1.b				color1.a				

Figure 3.1 – The GPU lines' buffer structure

This buffer is created with the following usage bits:

- `VK_BUFFER_USAGE_INDIRECT_BUFFER_BIT`
- `VK_BUFFER_USAGE_STORAGE_BUFFER_BIT`
- `VK_BUFFER_USAGE_TRANSFER_DST_BIT`

This buffer should be made available to all render passes you wish to be able to draw/generate lines from:

```
std::shared_ptr<VulkanCore::Buffer> gpuLineBuffer;
gpuLineBuffer = context.createBuffer(
    kGPULinesBufferSize,
    VK_BUFFER_USAGE_INDIRECT_BUFFER_BIT |
        VK_BUFFER_USAGE_STORAGE_BUFFER_BIT |
        VK_BUFFER_USAGE_TRANSFER_DST_BIT,
    static_cast<VmaMemoryUsage>(
        VK_MEMORY_PROPERTY_DEVICE_LOCAL_BIT));
```

2. The provided code snippet initializes a `gpuLineBuffer` buffer using the Vulkan API. This buffer, created via the `context.createBuffer` method, is given a specified size (`kGPULinesBufferSize`) and is designated for multiple purposes, including indirect draw commands, shader data storage, and as a destination for buffer-to-buffer copy operations. Additionally, the buffer's memory is set to reside on the GPU, ensuring fast access:

```
struct Line {
  vec3 v0;
  vec4 c0;
  vec3 v1;
  vec4 c1;
};
struct VkDrawIndirectCommand {
  uint vertexCount;
  uint instanceCount;
  uint firstVertex;
  uint firstInstance;
};
layout(set = 4, binding = 0) buffer GPULinesBuffer
{
  uint size;
  uint row;
  uint pad1;
  uint pad2;
  VkDrawIndirectCommand cmd;
  Line lines[];
} lineBuffer;

void addLine(vec3 v0, vec3 v1, vec4 c0, vec4 c1) {
  const uint idx =
      atomicAdd(lineBuffer.cmd.instanceCount, 1);

  if (idx >= lineBuffer.size) {
    atomicMin(lineBuffer.cmd.instanceCount,
              lineBuffer.size);
    return;
  }

  lineBuffer.lines[idx].v0 = v0;
  lineBuffer.lines[idx].v1 = v1;
  lineBuffer.lines[idx].c0 = c0;
  lineBuffer.lines[idx].c1 = c1;
}
```

The function first checks for the next available index for storing the line information by retrieving the number of lines already in the buffer with `atomicAdd`. If the index returned by the function is greater than the maximum number of lines that can fit into the buffer, the function returns early and is a no-op. Otherwise, the line data is stored in the buffer.

3. Rendering the lines is done with an extra render pass once all other passes have finished processing since the data from previous passes is required. The vertex shader code to render the lines looks like the following snippet:

```glsl
#version 460
#extension GL_EXT_nonuniform_qualifier : require

struct Line {
  vec3 v0;
  vec4 c0;
  vec3 v1;
  vec4 c1;
};

struct VkDrawIndirectCommand {
  uint vertexCount;
  uint instanceCount;
  uint firstVertex;
  uint firstInstance;
};

layout(set = 1, binding = 0) readonly buffer
GPULinesBuffer {
  Line lines[];
} lineBuffer;

layout (location = 0) out vec4 outColor;

void main() {
  if (gl_VertexIndex == 0) {
    vec3 vertex =
        lineBuffer.lines[gl_InstanceIndex].v0;
    gl_Position = vec4(vertex, 1.0).xyww;

    outColor =
        lineBuffer.lines[gl_InstanceIndex].c0;
  } else {
    vec3 vertex =
        lineBuffer.lines[gl_InstanceIndex].v1;
```

```
        gl_Position = vec4(vertex, 1.0).xyww;

        outColor =
            lineBuffer.lines[gl_InstanceIndex].c1;
    }
}
```

In the preceding code, two structures are introduced: `Line` and `VkDrawIndirectCommand`. The `Line` structure represents a colored line segment, defined by two 3D endpoints (`v0` and `v1`) and their corresponding colors (`c0` and `c1`). The `VkDrawIndirectCommand` structure represents a Vulkan command for indirect drawing. The shader also establishes a `GPULinesBuffer` buffer containing an array of `Line` structures. In the main function, depending on the value of `gl_VertexIndex`, the shader selects the starting or ending point of a line instance and assigns the respective color to `outColor`. Also, notice how in this shader, we only define the `GPULinesBuffer` structure without the header structure. That's because for drawing lines, we bind the buffer at an offset, bypassing the need to define the `Header` segment in the shader.

The fragment shader just outputs the color provided through the vertex shader:

```
#version 460

layout(location = 0) in vec4 inColor;
layout(location = 0) out vec4 outColor;

void main() {
  outColor = inColor;
}
```

Before rendering the lines, we need to make sure that the previous steps have finished writing into the buffer, so we issue a buffer barrier:

```
const VkBufferMemoryBarrier bufferBarrier = {
    .sType =
        VK_STRUCTURE_TYPE_BUFFER_MEMORY_BARRIER,
    .srcAccessMask = VK_ACCESS_SHADER_WRITE_BIT,
    .dstAccessMask =
        VK_ACCESS_INDIRECT_COMMAND_READ_BIT,
    .srcQueueFamilyIndex =
        VK_QUEUE_FAMILY_IGNORED,
    .dstQueueFamilyIndex =
        VK_QUEUE_FAMILY_IGNORED,
    .buffer = gpuLineBuffer->vkBuffer(),
    .offset = 0,
    .size = VK_WHOLE_SIZE,
};
```

```
vkCmdPipelineBarrier(
    commandBuffer,
    VK_PIPELINE_STAGE_FRAGMENT_SHADER_BIT,
    VK_PIPELINE_STAGE_DRAW_INDIRECT_BIT, 0, 0,
    nullptr, 1, &bufferBarrier, 0, nullptr);
```

After that, we issue an indirect draw command that derives its parameters directly from the buffer itself. We cleverly stored the number of lines stored in the buffer in the previous passes in `VkDrawIndirectCommand::instanceCount`:

```
vkCmdDrawIndirect(commandBuffer,
                  gpuLineBuffer->vkBuffer(),
                  sizeof(uint32_t) * 4, 1,
                  sizeof(VkDrawIndirectCommand));
```

4. The final step consists of clearing the buffer, which is required for clearing the number of lines in the buffer (`VkDrawIndirectCommand::instanceCount`). Before clearing the buffer, we must ensure that the GPU has finished drawing lines, which we can verify by issuing another buffer barrier:

```
const VkBufferMemoryBarrier bufferBarrierClear = {
    .sType =
        VK_STRUCTURE_TYPE_BUFFER_MEMORY_BARRIER,
    .srcAccessMask =
        VK_ACCESS_INDIRECT_COMMAND_READ_BIT,
    .dstAccessMask = VK_ACCESS_TRANSFER_WRITE_BIT,
    .srcQueueFamilyIndex =
        VK_QUEUE_FAMILY_IGNORED,
    .dstQueueFamilyIndex =
        VK_QUEUE_FAMILY_IGNORED,
    .buffer = gpuLineBuffer->vkBuffer(),
    .offset = 0,
    .size = VK_WHOLE_SIZE,
};

// Reset the number of lines in the buffer
vkCmdFillBuffer(commandBuffer,
                gpuLineBuffer->vkBuffer(),
                sizeof(uint32_t) * 5,
                sizeof(uint32_t), 0);
```

In this recipe, we have unpacked a powerful technique for rendering lines directly from shaders. The utility of this method extends to diverse rendering applications, and it lays the groundwork for more advanced graphical outputs, elevating your skills to an even higher level in the realm of GPU programming using Vulkan.

Expanding line-drawing techniques to render textual values from shaders

Continuing from our previous exploration, where we developed the capability to draw lines directly from shaders, our next challenge is to further refine this capability to facilitate the rendering of text values. Drawing inspiration from the foundational concepts established in the preceding recipe, we aim to implement a methodology that permits the conversion of numerical values into line segments, much like digital LCD displays. By doing so, not only do we breathe life into bare numerical data, making it more visual and interpretable, but we also harness the power and efficiency of shaders in crafting these representations. Upon completion, you will be equipped with a robust toolset, allowing them to render clear, scalable, and visually appealing textual data, right from their shaders.

Getting ready

Before diving into the recipe, you should make sure you have VS 2022 installed and that you are able to build the repository as per the steps provided in *Chapter 1, Vulkan Core Concepts*.

You should be able to launch the executable named Chapter03_GPU_Text.exe from VS 2022.

Since this recipe is heavily based on the previous recipe, we recommend reading the previous recipe on GPU line drawing first. The code covered in this recipe can be found in the repository, in chapter3/mainGPUText.cpp and chapter3/resources/shaders, in the gpuText.frag, gpuText.vert, gpuTextDraw.frag, and gpuTexDraw.vert files.

How to do it...

The idea is to decompose numbers into segments (like LCD segment displays) and print values by drawing lines for each digit. The previous recipe covered how to store and draw lines; this recipe builds on top of that to print numbers. Since in this recipe we need to draw numbers, we will need to parse numbers and decompose them into lines:

1. First, we need to use a strategy to represent digits with only lines. We chose to implement a simple 7-segment approach that can be used to display all digits from 0 to 9 plus a minus sign. We also added an extra segment to represent a decimal separator. *Figure 3.2* shows the seven segments plus the decimal separator and their indices as used by the code in the shader:

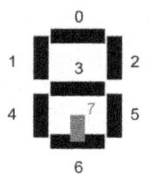

Figure 3.2 – Segments used to represent all digits from 0 to 9 plus a decimal separator and a minus sign

2. In addition to the structures defined in the previous recipe, we will replace the `pad0` member of the `GPULinesBuffer` buffer so that it stores the row number:

```
layout(set = 4, binding = 0) buffer GPULinesBuffer
{
   uint size;
   uint row;
   uint pad1;
   uint pad2;
   VkDrawIndirectCommand cmd;
   Line lines[];
} lineBuffer;
```

3. We'll also need the definition of the segments shown in *Figure 3.2* as two vectors:

```
vec2 v[] = {vec2(-0.5f,  1.0f), vec2(0.5f,  1.f),
            vec2(-0.5f,  0.0f), vec2(0.5f,  0.f),
            vec2(-0.5f, -1.0f), vec2(0.5f, -1.f),
            vec2( 0.0f, -0.8f), vec2(0.0f, -1.f) };

uvec2 i[] = {uvec2(0, 1), uvec2(2, 3), uvec2(4, 5), uvec2(0, 2),
uvec2(1, 3), uvec2(2, 4), uvec2(3, 5), uvec2(6, 7)};
```

Array `v` represents the coordinates of all vertices shown in *Figure 3.2* normalized into the range [-0.5, 0.5] in the *x* direction and [-1.0, 1.0] in the *y* direction. Array `i` describes all segments and their vertices. For instance, the first element of the array describes segment 0 in the picture, from vertex 0 (-0.5, 1.0) to vertex 1 (0.5, 1.0).

4. The `printSegment` function adds one segment, given its index, a scale, and a translation, to the GPU buffer where lines are stored:

```
void printSegment(int segment, vec2 pos, vec2 scale) {
   uint idx = i[segment].x;
   uint idy = i[segment].y;
   vec3 v0 = vec3(v[idx] * scale + pos, 1.0);
   vec3 v1 = vec3(v[idy] * scale + pos, 1.0);

   addLine(v0, v1, vec4(0,0,0,1), vec4(0,0,0,1));
}
```

This function calls the `addLine` function presented before to record the final vertices and colors of lines in the buffer.

5. The `printDigit` function prints all segments for a digit at a specific line and column, passed in as parameters:

   ```
   void printDigit(int digit, uint linenum,
                   uint column) {
     const float charWidthPixel = 10;
     const float charHeightPixels = 10;
     const float horSpacePixels = 5;
     const float verSpacePixels = 5;
     const float charWidthNDC =
         charWidthPixels / screenWidth;
     const float charHeightNDC =
         charHeightPixels / screenHeight;
     const float horSpaceNDC =
         horSpacePixels / screenWidth;
     const float verSpaceNDC =
         verSpacePixels / screenHeight;
     const float colx =
         (column + 1) *
         (charWidthNDC + horSpaceNDC);
     const float coly =
         (linenum + 1) *
         (charHeightNDC + 3 * verSpaceNDC);
   ```

   Initially, it calculates the width and height of the characters in **normalized device coordinates** (**NDC**) space as well as the spacing between them. For that, we need the dimensions of the viewport. A viewport is a 2D rectangle representing the area into which the rendering result will be displayed on the screen. The function uses a `switch` statement to decide which digit to print. The following snippet only shows how to print the digits 0 and 1, the decimal separator, and the minus sign for brevity:

   ```
   const vec2 pos(colx, coly);
   const vec2 scale(charWidthNDC, -charHeightNDC);
   switch (digit) {
   case 0:
     printSegment(0, pos, scale);
     printSegment(3, pos, scale);
     printSegment(4, pos, scale);
     printSegment(5, pos, scale);
     printSegment(6, pos, scale);
     printSegment(2, pos, scale);
     break;
   case 1:
     printSegment(4, pos, scale);
     printSegment(6, pos, scale);
   ```

```
      break;
    case 10: // decimal separator
      printSegment(7, pos, scale);
      break;
    case 11: // minus sign
      printSegment(1, pos, scale);
      break;
  }
}
```

The preceding code employs a switch-case structure to identify which segments should be activated based on the digit or symbol passed. For example, the number 0 requires several segments to depict its round shape. Therefore, when the digit is 0, multiple `printSegment` calls are made to render each segment required for the 0 digit. Similarly, 1 is formed using two segments on its side. Beyond the digits, the function also has provisions to depict a decimal separator and a minus sign, distinguished by their unique segment arrangements.

6. The `printNumber` function is designed to display an integer on a specified line, starting from a given column. After executing, it provides the next available column following the last digit printed. If the integer is zero, it simply prints '0'. For nonzero integers, the function efficiently computes the number of digits and iteratively prints each one, advancing the column accordingly:

```
uint printNumber(highp int value,
                 uint linenum, uint column) {
  if (value == 0) {
    printDigit(0, linenum, column);
    return column + 1;
  }

  int counter = 0;
  int copy = value;
  int tens = 1;
  while (copy > 0) {
    counter++;
    copy = copy / 10;
    tens *= 10;
  }
  tens /= 10;

  for (int i = counter; i > 0; --i) {
    int digit = int(value / tens);
    printDigit(digit, linenum, column);
    value = value - (digit * tens);
    tens /= 10;
```

```
      column++;
   }

   return column;
}
```

This function parses the integer parameter and prints each digit individually, while incrementing the `column` index.

7. Finally, the `parse` function parses a float and prints it with a certain number of decimal places:

```
void parse(float val, uint decimals) {
   int d = int(log(val));
   int base = int(pow(10, d));

   const float tens = pow(10, decimals);

   const uint line = atomicAdd(lineBuffer.row, 1);
   uint column = 0;

   // Minus sign
   if (val < 0) {
     printDigit(11, line, column);
     column++;
   }

   // Prints only positive values
   val = abs(val);

   // Integer part
   const int intPart = int(val);
   column = printNumber(intPart, line, column);

   // Decimal
   if (decimals > 0) {
     // Dot
     printDigit(10, line, column);
     column++;

     const int decimal =
         int(val * tens - intPart * tens);
     printNumber(decimal, line, column);
   }
}
```

The function splits the float into two parts, the integer part and the decimal part, and prints them separately. If the number is negative, it prints the minus sign.

8. The next step is to clear the buffer once the lines text has been rendered. In the previous recipe, we cleared the number of lines in the buffer. Here, we also need to clear the row number:

```
vkCmdFillBuffer(commandBuffer,
                gpuLineBuffer->vkBuffer(),
                sizeof(uint32_t),
                sizeof(uint32_t), 0);
```

9. The last step is to use the `parse` function. Just call it from any shader that includes those functions. Each call to `parse` will print the value on a new line. *Figure 3.3* shows the result of printing some values with the following code in the vertex shader:

```
if (gl_VertexIndex == 0) {
  parse(123456, 0);
  parse(789, 0);
  parse(780.12, 3);
  parse(-23, 1);
  parse(0.3, 2);
}
```

The following screenshot shows how we can use this technique for debugging purposes or to display text:

Figure 3.3 – The result of printing values from the vertex shader

In this recipe, we delved into the intricate process of representing numerical values using line segments, reminiscent of LCD displays. By breaking down numbers into their individual segments and leveraging our foundational line-drawing methods from shaders, we provided you with an innovative technique to visualize numbers. The end result is a seamless integration of numbers into your graphics, with clarity reminiscent of digital segment displays, enriching the overall visual experience.

Drawing text using SDF

In this recipe, we address the challenge of rendering crisp and scalable text, regardless of its size. By utilizing the principles of SDF, we transform traditional text rendering into a more fluid process, ensuring sharpness and clarity. The outcome is beautifully rendered text that remains clear and legible, whether you're zooming in closely or viewing from a distance.

SDFs provide a way to represent surfaces. An SDF is basically a function that, for every point in space, returns the shortest distance to the surface of the shape. SDFs can be used for a variety of use cases such as volume rendering or to perform operations on shapes such as dilation, erosion, and other morphological operations.

Traditionally, text is rendered using bitmap fonts. One can use a 2D canvas to render text and then use that as a texture to draw a quad in a 3D context. However, this method creates bitmaps that are resolution-dependent and need to be generated and uploaded to the device by the CPU. Each font style, such as bold, italics, and so on, also needs to be processed by the CPU, which causes an extra overhead for the computation and transfer of the textures for each style needed for rendering.

Rendering text using SDFs is a modern approach that uses distance fields for each character. These are grids in which each of the values represents the distance from each pixel to the nearest edge of the character. SDFs help avoid all the problems mentioned before by offering resolution-independent scaling as well as using the GPU for most of the work. Styles such as bold, outline, and so on require only changes to shaders.

Each letter of a font (a glyph) is described by a combination of straight lines and Bézier curves. One example of a glyph is shown in *Figure 3.4*, which shows the detail of a glyph's serif:

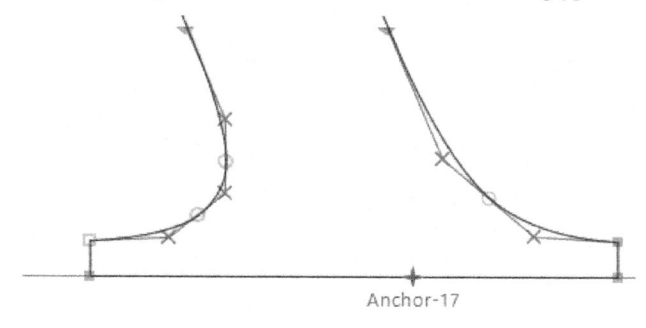

Figure 3.4 – Detail of a glyph definition: circles, triangles, and squares represent the start and end points of each segment (curves or straight lines)

Traditional SDF algorithms encode the distance from a pixel to the glyph's boundary for each pixel in a grid, store that information in a texture, and upload that to the CPU. The algorithm presented in this recipe implements a different approach, in which the distances from a pixel to the nearest curves are computed on the GPU. To do that, each glyph in the font is preprocessed on the CPU against a grid of fixed size of 8 x 8 cells. This preprocessing detects curves that intersect each cell and stores the information in a 32-bit integer, as shown in *Figure 3.5*:

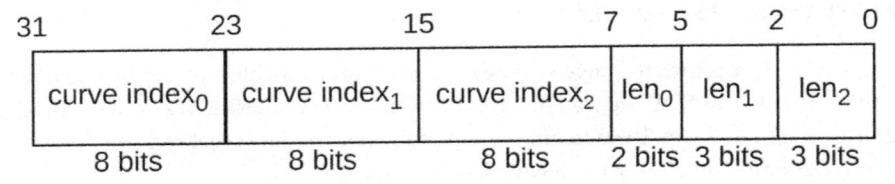

31	23	15	7	5	2	0
curve index$_0$	curve index$_1$	curve index$_2$	len$_0$	len$_1$	len$_2$
8 bits	8 bits	8 bits	2 bits	3 bits	3 bits

Figure 3.5 – Cell encoding stores the initial index of three separate curves that intersect the cell along with the length of each loop

Each cell contains the information of up to three loops that intersect it by storing the initial index of each loop plus their lengths. For example, the glyph shown in cell (2, 0) intersects two curves, curve 1 and curve 2. The information encoded for that cell would contain the index to curve 1 and a length of 2. The other indices would remain 0, as the cell doesn't intersect any other curves.

The following diagram demonstrates how the letter *S* can be represented using glyphs:

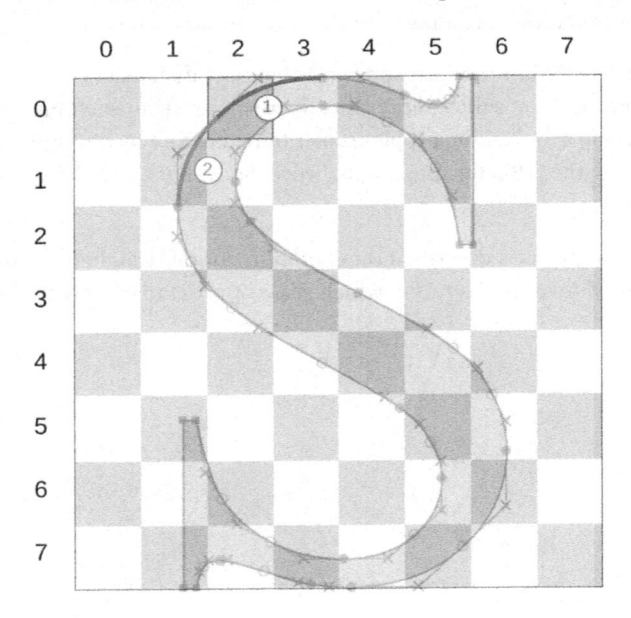

Figure 3.6 – Curves representing an S glyph; cell (2, 0) intersects two curves: curve 1 and curve 2

Drawing text using SDF

The vertex shader passes the cell indices for each corner of the rectangle to the fragment shader, which receives the interpolated coordinate of the cell, uses it to retrieve the information of which curve loops and their lengths to inspect, and calculates the minimum distance to each one of the curves in the three loops, choosing the minimum distance.

This information is then used to calculate the opacity of the current fragment, along with the color and the sharpness of the edge of the font.

In this recipe, we use a third-party library to capture the definition of the glyphs and store that information in a shader-friendly format. The library is authored by Dávid Kocsis and can be found here: `https://github.com/kocsis1david/font-demo`.

Getting ready

Before diving into the recipe, you should make sure you have VS 2022 installed and that you are able to build the repo as per the steps provided in *Chapter 1, Vulkan Core Concepts*.

You should be able to launch the executable named `Chapter03_GPU_Text_SDF.exe` from VS 2022.

A complete example with the code covered in this recipe can be found in the repository, in `chapter3/mainGPUTextSDF.cpp`, `chapter3/FontManager.hpp`, `chapter3/FontManager.cpp`, and `chapter3/resources/shaders`, in the `font.frag` and `font.vert` files.

How to do it...

The steps to render text using SDFs on the device are as follows:

1. The initial task involves loading the font file through the `FreeType` library. This step is crucial because it's where we obtain the glyph data for each character. Glyph data, in essence, represents the basic design of a character in a font, describing its unique shape and appearance. Once we have this, the subsequent objective is to transform this glyph data into outline data. The outline data captures the essence of the glyph's shape, breaking it down into components such as points, cells, and a bounding box specific to each character. These components essentially dictate how a character will be rendered on a screen or display. To achieve this transformation from `FreeType`'s intricate glyph data to more structured outline data, we employ the `fd_outline_convert` function. The data for each character is combined into a single stream of points and cells that is uploaded to the GPU as a *vertex buffer*:

```
FontManager fontManager;
const auto &glyphData = fontManager.loadFont(
    (fontsFolder / "times.ttf").string());

std::vector<GlyphInfo> glyhInfoData;
std::vector<uint32_t> cellsData;
std::vector<glm::vec2> pointsData;
```

```cpp
uint32_t pointOffset = 0;
uint32_t cellOffset = 0;

for (const auto &glyph : glyphData) {
  glyhInfoData.push_back(
      {glyph.bbox,
       glm::uvec4(pointOffset, cellOffset,
                  glyph.cellX,
                  glyph.cellY)});

  cellsData.insert(cellsData.end(),
                   glyph.cellData.begin(),
                   glyph.cellData.end());
  pointsData.insert(pointsData.end(),
                    glyph.points.begin(),
                    glyph.points.end());
  pointOffset += glyph.points.size();
  cellOffset += glyph.cellData.size();
}
```

The code delves deeply into font rendering by handling the glyphs, which are the backbone of font representation. One of the main elements here is the point data. This crucial piece captures every point that makes up the Bézier curves of each glyph. Right now, our focus is mainly on the uppercase letters. But looking at how the code is structured, it's clear that we could easily expand it to embrace other characters if we wished to. Parallel to the point data, we also work with the cell data. It has a special role when we're in the rendering phase, especially in the fragment shader. It's this data that aids in navigating the curves that intersect with a given cell, making sure that every glyph is depicted accurately and precisely on the screen. All in all, by marrying the point and cell data with the capabilities of the fragment shader, we're able to render the font's visual intricacies effectively.

2. Next, we build a buffer that contains the bounding rectangles of each glyph. This buffer serves as the vertex buffer, and we draw as many instances as the number of characters in the display string:

```cpp
std::string textToDisplay = "GPUSDFTEXTDEMO";
std::vector<CharInstance>
    charsData(textToDisplay.length());

int startX =
    context.swapchain()->extent().width / 6.0f;
int startY =
    context.swapchain()->extent().height / 2.0f;
const float scale = 0.09f;
```

```
for (int i = 0; i < textToDisplay.length();
    ++i) {
  int glpyIndex = textToDisplay[i] - 'A';
  charsData[i].glyphIndex = glpyIndex;
  charsData[i].sharpness = scale;
  charsData[i].bbox.x =
      (startX +
       glyphData[glpyIndex].bbox.x * scale) /
          (context.swapchain()
               ->extent()
               .width /
           2.0) -
      1.0;

  charsData[i].bbox.y =
      (startY -
       glyphData[glpyIndex].bbox.y * scale) /
          (context.swapchain()
               ->extent()
               .height /
           2.0) -
      1.0;

  charsData[i].bbox.z =
      (startX +
       glyphData[glpyIndex].bbox.z * scale) /
          (context.swapchain()
               ->extent()
               .width /
           2.0) -
      1.0;

  charsData[i].bbox.w =
      (startY -
       glyphData[glpyIndex].bbox.w * scale) /
          (context.swapchain()
               ->extent()
               .height /
           2.0) -
      1.0;

  startX += glyphData[glpyIndex]
```

```
                    .horizontalAdvance *
        scale;
}
```

The code snippet is dedicated to rendering the phrase `"GPUSDFTEXTDEMO"` onscreen. Here, `textToDisplay` holds the desired text, and `charsData` is primed to store individual character details. The starting position, calculated from the screen dimensions, suggests a slightly offset start from the left and a vertical centering of the text. A scaling factor shrinks the characters, likely aiding design or screen fit. As we progress character by character, a mapping correlates each letter to its respective data in `glyphData`. The bounding box coordinates for every character are meticulously scaled and normalized to ensure their optimal display on screen. To sidestep overlap, the horizontal placement (`startX`) gets an update for each character, relying on its width and the scaling factor. In sum, this snippet efficiently prepares the specifics for a neatly rendered, scaled, and centered display of `"GPUSDFTEXTDEMO"` on the screen.

3. In the following step, we transfer the points, cell data, glyph data, and string to the GPU as separate buffers. Subsequently, we execute a `vkCmdDraw` command:

```
// 4 vertex (Quad) and x (charData) instances
vkCmdDraw(commandBuffer, 4, charsData.size(), 0, 0);
```

4. The vertex shader needs access to an array of glyph data (`GlyphInfo`) that is packed into the `glyph_buffer` buffer. The other inputs are `in_rect`, `in_glyph_index`, and `in_sharpness`, which come from the *vertex buffer*:

```
#version 460

// Stores glyph information
struct GlyphInfo {
  vec4 bbox; // Bounding box of the glyph

  // cell_info.x: point offset
  // cell_info.x: cell offset
  // cell_info.x: cell count in x
  // cell_info.x: cell count in y
  uvec4 cell_info;
};

// Storage buffer object for glyphs
layout(set = 0, binding = 0) buffer GlyphBuffer {
  GlyphInfo glyphs[];
} glyph_buffer;

layout(location = 0) in vec4 in_rect;
layout(location = 1) in uint in_glyph_index;
```

```glsl
layout(location = 2) in float in_sharpness;

layout(location = 0) out vec2 out_glyph_pos;
layout(location = 1) out uvec4 out_cell_info;
layout(location = 2) out float out_sharpness;
layout(location = 3) out vec2 out_cell_coord;

void main() {
  // Get the glyph information
  GlyphInfo gi = glyph_buffer.glyphs[in_glyph_index];

  // Corners of the rectangle
  vec2 pos[4] = vec2[](
      vec2(in_rect.x, in_rect.y), // Bottom-left
      vec2(in_rect.z, in_rect.y), // Bottom-right
      vec2(in_rect.x, in_rect.w), // Top-left
      vec2(in_rect.z, in_rect.w)  // Top-right
  );

  // Corners of the glyph
  vec2 glyph_pos[4] = vec2[](
      vec2(gi.bbox.x, gi.bbox.y), // Bottom-left
      vec2(gi.bbox.z, gi.bbox.y), // Bottom-right
      vec2(gi.bbox.x, gi.bbox.w), // Top-left
      vec2(gi.bbox.z, gi.bbox.w)  // Top-right
  );

  // Cell coordinates
  vec2 cell_coord[4] = vec2[](
      vec2(0, 0), // Bottom-left
      vec2(gi.cell_info.z, 0), // Bottom-right
      vec2(0, gi.cell_info.w), // Top-left
      vec2(gi.cell_info.z,
           gi.cell_info.w) // Top-right
  );

  gl_Position = vec4(pos[gl_VertexIndex], 0.0, 1.0);
  out_glyph_pos = glyph_pos[gl_VertexIndex];
  out_cell_info = gi.cell_info;
  out_sharpness = in_sharpness;
  out_cell_coord = cell_coord[gl_VertexIndex];
}
```

The preceding vertex shader is tailored for glyph rendering. The shader works with a structure named `GlyphInfo` that encapsulates information about each glyph, including its bounding box and details related to the cell positioning of the glyph. Within the `main` function, the shader fetches data for a specific glyph using an input index. It subsequently determines the positions of both the input rectangle's corners and the corresponding glyph's bounding box and calculates the cell coordinates for the glyph. Using `gl_VertexIndex`, which indicates which vertex of the rectangle is currently being processed, the shader sets the position for that vertex and assigns necessary values to the output variables. This preprocessed information is leveraged by the fragment shader to produce a final visual representation of the glyph.

5. Next are the steps for calculating the text's glyph color using the fragment shader:

   - Calculates the cell index for a given fragment/pixel.
   - Fetches the cell from the cell buffer based on the cell index.
   - Calculates the SDF of the cell from the glyph's bounding box. Based on the distance, an alpha value is computed:

```
// Main function of the fragment shader
void main() {
  // Calculate the cell index
  uvec2 c = min(uvec2(in_cell_coord),
                in_cell_info.zw - 1);
  uint cell_index = in_cell_info.y +
                    in_cell_info.z * c.y + c.x;

  // Get the cell
  uint cell = cell_buffer.cells[cell_index];

  // Calculate the signed distance from the
  // glyph position to the cell
  float v = cell_signed_dist(
      in_cell_info.x, cell, in_glyph_pos);
  // Calculate the alpha value
  float alpha = clamp(v * in_sharpness + 0.5,
                      0.0, 1.0);
  out_color = vec4(1.0, 1.0, 1.0, alpha);
}
```

The result of the recipe can be seen in *Figure 3.7*:

Figure 3.7 – The output of the recipe

In this recipe, we showcased the application of SDF for rendering text with the assistance of a GPU.

See also

Inigo Quilez demonstrates how to use SDFs to create shapes in an excellent video:

`https://www.youtube.com/watch?v=8--5LwHRhjk`

There are multiple libraries that generate SDF textures – for example, `https://libgdx.com/wiki/tools/hiero` and `https://github.com/Chlumsky/msdfgen`.

Frustum culling using compute shaders

In this recipe, we will show how to do frustum culling using the GPU and compute shaders.

In the world of real-time rendering, efficient rendering is key to achieving smooth performance and high-quality visuals. One of the most widely used techniques to optimize rendering is frustum culling. Frustum culling is a process that improves rendering speed by ignoring or *culling* objects that are not visible within the camera's FOV, or *frustum*. The following diagram demonstrates it visually:

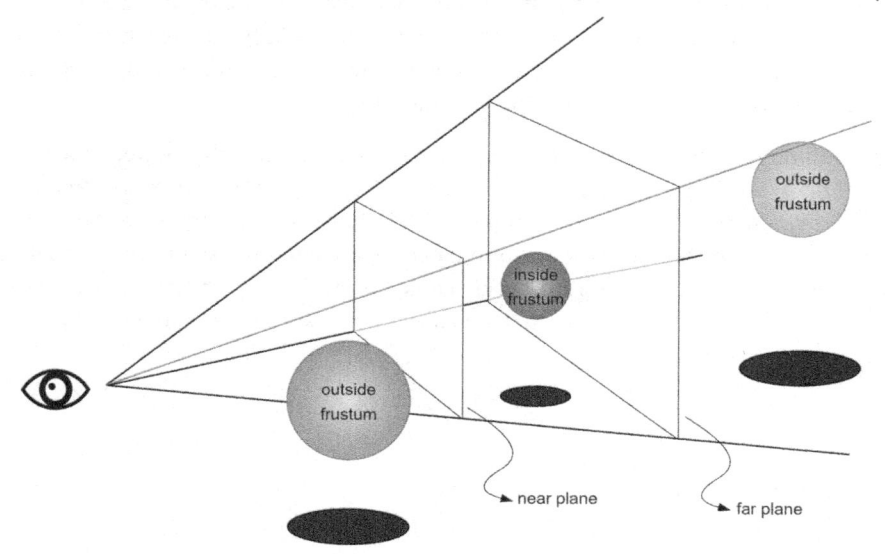

Figure 3.8 – Frustum culling works by ignoring objects that fall outside of the camera's view (the frustum)

Frustum culling works by testing each object in the scene to see if it lies within the camera's frustum. If an object is entirely outside the frustum, it gets culled; that is, it's not drawn. This can significantly reduce the number of primitives that need to be drawn. Traditionally, culling was done on the CPU, but this meant it needed to be done every time the camera moved. We demonstrate culling by using the compute shader, eliminating the need to upload data from the CPU to the GPU every time the view changes. Compute shaders do not necessarily need to be related to rendering and can process data structures and perform operations such as sorting, physics simulations, and, in our case, frustum culling.

Getting ready

Before diving into the recipe, you should make sure you have VS 2022 installed and that you are able to build the repository as per the steps provided in *Chapter 1, Vulkan Core Concepts*.

You should be able to launch the executable named `Chapter03_GPU_Culling.exe` from VS 2022.

This recipe is based on the *Implementing Programmable Vertex Pulling and Multi-Draw Indirect* recipe from *Chapter 2, Working with Modern Vulkan*. The code covered in this recipe can be found in the repository, in `chapter3/mainCullingCompute.cpp`, `chapter3/CullingComputePass.cpp`, and `chapter3/resources/shaders`, in the `gpuculling.comp`, `indirectdraw.frag`, and `indirectdraw.vert` files.

How to do it...

We will be building on a recipe from *Chapter 2, Working with Modern Vulkan*. that implemented Multi-Draw Indirect. We demonstrated during that recipe the use of `vkCmdDrawIndexedIndirect`. In this recipe, we will use a command that derives the number of its parameters from a device buffer, `vkCmdDrawIndexedIndirectCount`. This Vulkan API lets you specify a GPU buffer that contains the draw count instead of providing it by the CPU.

This recipe's technique relies on three buffers: the first two each contain the indirect draw parameters' structures, `InputIndirectDraws` and `OutputIndirectDraws` respectively; the third one contains the number of meshes to be rendered. The first buffer contains the parameters for all meshes in the scene. The second buffer is populated by the compute shader: meshes that are *not* culled have their indirect parameters atomically copied from the `InputIndirectDraws` buffer to `OutputIndirectDraws`; meshes that are culled don't have their parameters copied:

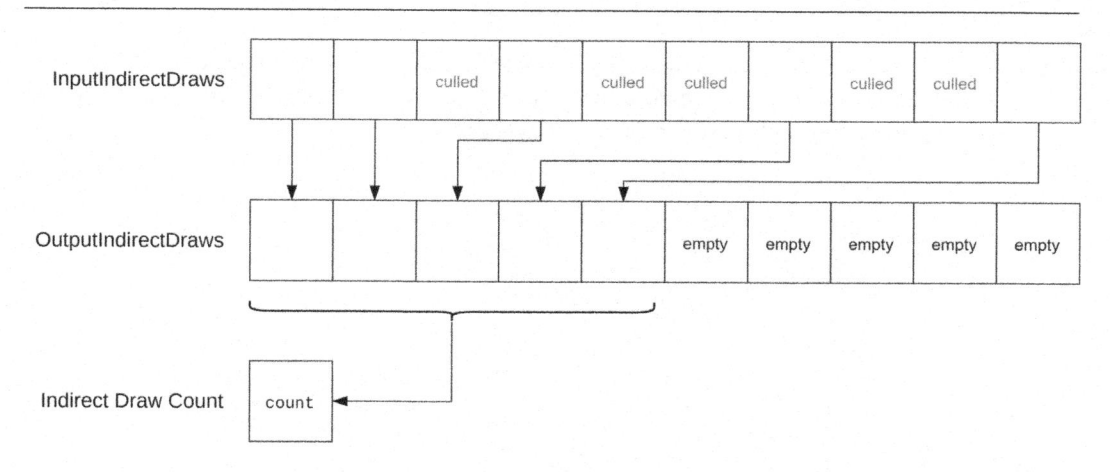

Figure 3.9 – Top buffer: all mesh parameters; bottom buffer: unculled meshes set to render

Additionally, the compute shader needs information about each mesh's bounding box and their center, and the six planes of the frustum. With this information, the compute pass can cull (or not) each mesh. At the end of the pass, the `OutputIndirectDraws` buffer contains parameters only for the meshes that will be rendered and is used by the indirect draw command.

Next is the recipe broken down into steps, along with snippets from `mainCullingCompute.cpp`. It provides a high-level view of how culling and drawing passes are used in tandem to perform frustum culling using compute shaders in Vulkan. The compute shader takes care of determining which meshes should be drawn, and then the graphics pipeline takes care of drawing those meshes.

1. Initialize the culling pass by using scene information and a scene buffer:

    ```
    cullingPass.init(&context, &camera,
                     *bistro.get(), buffers[3]);
    cullingPass.upload(commandMgr);
    ```

    The first step consists of initializing the two buffers shown in *Figure 3.9* and uploading them to the device. The details are encapsulated by the `CullingComputePass` class.

2. The compute pass is also encapsulated by the `CullingComputePass` class:

    ```
    auto commandBuffer = commandMgr.getCmdBufferToBegin();
    cullingPass.cull(commandBuffer, index);
    ```

    We will discuss the cull method shown next in more detail.

3. To prevent a race condition between the compute pass and the rendering pass, we add a barrier for the culled indirect draw and the draw count buffer. This is necessary because the subsequent drawing commands rely on the results of the culling pass:

```
cullingPass.addBarrierForCulledBuffers(
    commandBuffer,
    VK_PIPELINE_STAGE_DRAW_INDIRECT_BIT,
    context.physicalDevice()
        .graphicsFamilyIndex()
        .value(),
    context.physicalDevice()
        .graphicsFamilyIndex()
        .value());
```

4. The draw call is recorded with the `vkCmdDrawIndexedIndirectCount` command:

```
vkCmdDrawIndexedIndirectCount(
    commandBuffer,
    cullingPass.culledIndirectDrawBuffer()
        ->vkBuffer(),
    0,
    cullingPass
        .culledIndirectDrawCountBuffer()
        ->vkBuffer(),
    0, numMeshes,
    sizeof(
        EngineCore::
            IndirectDrawCommandAndMeshData));
```

Having grasped the essential elements of code for the culling pass, let's delve into its operational mechanism.

How it works...

The `CullingComputePass::cull` method is responsible for updating frustum data, binding the compute pipeline, updating push constants, and calling `vkCmdDispatch`. `vkCmdDispatch` dispatches the compute work to the GPU. The compute work is divided into smaller units, each of which is called a workgroup. The (`pushConst.drawCount / 256) + 1, 1, 1`) parameters specify the number of workgroups that are dispatched in the *x*, *y*, and *z* dimensions, respectively:

```
void CullingComputePass::cull(
   VkCommandBuffer cmd, int frameIndex) {
 GPUCullingPassPushConstants pushConst{
     .drawCount =
         uint32_t(meshesBBoxData_.size()),
 };
```

```cpp
// Compute and store the six planes of the frustum
for (int i = 0;
     auto &plane :
     camera_->calculateFrustumPlanes()) {
  frustum_.frustumPlanes[i] = plane;
  ++i;
}

// Upload the data to the device
camFrustumBuffer_->buffer()
    ->copyDataToBuffer(&frustum_,
                       sizeof(ViewBuffer));

// Bind the compute pipeline, update push constants
pipeline_->bind(cmd);
pipeline_->updatePushConstant(
    cmd, VK_SHADER_STAGE_COMPUTE_BIT,
    sizeof(GPUCullingPassPushConstants),
    &pushConst);

// Bind descriptor sets
pipeline_->bindDescriptorSets(
    cmd,
    {
        {.set = MESH_BBOX_SET,
         .bindIdx = 0},
        {.set = INPUT_INDIRECT_BUFFER_SET,
         .bindIdx = 0},
        {.set = OUTPUT_INDIRECT_BUFFER_SET,
         .bindIdx = 0},
        {.set =
             OUTPUT_INDIRECT_COUNT_BUFFER_SET,
         .bindIdx = 0},
        {.set = CAMERA_FRUSTUM_SET,
         .bindIdx = uint32_t(frameIndex)},
    });

// Update descriptor sets
pipeline_->updateDescriptorSets();
```

```cpp
    // Dispatch the compute pass
    vkCmdDispatch(
        cmd, (pushConst.drawCount / 256) + 1, 1, 1);
}
```

The `CullingComputePass::addBarrierForCulledBuffers` method adds a pipeline barrier that ensures the culling operation has finished before the results are read. The barrier is set up so that it blocks the indirect command read access (which will be used in the draw call) until the shader write (the culling operation) has completed:

```cpp
void CullingComputePass::
    addBarrierForCulledBuffers(
        VkCommandBuffer cmd,
        VkPipelineStageFlags dstStage,
        uint32_t computeFamilyIndex,
        uint32_t graphicsFamilyIndex) {
    std::array<VkBufferMemoryBarrier, 2> barriers{
        VkBufferMemoryBarrier{
            .sType =
                VK_STRUCTURE_TYPE_BUFFER_MEMORY_BARRIER,
            .srcAccessMask =
                VK_ACCESS_SHADER_WRITE_BIT,
            .dstAccessMask =
                VK_ACCESS_INDIRECT_COMMAND_READ_BIT,
            .srcQueueFamilyIndex =
                computeFamilyIndex,
            .dstQueueFamilyIndex =
                graphicsFamilyIndex,
            .buffer = outputIndirectDrawBuffer_
                        ->vkBuffer(),
            .size = outputIndirectDrawBuffer_
                        ->size(),
        },
        VkBufferMemoryBarrier{
            .sType =
                VK_STRUCTURE_TYPE_BUFFER_MEMORY_BARRIER,
            .srcAccessMask =
                VK_ACCESS_SHADER_WRITE_BIT,
            .dstAccessMask =
                VK_ACCESS_INDIRECT_COMMAND_READ_BIT,
            .srcQueueFamilyIndex =
                computeFamilyIndex,
            .dstQueueFamilyIndex =
                graphicsFamilyIndex,
```

```
            .buffer =
                outputIndirectDrawCountBuffer_
                    ->vkBuffer(),
            .size =
                outputIndirectDrawCountBuffer_
                    ->size(),
        },
    };

    vkCmdPipelineBarrier(
        cmd,
        VK_PIPELINE_STAGE_COMPUTE_SHADER_BIT,
        dstStage, 0, 0, nullptr,
        (uint32_t)barriers.size(),
        barriers.data(), 0, nullptr);
}
```

In the compute shader, we need a function that tells whether a bounding box falls completely outside of the frustum by comparing its extents and its center point against the six planes of the frustum:

```
void cullMesh(uint id) {
  MeshBboxData meshBBoxData = meshBboxDatas[id];
  bool isVisible = true;

  for (int i = 0; i < 6 && isVisible; i++) {
    vec3 planeNormal =
        viewData.frustumPlanes[i].xyz;
    float distFromPlane = dot(
        meshBBoxData.centerPos.xyz, planeNormal);
    float absDiff = dot(abs(planeNormal),
                        meshBBoxData.extents.xyz);
    if (distFromPlane + absDiff +
            viewData.frustumPlanes[i].w < 0.0) {
      isVisible = false;
    }
  }
  if (isVisible) {
    uint index = atomicAdd(outDrawCount.count, 1);
    outputIndirectDraws[index] = inputIndirectDraws[id];
  }
}
```

If the mesh is culled, the function returns early. Otherwise, it atomically increments the number of visible meshes in the `IndirectDrawCount` buffer and copies the indirect draw parameters from the input to the output buffer using the previous number of meshes in the buffer as the index of the destination.

The only remaining work for the main function is to call `cullMesh`:

```
layout(local_size_x = 256, local_size_y = 1,
       local_size_z = 1) in;
void main() {
  uint currentThreadId = gl_GlobalInvocationID.x;
  if (currentThreadId == 0) {
    atomicExchange(outDrawCount.count, 0);
  }
  barrier();
  if (currentThreadId < cullData.count) {
    cullMesh(currentThreadId);
  }
}
```

Through this recipe, we've harnessed the power of the GPU to effectively filter out non-essential objects, optimizing our rendering workflow. By implementing this method, you will achieve a more responsive and resource-efficient visualization, especially vital for intricate 3D scenes.

4

Exploring Techniques for Lighting, Shading, and Shadows

Welcome to an exploration of lighting and shading techniques designed to infuse realism into your scenes. In the world of graphics, both lighting and shading play an integral role in enhancing the aesthetic appeal and realism of 3D visuals. This chapter delves into these topics, presenting a spectrum of algorithms ranging from the fundamental to the complex which can add realism to your scenes. In this chapter, we will cover the following recipes:

- Implementing G-buffer for deferred rendering
- Implementing screen space reflections
- Implementing shadow maps for real-time shadows
- Implementing screen space ambient occlusion
- Implementing a lighting pass for illuminating the scene

By the end of this chapter, you will have a comprehensive understanding of these techniques, enabling you to adeptly implement them in your rendering projects.

Technical requirements

For this chapter, you will need to make sure you have VS 2022 installed along with the Vulkan SDK. Basic familiarity with the C++ programming language and an understanding of OpenGL or any other graphics API will be useful. Please revisit *Chapter 1, Vulkan Core Concepts*, under the T*echnical requirements* section for details on setting up and building executables for this chapter. We also assume that by now you are familiar with how to use the Vulkan API and various concepts that were introduced in previous chapters. All recipes for this chapter are encapsulated in a single executable and can be launched using `Chapter04_Deferred_Renderer.exe` executable.

Implementing G-buffer for deferred rendering

Deferred rendering is a technique that adds an additional render pass at the beginning of the scene rendering that accumulates various information about the scene in screen space, such as position, surface normal, surface color, and others. This extra information is stored in a buffer called the **geometry buffer** (**G-buffer**), where each one of the values computed during this step is stored for each pixel. Once this initial pass has finished, the final scene rendering can take place, and the extra information to improve the rendering quality by computing things such as reflections, ambient occlusion, atmospheric effects, and others can be used. The benefit of using deferred rendering is that it provides more efficient handling of complex scenes with many lights, as each light only needs to be calculated once per pixel, rather than once per object. We have essentially decoupled geometry and shading, which allows for more flexibility in the rendering pipeline. The technique also has some disadvantages, such as increased memory usage (for the G-buffer itself), and difficulty handling transparency and anti-aliasing.

In this tutorial, you will gain an understanding of the implementation of G-buffer for deferred rendering, its advantages in managing complex scenes with multiple lights, and the challenges it may present, such as increased memory usage.

Getting ready

Creating a G-buffer in Vulkan is somewhat straightforward. The bulk of the technique relies on creating a framebuffer that contains references to all render targets (textures) that will store the scene's information, such as position, normal, and material data. The render pass also needs to dictate how those render targets should be loaded and stored at the end of the pass. Finally, in the fragment shader, each render target is specified as an output variable and the value of each render target is written to the output that refers to the correct texture or storage buffer.

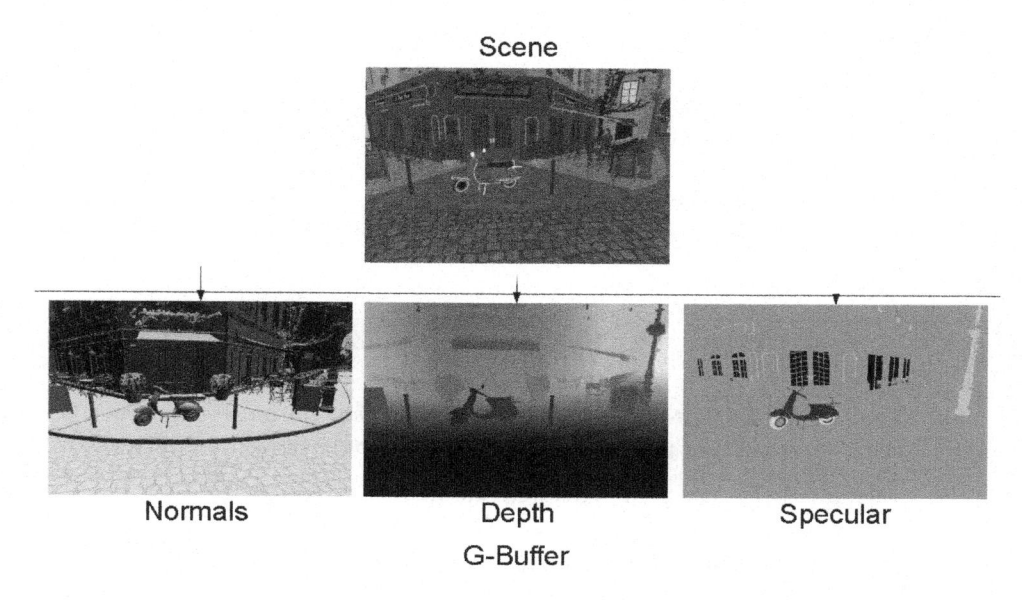

Figure 4.1 – G-buffer textures

In the repository, the G-buffer generation is encapsulated in the `GBufferPass` class.

How to do it...

To generate a G-buffer and its artifacts, we need to first create a framebuffer and a corresponding `RenderPass`. In the following steps, we will show you how to create targets for the base color of the material, the normal, and the depth components:

1. Before creating theFrambuffer object, it is necessary to create the textures (render targets) that will store the output of the G-buffer pass:

    ```
    gBufferBaseColorTexture_ = context->createTexture(
        VK_IMAGE_TYPE_2D, VK_FORMAT_R8G8B8A8_UNORM, 0,
        VK_IMAGE_USAGE_COLOR_ATTACHMENT_BIT |
            VK_IMAGE_USAGE_SAMPLED_BIT |
            VK_IMAGE_USAGE_STORAGE_BIT,...

    gBufferNormalTexture_ = context->createTexture(
        VK_IMAGE_TYPE_2D,
        VK_FORMAT_R16G16B16A16_SFLOAT, 0,
        VK_IMAGE_USAGE_COLOR_ATTACHMENT_BIT |
            VK_IMAGE_USAGE_SAMPLED_BIT |
            VK_IMAGE_USAGE_STORAGE_BIT,...
    ```

```
gBufferPositionTexture_ = context->createTexture(
    VK_IMAGE_TYPE_2D, VK_FORMAT_R16G16B16A16_SFLOAT, 0,
    VK_IMAGE_USAGE_COLOR_ATTACHMENT_BIT | VK_IMAGE_USAGE_
SAMPLED_BIT | VK_IMAGE_USAGE_STORAGE_BIT,…

depthTexture_ = context->createTexture(
    VK_IMAGE_TYPE_2D, VK_FORMAT_D24_UNORM_S8_UINT,
    0,
    VK_IMAGE_USAGE_DEPTH_STENCIL_ATTACHMENT_BIT |
        VK_IMAGE_USAGE_TRANSFER_DST_BIT |
        VK_IMAGE_USAGE_SAMPLED_BIT,…
```

2. The `Framebuffer` object references the preceding targets. The order is important here and should be mirrored in the shader where the outputs are specified:

```
frameBuffer_ = context->createFramebuffer(
    renderPass_->vkRenderPass(),
    {gBufferBaseColorTexture_, gBufferNormalTexture_,
gBufferEmissiveTexture_,
    gBufferSpecularTexture_, gBufferPositionTexture_,
depthTexture_},
    nullptr, nullptr, "GBuffer framebuffer ");
```

3. The `RenderPass` object describes how each render target should be loaded and stored. The operations should match the order of the targets used by the framebuffer:

```
renderPass_ = context->createRenderPass(
    {gBufferBaseColorTexture_, gBufferNormalTexture_,
gBufferEmissiveTexture_,
    gBufferSpecularTexture_, gBufferPositionTexture_,
depthTexture_},
        {VK_ATTACHMENT_LOAD_OP_CLEAR, VK_ATTACHMENT_LOAD_OP_CLEAR,
        VK_ATTACHMENT_LOAD_OP_CLEAR, VK_ATTACHMENT_LOAD_OP_CLEAR,
        VK_ATTACHMENT_LOAD_OP_CLEAR, VK_ATTACHMENT_LOAD_OP_
CLEAR},
        {VK_ATTACHMENT_STORE_OP_STORE, VK_ATTACHMENT_STORE_OP_
STORE,
        VK_ATTACHMENT_STORE_OP_STORE, VK_ATTACHMENT_STORE_OP_
STORE,
        VK_ATTACHMENT_STORE_OP_STORE, VK_ATTACHMENT_STORE_OP_
STORE},
        // final layout for all attachments
        {VK_IMAGE_LAYOUT_SHADER_READ_ONLY_OPTIMAL, VK_IMAGE_
LAYOUT_SHADER_READ_ONLY_OPTIMAL,
        VK_IMAGE_LAYOUT_SHADER_READ_ONLY_OPTIMAL, VK_IMAGE_
```

```
        LAYOUT_SHADER_READ_ONLY_OPTIMAL,
            VK_IMAGE_LAYOUT_SHADER_READ_ONLY_OPTIMAL,
            VK_IMAGE_LAYOUT_SHADER_READ_ONLY_OPTIMAL},
            VK_PIPELINE_BIND_POINT_GRAPHICS, "GBuffer RenderPass");
```

4. In the fragment shader, besides the input data originating from the previous stages in the pipeline, the output data is directed to each one of the targets using the layout keyword and the location qualifier. The location index must match the render target index on the framebuffer:

```
layout(location=0) in vec2 inTexCoord;
layout(location=1) in flat uint inflatMeshId;
layout(location=2) in flat int inflatMaterialId;
layout(location=3) in vec3 inNormal;
layout(location=4) in vec4 inTangent;

layout(location = 0) out vec4 outgBufferBaseColor;
layout(location = 1) out vec4 outgBufferWorldNormal;
layout(location = 2) out vec4 outgBufferEmissive;
layout(location = 3) out vec4 outgBufferSpecular;
layout(location = 4) out vec4 outgBufferPosition;

const vec3 n = normalize(inNormal);
const vec3 t = normalize(inTangent.xyz);
const vec3 b = normalize(cross(n,t) * inTangent.w);
const mat3 tbn =  mat3(t, b, n);
outgBufferWorldNormal.rgb = normalize(tbn *
normalize(normalTan));
```

In the preceding code snippet, the world normal is calculated based on the normal and tangent values and stored in the `outgBufferWorldNormal` location, which corresponds to the attachment with `index 1` (see code fragment in *step 2*).

Implementing screen space reflections

Physically correct reflections involve tracing the path of light rays as they bounce off surfaces. This process accounts for the geometry, material properties, and light sources in the scene, as well as the view angle. However, it is a very computationally intensive process, often too demanding for real-time rendering, especially in complex scenes or on less powerful hardware. To achieve a balance between visual quality and performance, an approximation technique known as **screen space reflection** (**SSR**) can be used. SSR is a method that approximates reflections by reusing data that has already been rendered to the screen. By utilizing a screen-space variant, the heavy computational cost associated with physically correct reflections can be significantly reduced, making it a viable technique for real-time rendering. In this recipe, we will explain how to compute reflections using buffers derived from the previous section, such as the normal and depth buffers.

Getting ready

SSR uses the depth buffer to find intersections between a reflected ray and the geometry's depth. The reflection ray is computed in world space based on the surface normal and the view direction and is marched in small increments until it leaves the screen bounds. For every step, the ray's location is projected onto the screen and its coordinates are compared against the depth buffer. If the difference between the ray's location and the depth buffer's depth is less than a small threshold, then the ray has collided with some geometry, and the ray's originating point on the surface is obscured. This reflection vector is then used to look up the color of the pixel in the already-rendered image at the reflected position. This color is then used as the reflected color, creating the illusion of a reflection. SSR can produce visually pleasing reflections that come close to those produced by much more computationally expensive physically correct reflection models; however, it can only reflect what's already visible on the screen, and it may produce inaccurate results for complex surfaces or at screen edges.

How to do it...

Once the depth and normal buffers have been calculated, the SSR can be easily computed in a render or compute pass:

1. The following SSR code is used by a compute pass and specifies the buffers used as input, generated by the deferred rendering step, as well as the transformation data it needs to perform the intersection in screen space:

```
layout(set = 0, binding = 0, rgba16f) uniform image2D
SSRIntersect;

layout(set = 1, binding = 0)uniform sampler2D
gBufferWorldNormal;
layout(set = 1, binding = 1)uniform sampler2D gBufferSpecular;
layout(set = 1, binding = 2)uniform sampler2D gBufferBaseColor;
layout(set = 1, binding = 3)uniform sampler2D hierarchicalDepth;

layout(set = 2, binding = 0)uniform Transforms
{
  mat4 model;
  mat4 view;
  mat4 projection;
  mat4 projectionInv;
  mat4 viewInv;
} cameraData;
```

2. Two auxiliary functions are defined in the shader. They perform the projection from a point in world space to screen space and calculate the projection from a screen space along with depth coordinate to world space:

    ```
    vec3 generatePositionFromDepth(vec2 texturePos, float depth);
    vec2 generateProjectedPosition(vec3 worldPos);
    ```

3. In this step, the data needed for the reflection calculations from the G-buffer is fetched. This includes the world normal, specular data, and base color for the current pixel. The UV coordinates are calculated, which are used to sample the base color from the G-buffer. The roughness, which controls how blurry or sharp the reflection is, is also extracted from the specular data. We also check the metalness value from the G-buffer specular data. If the material is not metallic (`metalness < 0.01`), it assumes it doesn't reflect and simply writes the base color to the result and exits:

    ```
    layout(local_size_x = 16, local_size_y = 16,
           local_size_z = 1) in;
    void main() {
      // Return if the coordinate is outside the screen
      ...

      imageStore(SSRIntersect,
                 ivec2(gl_GlobalInvocationID.xy),
                 vec4(0));

      vec2 uv = (vec2(gl_GlobalInvocationID.xy) +
                vec2(0.5f)) /
                vec2(pushConstant.textureResolution);
      ivec2 pixelPos = ivec2(gl_GlobalInvocationID.xy);

      vec4 gbufferNormalData =
          texelFetch(gBufferWorldNormal, pixelPos, 0);
      vec4 gbufferSpecularData =
          texelFetch(gBufferSpecular, pixelPos, 0);
      vec3 basecolor =
          texture(gBufferBaseColor, uv).xyz;

      float roughness = gbufferSpecularData.g;

      if (gbufferSpecularData.r <
          .01) { // Metal-ness check
    ```

```
        imageStore(SSRIntersect,
                  ivec2(gl_GlobalInvocationID.xy),
                  vec4(basecolor, 1.0));
    return;
}
```

4. The following snippet fetches the depth of the current pixel from the depth buffer and generates the world position of the pixel using the UV and depth. The view direction is calculated from the camera position to the pixel's world position. The reflection direction is then calculated using the view direction and the normal. The shader then performs ray marching along the reflection direction in screen space. It steps along the reflection ray and at each step, it checks whether the ray has intersected with any geometry, based on the depth difference between the current position of the ray and the depth at the corresponding screen position:

```
float z =
    texelFetch(hierarchicalDepth, pixelPos, 0).r;
vec3 position = generatePositionFromDepth(uv, z);
vec3 normal = normalize(gbufferNormalData.xyz);

vec3 camPos = cameraData.viewInv[3].xyz;

vec3 viewDirection = normalize(position - camPos);
vec3 reflectionDirection =
    reflect(viewDirection, normal);

;
float stepSize = 0.05; // Initial step size

vec3 currentPos = position;

for (int i = 0; i < 50; i++) {
  currentPos += reflectionDirection * stepSize;
  vec2 screenPos =
      generateProjectedPosition(currentPos);

  if (screenPos.x < 0.0 || screenPos.x > 1.0 ||
      screenPos.y < 0.0 || screenPos.y > 1.0) {
    break; // Ray went out of screen bounds
  }
```

```
           float depthAtCurrent =
               texture(hierarchicalDepth, screenPos).r;
           vec3 positionFromDepth =
               generatePositionFromDepth(screenPos,
                                         depthAtCurrent);
           float depthDifference =
               length(currentPos - positionFromDepth);
```

5. If an intersection is found, the code fetches the color at the intersection point and blends it with the base color. The blending is based on the roughness value, which represents a characteristic of the surface at the intersection point:

```
           if (depthDifference < 0.05) {
             vec3 hitColor =
                 texture(gBufferBaseColor, screenPos).xyz;
             if (hitColor.x <= .1 && hitColor.y <= .1 &&
                 hitColor.z <= .1 && hitColor.x >= .08 &&
                 hitColor.y >= .08 &&
                 hitColor.z >=
                     .08) { // .1 is considered sky color,
                            // ignore if we hit sky
               hitColor = basecolor;
             }

             vec3 blendColor =
                 hitColor * (1.0 - roughness) +
                 roughness * basecolor;

             imageStore(SSRIntersect,
                 ivec2(gl_GlobalInvocationID.xy),
                 vec4(blendColor, 1.0));
             return;
           }
         }

         // Fallback
         imageStore(SSRIntersect,
             ivec2(gl_GlobalInvocationID.xy),
             vec4(basecolor, 1.0));
       }
```

In the preceding code, we learned how SSR is computed using the depth and normal buffers.

See also

The following are some references that go into more detail on how to implement SSR; we suggest you go through these references to gain a more thorough understanding:

- `https://interplayoflight.wordpress.com/2022/09/28/notes-on-screenspace-reflections-with-fidelityfx-sssr/`
- `http://roar11.com/2015/07/screen-space-glossy-reflections/`
- `https://interplayoflight.wordpress.com/2019/09/07/hybrid-screen-space-reflections/`

Implementing shadow maps for real-time shadows

As the name implies, **shadow maps** are used to simulate shadows. The goal of shadow mapping is to determine which parts of a scene are in shadow and which parts are illuminated by a light source by first rendering the scene from the light's perspective, generating a depth map.

This depth map (also known as a shadow map) serves as a spatial record, storing the shortest distance from the light source to any point in the scene. By encapsulating the scene from the vantage point of the light source, the depth map effectively captures the areas of the scene that are directly visible to the light source and those that are occluded.

This depth map is then used during the main render pass to determine if the fragment can't be reached from the light by comparing its depth value with the one in the depth map. For each fragment in the scene, we perform a test to evaluate whether it lies in shadow. This is achieved by comparing the depth value of the fragment from the light source, derived from the main camera's perspective, with the corresponding depth value stored in the depth map.

If the fragment's depth value exceeds the value recorded in the depth map, it implies that the fragment is occluded by another object in the scene and is, therefore, in shadow. Conversely, if the fragment's depth value is less than or equal to the depth map value, it signifies that the fragment is directly visible to the light source and is thus illuminated.

In this recipe, you will learn how to implement shadow maps to create real-time shadows in your 3D scene. This involves understanding the theory of shadow mapping, generating a depth map from the light's perspective, and finally using this depth map in the main render pass to accurately determine which fragments of the scene are in shadow and which are illuminated.

Getting ready

To obtain the shadow map, we first need to render the scene from the light's perspective and retain the depth map. This render pass needs a depth texture that will store the depth information and simple vertex and fragment shaders. The main render pass, in which the scene is rendered, is where the depth map is used as a reference to determine if a pixel is lit or not and needs to refer to the shadow map generated in the previous step, along with a special sampler to access the depth map in the shader code. It also has code to perform the comparison between the fragment and the value stored in the depth map.

In the repository, a shadow map generation is encapsulated in the `ShadowPass` class, and usage of shadow depth texture is encapsulated in the `LightingPass` class.

How to do it...

We'll start with a walk-through of the shadow map pass first:

1. The shadow map is a regular texture with a format that supports depth values. Our depth texture is 4x the resolution of the normal texture and uses the `VK_FORMAT_D24_UNORM_S8_UINT` format:

    ```
    void ShadowPass::initTextures(
        VulkanCore::Context *context) {
      depthTexture_ = context->createTexture(
          VK_IMAGE_TYPE_2D, VK_FORMAT_D24_UNORM_S8_UINT,
          0,
          VK_IMAGE_USAGE_DEPTH_STENCIL_ATTACHMENT_BIT |
            VK_IMAGE_USAGE_TRANSFER_DST_BIT |
            VK_IMAGE_USAGE_SAMPLED_BIT,
          {
              .width =
                  context->swapchain()->extent().width *
                  4, // 4x resolution for shadow maps
              .height = context->swapchain()
                            ->extent()
                            .height *
                        4,
              .depth = 1,
          },
          1, 1, VK_MEMORY_PROPERTY_DEVICE_LOCAL_BIT,
          false, "ShadowMap Depth buffer");
    }
    ```

2. The render pass needs to clear the depth attachment at the beginning and then store it at the end. There are no color attachments in the shadow map render pass or in the framebuffer:

```
renderPass_ = context->createRenderPass(
    {depthTexture_}, {VK_ATTACHMENT_LOAD_OP_CLEAR},
    {VK_ATTACHMENT_STORE_OP_STORE},
    // final layout for all attachments
    {VK_IMAGE_LAYOUT_SHADER_READ_ONLY_OPTIMAL},
    VK_PIPELINE_BIND_POINT_GRAPHICS,
    "ShadowMap RenderPass");

frameBuffer_ = context->createFramebuffer(
    renderPass_->vkRenderPass(), {depthTexture_},
    nullptr, nullptr, "ShadowMap framebuffer ");
```

3. This render pass's pipeline definition needs to match the size of the viewport to the size of the shadow map and use the special vertex and fragment shaders for this pass. The fragment and vertex shader are conceptually identical to the G-buffer pass but they just need to output the depth buffer instead of multiple geometry buffers; it also needs a light view projection matrix instead of the camera's one. As a future optimization, you could use the specialization constant with the G-buffer pass instead of using a separate shader:

```
auto vertexShader = context->createShaderModule(
    (resourcesFolder / "shadowpass.vert").string(),
    VK_SHADER_STAGE_VERTEX_BIT, "shadowmap vertex");
auto fragmentShader = context->createShaderModule(
    (resourcesFolder / "empty.frag").string(),
    VK_SHADER_STAGE_FRAGMENT_BIT,
    "shadowmap fragment");
const VulkanCore::Pipeline::
    GraphicsPipelineDescriptor gpDesc = {
        .sets_ = setLayout,
        .vertexShader_ = vertexShader,
        .fragmentShader_ = fragmentShader,
        .dynamicStates_ =
            {VK_DYNAMIC_STATE_VIEWPORT,
             VK_DYNAMIC_STATE_SCISSOR},
        .colorTextureFormats = {},
        .depthTextureFormat =
            VK_FORMAT_D24_UNORM_S8_UINT,
        .sampleCount = VK_SAMPLE_COUNT_1_BIT,
        .cullMode = VK_CULL_MODE_BACK_BIT,
        .viewport = VkExtent2D(
            depthTexture_->vkExtents().width,
```

```
                    depthTexture_->vkExtents().height),
        .depthTestEnable = true,
        .depthWriteEnable = true,
        .depthCompareOperation = VK_COMPARE_OP_LESS,
    };

    pipeline_ = context->createGraphicsPipeline(
        gpDesc, renderPass_->vkRenderPass(),
```

4. The vertex shader needs the light's transformation matrix, which is set into the **model view projection** (**MVP**) matrix; the vertex shader is almost an identical copy of the G-buffer vertex shader. The shader applies the light transformation to the scene's vertices and sends the data to the fragment shader. The depth value of each mesh will be recorded in the depth map, guided by the depth-related parameters we've defined in the preceding step. These parameters – including depthTestEnable, depthWriteEnable, and depthCompareOperation – will govern how we evaluate and store depth information during this process:

    ```
    #version 460
    #extension GL_EXT_nonuniform_qualifier : require
    #extension GL_EXT_debug_printf : enable

    #extension GL_GOOGLE_include_directive : require
    #include "CommonStructs.glsl"
    #include "IndirectCommon.glsl"

    void main() {
      Vertex vertex = vertexAlias[VERTEX_INDEX]
                          .vertices[gl_VertexIndex];
      vec3 position =
          vec3(vertex.posX, vertex.posY, vertex.posZ);
      gl_Position = MVP.projection * MVP.view *
                    MVP.model * vec4(position, 1.0);
    }
    ```

5. The fragment shader is empty, as it doesn't need to output any color information:

    ```
    #version 460

    void main() {
    }
    ```

The main render (lighting) pass uses the shadow map calculated before as a reference to determine if a fragment is lit or not. There is no special setup for the scene, except for the sampler used with the shadow map, which needs to enable a comparison function. The vertex and fragment shaders also need some special treatment to perform the depth comparison against the shadow map.

6. The sampler used to access the shadow map in the shader needs to enable the comparison function. We use the `VK_COMPARE_OP_LESS_OR_EQUAL` function:

   ```
   samplerShadowMap_ = context.createSampler(
       VK_FILTER_NEAREST, VK_FILTER_NEAREST,
       VK_SAMPLER_ADDRESS_MODE_CLAMP_TO_EDGE,
       VK_SAMPLER_ADDRESS_MODE_CLAMP_TO_EDGE,
       VK_SAMPLER_ADDRESS_MODE_CLAMP_TO_EDGE, 1.0f,
       true, VK_COMPARE_OP_LESS_OR_EQUAL,
       "lighting pass shadow");
   ```

7. The fragment shader needs a shadow map as well as a light's view projection matrix. The following code includes the uniform `sampler2Dshadow`, which holds the depth map or shadow map. The uniform `Lights` structure contains information about the light source, including its position, direction, color, and the view projection matrix from the light's perspective:

   ```
   #version 460
   layout(set = 0, binding = 6)uniform sampler2DShadow shadowMap;

   layout(set = 1, binding = 1)uniform Lights
   {
       vec4 lightPos;
       vec4 lightDir;
       vec4 lightColor;
       vec4 ambientColor; // environment light color
       mat4 lightVP;
       float innerConeAngle;
       float outerConeAngle;
   } lightData;
   ```

8. We introduce a `computeShadow` auxiliary function that takes as input a position in light-projective space. It first converts this position into **normalized device coordinates** (**NDCs**), then it looks up the shadow map at the corresponding position and returns the shadow intensity at that point:

   ```
   #version 460
   layout(set = 0, binding = 6)uniform sampler2DShadow shadowMap;

   layout(set = 1, binding = 1)uniform Lights
   {
       vec4 lightPos;
       vec4 lightDir;
       vec4 lightColor;
   ```

```
    vec4 ambientColor; // environment light color
    mat4 lightVP;
    float innerConeAngle;
    float outerConeAngle;
} lightData;
```

9. Next, we introduce another auxiliary function, the `PCF` function. **Percentage closer filtering (PCF)** is a technique used in shadow mapping to create softer, more natural-looking shadows. Shadow mapping, by its nature, creates shadows with hard edges because each pixel is either fully in shadow or fully lit. This is because the shadow mapping algorithm simply checks if a pixel is occluded from the light source or not. However, in real life, shadows often have softer edges due to the scattering of light. In the case of PCF, instead of sampling the shadow map only once for each pixel, we sample the shadow map multiple times in a small area around the pixel and average the result; for example, in our implementation PCF sample, the shadow map at `16` different offsets around the pixel. Then, it would calculate the average of these samples to determine the final shadow value for the pixel. This averaging process results in pixels on the edge of shadows having intermediate shadow values between fully lit and fully shadowed, creating a soft transition that makes the shadow look more natural:

```
float PCF(vec4 shadowCoord) {
  vec2 texCoord = shadowCoord.xy / shadowCoord.w;
  texCoord = texCoord * .5 + .5;
  texCoord.y = 1.0 - texCoord.y;

  if (texCoord.x > 1.0 || texCoord.y > 1.0 ||
      texCoord.x < 0.0 || texCoord.y < 0.0) {
    return 1.0;
  }

  vec2 texSize = textureSize(shadowMap, 0);
  float result = 0.0;
  vec2 offset = (1.0 / texSize) * shadowCoord.w;

  for(float x = -1.5; x <= 1.5; x += 1.0) {
    for(float y = -1.5; y <= 1.5; y += 1.0) {
      result += computeShadow(shadowCoord + vec4(vec2(x, y) *
offset, 0.0, 0.0));
    }
  }

  return result / 16.0;
```

10. In the main function, we first retrieve the world position and base color of the fragment from the G-buffer. If the world position is zero (indicating no meaningful information), we simply set the output color to the base color and return early. As a next step, the world position is transformed into light-projective space using the light's view projection matrix and passes this position to the PCF function to compute the visibility factor, which represents how much the fragment is in shadow. If the visibility factor is below a threshold (meaning the fragment is in deep shadow), it sets the visibility to a fixed value for a minimum amount of ambient light. Finally, we multiply the computed outColor by the visibility factor to create the final color, which will be darker if the fragment is in shadow and lighter if it's lit:

```
void main() {

    vec4 worldPos =
        texture(gBufferPosition, fragTexCoord);

    vec3 basecolor =
        texture(gBufferBaseColor, fragTexCoord).rgb;

    if (worldPos.x == 0.0 && worldPos.y == 0.0 &&
        worldPos.z == 0.0 && worldPos.w == 0.0) {
      outColor = vec4(basecolor, 1.0);
      return;
    }

    // compute outColor …

    vec4 shadowProjPos =
        lightData.lightVP * vec4(worldPos.xyz, 1.0f);
    float vis = PCF(shadowProjPos);

    if (vis <= .001) {
      vis = .3;
    }

    outColor.xyz *= vis;
}
```

In the preceding section, we illustrated how to implement shadow pass, but there are limitations to this technique that will be discussed in the next section.

There's more ...

We have demonstrated the use of the basic shadow mapping technique; however, this technique has some limitations, as follows:

- **Aliasing and pixelation**: One of the primary issues with simple shadow mapping is the problem of **aliasing**, where shadows can appear pixelated or blocky. This is because the resolution of the shadow map directly affects the shadow's quality. If the shadow map's resolution is too low, the resulting shadows will be pixelated. While increasing the shadow map's resolution can mitigate this, it comes at the cost of increasing memory usage and computational load.
- **Hard shadow edges**: Basic shadow mapping produces shadows with hard edges since it uses a binary lit or unlit test for shadow determination. Shadows often have soft edges due to light scattering (penumbra).
- **Shadow acne or self-shadowing artifacts**: This problem arises when a surface incorrectly shadows itself due to precision errors in the depth test. Techniques such as biasing are used to handle this issue but choosing the right bias can be challenging.

  Some of these challenges can be overcome with more advanced techniques such as the following:

  - **Cascade shadow maps**: This technique addresses the issue of resolution by dividing the camera's view frustum into multiple **cascades** or sections, each with its own shadow map. This allows for higher-resolution shadow maps to be used close to the camera, where detail is more important, and lower-resolution shadow maps to be used farther away.
  - **Moment shadow maps**: This technique uses statistical moments to store more information about the depth distribution within a pixel, which can handle transparency and provide anti-aliased, soft shadows. Moment shadow maps require more memory and computation than basic shadow maps but can provide higher-quality shadows.

See also

The following are references that discuss and provide implementation details about advanced techniques such as cascade shadow maps and moment shadows:

- https://learn.microsoft.com/en-us/windows/win32/dxtecharts/cascaded-shadow-maps
- https://momentsingraphics.de/I3D2015.html

Implementing screen space ambient occlusion

Screen space ambient occlusion (SSAO) can be used to approximate the effect of ambient occlusion in real time. Ambient occlusion is a shading and rendering method used to calculate how exposed each point in a scene is to ambient lighting. This technique adds more realistic shadows where two surfaces or objects meet, or where an object blocks light from reaching another object.

In this recipe, you will learn how to implement SSAO to realistically estimate ambient occlusion in real time. You will grasp how to use this shading and rendering technique to calculate the exposure of each point in a scene to ambient lighting.

Getting ready

The algorithm described in this recipe calculates the difference between the depth of a pixel and its neighbors (samples) in a circular fashion. If a sample is closer to the camera than the central pixel, it contributes to the occlusion factor, making the pixel darker.

A depiction of the algorithm is shown in *Figure 4.2*. The code loops over several *rings* around a central point, the pixel being processed. Within each ring, it takes several samples, as seen in item (a).

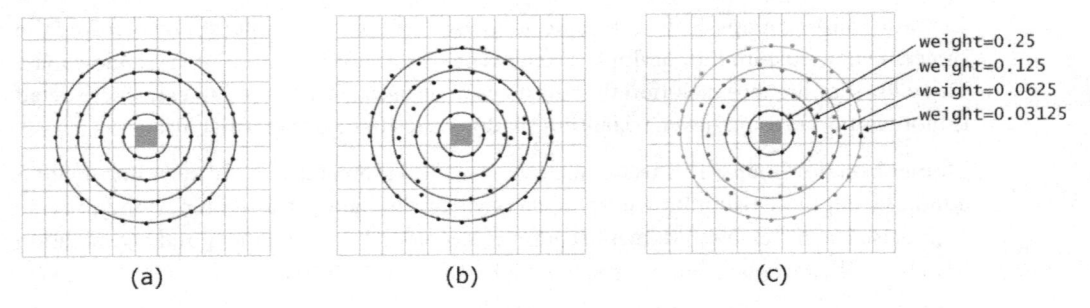

Figure 4.2 – SSAO sampling pattern

A small amount of noise is applied to each sample's location to avoid banding effects, as shown in item (b). Additionally, a weight is applied to samples on the same ring, with rings farther from the center with the smallest weights, as depicted in item (c).

How to do it...

The entire SSAO algorithm is implemented as a compute shader that writes its output to an image:

1. We start by declaring the inputs and outputs. The input is the depth buffer. The output is an image in which we'll store the result of the algorithm. We also need a function to generate noise in 2D. A small amount of noise is applied to each sample's location to avoid banding effects:

   ```
   #version 460

   layout(local_size_x = 16, local_size_y = 16,
          local_size_z = 1) in;

   layout(set = 0, binding = 0,
          rgba8) uniform image2D OutputSSAO;

   layout(set = 1, binding = 0) uniform sampler2D
       gBufferDepth;

   const float nearDistance = .1f;
   const float farDistance = 100.0f;

   vec2 generateRandomNoise(
       in vec2 coord) // generating random noise
   {
     float noiseX = (fract(
         sin(dot(coord, vec2(12.9898, 78.233))) *
         43758.5453));
     float noiseY = (fract(
         sin(dot(coord,
                 vec2(12.9898, 78.233) * 2.0)) *
         43758.5453));
     return vec2(noiseX, noiseY) * 0.004;
   }
   ```

2. We also need a function to convert the depth value from the depth buffer to a linear scale, as the values are not stored in a linear fashion:

```
float calculateLinearDepth(float depth) {
  return (2.0 * nearDistance) /
      (farDistance + nearDistance -
        depth * (farDistance - nearDistance));
}
```

3. The comparison between the depth value of the pixel being processed and the surrounding samples is done by the `compareDepths` function, which returns the difference between the samples:

```
float compareDepths(float depth1, float depth2) {
  const float aoCap = 0.5;
  const float aoMultiplier = 50.0;
  const float depthTolerance = 0.001;
  const float aoRange = 60.0;
  float depthDifference = sqrt(
      clamp(1.0 - (depth1 - depth2) /
                      (aoRange / (farDistance -
                                    nearDistance)),
            0.0, 1.0));
  float ao =
      min(aoCap, max(0.0, depth1 - depth2 -
                              depthTolerance) *
                      aoMultiplier) *
      depthDifference;
  return ao;
}
```

4. The main part of the algorithm starts by collecting the pixel's position and its depth value, which is converted to a linear scale. It also calculates the size of the buffers and calculates the noise:

```
void main() {
  if (gl_GlobalInvocationID.x >=
          pushConstant.textureResolution.x ||
      gl_GlobalInvocationID.y >=
          pushConstant.textureResolution.y) {
    return;
  }

  imageStore(OutputSSAO,
            ivec2(gl_GlobalInvocationID.xy),
            vec4(0));
```

```
            vec2 uv = (vec2(gl_GlobalInvocationID.xy) +
                      vec2(0.5f)) /
                     vec2(pushConstant.textureResolution);
            ivec2 pixelPos =
                ivec2(gl_GlobalInvocationID.xy);

            float depthBufferValue =
                texelFetch(gBufferDepth, pixelPos, 0).r;
            float depth =
                calculateLinearDepth(depthBufferValue);

            float textureWidth =
                float(pushConstant.textureResolution.x);
            float textureHeight =
                float(pushConstant.textureResolution.y);

            float aspectRatio =
                textureWidth / textureHeight;
            vec2 noise =
                generateRandomNoise(vec2(pixelPos));
```

5. The size of the area inspected for samples is proportional to the depth value of the pixel: the farther away the pixel is from the camera, the smaller the area is:

```
            float w = (1.0 / textureWidth) /
                         clamp(depth, 0.05, 1.0) +
                     (noise.x * (1.0 - noise.x));
            float h = (1.0 / textureHeight) /
                         clamp(depth, 0.05, 1.0) +
                     (noise.y * (1.0 - noise.y));

            w *= textureWidth / 2.0;
            h *= textureHeight / 2.0;

            float sampleWidth;
            float sampleHeight;

            float ao = 0.0;
            float totalSamples = 0.0;
            float fade = 1.0;

            const int NUM_RINGS = 3;
            const int NUM_SAMPLES = 6;
```

6. The bulk of the algorithm is where the ring radiuses and the number of samples are calculated. The number of samples is proportional to the ring's diameter. For each sample, we compare their depths, apply the ring weight, and accumulate the output, which is averaged out at the end of the function:

```
for (int i = 0; i < NUM_RINGS; i++) {
  fade *= 0.5;
  for (int j = 0; j < NUM_SAMPLES * i; j++) {
    float step = 3.14159265 * 2.0 /
                  float(NUM_SAMPLES * i);
    sampleWidth =
        (cos(float(j) * step) * float(i));
    sampleHeight =
        (sin(float(j) * step) * float(i));
    float newDepthValue =
        texelFetch(
            gBufferDepth,
            pixelPos +
                ivec2(int(sampleWidth * w),
                      int(sampleHeight * h)),
            0)
            .r;
    ao += compareDepths(depth,
                        calculateLinearDepth(
                            newDepthValue)) *
          fade;
    totalSamples += 1.0 * fade;
  }
}

ao /= totalSamples;
ao = 1.0 - ao;

imageStore(OutputSSAO, ivec2(gl_GlobalInvocationID.xy),
vec4(ao,ao,ao, 1.0));
```

This concludes our recipe for SSAO. For a deeper understanding and further exploration, we highly recommend visiting the various resources provided in the following section.

See also

For further understanding and an exploration of the topic of SSAO, you may find the following resources helpful:

- `https://github.com/NVIDIAGameWorks/HBAOPlus`
- `https://www.gamedevs.org/uploads/comparative-study-of-ssao-methods.pdf`
- `https://research.nvidia.com/sites/default/files/pubs/2012-06_Scalable-Ambient-Obscurance/McGuire12SAO.pdf`
- `https://www.ppsloan.org/publications/vo.pdf`
- `https://github.com/GameTechDev/XeGTAO`

Implementing a lighting pass for illuminating the scene

The last recipe in the book you how to implement a lighting pass; this is where we calculate the lighting for the scene. For each light in the scene, we draw a volume (for point lights, this would be a sphere; for directional lights, a full-screen quad; for spotlights, we would draw a cone) and for each pixel in that volume, we fetch the data from the G-buffer and calculate the lighting contribution of that light to the pixel. The results are then usually added together (blended) to a final render target to get the final image. In the demo, we only have one spotlight that is used as a demonstration, but we can easily add multiple lights. For each light in the scene, we will need to consider the area affected by the light (i.e., we use a shader that fetches the relevant data for each pixel from the G-buffer, which then uses this data to calculate how much this light source contributes to the final color of each pixel). For example, if we're dealing with a spotlight, this volume is a cone centered at the light's position, oriented in the light's direction, and with an angle that matches the spread of the spotlight. The length or height of the cone should be equal to the range of the spotlight. Lastly, we use a physically based lighting model (the **Cook-Torrance lighting model**), which is applied in the fragment shader. The inputs to the lighting model include the light's properties (color, intensity, position, etc.) and the surface properties (material color, shininess, normal, etc.), which are fetched from the G-buffer.

Getting ready

The recipe is implemented in the `LightingPass` class and the `Lighting.frag` shader. It simply uses a full-screen vertex shader to draw a full-screen quad.

As mentioned in the introduction of this recipe, we use the Cook-Torrance lighting model, which is a physically based rendering model that simulates how light interacts with a surface. It considers various factors such as the angle of incidence, surface roughness, and microfacet distribution to render realistic lighting effects. The algorithm uses the `Fresnel-Schlick` function, which is used to determine the proportion of light reflected versus refracted depending on the view angle. The GGX distribution function calculates the distribution of microfacets on the surface, which influences how rough or smooth a surface appears.

How to do it...

The entire algorithm is implemented as a full-screen space quad shader that writes its output to a final color texture:

1. We start by declaring the inputs and outputs. The inputs include the G-buffer data (normal, specular, base color, depth, and position), ambient occlusion map, shadow map, camera, and light data. The output is simply `fragColor`, which is written to the color attachment as specified by the render pass:

```
#version 460
#extension GL_EXT_nonuniform_qualifier : require
#extension GL_GOOGLE_include_directive : require

layout(set = 0, binding = 0)uniform sampler2D
gBufferWorldNormal;
layout(set = 0, binding = 1)uniform sampler2D gBufferSpecular;
layout(set = 0, binding = 2)uniform sampler2D gBufferBaseColor;
layout(set = 0, binding = 3)uniform sampler2D gBufferDepth;
layout(set = 0, binding = 4)uniform sampler2D gBufferPosition;
layout(set = 0, binding = 5)uniform sampler2D ambientOcclusion;
layout(set = 0, binding = 6)uniform sampler2DShadow shadowMap;

layout(set = 1, binding = 0)uniform Transforms
{
    mat4 viewProj;
    mat4 viewProjInv;
    mat4 viewInv;
} cameraData;

layout(set = 1, binding = 1)uniform Lights
{
    vec4 lightPos;
    vec4 lightDir;
    vec4 lightColor;
    vec4 ambientColor; // environment light color
```

```
        mat4 lightVP;
        float innerConeAngle;
        float outerConeAngle;
} lightData;


layout(location=0) in vec2 fragTexCoord;

layout(location = 0) out vec4 outColor;
```

2. Afterward, we define a few auxiliary functions; these will be used in the main function. These are defined in the `brdf.glsl` file.

   The `fresnelSchlick` function calculates the `Fresnel-Schlick` approximation, which models the amount of reflection and refraction based on the angle at which light hits the surface. The result is used to determine the specular color.

   The `distributionGGX` function calculates the distribution of microfacets on a surface. The result models how rough or smooth a surface appears, influencing the spread of the specular highlight.

   The `geometrySchlickGGX` function calculates the geometric attenuation term using **Schlick's approximation**. This term represents the probability that light isn't blocked by microfacets. The `geometrySmith` function calculates the total geometric attenuation considering both the view direction and the light direction. It calculates geometric attenuation for both view and light direction and multiplies both to get the final geometric attenuation, this function assumes that microfacet distribution is the same in all directions. These functions are combined in the `Cook-Torrance BRDF` model to account for microfacet occlusion and shadowing effects:

```
vec3 fresnelSchlick(float cosTheta, vec3 F0) {
    return F0 + (1.0 - F0) * pow(1.0 - cosTheta, 5.0);
}

float distributionGGX(vec3 N, vec3 H,
                      float roughness) {
    float a = roughness * roughness;
    float a2 = a * a;
    float NdotH = max(dot(N, H), 0.0);
    float NdotH2 = NdotH * NdotH;

    float nom = a2;
    float denom = (NdotH2 * (a2 - 1.0) + 1.0);
    denom = 3.14159265359 * denom * denom;

    return nom / denom;
}
```

```glsl
float geometrySchlickGGX(float NdotV,
                         float roughness) {
  float r = (roughness + 1.0) * 0.5;
  float r2 = r * r;

  float nom = NdotV;
  float denom = NdotV * (1.0 - r2) + r2;

  return nom / denom;
}

float geometrySmith(vec3 N, vec3 V, vec3 L,
                    float roughness) {
  float NdotV = max(dot(N, V), 0.0);
  float NdotL = max(dot(N, L), 0.0);
  float ggx2 = geometrySchlickGGX(NdotV, roughness);
  float ggx1 = geometrySchlickGGX(NdotL, roughness);

  return ggx1 * ggx2;
}
```

3. The shader first retrieves the base color, world position, camera position, specular data, and normal data from the G-buffer:

```glsl
void main() {

  vec4 worldPos =
      texture(gBufferPosition, fragTexCoord);

  vec3 basecolor =
      texture(gBufferBaseColor, fragTexCoord).rgb;

  if (worldPos.x == 0.0 && worldPos.y == 0.0 &&
      worldPos.z == 0.0 && worldPos.w == 0.0) {
    outColor = vec4(basecolor, 1.0);
    return;
  }

  vec2 gbufferSpecularData =
      texture(gBufferSpecular, fragTexCoord).rg;
```

```
        float metallic = gbufferSpecularData.r;
        float roughness = gbufferSpecularData.g;
        vec4 gbufferNormalData =
            texture(gBufferWorldNormal, fragTexCoord);
        vec3 N = normalize(gbufferNormalData.xyz);
```

4. In the next steps, it calculates the view vector (V), light vector (L), and half vector (H). These vectors are used in lighting calculations:

```
        vec3 camPos = cameraData.viewInv[3].xyz;
        vec3 V = normalize(camPos - worldPos.xyz);

        vec3 F0 = vec3(0.04);
        F0 = mix(F0, basecolor, metallic);
        vec3 L = normalize(
            lightData.lightDir.xyz -
            worldPos.xyz); // Using spotlight direction
        vec3 H = normalize(V + L);
```

5. During this part, the Fresnel-Schlick, distributionGGX, and geometrySmith functions are called to calculate the specular reflection:

```
        vec3 F = fresnelSchlick(max(dot(H, V), 0.0), F0);
        float D = distributionGGX(N, H, roughness);
        float G = geometrySmith(N, V, L, roughness);
        vec3 nominator = D * G * F;
        float denominator = 4.0 * max(dot(N, V), 0.0) *
                            max(dot(N, L), 0.0) +
                        0.001;
        vec3 specular = nominator / denominator;
```

6. In this step, the shader calculates the diffuse reflection. It's a simple model based on Lambert's cosine law, but it's modified by applying an energy conservation principle:

```
        vec3 kS = F;
        vec3 kD = vec3(1.0) - kS;
        kD *= 1.0 - metallic;

        float NdotL = max(dot(N, L), 0.0);
        vec3 diffuse = kD * basecolor / 3.14159265359;
```

7. In these last few steps, ambient light is calculated by simply multiplying the ambient light color by the base color. Here, we also calculate the attenuation based on the distance to the light, and the spot attenuation based on the angle between the light direction and the direction to the fragment. These are used to calculate the light intensity. The shader calculates the final color by adding the ambient, diffuse, and specular components together:

    ```
    vec3 ambient =
        lightData.ambientColor.rgb * basecolor;

    // Spotlight calculations
    vec3 lightToFragment =
        lightData.lightPos.xyz - worldPos.xyz;
    vec3 lightDirection =
        normalize(-lightData.lightDir.xyz);
    float distanceToLight = length(lightToFragment);
    float attenuation =
        1.0 /
        (1.0 + 0.1 * distanceToLight +
         0.01 * distanceToLight * distanceToLight);
    vec3 lightDir = normalize(lightToFragment);
    float cosTheta = dot(-lightDir, lightDirection);
    float spotAttenuation =
        smoothstep(lightData.outerConeAngle,
                   lightData.innerConeAngle, cosTheta);
    vec3 lightIntensity = spotAttenuation *
                          attenuation *
                          lightData.lightColor.rgb;

    // Final light contribution
    vec3 finalColor = (NdotL * (lightIntensity) *
                      (diffuse + specular)) +
                     ambient;
    ```

8. In the last step, the final color is then multiplied by the ambient occlusion factor (sampled from ambient occlusion texture calculated in the *Implementing screen space ambient occlusion* recipe) and the shadow visibility factor to account for shadows and ambient occlusion:

    ```
    float ao =
        texture(ambientOcclusion, fragTexCoord).r;
    finalColor *= ao;

    outColor = vec4(finalColor, 1.0);

    vec4 shadowProjPos =
    ```

```
        lightData.lightVP * vec4(worldPos.xyz, 1.0f);
float vis = PCF(shadowProjPos);

if (vis <= .001) {
  vis = .3;
}

outColor.xyz *= vis;
```

In the following screenshot, we present an image that shows a shadow created using the shadow map technique:

Figure 4.3 – A shadow using a shadow map

The following screenshot demonstrates the result of the SSR technique:

Figure 4.4 – SSR

In this chapter, we embarked on a journey to comprehend and implement some of the most influential techniques in 3D graphics for achieving real-time physically based effects using the Vulkan API. We began our exploration with the principles of G-buffer generation, a foundational concept of deferred rendering. This technique allows us to manage the complexity of modern lighting and shading, paving the way for the implementation of more advanced rendering effects. We then described techniques such as SSR and shadows, which are needed for simulating realism in rendered scenes. We also explored the complexities of lighting and shading with a deep dive into SSAO. This technique provided us with the tools to simulate the intricate ways light radiates in real life, adding depth and detail to corners in our 3D world. Finally, our exploration ended with the implementation of a lighting pass. By calculating the contributions of various light sources on each object in our scene, we successfully illuminated our 3D environment. We hope that you have gained a comprehensive understanding of several core techniques in modern lighting, shading, and shadows, which will empower you to create stunning and realistic 3D graphics with Vulkan.

5
Deciphering Order-Independent Transparency

Rendering transparent objects isn't always easy. While opaque objects can be rendered in any order, transparent objects need to be rendered from farthest to nearest relative to the camera, which implies an extra sorting step before performing the actual rendering. This depth sorting ensures that more distant objects are blended into the frame buffer first, followed by nearer objects, allowing for accurate composition of transparent layers.

Sorting can become computationally expensive and error-prone, especially when dealing with complex scenes, intersecting objects, or real-time rendering scenarios. Additionally, sorting fails to solve the problem of cyclic overlaps, where multiple objects interpenetrate in such a way that no single depth-sorting order can accurately represent their visual appearance.

Order-independent transparency techniques try to solve these problems by accumulating transparency information in a way that doesn't depend on the order in which objects are processed. This chapter delves into the complexities and challenges of rendering transparent objects, a task that requires precision and careful execution. In contrast to opaque objects, which can be rendered in any order, transparent objects necessitate rendering based on their depth in relation to the camera, from the farthest to the nearest. This involves an additional sorting step, which, while ensuring accurate composition of transparent layers, can prove to be computationally intensive and prone to errors.

In this chapter we're going to cover the following main topics:

- Implementing Depth-Peeling
- Implementing Dual Depth-Peeling
- Implementing Linked-List Order-Independent Transparency
- Implementing Weighted Order-Independent Transparency

Technical requirements

For this chapter, you will need to make sure you have VS 2022 installed along with the Vulkan SDK. Basic familiarity with the C++ programming language and an understanding of OpenGL or any other graphics API will be useful. Please revisit *Chapter 1, Vulkan Core Concepts*, under the *Technical requirements* section for details on setting up and building executables for this chapter. All recipes for this chapter are encapsulated in a single executable and can be launched using `Chapter05_Transparency.exe` executable.

Implementing Depth-Peeling

Depth Peeling was introduced in 2001 by Cass Everitt as a solution to render semi-transparent geometry without the need to sort the geometry from back-to-front. The technique consists of rendering the scene multiple times (passes). At each pass, only the nearest fragments to the camera are rendered and their depth is collected to be used on the next pass. On each pass, except for the first pass, fragments closer than the ones in the depth pass collected in the previous iteration are discarded. This process *peels* the scene into consecutive layers, from front to back. At the end of the process, all layers are blended into one final image, which is then blended once more with the background.

Getting ready

In the repository mentioned in *Technical requirements*, the Depth Peeling algorithm is implemented by the `DepthPeeling` class, located in `source/enginecore/passes/DepthPeeling.hpp` and `cpp` files. In this recipe, you will learn how to peel away or progressively remove layers of transparent objects in your rendering process. This technique ensures accurate rendering by handling each layer individually from the farthest to the nearest, thus improving the overall visual quality of scenes with complex overlapping transparencies.

The algorithm consists of rendering the scene repeatedly, storing the depth map at the end of each pass. The fragments nearest to the camera are blended with the previous pass (or an empty framebuffer for the first pass). The current pass fragment depth is discarded if it is smaller than the depth from the last pass, as summarized in *Figure 5.1*:

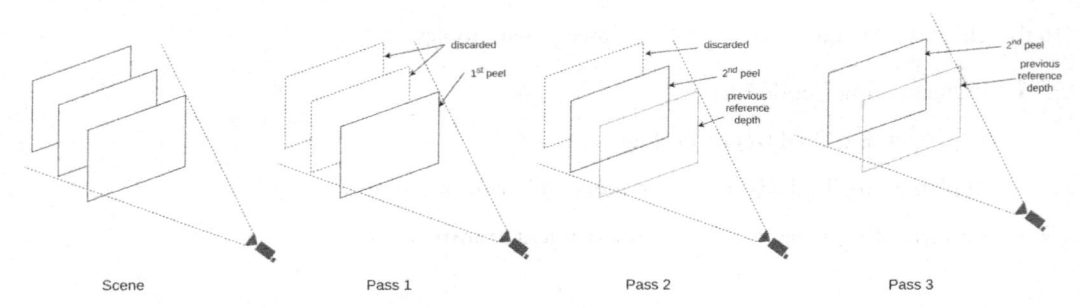

Figure 5.1 –Depth Peeling algorithm with 3 planes

Implementing Depth-Peeling

We've provided a foundational understanding of this technique in the preceding section. Moving forward, we will delve deeper, guiding you through a detailed, step-by-step process on how to practically implement this technique using Vulkan.

How to do it…

The algorithm uses two sets of depth maps and two sets of color attachments to perform a ping-pong operation between passes. The depth map obtained during one pass is used as a reference depth map on the next, while a second depth map is then used as a depth attachment. The same thing is done with two color attachments: one is used to store the blending of the current pass, while the other is used as the reference, generated in the previous pass. The subsequent steps will guide you through the actual execution of these operations. With the help of a detailed diagram provided below, you will be able to visualize and better understand the intricate workings of this algorithm.

Figure 5.2 effectively illustrates the described process, aiding in your comprehension and application of this intricate technique:

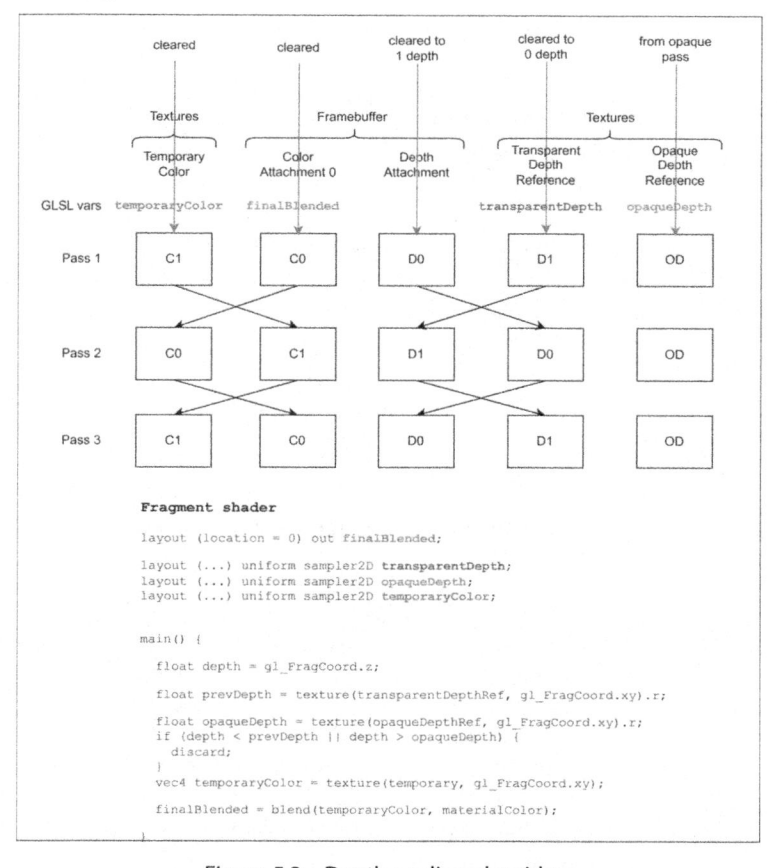

Figure 5.2 – Depth peeling algorithm

Now we will go through steps on how to perform this recipe.

1. The algorithm is performed by the `DepthPeeling::draw` method, which starts by clearing the depth map 1 and both color attachments:

```cpp
void DepthPeeling::draw(
    VkCommandBuffer commandBuffer, int index,
    const std::vector<
        std::shared_ptr<VulkanCore::Buffer>>
        &buffers,
    uint32_t numMeshes) {
{
  // Clear Depth 1
  vkCmdClearDepthStencilImage(
      commandBuffer,
      depthTextures_[1]->vkImage(),
      VK_IMAGE_LAYOUT_TRANSFER_DST_OPTIMAL,
      &clearDepth, 1, &range);
}
{
  // Clear color attachments
  vkCmdClearColorImage(
      commandBuffer,
      colorTextures_[0]->vkImage(),
      VK_IMAGE_LAYOUT_TRANSFER_DST_OPTIMAL,
      &clearColor, 1, &range);
  vkCmdClearColorImage(
      commandBuffer,
      colorTextures_[1]->vkImage(),
      VK_IMAGE_LAYOUT_TRANSFER_DST_OPTIMAL,
      &clearColor, 1, &range);
}
```

2. Both the color and depth attachments start with the color and depth attachments with index equal to 0:

```cpp
VulkanCore::DynamicRendering::
    AttachmentDescription colorAttachmentDesc{
        .imageView =
            colorTextures_[0]->vkImageView(),
        .imageLayout =
            VK_IMAGE_LAYOUT_COLOR_ATTACHMENT_OPTIMAL,
        .attachmentLoadOp =
            VK_ATTACHMENT_LOAD_OP_LOAD,
        .attachmentStoreOp =
```

```
            VK_ATTACHMENT_STORE_OP_STORE,
        .clearValue = clearValues[0],
    };

VulkanCore::DynamicRendering::
    AttachmentDescription depthAttachmentDesc{
        .imageView =
            depthTextures_[0]->vkImageView(),
        .imageLayout =
            VK_IMAGE_LAYOUT_DEPTH_STENCIL_ATTACHMENT_OPTIMAL,
        .attachmentLoadOp =
            VK_ATTACHMENT_LOAD_OP_CLEAR,
        .attachmentStoreOp =
            VK_ATTACHMENT_STORE_OP_STORE,
        .clearValue = clearValues[1],
    };
```

3. The algorithm repeats a number of times, equal to the number of passes. Care must be taken to transition each attachment to the correct layout, obeying the ping-ponging mechanism: a texture used as a color attachment before needs to be transitioned to a texture that will be read by a shader and vice-versa:

```
for (uint32_t currentPeel = 0;
    currentPeel < numPeels_; ++currentPeel) {

  colorTextures_[currentPeel % 2]
      ->transitionImageLayout(
          commandBuffer,
          VK_IMAGE_LAYOUT_COLOR_ATTACHMENT_OPTIMAL);
  colorTextures_[(currentPeel + 1) % 2]
      ->transitionImageLayout(
          commandBuffer,
          VK_IMAGE_LAYOUT_SHADER_READ_ONLY_OPTIMAL);

  depthTextures_[currentPeel % 2]
      ->transitionImageLayout(
          commandBuffer,
          VK_IMAGE_LAYOUT_DEPTH_STENCIL_ATTACHMENT_OPTIMAL);
  depthTextures_[(currentPeel + 1) % 2]
      ->transitionImageLayout(
          commandBuffer,
          VK_IMAGE_LAYOUT_SHADER_READ_ONLY_OPTIMAL);

  colorAttachmentDesc.imageView =
```

```
                colorTextures_[currentPeel % 2]
                    ->vkImageView();
        depthAttachmentDesc.imageView =
                depthTextures_[currentPeel % 2]
                    ->vkImageView();
```

4. Then we begin the render pass, issue the draw call, and end the pass:

```
        VulkanCore::DynamicRendering::beginRenderingCmd(
            commandBuffer,
            colorTextures_[currentPeel % 2]
                ->vkImage(),
            0,
            {{0, 0},
             {colorTextures_[currentPeel % 2]
                  ->vkExtents()
                  .width,
              colorTextures_[currentPeel % 2]
                  ->vkExtents()
                  .height}},
            1, 0, {colorAttachmentDesc},
            &depthAttachmentDesc, nullptr,
            colorTextures_[currentPeel % 2]
                ->vkLayout(),
            VK_IMAGE_LAYOUT_COLOR_ATTACHMENT_OPTIMAL);

        vkCmdSetViewport(commandBuffer, 0, 1,
                         &viewport_);
        vkCmdSetScissor(commandBuffer, 0, 1,
                        &scissor_);

        pipeline_->bind(commandBuffer);

        ... // Perform the draw call

        VulkanCore::DynamicRendering::endRenderingCmd(
            commandBuffer,
            colorTextures_[currentPeel % 2]
                ->vkImage(),
            VK_IMAGE_LAYOUT_UNDEFINED,
            VK_IMAGE_LAYOUT_UNDEFINED);
```

5. The images are transitioned to the correct layout by the render pass, so all we need to do is copy the result of the current pass into the other texture that will be used as the color attachment during the next pass:

```
vkCmdBlitImage(
    commandBuffer,
    colorTextures_[currentPeel % 2]
        ->vkImage(),
    VK_IMAGE_LAYOUT_TRANSFER_SRC_OPTIMAL,
    colorTextures_[(currentPeel + 1) % 2]
        ->vkImage(),
    VK_IMAGE_LAYOUT_TRANSFER_DST_OPTIMAL, 1,
    &region, VK_FILTER_NEAREST);
```

6. The vertex fragment is not special for depth peeling, but the fragment shader must discard fragments that are closer to the camera than the fragments collected in the previous pass. The fragment shader also performs the blending into the current attachment:

```
#version 460

layout(set = 1,
       binding = 0) uniform ObjectProperties {
  vec4 color;
  mat4 model;
}objectProperties;

layout(set = 2,
       binding = 0) uniform sampler2D depth;
layout(set = 2, binding = 2) uniform sampler2D
    temporaryColor;

layout(location = 0) out vec4 outColor;

void main() {
  float fragDepth = gl_FragCoord.z;

  float peelDepth =
      texture(depth, gl_FragCoord.xy /
                         textureSize(depth, 0))
          .r;

  if (fragDepth <= peelDepth) {
    discard;
  }
```

```
        vec4 tmpColor =
            texture(temporaryColor,
                    gl_FragCoord.xy /
                        textureSize(temporaryColor, 0));
        vec3 mulTmpColor = tmpColor.xyz * tmpColor.a;
        vec3 mulObjProp = objectProperties.color.xyz *
                            (1.0 - tmpColor.a);

        outColor = vec4(
            tmpColor.a * (objectProperties.color.a *
                            objectProperties.color.rgb) +
                tmpColor.rgb,
            (1 - objectProperties.color.a) *
                tmpColor.a);
    }
```

The blending equation is a special one, used for front-to-back compositing, as described by Louis Bavoil and Kevin Myers in 2008 in their *Order Independent Transparency with Dual Depth Peeling* paper. The blending equation is:

$C_{dst} = A_{dst}(A_{src}C_{src}) + C_{dst}$

$A_{dst} = (1 - A_{src})A_{dst}$

In the following recipe, we will explore how to enhance the depth-peeling technique, making it more efficient.

Implementing Dual Depth-Peeling

One of the main drawbacks of the Depth Peeling algorithm is that it requires multiple passes, each of which may consist of rasterizing the entire scene. The **Dual Depth-Peeling** algorithm extends the original Depth Peeling algorithm by peeling two layers at the same time, almost effectively cutting the number of passes by half. In this recipe, we will focus on implementing the Dual Depth-Peeling algorithm. We will address one of the key limitations of the Depth Peeling algorithm, namely its requirement for multiple passes which may involve rasterizing the entire scene. You'll learn how the Dual Depth-Peeling algorithm improves upon the original by peeling two layers concurrently, thus potentially reducing the number of passes by nearly half. This insight will empower you to handle complex scenes with greater efficiency and speed.

Getting ready

In the repository, the Depth Peeling algorithm is implemented by the `DualDepthPeeling` class, located in `source/enginecore/passes/DualDepthPeeling.hpp` and `cpp` files.

Before we begin, we need to set the `VkPhysicalDeviceFeatures::independentBlend` property to true. This property allows us to use different blending equations for each attachment associated with a graphics pipeline.

On each pass, a depth map with two components, R and G (in the code we use the `VK_FORMAT_R32G32_SFLOAT` format), is used to store both the front and the back peels simultaneously. The blend equation used with the map is `VK_BLEND_OP_MAX`. When storing the current fragment's depth, we encode it as `vec2(-depth, depth)`. The R component stores the negative depth of the front peel, while the G component stores the actual depth of the back peel, The Max blending equation ensures that we only store the nearest front peel by negating it. The back peels are guaranteed to always be the farthest because they are stored as positive depths.

The front peel is blended with the modified blend equation:

$$C_{dst} = A_{dst}(A_{src} C_{src}) + C_{dst}$$
$$A_{dst} = (1 - A_{src}) A_{dst}$$

While the back peel is blended with the regular back-to-front blend equation

$$C_{dst} = A_{src} C_{src} + (1 - A_{src}) C_{dst}$$

With the preparatory steps outlined, you are now ready to delve into the implementation of the Dual Depth-Peeling algorithm. In the next section, we will guide you through the step-by-step process of executing this algorithm, using the insights and techniques discussed above.

How to do it...

The algorithm in Vulkan consists of using 2 color attachments, one for the front peel and one for the back peel. It also uses 2 depth buffers with the same format. One is used for the even numbered passes, while the other for the odd even passes.

1. We start by specifying the blend operations for each attachment:

    ```
    const VkPipelineColorBlendAttachmentState
        depthBlendState = {
        .blendEnable = true,
        .srcColorBlendFactor =
            VK_BLEND_FACTOR_SRC_ALPHA,
        .dstColorBlendFactor =
            VK_BLEND_FACTOR_ONE_MINUS_SRC_ALPHA,
        .colorBlendOp = VK_BLEND_OP_MAX,
        .srcAlphaBlendFactor =
            VK_BLEND_FACTOR_SRC_ALPHA,
        .dstAlphaBlendFactor =
            VK_BLEND_FACTOR_DST_ALPHA,
    ```

```
        .alphaBlendOp = VK_BLEND_OP_MAX,
        .colorWriteMask =
            VK_COLOR_COMPONENT_R_BIT |
            VK_COLOR_COMPONENT_G_BIT |
            VK_COLOR_COMPONENT_B_BIT |
            VK_COLOR_COMPONENT_A_BIT,
};

const VkPipelineColorBlendAttachmentState
    frontBlendState = {
    // front color attachment
    .blendEnable = true,
    .srcColorBlendFactor =
        VK_BLEND_FACTOR_DST_ALPHA,
    .dstColorBlendFactor =
        VK_BLEND_FACTOR_ONE,
    .colorBlendOp = VK_BLEND_OP_ADD,
    .srcAlphaBlendFactor =
        VK_BLEND_FACTOR_ZERO,
    .dstAlphaBlendFactor =
        VK_BLEND_FACTOR_ONE_MINUS_SRC_ALPHA,
    .alphaBlendOp = VK_BLEND_OP_ADD,
    .colorWriteMask =
        VK_COLOR_COMPONENT_R_BIT |
        VK_COLOR_COMPONENT_G_BIT |
        VK_COLOR_COMPONENT_B_BIT |
        VK_COLOR_COMPONENT_A_BIT,
};
const VkPipelineColorBlendAttachmentState
    backBlendState = {
    // back color attachment
    .blendEnable = true,
    .srcColorBlendFactor =
        VK_BLEND_FACTOR_SRC_ALPHA,
    .dstColorBlendFactor =
        VK_BLEND_FACTOR_ONE_MINUS_SRC_ALPHA,
    .colorBlendOp = VK_BLEND_OP_ADD,
    .srcAlphaBlendFactor =
        VK_BLEND_FACTOR_ZERO,
    .dstAlphaBlendFactor =
        VK_BLEND_FACTOR_ONE_MINUS_SRC_ALPHA,
```

```
        .alphaBlendOp = VK_BLEND_OP_ADD,
        .colorWriteMask =
            VK_COLOR_COMPONENT_R_BIT |
            VK_COLOR_COMPONENT_G_BIT |
            VK_COLOR_COMPONENT_B_BIT |
            VK_COLOR_COMPONENT_A_BIT,
    };
```

These instances of the `VkPipelineColorBlendAttachmentState` structure are added to the `VkPipelineColorBlendStateCreateInfo` structure when creating a graphics pipeline and are provided in the order the attachments will be set in the framebuffers.

2. The algorithm, implemented by `DualDepthPeeling::draw` method, starts by clearing the depth buffers and the color attachments:

```
    void DualDepthPeeling::draw(
        VkCommandBuffer commandBuffer, int index,
        const std::vector<
            std::shared_ptr<VulkanCore::Buffer>>
            &buffers,
        uint32_t numMeshes) {
    // Clear Depth 0
    {
      vkCmdClearColorImage(
          commandBuffer,
          depthMinMaxTextures_[0]->vkImage(),
          VK_IMAGE_LAYOUT_TRANSFER_DST_OPTIMAL,
          &clearColor, 1, &range);
    }
    // Clear Depth 1
    {
      vkCmdClearColorImage(
          commandBuffer,
          depthMinMaxTextures_[1]->vkImage(),
          VK_IMAGE_LAYOUT_TRANSFER_DST_OPTIMAL,
          &clearColor, 1, &range);
    }
    // Clear color attachments
    {
      for (uint32_t i = 0;
           i < colorTextures_.size(); ++i) {
```

```
        vkCmdClearColorImage(
            commandBuffer,
            colorTextures_[i]->vkImage(),
            VK_IMAGE_LAYOUT_TRANSFER_DST_OPTIMAL,
            &clearColor, 1, &range);
    }
}
```

3. The depth textures are then transitioned for the first pass:

```
depthMinMaxTextures_[0]->transitionImageLayout(
    commandBuffer,
    VK_IMAGE_LAYOUT_COLOR_ATTACHMENT_OPTIMAL);
depthMinMaxTextures_[1]->transitionImageLayout(
    commandBuffer,
    VK_IMAGE_LAYOUT_SHADER_READ_ONLY_OPTIMAL);
```

4. Both the front and back textures are bound as attachments and are loaded and stored for each pass. One of the depth textures is also bound as an attachment and is cleared to (-99,999; 99,999) and stored after each pass. The other depth texture is bound as a texture for read by the fragment shader:

```
VulkanCore::DynamicRendering::AttachmentDescription
    colorAttachmentDesc_Front{
        .imageView = colorTextures_[0]
                        ->vkImageView(),
        .imageLayout =
            VK_IMAGE_LAYOUT_COLOR_ATTACHMENT_OPTIMAL,
        .attachmentLoadOp =
            VK_ATTACHMENT_LOAD_OP_LOAD,
        .attachmentStoreOp =
            VK_ATTACHMENT_STORE_OP_STORE,
    };
VulkanCore::DynamicRendering::AttachmentDescription
    colorAttachmentDesc_Back{
        .imageView = colorTextures_[1]
                        ->vkImageView(),
        .imageLayout =
            VK_IMAGE_LAYOUT_COLOR_ATTACHMENT_OPTIMAL,
        .attachmentLoadOp =
            VK_ATTACHMENT_LOAD_OP_LOAD,
        .attachmentStoreOp =
            VK_ATTACHMENT_STORE_OP_STORE,
    };
const VkClearValue clearDepthMinMax = {
```

```cpp
            .color = {-99999.0f, -99999.0f, 0.0f,
                      0.0f},
    };
    VulkanCore::DynamicRendering::AttachmentDescription
        depthMinMaxAttachmentDesc{
            .imageView =
                depthMinMaxTextures_[0]
                    ->vkImageView(),
            .imageLayout =
                VK_IMAGE_LAYOUT_COLOR_ATTACHMENT_OPTIMAL,
            .attachmentLoadOp =
                VK_ATTACHMENT_LOAD_OP_CLEAR,
            .attachmentStoreOp =
                VK_ATTACHMENT_STORE_OP_STORE,
            .clearValue = clearDepthMinMax,
    };
```

5. For each pass we start by transitioning the color and depth attachments to the correct layouts:

```cpp
    for (uint32_t currentPeel = 0;
         currentPeel < numPeels_;
         ++currentPeel) {
      const uint32_t readIdx = currentPeel % 2;

      colorTextures_[0]->transitionImageLayout(
          commandBuffer,
          VK_IMAGE_LAYOUT_COLOR_ATTACHMENT_OPTIMAL);
      colorTextures_[1]->transitionImageLayout(
          commandBuffer,
          VK_IMAGE_LAYOUT_SHADER_READ_ONLY_OPTIMAL);

      depthMinMaxTextures_[currentPeel % 2]
          ->transitionImageLayout(
              commandBuffer,
              VK_IMAGE_LAYOUT_COLOR_ATTACHMENT_OPTIMAL);
      depthMinMaxTextures_[(currentPeel + 1) %
                           2]
          ->transitionImageLayout(
              commandBuffer,
              VK_IMAGE_LAYOUT_SHADER_READ_ONLY_OPTIMAL);

      depthMinMaxAttachmentDesc.imageView =
          depthMinMaxTextures_[readIdx]
              ->vkImageView();
```

6. The attachments are provided for the render pass using dynamic rendering, the scene is rendered, and the pass is completed:

```
VulkanCore::DynamicRendering::
    beginRenderingCmd(
        commandBuffer,
        colorTextures_[0]->vkImage(), 0,
        {{0, 0},
         {colorTextures_[0]
             ->vkExtents()
             .width,
          colorTextures_[0]
             ->vkExtents()
             .height}},
        1, 0,
        {depthMinMaxAttachmentDesc,
         colorAttachmentDesc_Front,
         colorAttachmentDesc_Back},
        &depthAttachmentDesc, nullptr,
        colorTextures_[0]->vkLayout(),
        VK_IMAGE_LAYOUT_COLOR_ATTACHMENT_OPTIMAL);

vkCmdSetViewport(commandBuffer, 0, 1,
                &viewport_);
vkCmdSetScissor(commandBuffer, 0, 1,
                &scissor_);

pipeline_->bind(commandBuffer);

// Draw geometry

VulkanCore::DynamicRendering::
    endRenderingCmd(
        commandBuffer,
        colorTextures_[0]->vkImage(),
        VK_IMAGE_LAYOUT_UNDEFINED,
        VK_IMAGE_LAYOUT_UNDEFINED);
}
```

7. Once all the passes are completed, one last step remains which is consists of blending the last front and back peels. The front peel is provided as a color attachment and as a texture for the shader, while the back color is only provided as a texture for reading by the shader.

```
{
  {
    VulkanCore::DynamicRendering::
        beginRenderingCmd(...);

    vkCmdSetViewport(commandBuffer, 0, 1,
                     &viewport_);
    vkCmdSetScissor(commandBuffer, 0, 1,
                    &scissor_);

    pipelineFinal_->bind(commandBuffer);
    vkCmdDraw(commandBuffer, 4, 1, 0, 0);
    VulkanCore::DynamicRendering::
        endRenderingCmd(...);
  }
}
```

This last pass consists of drawing a rectangle the size of the viewport and used solely for blending the two peels

8. The main dual depth peeling fragment shader reads the depth value of the fragment output from the previous pass, decodes it, and decided whether the fragment should be discarded or not:

```
#version 460
const float MAX_DEPTH = 99999.0;
void main() {
  float fragDepth = gl_FragCoord.z;

  vec2 lastDepth =
      texture(depth,
              gl_FragCoord.xy /
                  textureSize(depth, 0)).rg;

  depthMinMax.rg = vec2(-MAX_DEPTH);
  frontColorOut = vec4(0.0f);
  backColorOut = vec4(0.0f);

  float nearestDepth = -lastDepth.x;
  float furthestDepth = lastDepth.y;
  float alphaMultiplier = 1.0 - lastFrontColor.a;
```

```glsl
    if (fragDepth < nearestDepth ||
        fragDepth > furthestDepth) {
      return;
    }
    if (fragDepth > nearestDepth &&
        fragDepth < furthestDepth) {
      depthMinMax = vec2(-fragDepth, fragDepth);
      return;
    }
    vec4 color = objectProperties.color;
    if (fragDepth == nearestDepth) {
      frontColorOut = vec4(
          color.rgb * color.a, color.a);
    } else {
      backColorOut = color;
    }
  }
```

9. The final pass, where the front and back peels are blended, uses a simple fragment shader:

```glsl
    #version 460
    layout(set = 0, binding = 0)
        uniform sampler2D front;
    layout(set = 0, binding = 1)
        uniform sampler2D back;

    layout(location = 0) in vec2
        fragTexCoord;

    layout(location = 0) out vec4 outColor;

    void main() {
      const vec4 frontColor =
          texture(front, fragTexCoord);
      const vec4 backColor =
          texture(back, fragTexCoord);
      outColor =
          vec4(((backColor)*frontColor.a +
               frontColor)
                  .rgb,
              (1.0 - backColor.a) *
                  frontColor.a);
    }
```

Having delved into the intricacies of the Dual Depth-Peeling algorithm, we will now shift our focus to another advanced technique in the next recipe.

Implementing Linked-List Order-Independent Transparency

Order Independent Transparency uses a per pixel linked list to handle transparency, it makes use of data structures, specifically linked lists, to store fragments for each pixel. Each node of the list contains information about a fragment's color and depth value, and the nodes are connected in a way that follows the order of fragments arrival, thus making sorting unnecessary.

This approach effectively eliminates overdrawing, and artifacts associated with depth sorting. By focusing on the depth value of each fragment, the approach provides a more accurate, visually pleasing representation of transparent objects. In this recipe, we will delve into the detailed process of implementing the Linked-List **Order-Independent Transparency** (**OIT**) technique. You'll learn how this technique leverages per pixel linked lists to efficiently manage transparency, eliminating the issues of overdrawing and depth sorting artifacts.

Getting ready

In the repository, the Linked list algorithm is implemented by the `OitLinkedListPass` class, located in `source/enginecore/passes/ OitLinkedListPass.hpp` and `cpp` files. The corresponding shaders are `source/enginecore/resources/shaders/OitLinkedListBuildPass.frag` and `source/enginecore/resources/shaders/ OITLinkedListCompositePass.frag`

The algorithm begins by initializing an empty list for each pixel, and as the scene is rendered, it adds nodes to the list in the order in which they are processed. This is done in a two-pass rendering stage. In the first pass, also known as the build pass, each fragment's depth, color, and next-node pointer are written into a buffer. The second pass, also known as resolve or composite pass, goes through the list from back-to-front for each pixel and blends the colors based on depth values, resulting in the final pixel color.

How to do it...

To implement a per pixel linked list, we need to maintain various buffers.

1. The `OitLinkedListPass::init` method is tasked with initializing a variety of resources. It establishes both the Build pass and the Composite pass pipelines. Furthermore, it arranges the necessary resources for the Build pass pipeline. The code snippet below highlights some key resources configured during the initialization phase.

A. `atomicCounterBuffer_`: This buffer is created to hold an atomic counter. The counter is used to allocate slots in the linked list buffer for storing new fragments.

B. `linkedListBuffer_`: This is the main buffer that holds the linked lists of fragments for each pixel. Each pixel can have multiple fragments, and each fragment is represented as a `Node` in the linked list. The size of this buffer is determined by the number of pixels in the swapchain's extent (its width and height), the number of slots per pixel, and the size of the Node structure.

C. `linkedListHeadPtrTexture_`: This buffer stores the head pointers for the linked lists of each pixel. A head pointer points to the first Node of a linked list. This buffer is created as a 2D texture (image) because it needs to store a pointer for each pixel in the swapchain's extents. The format `VK_FORMAT_R32_UINT` indicates that each element in the texture is a 32-bit unsigned integer, which is suitable for representing a pointer.

```
atomicCounterBuffer_ = context->createBuffer(
    sizeof(AtomicCounter), ...);

auto bufferSize = width * height *
                  slotsPerPixel *
                  sizeof(Node);

linkedListBuffer_ = context_->createBuffer(
    bufferSize, ...);

linkedListHeadPtrTexture_ =
    context->createTexture(...);
```

2. The actual magic of the algorithm happens during the `draw` function. As a first step, we are setting the pixels in `linkedListHeadPtrTexture_` to zero with `vkCmdClearColorImage` function, and filling the `linkedListBuffer_` and `atomicCounterBuffer_` with zeros using `vkCmdFillBuffer`, just to reset everything to null state before we begin writing to it.

```
vkCmdClearColorImage(
    commandBuffer,
    linkedListHeadPtrTexture_
        ->vkImage(),
    VK_IMAGE_LAYOUT_GENERAL,
    &clearColor, 1, &auxClearRanges);

vkCmdFillBuffer(
    commandBuffer,
    linkedListBuffer_->vkBuffer(), 0,
    VK_WHOLE_SIZE, 0);
vkCmdFillBuffer(
```

```
            commandBuffer,
            atomicCounterBuffer_->vkBuffer(), 0,
            VK_WHOLE_SIZE, 0);
```

3. The next step is to set up correct memory barriers. These barriers ensure that all clear operations finish before the shader starts reading from or writing to the buffers. The first barrier is a memory barrier:

```
      const VkPipelineStageFlags
          srcStageFlags =
              VK_PIPELINE_STAGE_TRANSFER_BIT;
      const VkPipelineStageFlags dstStageFlags =
          VK_PIPELINE_STAGE_FRAGMENT_SHADER_BIT;
      {
        const VkMemoryBarrier barrier = {
            .sType =
                VK_STRUCTURE_TYPE_MEMORY_BARRIER,
            .srcAccessMask =
                VK_ACCESS_TRANSFER_WRITE_BIT,
            .dstAccessMask =
                VK_ACCESS_SHADER_READ_BIT |
                VK_ACCESS_SHADER_WRITE_BIT,
        };
        vkCmdPipelineBarrier(
            commandBuffer, srcStageFlags,
            dstStageFlags,
            0,
            1, &barrier,
            0, VK_NULL_HANDLE,
            0, VK_NULL_HANDLE);
```

4. The other two barriers are buffer barriers, one for the linked list buffer and one for the atomic counter buffer:

```
        const VkBufferMemoryBarrier bufferBarriers[2] = {
            {
                .sType =
                    VK_STRUCTURE_TYPE_BUFFER_MEMORY_BARRIER,
                .srcAccessMask =
                    VK_ACCESS_TRANSFER_WRITE_BIT,
                .dstAccessMask =
                    VK_ACCESS_SHADER_READ_BIT |
                    VK_ACCESS_SHADER_WRITE_BIT,
                .buffer = linkedListBuffer_->vkBuffer(),
                .size = linkedListBuffer_->size(),
```

```
            },
            {
                .sType =
                    VK_STRUCTURE_TYPE_BUFFER_MEMORY_BARRIER,
                .srcAccessMask =
                    VK_ACCESS_TRANSFER_WRITE_BIT,
                .dstAccessMask =
                    VK_ACCESS_SHADER_READ_BIT |
                    VK_ACCESS_SHADER_WRITE_BIT,
                .buffer = atomicCounterBuffer_->vkBuffer(),
                .size = atomicCounterBuffer_->size(),
            },
        };
        vkCmdPipelineBarrier(
            commandBuffer, srcStageFlags,
            dstStageFlags, 0, 0, nullptr, 2,
            &bufferBarriers[0], 0, nullptr);
    }
```

5. In the next step descriptor sets are bound, updated, and the vertex and index buffers are bound to the pipeline. Then the indexed draw command is issued for each mesh.

```
pipeline_->bind(commandBuffer);
for (uint32_t meshIdx = 0;
     meshIdx < numMeshes; ++meshIdx) {
  // ...
  vkCmdDrawIndexed(commandBuffer,
              vertexCount, 1, 0, 0,
              0);
}
```

6. The vertex fragment is not special, but the fragment shader must maintain a linked list along with head pointer. Below we present the code breakdown for `OitLinkedListBuildPass.frag` which is responsible for the build pass of the linked list OIT algorithm:

   A. We start by defining a Node struct, which represents a node in a linked list for handling transparency. It contains the color and the index of the previous node. Afterwards, we declare several uniform and buffer variables, used for object properties, an atomic counter, a linked list of nodes, and an image for head pointers.

```
struct Node {
  vec4 color;
  uint previousIndex;
  float depth;
  uint padding1; // add 4 byte padding
```

```
                    // for alignment
    uint padding2; // add 4 byte padding
                    // for alignment
};

layout(set = 1, binding = 0) uniform
    ObjectProperties {
  vec4 color;
  mat4 model;
}
objectProperties;

layout(set = 2, binding = 0) buffer
    AtomicCounter {
  uint counter;
};
layout(set = 2,
       binding = 1) buffer LinkedList {
  Node transparencyList[];
}
transparencyLinkedList;

layout(set = 2, binding = 2,
       r32ui) uniform coherent uimage2D
    headPointers;
```

B. The main function performs an atomic add operation on the atomic counter to get a unique index for each fragment. After calculating the size of the image and ensuring the new node index doesn't exceed the maximum size of the linked list, it performs an atomic exchange operation to insert the new node at the beginning of the linked list. Finally, it sets the properties of the new node in the linked list.

```
void main() {
  // Set the output color to transparent
  outputColor = vec4(0.0);

  // Atomic operation to get unique
  // index for each fragment, don't
  // return 0 since that will be used as
  // ll terminator
  uint newNodeIndex =
      atomicAdd(counter, 1) + 1;

  ivec2 size = imageSize(headPointers);
```

```glsl
    // max size of linked list * width *
    // height
    if (newNodeIndex >
        (10 * size.x * size.y) - 1) {
      return;
    }

    // Atomic operation to insert the new
    // node at the beginning of the linked
    // list
    uint oldHeadIndex =
        imageAtomicExchange(
            headPointers,
            ivec2(gl_FragCoord.xy),
            newNodeIndex);

    transparencyLinkedList
        .transparencyList[newNodeIndex]
        .previousIndex = oldHeadIndex;
    transparencyLinkedList
        .transparencyList[newNodeIndex]
        .color = objectProperties.color;
    transparencyLinkedList
        .transparencyList[newNodeIndex]
        .depth = gl_FragCoord.z;
    transparencyLinkedList
        .transparencyList[newNodeIndex]
        .padding1 = 0;
    transparencyLinkedList
        .transparencyList[newNodeIndex]
        .padding2 = 0;
}
```

7. The next and final step is to draw a full screen quad. Before performing the full screen quad pass, we set up memory and buffer barriers to ensure synchronization for the `linkedListBuffer_` and the `linkedListHeadPtrTexture_` since these resources are used during the composite pass.

8. Lastly, the composite pass fragment shader starts by first getting the head of the linked list for the current pixel. The list is stored in a buffer, and each pixel corresponds to the first node of a linked list of all fragments that affect that pixel. An array to temporarily store the nodes for sorting is created. We then iterate over the linked list, retrieving each node and storing it in the temporary array. It continues until it reaches the end of the list (denoted by `nodeIndex` being 0) or when it has retrieved 20 nodes:

```
void main() {
  outputColor = vec4(0.0);
  // Get the head of the linked list for
  // the current pixel
  uint nodeIndex = imageLoad(headPointers,
              ivec2(gl_FragCoord.xy)).x;

  // Create a temporary array to store
  // the nodes for sorting
  Node nodes[20]; // Assuming a maximum
                  // of 20 overlapping
                  // fragments
  int numNodes = 0;
  // Iterate over the linked list
  while (nodeIndex != 0 &&
         numNodes < 20) {
    nodes[numNodes] = transparencyLinkedList.
transparencyList[nodeIndex];
    nodeIndex = nodes[numNodes].previousIndex;
    numNodes++;
  }
```

9. The nodes in the array are sorted in descending order based on their depth values using a simple bubble sort algorithm. This ensures that the nodes closest to the camera are blended last:

```
for (int i = 0; i < numNodes; i++) {
  for (int j = i + 1; j < numNodes; j++) {
    if (nodes[j].depth > nodes[i].depth) {
      Node temp = nodes[i];
      nodes[i] = nodes[j];
      nodes[j] = temp;
    }
  }
}
```

10. Finally, the colors of each node are blended from back to front using the mix function:

```
// Blend the colors from back to front
for (int i = 0; i < numNodes; i++) {
  outputColor = mix(outputColor, nodes[i].color,
         nodes[i].color.a);
}
}
```

This algorithm gives a very good result and is an excellent option if you value correctness. It's a bit slower than the one presented in the next recipe, but it is by far the most intuitive algorithm amongst all the different algorithms we discussed in this chapter.

There's more...

We would like to note an additional technique, known as **Tail Blending**, that can be effectively combined with the technique discussed above. One of the limitations of our approach is the maximum number of fragments that can be accommodated for each pixel, which is typically dictated by the anticipated depth complexity of the scene and the memory available. In more intricate scenes with numerous overlapping transparent objects, the fragment count for a pixel may surpass this limit. That's when Tail Blending becomes handy. When a linked list reaches its capacity, any extra fragments are directly blended with the color of the last node in the list, also known as the *tail*, hence the term *Tail Blending*. The benefit of tail blending is its ability to process scenes with extremely high depth complexity without the need to expand the maximum length of the linked list, thereby conserving memory. However, a potential drawback is that it might yield less precise results since blending is order-dependent and the fragments blended with the tail aren't arranged in relation to the other fragments in the list.

See also

Please see the following link on:

- Exploring and Expanding the Continuum of OIT Algorithms: http://cwyman.org/papers/hpg16_oitContinuum.pdf

Implementing Weighted Order-Independent Transparency

Weighted Order-Independent Transparency (WOIT) uses a different idea to tackle transparency, by using the concept of weighted averages rather than using data structures like linked lists or layers like depth peeling.

This method doesn't require sorting or linked lists or multiple passes, reducing the overhead associated with those operations. The final color is calculated by normalizing the color buffer with the weight buffer, which provides an aggregate view of the colors and their weights. Although it may not be as accurate as per-pixel linked lists in complex scenarios, WOIT offers a performance-efficient solution for handling transparency in scenes with lower depth complexity. In this recipe, you will gain an understanding of the WOIT technique. We will explore how this method employs weighted averages to handle transparency, eschewing the need for data structures like linked lists or multiple passes, thereby reducing associated overhead.

Getting ready

In the repository, the WOIT algorithm is implemented by the `OitWeightedPass` class, located in source `/enginecore/passes/ OitWeightedPass.hpp` and `cpp` files. The corresponding shaders are `source/enginecore/resources/shaders/OitWeighted.frag` and `source/enginecore/resources/shaders/ OITWeightedComposite.frag`

The WOIT algorithm begins by initializing two empty buffers for each pixel, one for accumulating color and the other for accumulating weights. As the scene is rendered, the algorithm processes each transparent fragment and updates these buffers in a single rendering pass. During this pass, each fragment's color is multiplied by its alpha value (the weight) and added to the color buffer, while the alpha value itself is added to the weight buffer. This process continues for all fragments, accumulating and blending their contributions based on their opacity. Once all fragments are processed, a final composite step is performed where the accumulated color in the color buffer is divided by the total weight in the weight buffer. This results in the final pixel color, providing a composite view of all transparent fragments based on their weights.

How to do it...

The following steps provides a guide on implementing the WOIT technique using the Vulkan API.

1. The `OitWeightedPass::init` method is tasked with initializing a variety of resources. It establishes both the Accumulation pass and the Composite pass pipelines. Furthermore, it arranges the necessary resources for the accumulation pass pipeline.

   The `colorTexture_` uses the `VK_FORMAT_R16G16B16A16_SFLOAT` format. This format represents 4 channels (R, G, B, A) of 16-bit floating point numbers, providing high precision for color representation. It's important for the color buffer to have a high precision format because during the accumulation pass, colors from various fragments are added together:

   ```
   colorTexture_ =
        context->createTexture(VK_IMAGE_TYPE_2D, VK_FORMAT_
   R16G16B16A16_SFLOAT ...
   ```

2. The `alphaTexture_` uses the `VK_FORMAT_R16_SFLOAT` format, which is a single 16-bit floating point number. This is adequate because we're only storing the alpha (opacity) value:

   ```
   alphaTexture_ =
        context->createTexture(VK_IMAGE_TYPE_2D, VK_FORMAT_R16_
   SFLOAT ...
   ```

3. Since WOIT depends upon blending, it's important to set up blending attachments correctly. The pipeline descriptor `gpDesc` below is created with two `VkPipelineColorBlendAttachmentState` structures, one for each attachment. For the first blend attachment (corresponding to the color texture), the blend factors are set to `VK_BLEND_FACTOR_ONE` for both the source and destination, and the blend operation is `VK_BLEND_OP_ADD`. This effectively implements additive blending, where the new fragment's color is added to the existing color in the color buffer.

```
const VulkanCore::Pipeline::
  GraphicsPipelineDescriptor gpDesc = {
    .blendAttachmentStates_ = {
      VkPipelineColorBlendAttachmentState{
        .blendEnable = VK_TRUE,
        .srcColorBlendFactor =
          VK_BLEND_FACTOR_ONE,
        .dstColorBlendFactor =
          VK_BLEND_FACTOR_ONE,
        .colorBlendOp = VK_BLEND_OP_ADD,
        .srcAlphaBlendFactor =
          VK_BLEND_FACTOR_ONE,
        .dstAlphaBlendFactor =
          VK_BLEND_FACTOR_ONE,
        .alphaBlendOp = VK_BLEND_OP_ADD,
        .colorWriteMask =
          VK_COLOR_COMPONENT_R_BIT |
          VK_COLOR_COMPONENT_G_BIT |
          VK_COLOR_COMPONENT_B_BIT |
          VK_COLOR_COMPONENT_A_BIT,
      },
```

4. For the second blend attachment (corresponding to the alpha texture), the source alpha blend factor is `VK_BLEND_FACTOR_ZERO`, and the destination alpha blend factor is `VK_BLEND_FACTOR_ONE_MINUS_SRC_COLOR`. This configuration ensures that the new fragment's alpha (or weight) is accumulated in the alpha buffer:

```
        VkPipelineColorBlendAttachmentState{
          .blendEnable = VK_TRUE,
          .srcColorBlendFactor =
            VK_BLEND_FACTOR_ZERO,
          .dstColorBlendFactor =
            VK_BLEND_FACTOR_ONE_MINUS_SRC_COLOR,
          .colorBlendOp = VK_BLEND_OP_ADD,
          .srcAlphaBlendFactor =
            VK_BLEND_FACTOR_ZERO,
```

```
                .dstAlphaBlendFactor =
                  VK_BLEND_FACTOR_ONE_MINUS_SRC_ALPHA,
                .alphaBlendOp = VK_BLEND_OP_ADD,
                .colorWriteMask =
                  VK_COLOR_COMPONENT_R_BIT |
                  VK_COLOR_COMPONENT_G_BIT |
                  VK_COLOR_COMPONENT_B_BIT |
                  VK_COLOR_COMPONENT_A_BIT,
            },
        },
    };
```

5. Next, we need to initialize the composite pipeline. This could be implemented as a Vulkan subpass, but for simplicity we have kept it as a separate pass. The composite pipeline is created with `VK_BLEND_FACTOR_ONE_MINUS_SRC_ALPHA` as `srcColorBlendFactor` and `VK_BLEND_FACTOR_SRC_ALPHA` as `dstColorBlendFactor`.

   This configuration causes the incoming fragment's color and alpha values to be blended with the current color and alpha in the frame buffer, with the incoming fragment's alpha value controlling how much of the incoming color overwrites the existing color.

6. The draw function is where the actual rendering occurs, the implementation is straightforward and uses `vkCmdDrawIndexed` to draw multiple meshes. Below we present the fragment shader used during this step. In this fragment shader, the view-space depth is scaled to provide depth weight; closer fragments are assigned larger weights. Then, the maximum color component multiplied by alpha is calculated to weigh vibrant pixels more. The calculated color weight is ensured to be no more than 1.0 and compared with the alpha to take the maximum value. The depth weight is then calculated and clamped within a specific range. The final weight is the product of color and depth weights. The color is then premultiplied by its alpha value to prevent over-saturation during blending. This shader outputs the weighted color and the original alpha of the fragment.

```
void main() {
  const float scaledDepth =
     -(inViewSpaceDepth * 3.0) / 200;
  float maxColorComponent =
     max(max(objectProperties.color.r,
             objectProperties.color.g),
         objectProperties.color.b);
  float weightedColor =
     maxColorComponent *
     objectProperties.color.a;
  float weightedColorAlpha =
     max(min(1.0, weightedColor),
```

```
            objectProperties.color.a);
    float depthWeight =
        0.03 /
        (1e-5 + pow(scaledDepth, 4.0));
    depthWeight =
        clamp(depthWeight, 0.01, 4000);
    const float weight =
        weightedColorAlpha * depthWeight;
    outputColor =
        vec4(objectProperties.color.rgb *
                objectProperties.color.a,
            objectProperties.color.a) *
        weight;
    outputAlpha =
        objectProperties.color.a;
}
```

7. The final step is drawing a full screen quad using composite pipeline, it reads the accumulated color and alpha from two textures (`colorData` and `alphaData`) for the current fragment. The accumulated color (`accumulateColor`) is the sum of the product of color, alpha, and weight for each fragment from the previous step. The alpha value (alpha) is the original alpha value of the fragment. In the output color (`outColor`), the RGB components of the accumulated color are divided by the accumulated alpha value to normalize them, with a minimum limit of 0.0001 to prevent division by zero. This is because the accumulated color was premultiplied by the alpha value (and weight) in the previous steps.

```
void main() {
  vec4 accumulateColor =
      texture(colorData, fragTexCoord);
  float alpha =
      texture(alphaData, fragTexCoord)
          .r;
  outColor = vec4(
      accumulateColor.rgb /
          max(accumulateColor.a, .0001),
      alpha);
}
```

This technique is faster than the linked-list one presented in recipe *Implementing Linked-List Order-Independent Transparency*, but it has its drawbacks, such as the weighting function which is prone to add artifacts to the result if not well designed and tested.

There's more...

In this chapter, we have explored various techniques for handling transparency. The following table highlights the advantages and disadvantages of each method:

Technique	Memory	Performance	Physically correct
Linked list OIT	High, depends upon scene complexity as well as maintained LinkedList size	Moderate speed, only requires two passes	Highly accurate, handles complex overlapping geometry very well
Dual Depth Peeling OIT	Moderate, requires storage of two depth buffer	Slower, since it requires multiple passes	Moderate accuracy, struggles with highly complex scene.
WOIT	Low, only needs to store weights & colors for each fragment.	Fast, since only single pass is required	Low accuracy, requires careful weight management that can depend upon scene.

Table 5.1 – Comparison of various techniques

We hope *Table 5.1* will help you decide which technique to use based upon your use case.

See also

Please see following link for more details on WOIT:

- WOIT: `https://jcgt.org/published/0002/02/09/`

6
Anti-Aliasing Techniques

Anti-aliasing can be achieved in many ways, the most common being the one usually provided by the graphics API. In this chapter, we start by looking at how to enable and use the anti-aliasing provided by Vulkan, going over a multitude of other techniques that are more suitable for other use cases that require better anti-aliasing or that need a different algorithm altogether, such as temporal anti-aliasing. In this chapter, we will guide you through various anti-aliasing techniques, starting from enabling and using the one provided by Vulkan to exploring other more advanced and suitable methods for different use cases. The goal is to empower you with the knowledge and skills to choose and implement the most appropriate anti-aliasing technique for your specific needs, thereby improving the visual quality of your rendered graphics.

In this chapter, we will cover the following recipes:

- Enabling and using Vulkan's MSAA
- Applying FXAA
- Utilizing TAA
- Applying DLSS

Technical requirements

For this chapter, you will need to make sure you have VS 2022 installed along with the Vulkan SDK. Basic familiarity with the C++ programming language and an understanding of OpenGL or any other graphics API will be useful. Please revisit *Chapter 1, Vulkan Core Concepts*, under the *Technical requirements* section for details on setting up and building executables for this chapter. This chapter has multiple recipes, which can be launched using the following executables:

1. Chapter06_MSAA.exe
2. Chapter06_FXAA.exe
3. Chapter06_TAA.exe
4. Chapter06_DLSS.exe

Enabling and using Vulkan's MSAA

MSAA is an anti-aliasing technique that is used to reduce the jagged edges that can appear on curved lines and diagonal edges. Here's an overview of how it works:

1. **Multiple samples**: Instead of sampling a pixel once (like in regular rendering), MSAA takes multiple samples within each pixel. For example, 4 x MSAA needs 4 samples while 8 x MSAA needs 8 samples. The fragment shader runs for each one of the samples, and their output is stored for processing in *step 3*.
2. **Edge detection**: MSAA only multi-samples pixels that are at the edges of geometry. This makes it more performance-efficient compared to techniques such as super-sampling, which samples the entire image at a higher resolution.
3. **Combining samples**: Once the samples are taken, they are averaged (or resolved) into a single-color value for the pixel. If some of the samples are within an object and some are outside it, the final pixel color will be a blend, creating a smoother transition and thereby reducing the appearance of jagged edges.

In this recipe, we will describe what steps you need to take to enable MSAA in Vulkan, as it is provided by the API.

Getting ready

Enabling MSAA in Vulkan requires changes to multiple locations in the source code. The following are high-level steps to implement MSAA:

1. First, you need to ensure that the system supports MSAA. Additionally, you need to determine the maximum number of samples per pixel that are supported.
2. Textures need to be created with the number of samples they support.
3. Additional textures need to be created to serve as the output after combining the samples (also referred to as resolve attachments).
4. Render passes need to specify the number of samples per attachment and provide extra information about the resolve attachments.
5. Finally, framebuffers need to refer to the resolve attachments.

Rendering with MSAA involves images with sample counts greater than 1. However, these multi-sampled images cannot be presented directly using `VK_IMAGE_LAYOUT_PRESENT_SRC_KHR`. The `VK_IMAGE_LAYOUT_PRESENT_SRC_KHR` layout is designed for single-sampled images that are ready for presentation, with one color value per pixel. That's why a *resolve* operation is needed to convert the multi-sampled image into a single-sampled image. The final anti-aliased output, which is suitable for presentation, needs to be written to another image with a sample count of `VK_SAMPLE_COUNT_1_BIT`. This implies that every color attachment with a sample count greater than 1 requires an associated attachment with a sample count equal to `VK_SAMPLE_COUNT_1_BIT`. These additional attachments, known as resolve attachments, are used to store the final anti-aliased output. During the resolve operation, the values from the multi-samples are combined and written into the *resolve* attachment, creating the final single-sample image that can be presented.

How to do it...

Enabling MSAA in Vulkan is not difficult but needs changes in multiple parts of the code. Here's a step-by-step guide on how to do it:

1. In the following code block, we deal with `VkPhysicalDeviceProperties` objects, specifically focusing on the `framebufferColorSampleCounts` and `framebufferDepthSampleCounts` properties. These properties help us determine the maximum number of samples per pixel supported for color and depth respectively. This capability is hardware-dependent, which makes it necessary to check it first before usage. The maximum supported value is found in the following:

   ```
   VkPhysicalDeviceProperties::limits::framebufferColorSampleCounts
   VkPhysicalDeviceProperties::limits::framebufferDepthSampleCounts
   ```

2. The maximum number of samples is provided as a bit field of type `VkSampleCountFlagBits`, with flags such as `VK_SAMPLE_COUNT_1_BIT`, `VK_SAMPLE_COUNT_2_BIT`, `VK_SAMPLE_COUNT_4_BIT`, and so on, up to `VK_SAMPLE_COUNT_64_BIT`.

3. During image creation, the number of samples that a texture supports must be specified. This is done by setting the `samples` member of the `VkImageCreateInfo` structure, which is of type `VkSampleCountFlagBits`, such as the following:

   ```
   VkImageCreateInfo newTexture = {
       ...
       .samples = VK_SAMPLE_COUNT_8_BIT,
   };
   ```

4. While creating a render pass, the attachment descriptions must indicate the sample count by setting the `VkAttachmentDescription::samples` field:

```
VkAttachmentDescription attachment = {
    ...
    .samples = VK_SAMPLE_COUNT_8_BIT,
};
```

5. An instance of the `VkAttachmentDescription` structure needs to be added to the render pass's list of attachments, `VkSubpassDescription::pColorAttachments`, for each resolve attachment in the render pass. The resolve attachments must have their samples field set to `VK_SAMPLE_COUNT_1_BIT`, as the resolution of the multi-sampled image results in a single sample per pixel. This is because the multiple samples from the multi-sampled image are resolved into one final color value for that pixel. Here is how you can create and configure such a `VkAttachmentDescription` instance:

```
VkAttachmentDescription resolveAttachment = {
    ...
    .samples = VK_SAMPLE_COUNT_1_BIT,
}
```

6. An instance of the `VkAttachmentReference` structure must be created to reference this resolve attachment:

```
VkAttachmentReference resolveAttachmentRef{
    .attachment = <index of resolve texture in the
attachmentDescriptor vector>,
    .layout =
        VK_IMAGE_LAYOUT_COLOR_ATTACHMENT_OPTIMAL,
}
```

The `VkAttachmentReference::attachment` field is an integer that points to the resolve attachment at the corresponding index of the `VkRenderPassCreateInfo::pAttachments` array.

7. Finally, the list of attachment references that describe the resolve attachments is added to the `VkSubpassDescription::pResolveAttachments` field.

Figure 6.1 illustrates how each component is set up and how they are referenced by a render pass and subpass description structures. The depth/stencil attachment must have the same sample count as the color attachments, and the number of resolve attachments must be equal to the number of color attachments.

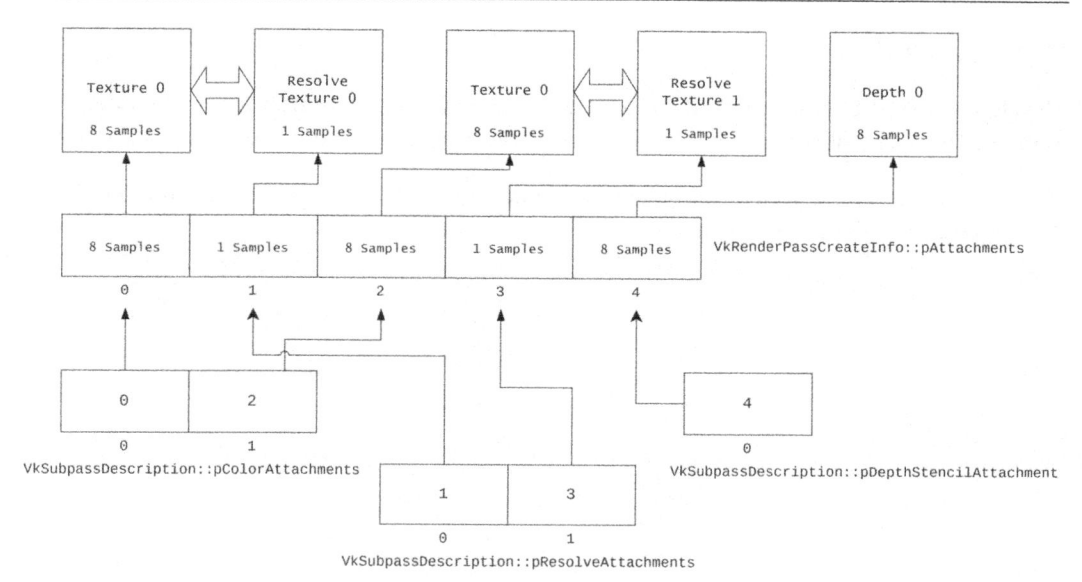

Figure 6.1 – Render pass configuration

In the preceding diagram, we showcased the configuration of texture sample count and its reference by both the render pass and subpass description structures. This arrangement is crucial for enabling MSAA in Vulkan.

Applying FXAA

FXAA is a screen-space anti-aliasing technique that can be implemented as an extra full-screen post-process pass. FXAA works by identifying edges in the image and then smoothing them to reduce the appearance of aliasing. Without the need for any additional information from the scene, FXAA can be easily integrated into existing code. It's also fast because it processes only the final rendered image pixels and some of their neighbors. In this recipe, you will learn about the FXAA technique. You will understand how it functions as a screen-space anti-aliasing method, how it can be applied through a post-process pass, and why it is a beneficial tool due to its ease of integration and speed. Note that FXAA is generally applied before gamma correction or any sRGB conversion. The reason for this is that FXAA works best on linear RGB data. If you apply FXAA after gamma correction or sRGB conversion, it may result in incorrect edge detection and thus less effective anti-aliasing.

Getting ready

The FXAA algorithm is implemented in our repository by the FXAAPass class, found in the source/enginecore/passes/FXAA.cpp and FXAA.hpp files. The shader used by the pass is located at source/enginecore/resources/shaders/fxaa.frag.

How to do it...

The algorithm can be implemented entirely in a fragment shader that uses the final render image as input. The shader also needs the size of the viewport, which can be provided as a push constant:

1. The shader is simple in terms of input and output and only needs an input texture and the size of the viewport for processing:

   ```
   #version 460

   layout(push_constant) uniform Viewport {
     uvec2 size;
   }
   ViewportSize;

   layout(set = 0, binding = 0) uniform sampler2D
       inputTexture;

   layout(location = 0) out vec4 outColor;
   ```

2. The FXAA algorithm operates on the luminance of the pixels, so we need a function to convert RGB values to luminance:

   ```
   float rgb2luma(vec3 rgb) {
     return dot(rgb, vec3(0.299, 0.587, 0.114));
   }
   ```

3. Here are some constants for the edge-detection part:

   ```
   const float EDGE_THRESHOLD_MIN = (1.0 / 16.0);
   const float EDGE_THRESHOLD_MAX = (1.0 / 8.0);
   const float PIXEL_BLEND_LIMIT_TO_REDUCE_BLURRING =
       (3.0 / 4.0);
   const float MIN_PIXEL_ALIASING_REQUIRED =
       (1.0 / 8.0);
   const float NUM_LOOP_FOR_EDGE_DETECTION = 1;
   ```

4. To simplify the code, we'll use an array to store the luminance and RGB values for the neighboring pixels. We'll also use constants to help refer to elements of the vector without using just integers:

   ```
   const int Center   = 0;
   const int Top      = 1;
   const int Bottom   = 2;
   const int Left     = 3;
   const int Right    = 4;
   const int TopRight = 5;
   ```

```
const int BottomRight = 6;
const int TopLeft     = 7;
const int BottomLeft  = 8;
vec2 offsets[] = {
    vec2( 0,  0), vec2( 0, -1), vec2( 0,  1),
    vec2(-1,  0), vec2( 1,  0), vec2( 1, -1),
    vec2( 1,  1), vec2(-1, -1), vec2(-1,  1) };
```

5. The algorithm is encapsulated in the `applyFXAA` function that takes the screen coordinates in pixels, the rendered image to be processed, and the size of the viewport:

   ```
   vec4 applyFXAA(vec2 screenCoord,
                  sampler2D inputTexture,
                  uvec2 viewportSize) {
   ```

6. The first step is to compute the luminance and the RGB values of all eight neighboring pixels, as well as the range between the lowest and the highest luminance. If the value is below a certain threshold, we don't perform the anti-aliasing. The **threshold** is used to determine whether a pixel is on an edge; its value represents the minimum difference in luminance that must exist between a pixel and its neighbors for that pixel to be considered part of an edge:

   ```
   const vec2 viewportSizeInverse = vec2(
       1.0 / viewportSize.x, 1.0 / viewportSize.y);
   const vec2 texCoord =
       screenCoord * viewportSizeInverse;

   float minLuma = 100000000;
   float maxLuma = 0;
   float lumas[9];
   vec3 rgb[9];
   vec3 rgbSum = vec3(0, 0, 0);
   for (int i = 0; i < 9; ++i) {
     rgb[i] =
         texture(inputTexture,
                 texCoord +
                     offsets[i] *
                         viewportSizeInverse)
             .rgb;
     rgbSum += rgb[i];
     lumas[i] = rgb2luma(rgb[i]);
     if (i < 5) {
       minLuma = min(lumas[i], minLuma);
       maxLuma = max(lumas[i], maxLuma);
     }
   ```

```
}
const float rangeLuma = maxLuma - minLuma;
if (rangeLuma <
    max(EDGE_THRESHOLD_MIN,
        EDGE_THRESHOLD_MAX * maxLuma)) {
  return vec4(rgb[Center], 1.0);
}
```

7. The difference between the average luminance of all neighboring pixels and the center pixels tells us whether we need to perform the anti-aliasing algorithm and the amount of blending required. It also clamps the blend amount between 0 and PIXEL_BLEND_LIMIT_TO_REDUCE_BLURRING to reduce blurring:

```
const float lumaTopBottom =
    lumas[Top] + lumas[Bottom];
const float lumaLeftRight =
    lumas[Left] + lumas[Right];
const float lumaTopCorners =
    lumas[TopLeft] + lumas[TopRight];
const float lumaBottomCorners =
    lumas[BottomLeft] + lumas[BottomRight];
const float lumaLeftCorners =
    lumas[TopLeft] + lumas[BottomLeft];
const float lumaRightCorners =
    lumas[TopRight] + lumas[BottomRight];
const float lumaTBLR =
    lumaTopBottom + lumaLeftRight;

const float averageLumaTBLR = (lumaTBLR) / 4.0;
const float lumaSubRange =
    abs(averageLumaTBLR - lumas[Center]);
float pixelblendAmount =
    max(0.0, (lumaSubRange / rangeLuma) -
                 MIN_PIXEL_ALIASING_REQUIRED);
pixelblendAmount = min(
    PIXEL_BLEND_LIMIT_TO_REDUCE_BLURRING,
    pixelblendAmount *
        (1.0 /
            (1.0 - MIN_PIXEL_ALIASING_REQUIRED)));
```

8. The next step consists of determining whether the edge is more vertical than horizontal and initializing the variables that will be used to find the edge endpoints, with the `findEndPointPosition` function:

```
    const vec3 averageRGBNeighbor =
        rgbSum * (1.0 / 9.0);
    const float verticalEdgeRow1 =
        abs(-2.0 * lumas[Top] + lumaTopCorners);
    const float verticalEdgeRow2 =
        abs(-2.0 * lumas[Center] + lumaLeftRight);
    const float verticalEdgeRow3 = abs(
        -2.0 * lumas[Bottom] + lumaBottomCorners);
    const float verticalEdge =
        (verticalEdgeRow1 + verticalEdgeRow2 * 2.0 +
         verticalEdgeRow3) /
        12.0;
    const float horizontalEdgeCol1 =
        abs(-2.0 * lumas[Left] + lumaLeftCorners);
    const float horizontalEdgeCol2 =
        abs(-2.0 * lumas[Center] + lumaTopBottom);
    const float horizontalEdgeCol3 =
        abs(-2.0 * lumas[Right] + lumaRightCorners);
    const float horizontalEdge =
        (horizontalEdgeCol1 +
         horizontalEdgeCol2 * 2.0 +
         horizontalEdgeCol3) /
        12.0;
    const bool isHorizontal =
        horizontalEdge >= verticalEdge;

    const float luma1 =
        isHorizontal ? lumas[Top] : lumas[Left];
    const float luma2 =
        isHorizontal ? lumas[Bottom] : lumas[Right];
    const bool is1Steepest =
        abs(lumas[Center] - luma1) >=
        abs(lumas[Center] - luma2);
    float stepLength =
        isHorizontal ? -screenCoordToTextureCoord.y
                     : -screenCoordToTextureCoord.x;
    float lumaHighContrastPixel;
    if (is1Steepest) {
      lumaHighContrastPixel = luma1;
    } else {
```

Anti-Aliasing Techniques

```
        lumaHighContrastPixel = luma2;
        // Also reverse the direction:
        stepLength = -stepLength;
    }
    vec2 outPosToFetchTexelForEdgeAntiAliasing;
    vec3 rgbEdgeAntiAliasingPixel = rgb[Center];
```

9. The `findEndPointPosition` function returns 1 if it deems antialiasing is needed and 0 otherwise. It also returns the coordinate of the texel that will be blended with the pixel being anti-aliased. We will investigate the `findEndPointPosition` function in *step 11*:

```
    const float res = findEndPointPosition(
        inputTexture, texCoord,
        lumas[Center], lumaHighContrastPixel,
        stepLength, screenCoordToTextureCoord,
        isHorizontal,
        outPosToFetchTexelForEdgeAntiAliasing);
```

10. If the return value is `1.0`, we perform the antialiasing by blending the original pixel's color with the color from the texel at the `outPosToFetchTexelForEdgeAntiAliasing` coordinate. The blending factor to use (`pixelblendAmount`) was computed previously, in *step 7*:

```
    if (res == 1.0) {
      rgbEdgeAntiAliasingPixel =
          texture(
              inputTexture,
              outPosToFetchTexelForEdgeAntiAliasing)
              .rgb;
    }

    return vec4(mix(rgbEdgeAntiAliasingPixel,
                    averageRGBNeighbor,
                    pixelblendAmount),
                1.0);
}
```

11. The `findEndPointPosition` function performs an important task – it traverses the image in search of edge endpoints, moving in both directions from the central pixel that's being processed. To accomplish this, it requires several pieces of information. First, it needs the texture that's being processed, which is the image that the function will traverse. Next, it requires the coordinate of the pixel being processed, which serves as the starting point for the function's traversal. The function also needs to know the luminance, or brightness, of the pixel.

In addition, it must be aware of the luminance of the highest contrast pixel, an element that is determined based on whether the edge being examined is more horizontal or more vertical. Another crucial piece of information is the step length, which, like the luminance of the highest contrast pixel, is also dependent on the angle of the edge. The function needs the length of one pixel in texture coordinates for accurate image traversal. Finally, it requires a flag that indicates whether the edge is more horizontal or more vertical to correctly understand the edge's orientation. It returns 1 if it deems anti-aliasing needs to be performed and 0 otherwise. It also returns the coordinate of the pixel that contains the RGB value to be used for the anti-aliasing:

```
float findEndPointPosition(
    sampler2D inputTexture,
    vec2 textureCoordMiddle, float lumaMiddle,
    float lumaHighContrastPixel, float stepLength,
    vec2 screenCoordToTextureCoord,
    bool isHorizontal,
    out vec2
        outPosToFetchTexelForEdgeAntiAliasing) {
```

12. Depending on whether the edge is horizontal or not, the function initializes the direction and position of the high-contrast pixel:

```
vec2 textureCoordOfHighContrastPixel =
    textureCoordMiddle;

// Direction of the edge
vec2 edgeDir;

if (isHorizontal) {
  textureCoordOfHighContrastPixel.y =
      textureCoordMiddle.y + stepLength;
  textureCoordOfHighContrastPixel.x =
      textureCoordMiddle.x;
  edgeDir.x = screenCoordToTextureCoord.x;
  edgeDir.y = 0.0;
} else {
  textureCoordOfHighContrastPixel.x =
      textureCoordMiddle.x + stepLength;
  textureCoordOfHighContrastPixel.y =
      textureCoordMiddle.y;
  edgeDir.y = screenCoordToTextureCoord.y;
  edgeDir.x = 0.0;
}
```

13. Before we proceed to start looking for the edge endpoints, we need to set up some variables used in the loop:

    ```
    // Prepare for the search loop:
    float lumaHighContrastPixelNegDir;
    float lumaHighContrastPixelPosDir;
    float lumaMiddlePixelNegDir;
    float lumaMiddlePixelPosDir;
    bool doneGoingThroughNegDir = false;
    bool doneGoingThroughPosDir = false;
    vec2 posHighContrastNegDir =
        textureCoordOfHighContrastPixel - edgeDir;
    vec2 posHighContrastPosDir =
        textureCoordOfHighContrastPixel + edgeDir;
    vec2 posMiddleNegDir =
        textureCoordMiddle - edgeDir;
    vec2 posMiddlePosDir =
        textureCoordMiddle + edgeDir;
    ```

14. The loop iterates a maximum of NUM_LOOP_FOR_EDGE_DETECTION times. It checks for edges by looking at the luminance differences in both the positive and negative directions from the middle pixel. The edge is detected when the luminance difference between two consecutive points in one direction exceeds a threshold (we will look at the processDirection function in *step 20*):

    ```
    for (int i = 0; i < NUM_LOOP_FOR_EDGE_DETECTION;
      ++i) {
    // Negative direction processing
    if (!doneGoingThroughNegDir) {
      processDirection(doneGoingThroughNegDir,
                       posHighContrastNegDir,
                       posMiddleNegDir, -edgeDir,
                       lumaHighContrastPixel,
                       lumaMiddle);
    }

    // Positive direction processing
    if (!doneGoingThroughPosDir) {
      processDirection(doneGoingThroughPosDir,
                       posHighContrastPosDir,
                       posMiddlePosDir, edgeDir,
                       lumaHighContrastPixel,
                       lumaMiddle);
    ```

```
        }
        // If both directions are done, exit the loop
        if (doneGoingThroughNegDir &&
            doneGoingThroughPosDir) {
          break;
        }
      }
```

15. The function now calculates the distances from the middle pixel to the detected edge endpoints, in both the negative and positive directions:

    ```
    float dstNeg;
    float dstPos;
    if (isHorizontal) {
      dstNeg =
          textureCoordMiddle.x - posMiddleNegDir.x;
      dstPos =
          posMiddlePosDir.x - textureCoordMiddle.x;
    } else {
      dstNeg =
          textureCoordMiddle.y - posMiddleNegDir.y;
      dstPos =
          posMiddlePosDir.y - textureCoordMiddle.y;
    }
    ```

16. It also checks which endpoint is closer to the middle pixel:

    ```
    bool isMiddlePixelCloserToNeg = dstNeg < dstPos;
    float dst = min(dstNeg, dstPos);
    float lumaEndPointOfPixelCloserToMiddle =
        isMiddlePixelCloserToNeg
            ? lumaMiddlePixelNegDir
            : lumaMiddlePixelPosDir;
    ```

17. Anti-aliasing is deemed necessary, based on the luminance difference between the endpoint that is closer to the middle pixel and the middle pixel itself:

    ```
    bool edgeAARequired =
        abs(lumaEndPointOfPixelCloserToMiddle -
            lumaHighContrastPixel) <
        abs(lumaEndPointOfPixelCloserToMiddle -
            lumaMiddle);
    ```

18. Using the distances to the edge endpoints, the following code snippet calculates the pixel offset that is required for anti-aliasing:

    ```
    float negInverseEndPointsLength =
        -1.0 / (dstNeg + dstPos);
    float pixelOffset =
        dst * negInverseEndPointsLength + 0.5;
    outPosToFetchTexelForEdgeAntiAliasing =
        textureCoordMiddle;
    if (isHorizontal) {
      outPosToFetchTexelForEdgeAntiAliasing.y +=
          pixelOffset * stepLength;
    } else {
      outPosToFetchTexelForEdgeAntiAliasing.x +=
          pixelOffset * stepLength;
    }
    ```

19. The function returns `1.0` if edge anti-aliasing is required and `0.0` otherwise:

    ```
    return edgeAARequired ? 1.0 : 0.0;
    }
    ```

20. The `processDirection` inspects the luma values of pixels in a certain direction (given by `edgeIncrement`) to check for high contrast or edges. It will continue to inspect positions in this direction until a certain contrast condition is met. Once the condition is met, it will set the `doneGoingThroughDir` flag to `true`, signaling that it's done processing in this direction:

    ```
    void processDirection(inout bool doneGoingThroughDir,
                          inout vec2 posHighContrast,
                          inout vec2 posMiddle,
                          float edgeIncrement,
                          float lumaHighContrastPixel,
                          float lumaMiddle) {
      float lumaHighContrastPixelDir = rgb2luma(
          texture(inputTexture, posHighContrast).rgb);
      float lumaMiddlePixelDir = rgb2luma(
          texture(inputTexture, posMiddle).rgb);

      doneGoingThroughDir =
          abs(lumaHighContrastPixelDir -
              lumaHighContrastPixel) >
    ```

```
               abs(lumaHighContrastPixelDir -
                   lumaMiddle) ||
           abs(lumaMiddlePixelDir - lumaMiddle) >
               abs(lumaMiddlePixelDir -
                   lumaHighContrastPixel);

    // Update position for next iteration if not
    // done
    if (!doneGoingThroughDir) {
      posHighContrast += edgeIncrement;
      posMiddle += edgeIncrement;
    }
  }
```

21. The fragment code calls `applyFXAA`, which returns the new color to output from the shader:

    ```
    void main() {
      outColor =
          applyFXAA(gl_FragCoord.xy, inputTexture,
                    ViewportSize.size);
    }
    ```

And there you have it – the recipe for applying FXAA, a powerful tool for smoothing out jaggies in your graphics. As we wrap this up, remember that the beauty of FXAA lies not just in its ability to enhance visual output but also in its flexibility and ease of integration into existing systems.

Utilizing TAA

Unlike the previously discussed anti-aliasing methods, which only consider spatial information, TAA is based on temporal information – that is, it utilizes both the current and previous frames to smooth out these aliasing artifacts. The reason aliasing artifacts happens is because of insufficient samples; TAA solves this by sampling data over the frame sequence, significantly reducing the pressure on a single frame.

The basic idea is to apply subpixel jittering – that is, slightly shift the projection matrix of the camera for each new frame. This results in slightly different viewpoints for each frame, giving us more information about the scene than a static viewpoint would. When sampling textures during rendering, the resulting color value can be different due to the jitter. This creates a different aliasing pattern per frame, which, when accumulated over time, averages out and reduces the visible aliasing in the scene. This is demonstrated in the following screenshot in *Figure 6.2*:

Anti-Aliasing Techniques

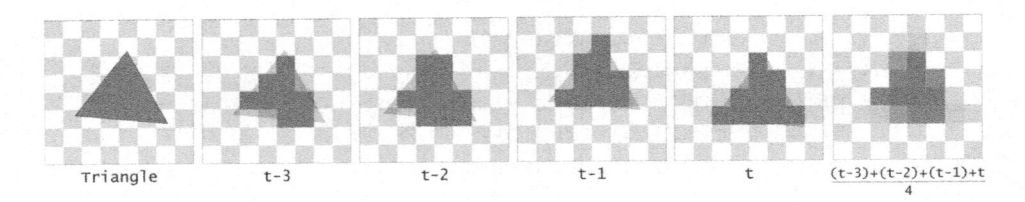

Figure 6.2 – A temporal anti-aliasing overview

The concept outlined here performs exceptionally well for static scenes. However, in scenarios where either the objects or the camera is in motion, consecutive frames can exhibit substantial differences. This can lead to a visual artifact where moving objects appear to leave behind a series of their *ghosts*, creating what is known as the **ghosting** effect.

To get rid of ghosting, we use what is commonly called a **velocity** buffer, and the motion in the scene is captured using motion vectors. For each pixel, a motion vector is calculated that represents how much a pixel has moved compared to the previous frame. The result is a velocity buffer that stores these motion vectors. The previously rendered frame is then re-projected onto the current frame using the velocity buffer. This means that for each pixel, the color of the corresponding pixel in the previous frame is looked up using the motion vector. This color is then blended with the current color of the pixel, which results in a smoothing of the colors over time.

Figure 6.3 shows a high-level overview of the TAA algorithm:

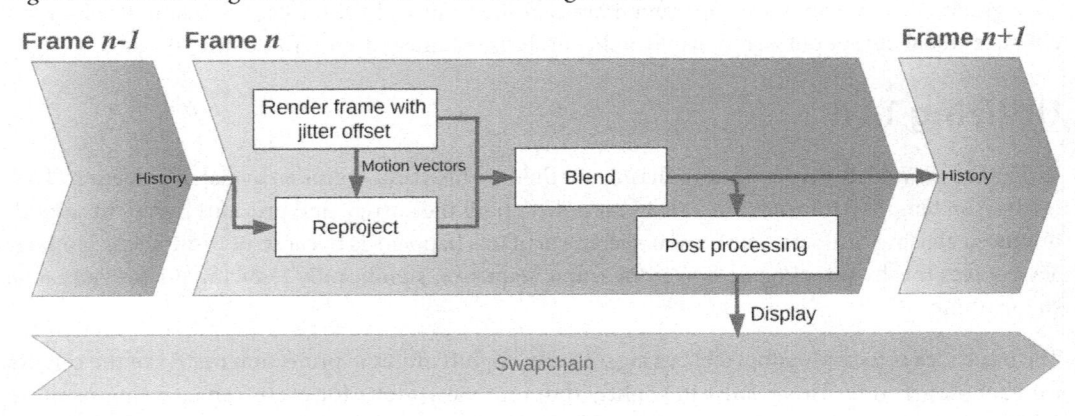

Figure 6.3 – A TAA frame overview

In this recipe, you will learn how to implement TAA, an advanced technique that can significantly reduce flickering and provide smoother visuals in your graphics. You'll understand the intricacies of TAA and how to adeptly integrate it into your code, adding another powerful tool to your graphics rendering toolbox.

Getting ready

In the repository, the TAA algorithm is implemented by the TAAComputePass class, located in the source/enginecore/passes/TAAComputePass.hpp and cpp files. The shaders are implemented using a compute shader, located in source/enginecore/resources/shaders/taaresolve.comp and source/enginecore/resources/shaders/taahistorycopyandsharpen.comp. TAA example can be launched by running the Chapter06_TAA executable.

Figure 6.4 illustrates the flow of the TAA algorithm:

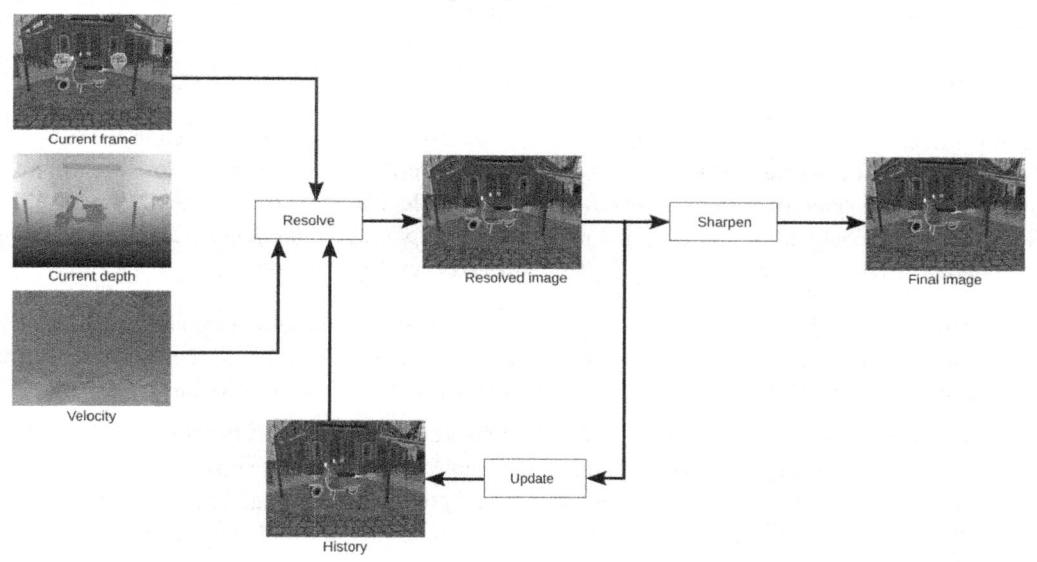

Figure 6.4 – A TAA algorithm in a deferred renderer

TAA is implemented as a two-step compute shader:

1. The first step is the TAA resolve shader, which takes ColorTexture, DepthTexture, HistoryTexture, and VelocityTexture as input and writes to an intermediate image. The velocity, color, and depth texture are produced from the Gbuffer pass in the given example; however, conceptually, the same could be produced in forward rendering as well.

2. The second step is running a compute shader that is responsible for the following:

   A. Copying the results of the previously produced intermediate texture into a history texture.

   B. Refining these intermediate results, we don't need to generate an additional texture to store the refined results, instead, we can utilize the provided ColorTexture in the TAA resolve shader. This is the same ColorTexture that eventually gets displayed. A known downside of TAA is the potential of causing a minor blur in the image. To mitigate this, a sharpening filter is applied post-TAA. This sharpening phase is designed to intensify the edges and intricate details in the image, thereby reinstating some of the sharpness that might have been compromised during the TAA resolve process.

How to do it...

To implement TAA, we first need to construct a jitter matrix. This matrix will be used in tandem with the **Model-View-Projection (MVP)** matrix during the rendering process. Furthermore, we will need color, depth, and velocity buffers. Conveniently, these buffers are already generated as part of the G-buffer pipeline, which we implemented in *Chapter 4, Exploring Techniques for Lighting, Shading, and Shadows* in the *Implementing the G-buffer for deferred rendering* recipe:

1. The TAAComputePass::init method is in charge of initializing various resources. It establishes two pipelines – one for resolving to an output color, and another for transferring the output color into a history texture and enhancing the output color's sharpness.

2. The majority of work happens in the TAAComputePass::doAA function. This function simply operates the resolve compute pipeline, followed by the pipeline that handles the copying of the history texture and the sharpening of the output color. We've highlighted key components of the doAA function as follows, omitting less critical parts to avoid verbosity:

```
void TAAComputePass::doAA(VkCommandBuffer cmd,
                          int frameIndex,
                          int isCamMoving) {
    pipeline_->bind(cmd);
    outColorTexture_->transitionImageLayout(
        cmd, VK_IMAGE_LAYOUT_GENERAL);
    historyTexture_->transitionImageLayout(
        cmd, VK_IMAGE_LAYOUT_GENERAL);
    vkCmdDispatch(...);
    VkImageMemoryBarrier barriers[2] = {
        {
            ...
        }
    };
```

```cpp
    vkCmdPipelineBarrier(
        cmd, VK_PIPELINE_STAGE_COMPUTE_SHADER_BIT,
        VK_PIPELINE_STAGE_COMPUTE_SHADER_BIT, 0, 0,
        nullptr, 0, nullptr, 2, barriers);
    colorTexture_->transitionImageLayout(
        cmd, VK_IMAGE_LAYOUT_GENERAL);
    sharpenPipeline_->bind(cmd);
    vkCmdDispatch(…);
    colorTexture_->transitionImageLayout(
        cmd,
        VK_IMAGE_LAYOUT_SHADER_READ_ONLY_OPTIMAL);
    outColorTexture_->transitionImageLayout(
        cmd,
        VK_IMAGE_LAYOUT_SHADER_READ_ONLY_OPTIMAL);
}
```

3. The actual magic happens in the two compute shaders; specifically, the resolve shader is the most important. The resolve shader is implemented in `taaresolve.comp`. Let's look at how the shaders work.

4. First, we will expand on some auxiliary functions. `catmullRomTextureFiltering` helps smooth out the temporal aliasing by blending the colors of pixels between frames, using Catmull-Rom interpolation. Catmull-Rom interpolation is a form of cubic interpolation that provides a smoother appearance than linear interpolation. The function uses the Catmull-Rom weights (`w0`, `w1`, `w2`, `w3`) to calculate the weight for the center (`w12`) and the offset from the center (`offset12`). Then, the function calculates three new texture positions (`texPos0`, `texPos3`, and `texPos12`) and adjusts these positions to match the texture resolution. The function then uses these weights and texture positions to calculate the resulting pixel color, by accessing the history buffer texture at the specific positions, multiplying the retrieved color by the respective weights, and summing them together.

The `varianceClampColor` function is used in anti-aliasing TAA to deal with issues of ghosting and blurring that can occur, due to the temporal reprojection of color data. The function works by limiting the color value of a given pixel, based on the color variance of its surrounding pixels. It loops over a 3x3 neighborhood around the current pixel. For each neighboring pixel, the function retrieves its color data (`neighColor`) and calculates a weight (`w`), based on the Euclidean distance from the current pixel. This weight is designed to give closer pixels more influence over the final color result.

The `calculateBlendFactor` function is responsible for performing calculations to determine the blend factor of a pixel, based on its velocity and luminance. Firstly, the pixel movement is calculated on two levels, the overall motion and the tiny subpixel motion, resulting in values called `subpixelMotion` and `dynamicBlendFactor` respectively. Then, to adjust the pixel's brightness or luminance, the difference between the current color and the previous frame color is determined. This entire process enhances the realism of the pixel's movement and color changes over time, significantly improving the overall image quality when there's movement of objects or camera. The implementation of `catmullRomTextureFiltering` and `varianceClampColor` are very verbose; we suggest looking at `taaresolve.comp` for implementation details.

5. Next, we present the `main` function; this helps to produce a smoother, more stable image by reducing flickering and ghosting artifacts that can occur, due to the rapid movement of the camera or objects in a scene. The following sub-steps will walk you through the specifics of its implementation:

    A. Calculate the closest depth and corresponding velocity around the current pixel:

    ```
    void main() {
      vec2 velocity;
      const float closestDepth =
          closestVelocityAndDepth(velocity);
    ```

    B. Reproject the current pixel position to its position in the previous frame using the calculated velocity:

    ```
      vec2 reprojectedUV = uv - velocity;
    ```

    C. Calculate `velocityLerp` using the history buffer at the reprojected location. Note the use of `taaConstData.isFirstFrame`, which helps to determine whether we are dealing with the first frame of the sequence or not. If it is the first frame, `velocityLerp` is simply initialized to `0.0f`. In the context of camera cuts or teleports (i.e., a sudden change from one perspective to another), the first frame assumption is also applicable. Whenever these events occur, the scene changes dramatically from one frame to another. In such cases, it's beneficial to treat the frame right after the cut or teleport as a first frame. This is because the data from the previous frame is no longer a good reference for the current frame, due to the drastic changes in scene content:

    ```
      float velocityLerp =
          (taaConstData.isFirstFrame != 0)
            ? texture(inHistoryBuffer,
                      reprojectedUV)
                  .w
            : 0.0f;
    ```

D. Load the current frame color (`colorIn`) and calculate `colorHistory` using `catmullRomTextureFiltering`:

```
vec3 colorIn = getColorData(
    ivec2(gl_GlobalInvocationID.xy));

vec3 colorHistory = catmullRomTextureFiltering(
    reprojectedUV, vec2(workSize));
```

E. Define two constants, `boxSizeWhenMoving` and `boxSizeWhenStationary`. We determine value of `boxSize` based on whether the camera is moving or not and is interpolated between the stationary and moving values, based on `velocityLerp`:

```
const float boxSizeWhenMoving = 2000.0f;
const float boxSizeWhenStationary = 100.0f;
float boxSize =
    (taaConstData.isCameraMoving == 0)
        ? boxSizeWhenStationary
        : mix(boxSizeWhenStationary,
            boxSizeWhenMoving, velocityLerp);
boxSize = mix(
    0.5f, boxSize,
    noGeometry ? 0.0f
               : smoothstep(0.02f, 0.0f,
                    length(velocity)));
```

F. Historical color (`colorHistory`) is then clamped using the `varianceClampColor` function to ensure that the color is within a certain range, based on the variance of surrounding pixels:

```
vec3 clampHistory =
    varianceClampColor(colorHistory, boxSize);
```

G. Calculate `blendFactor`, which determines how much of the current color and the historical color should be used to get the final color:

```
float blendFactor = calculateBlendFactor(
    closestDepth, velocity, noGeometry,
    workSize, colorIn, clampHistory,
    velocityLerp);
```

H. Compute the final color (`colorResolve`) as a mix of the clamped historical color and the current color, based on `blendFactor`; also, store `velocityLerp` in the `alpha` channel:

```
vec3 colorResolve =
    mix(clampHistory, colorIn, blendFactor);
```

```
       imageStore(outColorImage,
               ivec2(gl_GlobalInvocationID.xy),
               vec4(colorResolve, velocityLerp));
}
```

6. Next, we will show how `taahistorycopyandsharpen.comp` works; this shader is responsible for copying the data into history texture, as well as sharpening the results produced by *step 5* (`taaresolve.comp`). The main function is presented as follows, and the code is simple – it first copies `incolor` (which is the image produced by previous *step 5*) into the history texture. Then, the `sharpen` method is called. This method works by first loading pixel colors from the center and four directly adjacent locations (top, left, right, and bottom). It then uses an unsharp masking technique, which involves subtracting a blurred or *unsharp* version of the image from the original image to create a mask that represents the detail of the image. The function applies this mask to enhance the original image, making it appear sharper. The final color produced by the `sharpen` method is stored in `outColorImage`, which is finally copied to the swapchain image. For the sake of brevity, we're not detailing the `sharpen` function here. However, you can review its implementation in the `taahistorycopyandsharpen.comp` file:

```
void main() {
  vec4 incolor = imageLoad(inColorImage, ivec2(gl_
GlobalInvocationID.xy));
    imageStore(outHistory, ivec2(gl_GlobalInvocationID.xy),
incolor);
    vec3 color = sharpen();
    imageStore(outColorImage, ivec2(gl_GlobalInvocationID.xy),
vec4(color, 1.0f));
}
```

Despite its widespread use and numerous benefits, TAA isn't without its shortcomings:

- When object motion uncovers new areas on a screen, these areas are either not present in the history buffer or are inaccurately depicted by the motion vectors. Additionally, camera rotation and reverse translation can lead to extensive uncovered areas at the screen's edges.

- Features with subpixel dimensions, such as wires, may be missed by a consecutive frame, leading to their absence in motion vectors in the subsequent frame. Transparent surfaces can generate pixels where the motion vectors from opaque objects don't align with the overall movement of the objects depicted. Lastly, shadows and reflections don't follow the direction of the motion vectors of the surfaces they shade.

When TAA doesn't work properly, it either results in ghosting (a blurring effect caused by integrating incorrect values) or it exposes the original aliasing, leading to jagged edges, flickering, and noise.

See also

For further reading and a deeper understanding of TAA, consider exploring the following resources. These references will provide you with more detailed information, practical applications, and insights into the latest advancements:

- `https://research.nvidia.com/publication/2019-03_improving-temporal-antialiasing-adaptive-ray-tracing`
- `https://community.arm.com/arm-community-blogs/b/graphics-gaming-and-vr-blog/posts/temporal-anti-aliasing`

Applying DLSS

DLSS is an AI-powered technology developed by NVIDIA for their RTX series of graphics cards. DLSS uses the power of machine learning and AI to increase the resolution of rendered frames by intelligently upscaling lower resolution images in real time. This results in a high-quality, high-resolution image that requires less computational power to produce. We can also use DLSS to render frames at a lower base resolution and then use AI to upscale the image to a higher resolution.

Note that to use DLSS, you must have an NVIDIA RTX series graphics card.

In this recipe, you'll learn how to apply DLSS, an innovative technique for enhancing the resolution of rendered frames in real time. You will gain an understanding of how DLSS leverages machine learning and AI to upscale lower-resolution images intelligently, thereby achieving superior image quality with less computational power.

Getting ready

In the repository, DLSS is implemented by the `DLSS` class, located in the `source/enginecore/DLSS.hpp` and `cpp` files. The DLSS example can be launched by running the `chapter06_DLSS` executable.

DLSS also requires color, depth and velocity textures, the same textures that were used by the TAA algorithm.

How to do it...

The DLSS is integrated using the following steps:

1. First, we need to query the device and instance extensions that are required for DLSS; these extensions need to be enabled before Vulkan is initialized. NVIDIA's DLSS SDK provides NVSDK_NGX_VULKAN_RequiredExtensions, which needs to be used to query extensions. The following code block presents a static function that can append extensions required by DLSS; this needs to be called before initializing the Vulkan device:

```
void DLSS::requiredExtensions(std::vector<std::string>& instanceExtensions,
                                    std::vector<std::string>& deviceExtensions) {
  unsigned int instanceExtCount;
  const char** instanceExt;
  unsigned int deviceExtCount;
  const char** deviceExt;
  auto result = NVSDK_NGX_VULKAN_RequiredExtensions(
      &instanceExtCount, &instanceExt, &deviceExtCount, &deviceExt);

  for (int i = 0; i < instanceExtCount; ++i) {
    if (std::find(instanceExtensions.begin(), instanceExtensions.end(),
                  instanceExt[i]) == instanceExtensions.end()) {
      instanceExtensions.push_back(instanceExt[i]);
    }
  }
  for (int i = 0; i < deviceExtCount; ++i) {
    if (std::find(deviceExtensions.begin(), deviceExtensions.end(),
                  deviceExt[i]) == deviceExtensions.end()) {
      deviceExtensions.push_back(deviceExt[i]);
      if (deviceExtensions.back() ==
          "VK_EXT_buffer_device_address") {  // we are using 1.3, this extension
                                             // has been promoted
        deviceExtensions.pop_back();
      }
    }
  }
}
```

2. Next, we will look at `DLSS init` method. This method is responsible for initializing the DLSS feature provided by the NVSDK. It takes the current width and height of the viewport, an upscale factor, and a reference to a `CommandQueueManager` object. The function first sets the upscale factor and then determines the optimal settings for DLSS, based on the current viewport size and desired quality level. It then configures DLSS features such as motion vector resolution, frame sharpening, and others based on specific flags. Finally, it creates the DLSS feature and submits the command to the Vulkan command buffer:

```
void DLSS::init(int currentWidth, int currentHeight,
float upScaleFactor, VulkanCore::CommandQueueManager&
commandQueueManager) {
  NVSDK_NGX_Result result = NGX_DLSS_GET_OPTIMAL_
SETTINGS(paramsDLSS_, currentWidth, currentHeight, dlssQuality,
  &optimalRenderWidth, &optimalRenderHeight, &minRenderWidth,
  &minRenderHeight, &maxRenderWidth, &maxRenderHeight,
  &recommendedSharpness);
  int dlssCreateFeatureFlags = NVSDK_NGX_DLSS_Feature_Flags_
None;
  dlssCreateFeatureFlags |= NVSDK_NGX_DLSS_Feature_Flags_
MVLowRes;
  dlssCreateFeatureFlags |= NVSDK_NGX_DLSS_Feature_Flags_
DoSharpening;
  NVSDK_NGX_DLSS_Create_Params dlssCreateParams{
      .Feature =
          {
              .InWidth = unsigned int(currentWidth),
              .InHeight = unsigned int(currentHeight),
              .InTargetWidth = unsigned int(currentWidth *
upScaleFactor),
              .InTargetHeight = unsigned int(currentHeight *
upScaleFactor),
              .InPerfQualityValue = NVSDK_NGX_PerfQuality_Value_
MaxQuality,
          },
      .InFeatureCreateFlags = dlssCreateFeatureFlags,
  };
  auto commmandBuffer = commandQueueManager.
getCmdBufferToBegin();
  constexpr unsigned int creationNodeMask = 1;
  constexpr unsigned int visibilityNodeMask = 1;
  NVSDK_NGX_Result createDlssResult = NGX_VULKAN_CREATE_DLSS_
EXT(commmandBuffer, creationNodeMask, visibilityNodeMask,
  &dlssFeatureHandle_, paramsDLSS_, &dlssCreateParams);
  ASSERT(createDlssResult == NVSDK_NGX_Result_Success, "Failed
to create NVSDK NGX DLSS feature");
  commandQueueManager.endCmdBuffer(commmandBuffer);
  VkSubmitInfo submitInfo{
```

```
        .sType = VK_STRUCTURE_TYPE_SUBMIT_INFO,
        .commandBufferCount = 1,
        .pCommandBuffers = &commmandBuffer,
};
commandQueueManager.submit(&submitInfo);
commandQueueManager.waitUntilSubmitIsComplete();
}
```

3. The next step is to call DLSS's `render` method, which is responsible for applying DLSS to the provided input textures to enhance the image quality. It takes a Vulkan command buffer and several texture objects as inputs – color, depth, motion vector, and output color texture, along with a 2D vector for the camera jitter. Firstly, we create resources for each of the input textures using the `NVSDK_NGX_Create_ImageView_Resource_VK` function; afterward, we transition the layout of the output color texture to `VK_IMAGE_LAYOUT_GENERAL` to prepare it for writing. Next, this function sets up the parameters for the DLSS evaluation, including input color and output resources, sharpness level, depth resource, motion vector resource, and camera jitter offsets. The last part is to call `NGX_VULKAN_EVALUATE_DLSS_EXT` to apply DLSS to the images, which enhances the image quality, based on the parameters provided:

```
void DLSS::render(VkCommandBuffer commandBuffer,
VulkanCore::Texture& inColorTexture, VulkanCore::Texture&
inDepthTexture, VulkanCore::Texture& inMotionVectorTexture,
VulkanCore::Texture& outColorTexture, glm::vec2 cameraJitter) {
  NVSDK_NGX_Resource_VK inColorResource = NVSDK_NGX_Create_
ImageView_Resource_VK(
          inColorTexture.vkImageView(), inColorTexture.
vkImage(),
          {VK_IMAGE_ASPECT_COLOR_BIT, 0, 1, 0, 1}, VK_FORMAT_
UNDEFINED,
          inColorTexture.vkExtents().width, inColorTexture.
vkExtents().height,
          true);
  NVSDK_NGX_Resource_VK outColorResource = NVSDK_NGX_Create_
ImageView_Resource_VK(...);
  NVSDK_NGX_Resource_VK depthResource = NVSDK_NGX_Create_
ImageView_Resource_VK(...);
  NVSDK_NGX_Resource_VK motionVectorResource = NVSDK_NGX_Create_
ImageView_Resource_VK(...);
  outColorTexture.transitionImageLayout(commandBuffer, VK_IMAGE_
LAYOUT_GENERAL);
  NVSDK_NGX_VK_DLSS_Eval_Params evalParams = {
      .Feature =
          {
              .pInColor = &inColorResource,
              .pInOutput = &outColorResource,
              .InSharpness = 1.0,
```

```cpp
            },
        .pInDepth = &depthResource,
        .pInMotionVectors = &motionVectorResource,
        .InJitterOffsetX = cameraJitter.x,
        .InJitterOffsetY = cameraJitter.y,
        .InRenderSubrectDimensions =
            {
                .Width =
                    static_cast<unsigned int>(inColorTexture.
vkExtents().width),
                .Height =
                    static_cast<unsigned int>(inColorTexture.
vkExtents().height),
            },
        .InReset = 0,
        .InMVScaleX = -1.0f * inColorResource.Resource.
ImageViewInfo.Width,
        .InMVScaleY = -1.0f * inColorResource.Resource.
ImageViewInfo.Height,
        .pInExposureTexture = nullptr,
    };
    NVSDK_NGX_Result result = NGX_VULKAN_EVALUATE_DLSS_
EXT(commandBuffer, dlssFeatureHandle_, paramsDLSS_,
&evalParams);
    ASSERT(result == NVSDK_NGX_Result_Success, "Failed to evaluate
DLSS feature");
    if (result != NVSDK_NGX_Result_Success) {
      auto store = GetNGXResultAsString(result);
    }
}
```

In the next section, we present valuable links for further reading and deeper understanding of the topic.

See also

For more in-depth knowledge and practical insights on DLSS, the following resource will prove invaluable:

- `https://github.com/NVIDIA/DLSS/blob/main/doc/DLSS_Programming_Guide_Release.pdf`

In this chapter, we started with Vulkan's MSAA. This is a method used to combat the spatial aliasing of high-contrast edges, often seen as jagged or staircase lines in the rendered image. We discussed the process of enabling MSAA in Vulkan, which involves configuring the multi-sample state during pipeline creation and allocating a separate multi-sample image. We also covered how MSAA operates by averaging the color of multiple sample points, reducing the jagged appearance, and providing a smoother, more natural look to the edges.

Then, we addressed FXAA. This technique is a screen-space, post-processing method, meaning that it works directly on the final image. Its primary advantage is its speed and simplicity, offering a good trade-off between performance and quality. FXAA smooths edges by finding high-contrast pixels and blending them with their surroundings. Despite being an approximation, FXAA can often provide a significant improvement in perceived image quality, particularly in scenes with many high-contrast edges.

The third technique we discussed was TAA. This method uses the concept of temporal reprojection, where it leverages information from previous frames to minimize aliasing artifacts in the current frame. We covered how TAA operates by accumulating samples over multiple frames and applying a filter to reduce the temporal aliasing effects, such as crawling and flickering. When implemented correctly, TAA can offer superior results over purely spatial techniques, particularly in scenes with high levels of motion and detail.

Lastly, we explored the cutting-edge technique of DLSS. Powered by AI, DLSS is a proprietary technology developed by NVIDIA. It works by training a deep learning model to predict high-resolution images from lower-resolution inputs. The trained model is then used to upscale images in real time. We also talked about how DLSS can maintain or even improve visual fidelity while significantly boosting performance.

This chapter provided a comprehensive overview of various anti-aliasing techniques, each with its strengths and use cases. By understanding these methods, you can make informed choices on which technique to implement, based on the specific needs of your Vulkan applications.

7
Ray Tracing and Hybrid Rendering

In this chapter, we venture into the fascinating world of **ray tracing** and **hybrid rendering**. Ray tracing, to put it simply, is a special technique used in computer graphics that simulates how light interacts with objects. This results in images that are so lifelike, they can be mistaken for reality. However, pure ray tracing is computationally intensive and requires significant hardware resources, which makes it unfeasible for real-time applications with the current generation of hardware. On the other hand, there's hybrid rendering, which is a mix of conventional rasterization techniques and the realism of ray tracing. This blend offers both good performance and stunning visuals. This chapter will take you through how these techniques can be implemented using Vulkan. We'll show you how to set up a ray tracing pipeline and guide you on how to integrate hybrid rendering into your work. By the end of this chapter, you will have a deeper understanding of how these advanced techniques work. More importantly, you'll learn how to use them in your own projects.

The first part of the chapter focuses on developing a GPU-based ray tracer. We'll elaborate on how to effectively develop this GPU-based ray tracer, detailing the steps involved, and how each function contributes to the final lifelike image. The second part of our chapter will revolve around the integration of shadows from a ray tracer along with rasterized deferred rendering. We will delve into how the shadows generated from a ray tracer can be combined with the rasterization technique of deferred rendering, a technique commonly referred to as hybrid rendering.

In this chapter, we will cover the following recipes:

- Implementing a GPU ray tracer
- Implementing a hybrid renderer

Technical requirements

For this chapter, you will need to make sure you have Visual Studio 2022 installed along with the Vulkan SDK. Basic familiarity with the C++ programming language and an understanding of ray tracing concepts would be useful. Please revisit *Chapter 1, Vulkan Core Concepts,* for details about setting up and building the code in the repository. We also assume that by now you are familiar with the Vulkan API and various concepts that were introduced in previous chapters. This chapter has multiple recipes, which can be launched using the following executables:

1. `Chapter07_RayTracer.exe`
2. `Chapter07_HybridRenderer.exe`

The code files for this chapter can be found here: https://github.com/PacktPublishing/The-Modern-Vulkan-Cookbook.

Implementing a GPU ray tracer

Ray tracing is a rendering technique that simulates the physical behavior of light to generate highly realistic graphics. Ray tracing works by tracing the path of light from a pixel in the image sensor back to its source. Each ray of light can interact with the objects in the scene, causing a variety of effects such as reflection, refraction, or absorption. This allows for the creation of realistic shadows, reflections, and light dispersion effects in complex 3D scenes. In previous chapters, specifically *Chapter 4, Exploring Techniques for Lighting, Shading, and Shadows*, we explored **rasterization**. It takes a more direct approach, converting 3D polygons that make up a scene directly into a 2D image. It essentially fills in the pixels of each polygon based on its color and texture. On the other hand, ray tracing simulates the path of light rays from the camera to the scene, accounting for how these rays interact with the scene's objects.

Before we delve into the specifics of how ray tracing is implemented in Vulkan, it is beneficial to gain an understanding of how ray tracing operates, along with several fundamental concepts such as the **bidirectional reflectance distribution function** (**BRDF**), radiance, and irradiance. These concepts play a crucial role in determining how light interacts with surfaces in a scene and subsequently influences the final rendered image.

To simplify understanding, let's break down the flow of the ray tracing algorithm, as depicted in *Figure 7.1*:

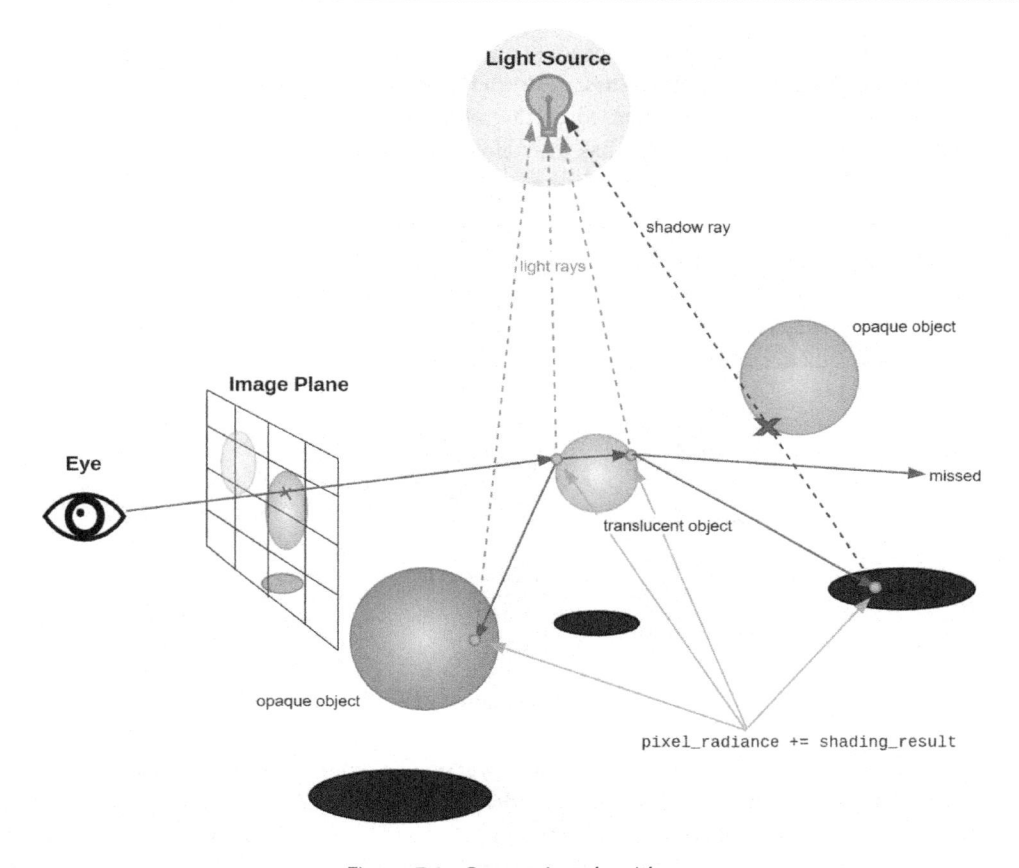

Figure 7.1 – Ray tracing algorithm

In the following section, we will outline the fundamental principles of the ray tracing algorithm:

1. For each pixel on the screen, a ray is projected from the viewpoint or "eye" into the scene. This is the initial step in ray tracing and sets the stage for further calculations.
2. The algorithm then calculates the point of intersection between the ray and the objects within the scene. It identifies the closest object that is hit by the ray, along with the exact hit point on the object's geometry.
3. Once the intersection point is determined, shading is performed at the hit point. The color and lighting information calculated at this point is added to the radiance value for the pixel, which contributes to the final color of the pixel in the rendered image.
4. The ray doesn't stop at the first hit. It can continue to propagate due to phenomena such as reflection or refraction. The rays resulting from reflection or refraction are assigned a throughput value, which represents the remaining energy of the light.

5. The recursive process can potentially go on indefinitely, which is computationally expensive. To handle this, techniques such as **Russian Roulette** are used. In Russian Roulette, the recursion is probabilistically terminated based on the remaining energy in the ray. If the ray's energy falls below a certain threshold, it has a certain chance of being terminated early, which helps to control the computational cost of the algorithm.

6. Now that we understand how the ray tracing algorithm functions, it's beneficial to delve into the principles of **radiometry**. Radiometry is a branch of physics that quantifies light's behavior, providing a series of methods and units to describe and measure different aspects of light in a scene. Several key concepts that are fundamental to understanding radiometry include radiant intensity, irradiance, and radiance. The following diagram (*Figure 7.2*) can help you remember these concepts:

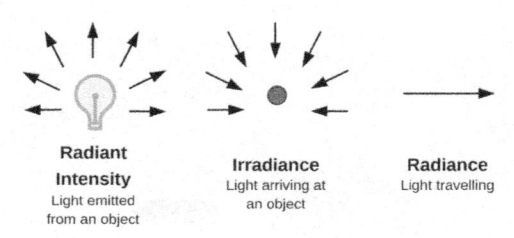

Figure 7.2 – Radiometry basics

- **Radiant intensity**: This is a measure of the power of light emitted, or radiant flux, per unit solid angle, typically measured in **watts per steradian (W/sr)**. The steradian, analogous to the radian in angular measure, quantifies solid angles in 3D space. In the context of ray tracing, it serves as a pivotal unit when calculating radiant intensity, capturing how light spreads across surfaces within the simulated environment. It is directional in nature, meaning it varies depending on the direction from which the light is observed.

- **Irradiance**: Irradiance measures the power of radiant flux incident upon a surface per unit area, typically measured in **watts per square meter (W/m²)**. In the context of ray tracing, irradiance is used to calculate the amount of light energy striking a surface, which is then used for shading calculations. It plays a key role in determining how bright an object appears in the scene.

- **Radiance**: Radiance refers to how much light is either coming from a specific area or passing through it, considering the particular direction or viewpoint from which the light is observed. It is used to describe the amount of light that reaches the camera from a specific point in the scene, through a specific direction. It's measured in **watts per square meter per steradian (W/m²/sr)**. Radiance is a critical concept in ray tracing as it integrates both directional and positional information, helping to generate accurate shading and lighting effects.

As the next step, we will learn a bit about the **rendering equation** used in ray tracing. The equation essentially depicts that the light leaving a point in a certain direction is equal to the light emitted by the point in that direction plus the light reflected by the point in that direction. The reflected light is integral over all directions of incoming light, where each incoming direction is weighted by the BRDF and the cosine of the angle between the incoming light and the surface normal. The link provided below offers a simplified explanation of the rendering equation: https://twitter.com/KostasAAA/status/1379918353553371139/photo/1.

- $L_o(x, \omega_o)$ is the total amount of radiance (light), leaving point $xs(x, \omega_o)$ is the emitted light from the point x in the direction ω_o. This term is usually only non-zero for light sources.
- The term $\int_\Omega$ represents an integral over the entire hemisphere Ω above point x.
- $f_r(x, \omega_i \rightarrow \omega_o)$ is the BRDF at point x, which defines how much light is reflected off x in the direction ω_o when light comes in from direction ω_i.
- $L_i(x, \omega_i)$ is the incoming light at point p from direction ω_i.
- $\omega_i \cdot n$ is the cosine of the angle between ω_i and the normal at point x. This accounts for the fact that light arriving at a shallow angle spread over a larger area. $d\omega_i$ is a small amount of solid angle around direction ω_i.

Monte Carlo method

Next, we will discuss the **Monte Carlo method**, which is a statistical technique that allows for numerical solutions to complex problems by performing repeated random sampling. Suppose you want to calculate the area under a curve described by the function $f(x) = x^2$ between $x = 0$ and $x = 1$. Mathematically, you'd solve this using calculus with an integral. However, imagine now that the function is extremely complex or has many variables, such that you can't easily integrate it using standard calculus techniques. This is where the Monte Carlo method comes into play. Instead of trying to compute the integral exactly, we can estimate it using random sampling. In the case of ray tracing, the rendering equation, which models how light interacts with surfaces, is quite complex, especially because it involves an integral over all possible directions of incoming light. This is the reason Monte Carlo is used. Instead of trying to calculate the exact value of the integral, we can approximate it by randomly sampling directions of incoming light, evaluating the integrand for each of these samples, and then averaging the results. This process is repeated many times to get a more accurate estimate.

We briefly talked about the BRDF during the rendering equation; it tells us how light bounces off a surface. When light hits a surface, it doesn't just bounce back in one direction but scatters in many directions. The BRDF gives us a way to predict this behavior. It considers two directions: the direction from which the light is coming, and the direction in which it's going after it hits the surface.

Imagine the sun shining on the surface. The BRDF helps us figure out how much light from the sun is reflected off that surface and in what direction it goes. This is important for calculating the color and brightness that we see in a rendered image. Here's where the concept of throughput or contribution comes in. It's like a measure of how much light energy is retained or lost when the light bounces off the surface. Think of it as the efficiency of light reflection. We need to include this in our calculations to get accurate results.

The **probability density function** (**PDF**) is a statistical tool that helps us handle the randomness involved in these calculations. When light hits the surface, it can bounce off in many different directions, and the PDF helps us figure out the likelihood of each possible direction.

Importance sampling is a technique used in ray tracing where we choose to send more rays in directions where the BRDF is high and fewer rays in directions where it is low. This helps us get a more accurate result with fewer rays, which can be computationally cheaper. However, since we're sending more rays in certain directions and fewer in others, we're biasing our sampling toward those directions. We divide our BRDF result by the PDF to get our result. The reason we divide the BRDF by a PDF is essentially to correct for bias that was introduced when we used importance sampling to choose the next direction in which to trace the ray.

In ray tracing, each light ray carries its own energy. Each time it bounces, we add the energy it carries times the BRDF to the overall brightness of the image.

In Vulkan, ray tracing is implemented through a series of distinct shader stages. In this recipe, we will guide you through the process of implementing a GPU ray tracer with Vulkan, providing a step-by-step walkthrough on how to set up each shader stage involved in the ray tracing process. By the end of this recipe, you'll be able to create your own ray tracer that can produce highly realistic graphics by accurately simulating the behavior of light.

The shader stages include the following:

- **Ray generation shader**: This is the starting point of the ray tracing process
- **Intersection shader**: This shader calculates how rays intersect with the scene's geometry
- **Miss and hit shaders**: These define how rays behave when they hit or miss an object

By understanding and implementing each of these stages, you'll be well on your way to creating visually stunning and realistic graphics.

Getting ready

The ray tracing pipeline in Vulkan is made up of six stages: ray generation, intersection, any-hit, closest hit, miss, and callable. *Figure 7.3* shows the stages and their general layout in the pipeline. Another key component of Vulkan ray tracing is **acceleration structure**. This structure is pivotal in efficiently handling the large amount of geometric data involved in ray tracing. The role of the acceleration structure is to organize data in a way that allows for rapid ray tracing calculations. **Bounding volume hierarchy** (**BVH**) is an algorithmic tree structure on a set of geometric objects. All geometric objects are wrapped in bounding volumes that form the leaf nodes of the tree. These nodes are then paired, bounded, and connected to form a parent node. This process continues up the tree until there is only one bounding volume remaining: the root of the tree. This structure allows the ray tracing algorithm to efficiently discard many objects that the ray cannot intersect, thereby speeding up the process significantly.

The acceleration structure is divided into two levels: the **bottom level acceleration structures** (**BLASs**) and the **top level acceleration structures** (**TLASs**):

- **BLAS**: BLASs are responsible for storing the geometric data for individual objects in the scene. Each object can have one or more BLAS associated with it, and each BLAS can contain one or more geometric primitives, such as triangles or instances of other BLASs. The BLAS is responsible for determining how rays intersect with the geometry they contains, making it a fundamental part of the ray tracing process.

- **TLAS**: The TLAS, on the other hand, does not contain geometric data. Instead, it contains instances of BLASs. Each instance defines a transformation (such as translation, rotation, or scaling) and a BLAS to apply it to. When ray tracing, the system starts from the TLAS and works its way down to the appropriate BLAS. The TLAS essentially acts as a directory that guides the system to the correct BLAS based on the ray's path.

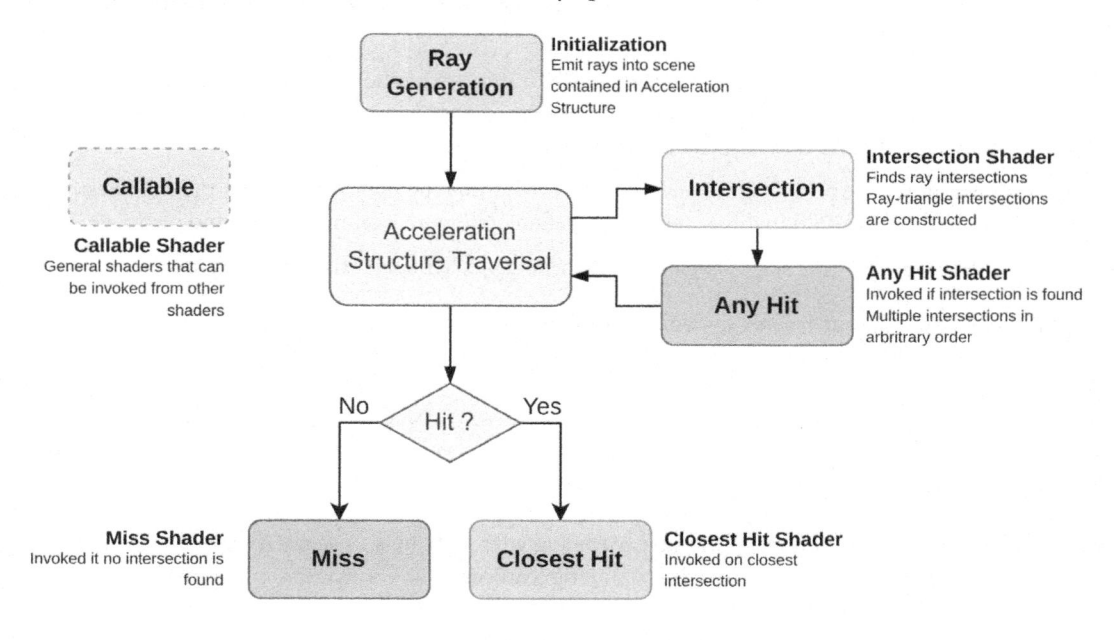

Figure 7.3 – Ray tracing pipeline and its stages

The shader stages are as follows:

1. **Ray generation stage**: The ray generation shader is essentially the starting point for ray tracing. Its primary function is to generate the initial or primary rays that are shot from the camera. This is accomplished by utilizing the traceRayExt function. These rays are what will eventually interact with the objects in the scene to create the final rendered image.

2. **Acceleration structure traversal**: The acceleration structure is a key component in optimizing the process of ray tracing. It functions as a scene management tree, akin to a BVH. Its primary use is to speed up collision detection between rays and objects within the scene. This part of the pipeline is fixed, meaning Vulkan has already implemented the logic behind it.

3. **Intersection stage**: As the rays traverse the BVH, they may call upon an intersection shader. This shader is particularly useful when dealing with custom types but isn't necessary when using the default triangle mesh primitive. This is because Vulkan has already incorporated the logic required for these default primitives, thereby bypassing the need for the intersection shader.

4. **Any-hit stage**: This stage processes intersection events found in the intersection stage; in case of an intersection, the any-hit shader is invoked. The any-hit shader determines the subsequent steps after the intersection of light and material occurs, such as whether to abandon the intersection and so on. Depending on the specific requirements, the intersection point can be discarded, at which point it is considered that no intersection took place. This process is then returned to the BLAS traversal.

5. **Closest hit stage**: This shader is responsible for processing the intersection that is currently the closest to the ray origin and has not yet been discarded by an any-hit stage. It typically involves applying light and material calculations to render the final color of the pixel.

6. **Miss stage**: The miss stage determines how to handle the light in the event the ray doesn't hit anything. This could involve assigning a default color, environment color, and so on.

7. **Callable stage**: This stage may be called from any other stage (from their shader code).

In the repository, the ray tracing code is encapsulated in the `RayTracer` class.

How to do it...

As a first step, we will look at the code that needs to be executed on the host side; most of the implementation is inside the `RayTracer` class:

1. The first critical step in setting up ray tracing with Vulkan is to verify if our physical device (GPU) supports ray tracing features. This verification is achieved by adding `VkPhysicalDeviceRayTracingPipelineFeaturesKHR` and `VkPhysicalDeviceAccelerationStructureFeaturesKHR` to the list of physical features that are checked for support. This feature-checking operation is implemented in the `PhysicalDevice` class. Here, these specific features are added to the `VkPhysicalDeviceFeatures2` structure's chain, serving as a mechanism to query the support for a set of features. This class also supplies the `isRayTracingSupported` function, which is utilized to activate the necessary features for ray tracing during the Vulkan device's creation process. In the `Context` class, we introduce specific features for `VkPhysicalDeviceAccelerationStructureFeaturesKHR` and

VkPhysicalDeviceRayTracingPipelineFeaturesKHR. However, these features are only activated during the construction of the Vulkan device if the demo application has ray tracing enabled and the physical device confirms its support for these features. Please also note that the demo application will only run if your GPU supports Vulkan ray tracing.

2. Next, we create shader modules for each of the shaders that will be used by the ray tracing pipeline:

```
auto rayGenShader = context_->createShaderModule(
  (resourcesFolder / "raytrace_raygen.rgen")
    .string(),
  VK_SHADER_STAGE_RAYGEN_BIT_KHR,
  "RayTracer RayGen Shader");

auto rayMissShader = context_->createShaderModule(
  (resourcesFolder / "raytrace_miss.rmiss")
    .string(),
  VK_SHADER_STAGE_MISS_BIT_KHR,
  "RayTracer Miss Shader");

auto rayMissShadowShader =
  context_->createShaderModule(
    (resourcesFolder / "raytrace_shadow.rmiss")
      .string(),
    VK_SHADER_STAGE_MISS_BIT_KHR,
    "RayTracer Miss Shadow Shader");

auto rayClosestHitShader =
  context_->createShaderModule(
    (resourcesFolder /
     "raytrace_closesthit.rchit")
      .string(),
    VK_SHADER_STAGE_CLOSEST_HIT_BIT_KHR,
    "RayTracer Closest hit Shader");
```

3. Next, we create a ray tracing pipeline by calling Pipeline::createRayTracingPipeline(). To facilitate creating a ray tracing pipeline, we added a helper structure, called Pipeline::RayTracingPipelineDescriptor, which stores the descriptor sets and their bindings (just like in the graphics and compute pipelines descriptors), and all shaders required to create a ray tracing pipeline. An instance of this structure must be passed to the constructor of the VulkanCore::Pipeline class:

```
struct RayTracingPipelineDescriptor {
  std::vector<SetDescriptor> sets_;
  std::weak_ptr<ShaderModule> rayGenShader_;
```

```
    std::vector<std::weak_ptr<ShaderModule>>
      rayMissShaders_;
    std::vector<std::weak_ptr<ShaderModule>>
      rayClosestHitShaders_;
    std::vector<VkPushConstantRange> pushConstants_;
};
```

A ray tracing pipeline in Vulkan necessitates an array of shader group structures. Rather than holding a list of shaders, each **shader group** serves as a mapping structure, detailing the association of shaders to their designated pipeline stages. At the time of creating the ray tracing pipeline, an array of all the shaders used by the pipeline must be provided, alongside the corresponding shader groups. Here's the definition of the shader group (VkRayTracingShaderGroupCreateInfoKHR) structure:

```
typedef struct VkRayTracingShaderGroupCreateInfoKHR {
    VkStructureType sType;
    const void *pNext;
    VkRayTracingShaderGroupTypeKHR type;
    uint32_t generalShader;
    uint32_t closestHitShader;
    uint32_t anyHitShader;
    uint32_t intersectionShader;
    const void *pShaderGroupCaptureReplayHandle;
} VkRayTracingShaderGroupCreateInfoKHR;
```

The structure contains fields to specify shaders for only four different stages of the pipeline (generalShader, closestHitShader, anyHitShader, and intersectionShader). That's because the indices of shaders for the miss and callable stages are provided in the generalShader field. It's important to note that the function of these fields depends on the value of the type member in the structure.

4. For the sake of brevity, we show here only the creation of one shader stage and one shader group. The other shader modules passed along with the pipeline descriptor are grouped into their own shader groups. In the provided code snippet, we demonstrate the construction of a shader group specifically for a ray generation shader. It's crucial to understand that each type of shader utilized in Vulkan ray tracing requires its own individual shader group. It's necessary because the design of the Vulkan ray tracing pipeline is such that it allows for different types of shaders to operate independently, each performing a unique task in the ray tracing process. By structuring each type of shader in its own shader group, we ensure that the corresponding tasks are executed independently and efficiently, aiding in the parallel computation capabilities of the GPU. Please refer to the code in Pipeline::createrayTracingPipeline() for more details:

```
    std::vector<VkPipelineShaderStageCreateInfo>
      shaderStages;
```

```cpp
    std::vector<VkRayTracingShaderGroupCreateInfoKHR>
      shaderGroups;

    const VkPipelineShaderStageCreateInfo
      rayGenShaderInfo{
        .sType =
          VK_STRUCTURE_TYPE_PIPELINE_SHADER_STAGE_CREATE_INFO,
        .stage = rayGenShader->vkShaderStageFlags(),
        .module = rayGenShader->vkShaderModule(),
        .pName = rayGenShader->entryPoint().c_str(),
      };
    shaderStages.push_back(rayGenShaderInfo);

    const VkRayTracingShaderGroupCreateInfoKHR
      shaderGroup{
        .sType =
          VK_STRUCTURE_TYPE_RAY_TRACING_SHADER_GROUP_CREATE_INFO_KHR,
        .type =
          VK_RAY_TRACING_SHADER_GROUP_TYPE_GENERAL_KHR,
        .generalShader =
          static_cast<uint32_t>(shaderStages.size()) -
          1,
        .closestHitShader = VK_SHADER_UNUSED_KHR,
        .anyHitShader = VK_SHADER_UNUSED_KHR,
        .intersectionShader = VK_SHADER_UNUSED_KHR,
      };
    shaderGroups.push_back(shaderGroup);
```

5. Finally, here's how you create a ray tracing pipeline:

```cpp
    VkRayTracingPipelineCreateInfoKHR rayTracingPipelineInfo{
        .sType = VK_STRUCTURE_TYPE_RAY_TRACING_PIPELINE_CREATE_INFO_KHR,
        .stageCount = static_cast<uint32_t>(shaderStages.size()),
        .pStages = shaderStages.data(),
        .groupCount = static_cast<uint32_t>(shaderGroups.size()),
        .pGroups = shaderGroups.data(),
        .maxPipelineRayRecursionDepth = 10,
        .layout = vkPipelineLayout_,
```

```
    };
    VK_CHECK(vkCreateRayTracingPipelinesKHR(context_->device(),
VK_NULL_HANDLE,
                                              VK_NULL_HANDLE, 1,
    &rayTracingPipelineInfo,
                                              nullptr,
    &vkPipeline_));
```

6. The next step is to create the **shader binding table** (**SBT**). This structure facilitates the linking of shaders to the specific parts of the scene where they will be applied. In the repository, we define a structure for the SBT, which contains a buffer to store the binding table and a `VkStridedDeviceAddressRegionKHR` structure that describes the location and structure of the SBT in memory:

```
struct SBT {
  std::shared_ptr<VulkanCore::Buffer> buffer;
  VkStridedDeviceAddressRegionKHR sbtAddress;
};
```

7. The `createShaderBindingTable()` function is where the SBT is created. This function begins by defining several variables to store the sizes and counts of various shader types in the application. In the code, `handleSize` and `handleSizeAligned` represent the size of a single shader group handle in the SBT, with the latter ensuring correct memory alignment:

```
void EngineCore::RayTracer::
createShaderBindingTable() {
const uint32_t handleSize =
  context_->physicalDevice()
    .rayTracingProperties()
    .shaderGroupHandleSize;
const uint32_t handleSizeAligned =
  alignedSize(context_->physicalDevice()
                .rayTracingProperties()
                .shaderGroupHandleSize,
              context_->physicalDevice()
                .rayTracingProperties()
                .shaderGroupHandleAlignment);
```

`numRayGenShaders`, `numRayMissShaders`, and `numRayClosestHitShaders` represent the number of each type of shader used in the pipeline. Next, we calculate the total size of the SBT (`sbtSize`) and create a `shaderHandleStorage` vector to store the shader handles:

```
const uint32_t numRayGenShaders = 1;
const uint32_t numRayMissShaders =
  2; // 1 for miss and 1 for shadow
```

```
        const uint32_t numRayClosestHitShaders = 1;

        const uint32_t numShaderGroups =
          numRayGenShaders + numRayMissShaders +
          numRayClosestHitShaders;
        const uint32_t groupCount =
          static_cast<uint32_t>(numShaderGroups);
        const uint32_t sbtSize =
          groupCount * handleSizeAligned;
```

8. The vkGetRayTracingShaderGroupHandlesKHR Vulkan function is then called to retrieve the shader group handles. These handles are unique identifiers for the shader groups in the pipeline. Afterward, we create separate buffers for each shader type (**RayGen**, **RayMiss**, and **RayClosestHit**) and set the stride, size, and device address for each. For each buffer, the copyDataToBuffer method is called to copy the relevant shader handles from shaderHandleStorage into the buffer. We recommend looking at the createShaderBindingTable function:

```
    std::vector<uint8_t> shaderHandleStorage(sbtSize);
    VK_CHECK(vkGetRayTracingShaderGroupHandlesKHR(
        context_->device(), pipeline_->vkPipeline(), 0,
        groupCount, sbtSize,
        shaderHandleStorage.data()));
```

9. Each buffer and its respective VkStridedDeviceAddressRegionKHR need to be filled. Here, we only show how ray generation is populated. The other groups follow a similar pattern:

```
    raygenSBT_.buffer = context_->createBuffer(
      context_->physicalDevice()
          .rayTracingProperties()
          .shaderGroupHandleSize *
        numRayGenShaders,
      VK_BUFFER_USAGE_SHADER_BINDING_TABLE_BIT_KHR |
        VK_BUFFER_USAGE_SHADER_DEVICE_ADDRESS_BIT,
      VMA_MEMORY_USAGE_CPU_ONLY, "RayGen SBT Buffer");

    raygenSBT_.sbtAddress.deviceAddress =
      raygenSBT_.buffer->vkDeviceAddress();
    raygenSBT_.sbtAddress.size =
      handleSizeAligned * numRayGenShaders;
    raygenSBT_.sbtAddress.stride = handleSizeAligned;

    raygenSBT_.buffer->copyDataToBuffer(
      shaderHandleStorage.data(),
      handleSize *numRayGenShaders);
```

10. Next, we need to load the environment map along with its acceleration structure. The `RayTracer::loadEnvMap()` method performs the loading of the environment map and the creation of the acceleration structure. It loads a **high dynamic range** (**HDR**) file and creates a corresponding Vulkan texture by calling `context_->createTexture()`. It then calls `createEnvironmentAccel()`, which is responsible for creating an acceleration data structure for importance sampling of the environment map. This function computes a vector of `EnvAccel` structures, one for each texel of the map. This data is uploaded to a device-only buffer.

11. Next, we create TLASs and BLASs with the `RayTracer::initBottomLevelAccelStruct()` and `RayTracer::initTopLevelAccelStruct()` methods.

    In the following steps, you will learn how to set up BLAS using Vulkan:

    A. **Creating acceleration structure geometry**: This describes the data used to build the acceleration structure. In this case, it's a triangle geometry (VK_GEOMETRY_TYPE_TRIANGLES_KHR) with vertices and indices from the model's buffers:

```
VkAccelerationStructureGeometryKHR
  accelerationStructureGeometry{
    .sType =
      VK_STRUCTURE_TYPE_ACCELERATION_STRUCTURE_GEOMETRY_KHR,
    .geometryType = VK_GEOMETRY_TYPE_TRIANGLES_KHR,
    .geometry = {
      .triangles = {
        .sType =
          VK_STRUCTURE_TYPE_ACCELERATION_STRUCTURE_GEOMETRY_TRIANGLES_DATA_KHR,
        .vertexFormat =
          VK_FORMAT_R32G32B32_SFLOAT,
        .vertexData = vertexBufferDeviceAddress,
        .vertexStride =
          sizeof(EngineCore::Vertex),
        .maxVertex = numVertices,
        .indexType = VK_INDEX_TYPE_UINT32,
        .indexData = indexBufferDeviceAddress,
      },
    },
  };
```

B. **Getting the required sizes to build the acceleration structure**: The `vkGetAccelerationStructureBuildSizesKHR` function call returns the size information needed to allocate the acceleration structure and the build scratch buffer. The `bLAS_[meshIdx].buffer` buffer is populated as a direct result of the `vkGetAccelerationStructureBuildSizesKHR` function call:

```
VkAccelerationStructureBuildSizesInfoKHR
  accelerationStructureBuildSizesInfo{
    .sType =
      VK_STRUCTURE_TYPE_ACCELERATION_STRUCTURE_BUILD_SIZES_INFO_KHR,
  };
vkGetAccelerationStructureBuildSizesKHR(
  context_->device(),
  VK_ACCELERATION_STRUCTURE_BUILD_TYPE_DEVICE_KHR,
  &accelerationStructureBuildGeometryInfo,
  &numTriangles,
  &accelerationStructureBuildSizesInfo);
```

C. **Building the acceleration structure**: After setting up the necessary data, the acceleration structure is finally built using a command buffer. First, we create a buffer named `bLAS_[meshIdx].buffer`, which is used to store the BLAS structure. We then create a structure of the `VkAccelerationStructureCreateInfoKHR` type, to which we provide the buffer just created, its size, and specify that it's a BLAS. Next, we call `vkCreateAccelerationStructureKHR` to create the actual acceleration structure and store the handle to it in `bLAS_[meshIdx].handle`. We created a temporary buffer named `tempBuffer` to store the temporary data needed when building the acceleration structure. When you are building an acceleration structure in Vulkan, the build procedure often needs some temporary space to perform its calculations. This temporary space is also referred to as a scratch buffer. We then fill a `VkAccelerationStructureBuildGeometryInfoKHR` structure with the details of the acceleration structure build, including the handle of the acceleration structure, the geometry, and the device address of `tempBuffer`. Next, we create a `VkAccelerationStructureBuildRangeInfoKHR` structure to specify the range of geometries to be used in the build. The `vkCmdBuildAccelerationStructuresKHR` function records the command to build the acceleration structure into the command buffer:

```
// Creating buffer to hold the acceleration structure
bLAS_[meshIdx].buffer = context_->createBuffer(...);
// Creating acceleration structure
VkAccelerationStructureCreateInfoKHR
  accelerationStructureCreateInfo{
    .sType = VK_STRUCTURE_TYPE_ACCELERATION_STRUCTURE_CREATE_INFO_KHR,
    .buffer = bLAS_[meshIdx].buffer->vkBuffer(),
```

```
        .size = accelerationStructureBuildSizesInfo.
accelerationStructureSize,
        .type = VK_ACCELERATION_STRUCTURE_TYPE_BOTTOM_LEVEL_KHR};
VK_CHECK(vkCreateAccelerationStructureKHR(context_->device(),

    &accelerationStructureCreateInfo, nullptr,

    &bLAS_[meshIdx].handle));

// Creating temporary buffer
auto tempBuffer = context_->createBuffer(...);

// Setting up geometry and build range info for acceleration
structure
VkAccelerationStructureBuildGeometryInfoKHR
accelerationBuildGeometryInfo{
    .sType = VK_STRUCTURE_TYPE_ACCELERATION_STRUCTURE_BUILD_
GEOMETRY_INFO_KHR,
    .dstAccelerationStructure = bLAS_[meshIdx].handle,
    .scratchData = {.deviceAddress = tempBuffer-
>vkDeviceAddress()}};
VkAccelerationStructureBuildRangeInfoKHR
accelerationStructureBuildRangeInfo{
    .primitiveCount = numTriangles};

// Building acceleration structure
const auto commandBuffer = commandQueueMgr.
getCmdBufferToBegin();
vkCmdBuildAccelerationStructuresKHR(
    commandBuffer, 1, &accelerationBuildGeometryInfo,
    &accelerationStructureBuildRangeInfo);
```

12. In the following steps, you will learn how to set up a TLAS in Vulkan:

    A. **Creating the acceleration structure instances**: The following loop creates the instances, each of which references a BLAS. Instances contain information about the transformation matrix, mask, flags, and the device address of the BLAS it references:

    ```
    for (int meshIdx = 0; meshIdx < model->meshes.size();
         ++meshIdx) {
      VkAccelerationStructureInstanceKHR instance{};
      ...
      instance.accelerationStructureReference =
        bLAS_[meshIdx].buffer->vkDeviceAddress();
      accelarationInstances_.push_back(instance);
    }
    ```

B. **Creating acceleration structure geometry**: The following code describes the data used to build the acceleration structure. In this case, it's a set of instances (VK_GEOMETRY_TYPE_INSTANCES_KHR):

```
VkAccelerationStructureGeometryKHR
  accelerationStructureGeometry{
    .sType = VK_STRUCTURE_TYPE_ACCELERATION_STRUCTURE_GEOMETRY_KHR,
    .geometryType = VK_GEOMETRY_TYPE_INSTANCES_KHR,
    .geometry = {
      .instances = {
        .sType = VK_STRUCTURE_TYPE_ACCELERATION_STRUCTURE_GEOMETRY_INSTANCES_DATA_KHR,
        .data = instanceDataDeviceAddress,
      },
    },
    .flags = VK_GEOMETRY_OPAQUE_BIT_KHR,
};
```

C. **Getting the required sizes to build the acceleration structure**: The vkGetAccelerationStructureBuildSizesKHR function call returns the size information needed to allocate the acceleration structure and the build scratch buffer:

```
VkAccelerationStructureBuildSizesInfoKHR
  accelerationStructureBuildSizesInfo{
    .sType =
      VK_STRUCTURE_TYPE_ACCELERATION_STRUCTURE_BUILD_SIZES_INFO_KHR,
  };
vkGetAccelerationStructureBuildSizesKHR(
  context_->device(),
  VK_ACCELERATION_STRUCTURE_BUILD_TYPE_DEVICE_KHR,
  &accelerationStructureBuildGeometryInfo,
  &primitiveCount,
  &accelerationStructureBuildSizesInfo);
```

D. **Creating the acceleration structure**: The acceleration structure is created using the previously obtained size information. Notice the use of VK_ACCELERATION_STRUCTURE_TYPE_TOP_LEVEL_KHR in the type field since we are building a TLAS. The final part is to record the vkCmdBuildAccelerationStructuresKHR command on the command buffer which is executed when the command buffer is submitted:

```
VkAccelerationStructureCreateInfoKHR
  accelerationStructureCreateInfo{
    .sType =
      VK_STRUCTURE_TYPE_ACCELERATION_STRUCTURE_CREATE_INFO_KHR,
```

```
        .buffer = tLAS_.buffer->vkBuffer(),
        .size = accelerationStructureBuildSizesInfo
                  .accelerationStructureSize,
        .type =
          VK_ACCELERATION_STRUCTURE_TYPE_TOP_LEVEL_KHR,
    };
    VK_CHECK(vkCreateAccelerationStructureKHR(
      context_->device(),
      &accelerationStructureCreateInfo, nullptr,
      &tLAS_.handle));

    vkCmdBuildAccelerationStructuresKHR(
      commandBuffer, 1, &accelerationBuildGeometryInfo,
      accelerationBuildStructureRangeInfos.data());
```

13. We also create a `RayTraced` storage image (encapsulated in `initRayTracedStorageImages`) and bind resources by calling `bindResource` on the pipeline during the initialization.

14. To execute a ray tracer, we need to call `RayTracer::execute()`, which is responsible for copying the camera data, binding the pipeline, and calling `vkCmdTraceRaysKHR`. This Vulkan function launches the `RayGen` shader.

Now that we have understood the steps on the host side, it's time to understand the device-side code. The device-side code for ray tracing is implemented using several shaders including `raytrace_raygen.rgen`, `raytrace_miss.rmiss`, `raytrace_closesthit.rchit`, and `raytrace_shadow.rmiss`:

1. The process begins with the invocation of the `raytrace_raygen.rgen` shader via `vkCmdTraceRaysKHR`. In the following shader code block, the ray tracing process initiates by generating rays for each pixel sample through a unique seed for randomness. These rays, defined by their origin and direction, are traced into the scene within a loop until either the maximum number of bounces is reached, or an exit condition is met in the payload. The payload carries essential information such as origin, direction, and bounce index. Once the final color for the pixel is calculated using an average from all samples, it is stored in the output image. If temporal accumulation is applied, the shader retrieves and adds colors from previous frames. Temporal accumulation is beneficial in ray tracing as it helps to reduce noise and improve image quality. Accumulating or averaging the color samples over multiple frames effectively increases the number of rays traced per pixel without the cost of tracing extra rays in a single frame:

```
void main() {
  // Ray Generation
  // tea refers to Tiny Encryption Algorithm, used to generate a
  unique and reproducible seed for each task and frame.
  uint seed =
    tea(gl_LaunchIDEXT.y * gl_LaunchIDEXT.x +
```

```glsl
                gl_LaunchIDEXT.x,
        camProps.frameId);
  vec3 finalOutColor = vec3(0);
  vec2 pixelCenter = vec2(gl_LaunchIDEXT.xy) +
                     vec2(0.5) +
                     vec2(rand(seed), rand(seed));
  vec4 target =
    camProps.projInverse *
    vec4(pixelCenter / vec2(gl_LaunchSizeEXT.xy) *
             2.0 -
           1.0,
         1, 1);
  vec4 direction =
    camProps.viewInverse *
    vec4(normalize(target.xyz / target.w), 0);

  // Initial Payload Setup
  rayPayload.currentBounceIndex = 0;
  rayPayload.exit = false;
  rayPayload.origin =
    (camProps.viewInverse * vec4(0, 0, 0, 1)).xyz;
  rayPayload.direction = direction.xyz;

  // Ray Tracing Loop
  for (int j = 0; j < MAX_BOUNCES; ++j) {
    rayPayload.currentBounceIndex = j;
  // Traces a ray using a culling mask of 0xff to include all
potential intersections.
    traceRayEXT(topLevelAccelStruct,
                gl_RayFlagsOpaqueEXT, 0xff, 0, 0, 0,
                rayPayload.origin.xyz, 0.001,
                rayPayload.direction.xyz, 10000.0, 0);
    if (rayPayload.exit)
      break;
  }

  // Final Color Calculation and Image Store
  finalOutColor += rayPayload.radiance / MAX_SAMPLES;
  imageStore(outputImage, ivec2(gl_LaunchIDEXT.xy),
             vec4(linear2sRGB(finalOutColor), 0.0));
}
```

2. The `raytrace_miss.rmiss` shader is pretty simple: it is invoked if the ray doesn't intersect any object. In such scenarios, the shader takes a sample from the environment map, determining the color based on the point of interaction between the ray and the environment. The `envMapColor` function takes a 3D direction vector as an input, normalizes it, and converts it into spherical coordinates (theta and phi). It then maps these coordinates onto a 2D plane (UV) and retrieves the corresponding color from the environment map texture. The following code block simply calls the `envMapColor` function to get the radiance for the current ray payload:

```
void main() {
  rayPayload.radiance =
    envMapColor(gl_WorldRayDirectionEXT);
  rayPayload.exit = true;
}
```

3. The `raytrace_closesthit.rchit` shader is where most of the magic, including a calculation for shading and determining the subsequent direction of the ray, happens:

   A. The initial stage of the process involves extracting the vertex and material data for the mesh that has been struck by the ray. This is achieved by utilizing the `gl_InstanceID` and `gl_PrimitiveID` variables, which are populated with the relevant data by the intersection shader. The hit shader also provides access to `hitAttributeEXT vec2 attribs`. In the context of triangles, these attributes represent the barycentric coordinates of the intersection point. Barycentric coordinates are a form of coordinate system used to specify the position of a point within a triangle. They are particularly useful in computer graphics because they allow for easy interpolation across a triangle. By using these coordinates, we can interpolate the positions of the vertices to determine the precise point of intersection within the triangle where the ray has made contact. Please refer to the code in `raytrace_closesthit.rchit` to understand how we use barycentric coordinates to get world space position.

   B. The next step is to call the `envSample()` function. This function is a crucial part of the ray tracing process, responsible for sampling the HDR environment map using importance sampling. The environment map is represented as a 2D texture (latitude-longitude format) and contains the illumination data of the surrounding environment. The function starts by uniformly picking a texel index in the environment map. It fetches the sampling data for that texel, which includes the ratio between the texel's emitted radiance and the environment map's average, the texel alias, and the distribution function values for that texel and its alias. The function then decides to either pick the texel directly or pick its alias based on a random variable and the intensity ratio. It computes the 2D integer coordinates of the chosen texel and uniformly samples the solid angle subtended by the pixel. The function converts the sampled UV coordinates to a direction in spherical coordinates, which is then converted to a light direction vector in Cartesian coordinates. This light direction vector is then returned along with the texel's PDF:

```
vec3 envLightColor = vec3(0);
vec4 dirPdf =
  envSample(envLightColor, rayPayload.seed);
vec3 lightDir = dirPdf.xyz;
float lightPdf = dirPdf.w;
```

C. Shadow rays play a crucial role in the ray tracing process. They help in creating realistic lighting effects by determining which parts of the scene are in shadow, thus adding depth and realism to the rendered image. The next step is to trace a shadow ray from the intersection point towards the light source to check for any occluding objects. This is a critical step in determining whether a point is in shadow or not. The `inshadow` variable is declared using `layout(location = 1) rayPayloadEXT bool inshadow`. When a ray is traced in a ray tracing shader, it carries with it a payload. This payload can be used to store information that needs to be passed between different stages of the ray tracing pipeline, such as from the closest hit shader to the ray generation shader. The `inshadow` variable is a Boolean that is used to store the information of whether a particular point is in shadow. When the shadow ray (a ray traced from the intersection point towards the light) is occluded by another object, this variable will be set to true, indicating that the point is in shadow. Please be aware that in the `traceRayEXT` function, the 6th parameter is set to `1`. This value serves as an index to specify which miss shader should be invoked. In this context, it refers to the miss shader found in `raytrace_shadow.miss`:

```
inshadow = true;
const int layoutLocation = 1;
// Trace the shadow ray
traceRayEXT(topLevelAccelStruct, rayFlags, cullMask,
            0, 0, 1, worldPosition, rayMinDist,
            lightDir, rayMaxDist, layoutLocation);
```

The next step is responsible for lighting calculation using the **physically based rendering** (**PBR**) model. The PBR model is evaluated with inputs such as the material's properties, incoming light direction, and the normal at the point of intersection. The resulting color is then calculated based on the light's color, the evaluated PBR, and the cosine of the angle between the light direction and the normal. The `PbrEval` function evaluates the PBR model for a given set of inputs. It uses the material properties (such as base color, specular color, roughness, and metallic factors), **view direction** (**V**), **normal** (**N**), and **light direction** (**L**) to compute the BRDF. This function handles both diffuse and specular contributions using the **Graphics Library Transmission Format's** (**glTF**) PBR model, with respect to the Fresnel equations. The function balances these contributions based on the metallic factor and returns the combined BRDF and its associated PDF. The final step is an accumulation of the light contribution (radiance) that a ray receives as it travels through the scene; `rayPayload.radiance` is the accumulated color or light contribution that the ray has gathered from all the light sources it has encountered up until now. `rayPayload.throughput` is a measure of how much light makes it through a certain path without being absorbed or scattered. Essentially, it's a measure of the energy left of a light path. For details on PBR theory, please visit `https://learnopengl.com/PBR/Theory`:

```
if (!inshadow) {
  float pdf;
  // returns diffuse & specular both
  vec3 F =
    PbrEval(eta, metallic, roughness, baseColor.rgb,
            specularColor, -rayPayload.direction, N,
            lightDir, pdf);
  float cosTheta = abs(dot(lightDir, N));
  float misWeight =
    max(0.0, powerHeuristic(lightPdf, pdf));
  if (misWeight > 0.0) {
    directLightColor += misWeight * F * cosTheta *
                        envLightColor /
                        (lightPdf + EPS);
  }
}
rayPayload.radiance +=
  directLightColor * rayPayload.throughput;
```

A. The final part is to figure out the next ray direction as well as the throughput (energy left) for the next ray. It starts by sampling a direction for the next ray (`bsdfDirNextRay`) using the `PbrSample` function, which uses the material properties and the current ray direction to generate this direction. We calculate `cosTheta`, which is the cosine of the angle between the surface normal and the direction of the next ray. This is used in the calculation of the new throughput because the amount of light reflected is proportional to the cosine of this angle (**Lambert's cosine law**). Finally, we update the ray's direction and origin for the next bounce. The direction is the sampled direction `bsdfDirNextRay`, and the origin is slightly offset from the current position to avoid self-intersection. Please note `PBREval` is used to evaluate the BRDF in a specific direction while `PBRSample` is used to generate a new direction and evaluate the BRDF in that direction:

```
Vec3 F = PbrSample(baseColor.rgb, specularColor, eta,
                   materialIOR, metallic, roughness,
                   T, B, -rayPayload.direction,
                   ffnormal, bsdfDirNextRay,
```

```
                        bsdfpdfNextRay, rayPayload.seed);
float cosTheta = abs(dot(N, bsdfDirNextRay));
rayPayload.throughput *=
  F * cosTheta / (bsdfpdfNextRay);
// Russian roulette
float rrPcont =
  min(max3(rayPayload.throughput) * eta * eta + 0.001,
      0.95);
rayPayload.throughput /= rrPcont;
// update new ray direction & position
rayPayload.direction = bsdfDirNextRay;
rayPayload.origin = offsetRay(
  worldPosition, dot(bsdfDirNextRay, worldNormal) > 0
                   ? worldNormal
                   : -worldNormal);
```

This concludes various parts of how to implement a simple GPU-based ray tracer in Vulkan.

See also

We recommend reading the *Ray Tracing in One Weekend* book series:

- `https://github.com/RayTracing/raytracing.github.io`

Adam Celarek and Bernhard Kerbl's YouTube channel contains a trove of information about lighting and ray-tracing:

- `https://www.youtube.com/playlist?list=PLmIqTlJ6KsE2yXzeq02hqCDpOdtj6n6A9`

Implementing hybrid rendering

In this recipe, we will explore the integration of rasterization, specifically deferred rendering, with ray-traced shadows.

In *Chapter 4, Exploring Techniques for Lighting, Shading, and Shadows*, we implemented deferred rendering, incorporating techniques such as shadow mapping, screen space AO, and screen space reflections. These techniques allowed us to generate multiple textures, which were then composited during the lighting pass. Within this recipe, you will gain insights into generating shadow textures using ray tracing, which will help in overcoming challenges associated with techniques such as screen space shadow mapping. Screen space shadow mapping relies on the information available in the rendered image. It doesn't have complete access to the entire 3D scene geometry. This limitation can result in inaccuracies and artifacts. Screen space shadow mapping is susceptible to aliasing issues, particularly along edges and boundaries due to the resolution of the screen space texture. The ray tracing approach doesn't have these problems as it works on a full scene.

Getting ready

Within the code repository, the hybrid rendering functionality is realized through the `RayTracedShadowPass` and `LightingPassHybridRenderer` classes.

The process begins with the execution of the `Gbuffer` pass, generating G-buffer textures based on the concepts discussed in *Chapter 4, Exploring Techniques for Lighting, Shading, and Shadows*. Following this, `RayTracedShadowPass` is initiated, employing the ray tracing stages outlined in the preceding section. However, in this pass, ray tracing is specifically employed to generate the shadow texture. The final step involves employing `LightingPassHybridRenderer` to compose information from the G-buffer and the ray-traced shadow texture, culminating in the production of a final image for display.

The device side code for the ray tracing shader is in the following:

```
raytrace_raygen_shadow_hybrid.rgen, raytrace_miss_shadow_hybrid.rmiss, raytrace_closesthit_shadow_hybrid.rchit
```

The device side code for compositing is in the following:

```
hybridRenderer_lighting_composite.frag.
```

Now that we have understood the code structure, we will investigate how to implement it in the following section.

How to do it...

The host side part of the code is in `RayTracedShadowPass` and the setup for it is very similar to what we described during the previous recipe. We will focus on the device side code to look at how we generate shadows:

1. As usual, we start the shader with a declaration for the input and uniform variables that the shader will use. The `layout(location = 0) rayPayloadEXT float visibilityRayPayload;` line defines the payload that will be returned by the ray tracing operation. The other uniform variables declared are for the acceleration structure, output image, and textures for the normal and position G-buffers:

```
layout(location = 0) rayPayloadEXT
  float visibilityRayPayload;
layout(set = 0, binding = 0) uniform
  accelerationStructureEXT topLevelAccelStruct;
layout(set = 0, binding = 1,
       rgba8) uniform image2D outputImage;
layout(set = 1,
       binding = 0) uniform sampler2D gbufferNormal;
layout(set = 1,
       binding = 1) uniform sampler2D gbufferPosition;
```

2. The `main` function is where the actual computation happens. It starts by calculating the pixel center and the UV coordinates for the current pixel (or launch). Then, it fetches the normal and world position from the G-buffers using the UV coordinates. `rayOrigin` is calculated by offsetting the world position slightly along the normal direction. This is to prevent **self-intersection**, where the ray might incorrectly intersect with the surface it was launched from:

   ```
   const vec2 pixelCenter =
     vec2(gl_LaunchIDEXT.xy) + vec2(0.5);
   const vec2 inUV =
     pixelCenter / vec2(gl_LaunchSizeEXT.xy);
   vec3 normal =
     normalize(texture(gbufferNormal, inUV).xyz);
   vec3 worldPosition =
     texture(gbufferPosition, inUV).xyz;
   vec3 rayOrigin = worldPosition + normal * 0.1f;
   ```

3. The shader launches multiple shadow rays towards random points on the light source. The loop runs for several samples, generating a random point on the light source for each sample, and then calculates the direction to that point. The `traceRayEXT` function is called to trace a ray from `rayOrigin` toward the light source. If the ray hits something before it reaches the light, the payload will be 0, indicating that the light source is occluded. If the ray reaches the light source without hitting anything, the payload will be 1, indicating that the light source is visible. The visibility for each sample is accumulated in the `visible` variable. The accumulated visibility for each sample, represented by the `visible` variable, is then stored in the corresponding location of the final image:

   ```
   for (int i = 0; i < numSamples; i++) {
     vec3 randomPointOnLight =
       lightData.lightPos.xyz +
       (rand3(seed) - 0.5) * lightSize;
     vec3 directionToLight =
       normalize(randomPointOnLight - worldPosition);
     // Start the raytrace
     traceRayEXT(topLevelAccelStruct, rayFlags, 0xFF, 0,
                 0, 0, rayOrigin.xyz, tMin,
                 directionToLight.xyz, tMax, 0);
     visible += visibilityRayPayload;
   }
   visible /= float(numSamples);
   ```

4. `raytrace_miss_shadow_hybrid.rmiss` and `raytrace_closesthit_shadow_hybrid.rchit` are pretty straightforward; they simply set `visibilityRayPayload` to 1.0 if it's a miss and 0.0 in case we hit something.

5. The last step is the compositing step. This is the same as the lighting pass we discussed in *Chapter 4, Exploring Techniques for Lighting, Shading, and Shadows*, the only difference being that now we are using a shadow texture that has been created using ray tracing.

In this chapter, we explored the world of ray tracing and hybrid rendering in Vulkan. We delved into these advanced graphical techniques, understanding how they can provide unprecedented levels of realism in rendered images. We learned how ray tracing algorithms work, tracing the path of rays of light to create highly detailed and physically accurate reflections and shadows in a 3D scene. Through hybrid rendering, we uncovered the process of combining traditional rasterization with ray tracing to achieve a balance between performance and visual fidelity. This blend allows for the high speed of rasterization where the utmost precision isn't required while using ray tracing to handle complex light interactions that rasterization struggles with. Vulkan's robust support for both techniques was explored, leveraging its efficient capabilities and explicit control over hardware resources.

8

Extended Reality with OpenXR

Similar to what Vulkan is for graphics, OpenXR, an integral part of the world of **Extended Reality** (**XR**), is an API that serves as a powerful tool for implementing XR applications. This chapter provides an overview of OpenXR and how to use it in conjunction with Vulkan. We start with a basic introduction to OpenXR, explaining its role and significance in XR applications, and follow with recipes that may be used to improve your XR applications, such as **single pass multiview** rendering, a technique that optimizes the rendering of stereo scenes. The chapter further expands into the realm of foveated rendering, a method that significantly bolsters **Frames Per Second** (**FPS**) by rendering different sections of the screen at diverse resolutions. We delve into the implementation of this technique using the **fragment shading rate** feature of the Vulkan extension, providing you with a practical understanding of its application. Lastly, we delve into the use of **half floats**, a practical aid in conserving memory space on **Head-Mounted Displays** (**HMDs**). By the end of this chapter, you will have gained an understanding of these concepts and will be equipped with the skills to apply them effectively in your XR projects.

In this chapter, we will cover the following recipes:

- Getting started with OpenXR
- How to implement single pass multiview rendering
- Implementing static foveated rendering with a fragment density map
- Retrieving eye gaze information from OpenXR in your app
- Implementing dynamic foveated rendering using Qualcomm's fragment density map Offset extension
- Using half floats to reduce memory load

Technical requirements

For this chapter, you will need to install Android Studio and will also need a Meta Quest 2 or Meta Quest Pro to run the **Virtual Reality** (**VR**) sample application provided in the repository. Please follow these steps to install the tools needed to build, install, and run an application on the device:

- Download and install the Android Studio Hedgehog version from https://developer.android.com/studio/releases.

- We also recommend installing the Meta Quest developer hub from https://developer.oculus.com/downloads/package/oculus-developer-hub-win. This tool provides several features that help the development of XR applications.

- Please follow the steps outlined in the following link to make sure that your device is developer-ready—that is, you can debug, deploy, and test VR apps: https://developer.oculus.com/documentation/native/android/mobile-device-setup/.

To launch the project, simply launch Android Studio and open this chapter's `project` folder located in `source/chapter8` directory.

Getting started with OpenXR

Before we dive into how our application code is structured, let's talk about some important OpenXR concepts:

- `XrInstance`: This is the starting point for an OpenXR application. It represents the application's connection to an OpenXR runtime. It is the first object you create and the last thing you destroy.

- `XrSystemId`: After creating an instance, the application queries for a system ID, which represents a specific device or group of devices, such as a VR headset.

- `XrViewConfigurationType`: This is used to select a view configuration that the application will use to display images. Different configurations can represent different display setups, such as monoscopic, stereoscopic, and so on.

- `XrSession`: Once the instance is set up and the system ID and view configuration are determined, a session is created. A session represents the application's interaction with a device. The session manages the life cycle, rendering parameters, and input data for the device.

- `XrSpace`: Spaces represent coordinate systems within the XR environment. They are used to position objects in 3D space.

- `XrSwapchain`: A swapchain is a collection of textures used to buffer images for display. After the session has been established, the swapchain is created to handle the rendering.

- `xrBeginFrame` and `xrEndFrame`: These are functions used to start and end the rendering of a frame. The `xrBeginFrame` function signals the start of a rendering frame, and `xrEndFrame` signals the end of a frame. They are called for each frame in the render loop.

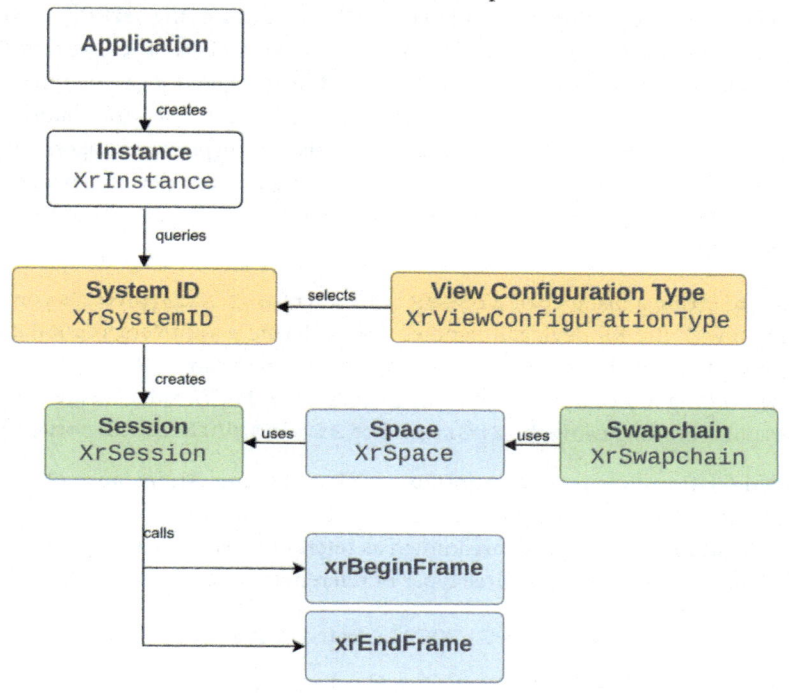

Figure 8.1 depicts the basic idea about how to use OpenXR:

Figure 8.1 – OpenXR object interaction diagram

In this recipe, we will learn about the main OpenXR initialization events, and which functions we need to use to render a frame and display them on a device. The recipe will also cover how the OpenXR code is handled in the repository.

Getting ready

The first step in creating an OpenXR application involves setting up an `XrInstance`. This instance is the primary connection between your application and the OpenXR runtime. To create an `XrInstance`, you'll need to call the `xrCreateInstance` function. Before you do this, you will need to decide which extensions your application requires. At the very least, your application will need to enable a graphics binding extension, which specifies the graphics API that will be used. You can also use `xrEnumerateInstanceExtensionProperties` to enumerate all extensions supported by the platform. Additionally, before calling `xrCreateInstance`, you will need to populate the `XrApplicationInfo` structure. This structure holds essential details about your application, such as the application's name, engine name, and version information.

After these details are set, you can call `xrCreateInstance`, which will return an instance handle upon successful creation. Following the creation of the `XrInstance`, the next step involves querying for a `SystemId` and selecting an `XrViewConfigurationView`. The `SystemId` represents a specific XR device or a group of devices, such as a VR headset, and it can be retrieved using the `xrGetSystem` function. `XrViewConfigurationView`, on the other hand, allows you to choose the view configuration that your application will use for displaying images. This could range from monoscopic to stereoscopic configurations, depending on your device type. In the recipes in this chapter, we will be using the stereo view by specifying XR_VIEW_CONFIGURATION_TYPE_PRIMARY_STEREO.

The next step is to create a instance of `XrSession`. A `XrSession` represents your application's active interaction with the XR device. It handles the rendering parameters, input data, and overall life cycle of the application's interaction with the device. To create an `XrSession`, we will need to fill the graphics binding information in `XrSessionCreateInfo`. Since we are using Vulkan, we will specify graphics binding using the `XrGraphicsBindingVulkanKHR` structure.

Tracking spatial relationships is very important in XR platforms. An instance of `XrSpace` class represent something that is being tracked by the XR system. To interact with tracked objects, we will use `XrSpace` handles. Several spaces are known as reference spaces, which can be accessed using sessions and enumerations. There are three types of reference spaces in OpenXR:

- XR_REFERENCE_SPACE_TYPE_LOCAL: Seated or static space
- XR_REFERENCE_SPACE_TYPE_VIEW: Head locked space
- XR_REFERENCE_SPACE_TYPE_STAGE: An area bounded by an environment in which the user can move around

To get an `XrSpace` from these enumerations, you will use `xrCreateReferenceSpace`. Another kind of space you can create is `xrCreateActionSpace`, which is used when you need to create a space from a pose action. For instance, we use it to create an `XrSpace` for gaze location and orientation. `xrLocateSpace` is an API which is used to determine transform relative to other spaces.

To render graphics, we will need to create a swapchain, just like in Vulkan. To create one, you need to call `xrCreateSwapchain`. Next, we will use `xrEnumerateSwapchainImages` to acquire multiple `XrSwapchainImageVulkanKHR` instances that hold a reference to `vkImage`.

In OpenXR, a key concept is that of layers. Imagine layers as distinct sections or elements of the final rendered scene in a virtual or augmented reality experience. Rather than presenting a flat, single-image view, OpenXR creates a multi-dimensional perspective by independently rendering each layer and then compositing them to form the final image. The most frequently used layer is `XrCompositionLayerProjection`. This layer is responsible for rendering the main scene. To create a sense of depth and immersion typical of VR experiences, this layer incorporates multiple views—one for each eye in a VR headset. This arrangement produces a stereoscopic 3D effect. But `XrCompositionLayerProjection` isn't the only layer at work. OpenXR also employs layers such as `XrCompositionLayerQuad`, `XrCompositionLayerCubeKHR`, and `XrCompositionLayerEquirectKHR`. Each of these plays a unique role in enhancing the rendering of the final image.

Now we will move to the render loop; the application render loop consists of three main functions:

1. `xrWaitFrame` blocks until the OpenXR runtime determines that it's the right time to start the next frame. This includes computations and rendering based on the user's head pose.
2. `xrBeginFrame` is called by the application to mark the start of rendering for the given frame.
3. `xrEndFrame` submits the frame for display.

The next part is acquiring and releasing swapchain images: `xrAcquireSwapchainImage` gives the index of the current swapchain image but it doesn't give you permission to write to the image. To write to the swapchain image, you will need to call `xrWaitSwapchainImage`. `xrReleaseSwapchainImage` is called just before `xrEndFrame`, before the rendering is done. `xrEndFrame` will use the most recently released swapchain image for displaying to the device.

The last important call is `xrPollEvents`, which is used to retrieve events from the event queue. Events in OpenXR represent various types of occurrences, such as changes in session state, input from the user, or changes in the environment. For instance, an event might be generated when the user puts on or takes off their headset, when they press a button on a controller, or when the tracking system loses or regains sight of a tracked object. It's usually called once a frame.

In the repository, the code for OpenXR is encapsulated in the `OXR::Context` and `OXR::OXRSwapchain` classes.

How to do it...

The `OXR::Context` class in the repository manages most of OpenXR calls and states. In this recipe, we will show you the details of these functions and how to use them to initialize the OpenXR sample app in the repository:

1. The `OXR::Context::initializeExtensions` method finds the extensions available in the OpenXR runtime and filters out the requested extensions that aren't supported. Once the available extensions are fetched, it iterates through the requested extensions, eliminating any that aren't available. That results in a list of extensions that are both requested and supported:

```
void Context::initializeExtensions() {
  uint32_t numExtensions = 0;
  xrEnumerateInstanceExtensionProperties(
    nullptr, 0, &numExtensions, nullptr);

  availableExtensions_.resize(
    numExtensions,
```

```cpp
      {XR_TYPE_EXTENSION_PROPERTIES});

  xrEnumerateInstanceExtensionProperties(
    nullptr, numExtensions, &numExtensions,
    availableExtensions_.data());
  requestedExtensions_.erase(

    std::remove_if(
      requestedExtensions_.begin(),
      requestedExtensions_.end(),
      [this](const char *ext) {
        return std::none_of(
          availableExtensions_.begin(),
          availableExtensions_.end(),
          [ext](
            const XrExtensionProperties &props) {
            return strcmp(props.extensionName,
                          ext) == 0;
          });
      }),
    requestedExtensions_.end());
}
```

2. The `Context::createInstance()` method is responsible for creating an OpenXR instance with basic application information and the extension details:

```cpp
bool Context::createInstance() {

  const XrApplicationInfo appInfo = {
    .applicationName = "OpenXR Example",
    .applicationVersion = 0,
    .engineName = "OpenXR Example",
    .engineVersion = 0,
    .apiVersion = XR_CURRENT_API_VERSION,
  };

  const XrInstanceCreateInfo instanceCreateInfo =
    {
      .type = XR_TYPE_INSTANCE_CREATE_INFO,
      .createFlags = 0,
      .applicationInfo = appInfo,
      .enabledApiLayerCount = 0,
      .enabledApiLayerNames = nullptr,
      .enabledExtensionCount =
```

```
                static_cast<uint32_t>(
                    requestedExtensions_.size()),
            .enabledExtensionNames =
                requestedExtensions_.data(),
        };

        XR_CHECK(xrCreateInstance(&instanceCreateInfo,
                                  &instance_));
        XR_CHECK(xrGetInstanceProperties(
            instance_, &instanceProps_));
    }
```

3. The `Context::systemInfo` method retrieves and stores the properties of the OpenXR system for a head-mounted display. It fetches the system ID and its properties, including system name, vendor ID, graphics properties, tracking properties, and eye gaze support:

```
    void Context::systemInfo() {
      const XrSystemGetInfo systemGetInfo = {
        .type = XR_TYPE_SYSTEM_GET_INFO,
        .formFactor =
            XR_FORM_FACTOR_HEAD_MOUNTED_DISPLAY,
      };
      XR_CHECK(xrGetSystem(instance_, &systemGetInfo,
                           &systemId_));
      XR_CHECK(xrGetSystemProperties(
        instance_, systemId_, &systemProps_));
    }
```

4. The `Context::enumerateViewConfigurations` function enumerates all the view configurations supported by the system and then selects and stores properties of the one that matches the predefined supported configuration. If the selected configuration supports the required number of viewports, it stores the configuration properties and the view configuration views.

5. The `Context::initGraphics` function is designed to initialize the graphics requirements for Vulkan. It achieves this by obtaining key components such as the Vulkan instance and device extensions. `xrGetVulkanInstanceExtensionsKHR` and `xrGetVulkanDeviceExtensionsKHR` are functions used in the OpenXR API to retrieve the names of Vulkan instance and device extensions, respectively, that are needed by a particular OpenXR runtime:

```
    void Context::initGraphics() {

      uint32_t bufferSize = 0;

      pfnGetVulkanInstanceExtensionsKHR(
```

```
      instance_, systemId_, 0, &bufferSize, NULL);

    requiredVkInstanceExtensionsBuffer_.resize(
      bufferSize);

    pfnGetVulkanInstanceExtensionsKHR(
      instance_, systemId_, bufferSize, &bufferSize,
      requiredVkInstanceExtensionsBuffer_.data());

    pfnGetVulkanDeviceExtensionsKHR(
      instance_, systemId_, 0, &bufferSize, NULL);

    requiredVkDeviceExtensionsBuffer_.resize(
      bufferSize);

    pfnGetVulkanDeviceExtensionsKHR(
      instance_, systemId_, bufferSize, &bufferSize,
      requiredVkDeviceExtensionsBuffer_.data());
}
```

6. The `Context::initializeSession` function creates a new OpenXR session. It begins by creating an `XrGraphicsBindingVulkanKHR` object, which is used to bind Vulkan to the XR session. This object is populated with the Vulkan instance, physical device, and device, as well as the queue family index. This information allows the OpenXR runtime to interface with the Vulkan API. Then, an `XrSessionCreateInfo` object is created, which is used to specify the parameters for creating a new session. This object attributes are populated with the nature of the session to be created, the graphics binding, and the system ID. Finally, the `xrCreateSession` function is called to create the session:

```
bool Context::initializeSession(
  VkInstance vkInstance,
  VkPhysicalDevice vkPhysDevice,
  VkDevice vkDevice, uint32_t queueFamilyIndex) {
  // Bind Vulkan to XR session
  const XrGraphicsBindingVulkanKHR
    graphicsBinding = {
      XR_TYPE_GRAPHICS_BINDING_VULKAN_KHR,
      NULL,
      vkInstance,
      vkPhysDevice,
      vkDevice,
      queueFamilyIndex,
      0,
    };
```

Getting started with OpenXR 277

```
    const XrSessionCreateInfo sessionCreateInfo = {
      .type = XR_TYPE_SESSION_CREATE_INFO,
      .next = &graphicsBinding,
      .createFlags = 0,
      .systemId = systemId_,
    };

    XR_CHECK(xrCreateSession(
      instance_, &sessionCreateInfo, &session_));

    return true;
  }
```

7. The `Context::enumerateReferenceSpaces` function retrieves the types of reference spaces available for the current OpenXR session. It calls `xrEnumerateReferenceSpaces` to fill a vector of `XrReferenceSpaceType` structures with the available reference space types. Finally, it checks whether the `XR_REFERENCE_SPACE_TYPE_STAGE` type is available and stores this information in the `stageSpaceSupported_` variable. The `XR_REFERENCE_SPACE_TYPE_STAGE` type represents a standing-scale experience where the user has a small amount of room to move around.

8. The `Context::createSwapchains` function is responsible for creating the swapchains needed for rendering. Based on the value of `useSinglePassStereo_`, it either creates a single swapchain that will be used for both views (in case of single-pass stereo rendering), or separate swapchains for each view. For each swapchain, it creates a new `OXRSwapchain` instance. The `OXRSwapchain` constructor is called with the Vulkan context, the OpenXR session, the viewport for the swapchain, and the number of views per swapchain. We call the `initialize` function to initialize the `OXRSwapchain` instance. The `initialize` function in the `OXRSwapchain` class sets up the color and depth swapchains for an OpenXR session by calling the `xrCreateSwapchain` function. Once `XrSwapchain` is created, we call `enumerateSwapchainImages` in `OXRSwapchain`, which is responsible for creating a vector of `XrSwapchainImageVulkanKHR`:

```
  void Context::createSwapchains(
    VulkanCore::Context &ctx) {
    const uint32_t numSwapchainProviders =
      useSinglePassStereo_ ? 1 : kNumViews;
    const uint32_t numViewsPerSwapchain =
      useSinglePassStereo_ ? kNumViews : 1;
    swapchains_.reserve(numSwapchainProviders);

    for (uint32_t i = 0; i < numSwapchainProviders;
         i++) {
```

```
            swapchains_.emplace_back(
              std::make_unique<OXRSwapchain>(
                ctx, session_, viewports_[i],
                numViewsPerSwapchain));
            swapchains_.back()->initialize();
        }
    }
```

9. `OXRSwapchain` also provides functions such as `getSurfaceTexture` and `releaseSwapchainImages`. `getSurfaceTexture` is responsible for acquiring a swapchain by calling `xrAcquireSwapchainImage` and `xrWaitSwapchainImage`.

10. Before starting to render, `OXR::Context::beginFrame` first synchronizes frame submission with the display by calling `xrWaitFrame`, which returns an `XrFrameState` structure. The frame state specifies a predicted display time when the runtime predicts a frame will be displayed. The function also calls `xrBeginFrame`, which must be called before rendering starts, and retrieves some other important information, such as the head and view poses, and calculates view and camera transformations:

```
XrFrameState Context::beginFrame() {
  const XrFrameWaitInfo waitFrameInfo = {
    XR_TYPE_FRAME_WAIT_INFO};
  XrFrameState frameState = {XR_TYPE_FRAME_STATE};
  XR_CHECK(xrWaitFrame(session_, &waitFrameInfo,
                       &frameState));

  XrFrameBeginInfo beginFrameInfo = {
    XR_TYPE_FRAME_BEGIN_INFO};
  XR_CHECK(
    xrBeginFrame(session_, &beginFrameInfo));

  XrSpaceLocation loc = {
    loc.type = XR_TYPE_SPACE_LOCATION};
  XR_CHECK(xrLocateSpace(
    headSpace_, stageSpace_,
    frameState.predictedDisplayTime, &loc));
  XrPosef headPose = loc.pose;

  XrViewState viewState = {XR_TYPE_VIEW_STATE};
  const XrViewLocateInfo projectionInfo = {
    .type = XR_TYPE_VIEW_LOCATE_INFO,
```

```
        .viewConfigurationType =
          viewConfigProps_.viewConfigurationType,
        .displayTime =
          frameState.predictedDisplayTime,
        .space = headSpace_,
    };

    uint32_t numViews = views_.size();
    views_[0].type = XR_TYPE_VIEW;
    views_[1].type = XR_TYPE_VIEW;

    XR_CHECK(xrLocateViews(
      session_, &projectionInfo, &viewState,
      views_.size(), &numViews, views_.data()));

}
```

11. Once rendering has been completed, the application must call the OXR::endFrame method, which in turn calls xrEndFrame. The XrFrameEndInfo structure specifies the type of layer being presented (and its flags) and its associated spaces (with its poses and field of view angles and maybe depth information) and how the image(s) should be blended with underlying layers. Note that, for the sake of conciseness, only the critical sections of the code are displayed here. For a comprehensive understanding, please refer to the full code in the original source:

```
void Context::endFrame(XrFrameState frameState) {
    const XrFrameEndInfo endFrameInfo = {
      .type = XR_TYPE_FRAME_END_INFO,
      .displayTime =
        frameState.predictedDisplayTime,
      .environmentBlendMode =
        XR_ENVIRONMENT_BLEND_MODE_OPAQUE,
      .layerCount = 1,
      .layers = layers,
    };
    XR_CHECK(xrEndFrame(session_, &endFrameInfo));
}
```

12. The android_main function, outside of the OXR::Context class, serves as the main entry point for a native Android activity. It initializes both OpenXR (oxrContext) and Vulkan (vkContext) contexts and sets up their required extensions and features. After creating an instance, it establishes a session and creates swapchains for rendering. Shader modules for

vertex and fragment shaders are also created. The function then enters a loop where it handles OpenXR events, begins a frame, carries out rendering actions, and ends the frame. This loop continues until the app is requested to be destroyed. Please note that, for brevity, a significant amount of detail has been omitted from this summary. You are encouraged to review the actual code in the repository for a comprehensive understanding:

```
void android_main(struct android_app *pApp) {

  OXR::Context oxrContext(pApp);
  oxrContext.initializeExtensions();
  oxrContext.createInstance();

  VulkanCore::Context vkContext(
    VkApplicationInfo{});
  vkContext.createVkDevice(
    oxrContext.findVkGraphicsDevice(
      vkContext.instance()),
    oxrContext.vkDeviceExtensions(),
    VK_QUEUE_GRAPHICS_BIT);

  oxrContext.initializeSession(
    vkContext.instance(),
    vkContext.physicalDevice().vkPhysicalDevice(),
    vkContext.device(),
    vkContext.physicalDevice()
      .graphicsFamilyIndex()
      .value());

  oxrContext.createSwapchains(vkContext);

  auto commandMgr =
    vkContext.createGraphicsCommandQueue(3, 3);

  do {
    auto frameState = oxrContext.beginFrame();
    if (frameState.shouldRender == XR_FALSE) {
      oxrContext.endFrame(frameState);
      continue;
    }
    auto commandBuffer =
      commandMgr.getCmdBufferToBegin();
    vkCmdDrawIndexedIndirect(
      commandBuffer, buffers[3]->vkBuffer(), 0,
      numMeshes,
```

```
            sizeof(EngineCore::
                IndirectDrawCommandAndMeshData));

    commandMgr.submit(
      &vkContext.swapchain()->createSubmitInfo(
        &commandBuffer,
        &VK_PIPELINE_STAGE_COLOR_ATTACHMENT_OUTPUT_BIT,
        false, false));

    commandMgr.goToNextCmdBuffer();
    oxrContext.swapchain(0)
      ->releaseSwapchainImages();

    oxrContext.endFrame(frameState);

  } while (!pApp->destroyRequested);
}
```

This recipe involves a sequence of steps starting from initializing the OpenXR and Vulkan contexts to entering a game event loop for handling OpenXR events and rendering. The process is intricate and involves enabling specific features, handling graphics commands, and managing frames. This guide has provided a simplified overview, and we strongly recommend reviewing the full code in the repository for a complete understanding.

See also

For more details, please refer to the OpenXR guide by Khronos:

- `https://www.khronos.org/files/openxr-10-reference-guide.pdf`

How to implement single pass multiview rendering

XR devices must render scenes at least twice for each frame, generating one image for each eye. Single pass multiview rendering is a technique used to enhance the performance of XR applications by allowing the rendering of multiple views in a single pass. This effectively enables the rendering of the scene from both eye's perspectives with one draw call.

In this recipe, we will navigate how to enable the Multiview rendering feature in Vulkan and how to use it to render the scene for both eyes in one render pass.

Getting ready

In the context of Vulkan, the `VK_STRUCTURE_TYPE_PHYSICAL_DEVICE_MULTIVIEW_FEATURES` extension specifies whether multiple views are supported in a single rendering pass. Once the feature is enabled, you can specify multiple viewports and scissor rectangles for your rendering pass. The graphics pipeline will then render the scene from different perspectives in a single pass, reducing the need for duplicate operations.

Besides enabling a Vulkan extension, you will also need to enable the `GL_EXT_multiview` extension in your shader code. `GL_EXT_multiview` is a GLSL extension that allows multiple views to be rendered in a single pass. `GL_EXT_multiview` introduces a new built-in variable, `gl_ViewIndex`, that can be used in your shaders to determine which view is being rendered. It contains the index of the current view being processed and can be used to adjust your drawing based on the view index (for instance, index `0` may represent the left eye, while index `1` can represent the right eye).

We also need the ability to query whether multiview is supported by hardware or not using `VkPhysicalDeviceMultiviewFeatures`. Additionally, we need to specify that we will be using multiple views when creating the render pass. This is done by adding an instance of the `VkRenderPassMultiviewCreateInfo` structure to the `pNext` chain of the `VkRenderPassCreateInfo` structure. One other important part is that swapchain images need to have multiple layers (in our case, two—one for each eye), and the results of the rendering go to different layers of the attachments. You may think that we could have rendered the same scene twice (one for left and one for right), but that would mean we build a command buffer that sends all the geometry and textures twice. This extension helps us send data only once and only shaders are fired twice (for each view ID). The only difference between these two executions is uniform data for the camera.

To support multiview, code changes are required in various areas of the code base. In this case, we needed to change `Texture`, `RenderPass`, `Context` classes, and shader files.

How to do it...

In the following steps, we will go through details on how to implement this recipe:

1. Extend `VulkanCore::Texture` to support `vkImageView` created using `VK_IMAGE_VIEW_TYPE_2D_ARRAY`; this is necessary if we have multiple layers in the same texture.

2. Add support for multiview in `VulkanCore::RenderPass`; this is achieved by connecting `VkRenderPassMultiviewCreateInfo` to `VkRenderPassCreateInfo`.

3. Add support to enable multiview extension in `VulkanCore::Context`; this is abstracted in a function named `enableMultiView`, which simply enables `VkPhysicalDeviceMultiviewFeatures` if it is supported by a physical device.

4. The vertex shader is now passed two **Model View Projection** (**MVP**) matrices, one for the left eye and the other for the right eye. A function named `Context::mvp(index)` was introduced, so that we can query MVP for the left and right eye.

5. We also introduced a constant named `kUseSinglePassStereo` that can be used to control whether we want to use a single pass or not.

Given that the code is distributed across various files, we strongly suggest delving into the repository for a comprehensive review of the implementation. Specifically, the file located at `source/chapter8/app/src/main/cpp/main.cpp` should warrant your particular attention.

Implementing static foveated rendering with a fragment density map

Foveated rendering is a cutting-edge graphics rendering technique that leverages the human eye's natural tendency to focus on specific regions of a scene, optimizing computational resources by allocating higher detail and resolution to the central, foveal vision, and progressively reducing it toward the peripheral vision. This mimics the way the human eye perceives detail, offering a substantial performance boost in graphics rendering without sacrificing visual quality.

In this recipe, we will see how to implement fixed foveated rendering by using the **fragment density map** (**FDM**) extension.

Getting ready

The FDM device extension in Vulkan (`VK_EXT_fragment_density`) enables an application to specify different levels of detail to use in different areas of the render target by means of a texture that encodes how many times a fragment shader will be invoked for that area. The FDM may be modified on each frame to accommodate the user's eye gaze direction. This recipe only works with HMDs that provide eye gaze detection, such as Meta's Quest Pro. The recipe presented here works for a single-pass stereo rendering approach.

How to do it...

Before creating and using an FDM and the FDM Offset extension, we need to enable the extensions:

1. Before enabling the feature, it is necessary to check whether the physical device supports it. Doing so requires appending an instance of the `VkPhysicalDeviceFragmentDensityMapFeaturesEXT` structure to the pNext chain of `VkPhysicalDeviceFeatures2` passed to the `vkGetPhysicalDeviceFeatures2` function.

   `VkPhysicalDeviceFragmentDensityMapFeaturesEXT::fragmentDensityMap` specifies whether the device supports the FDM extension.

2. The extension has properties that need to be queried to be used properly. To do that, also include an instance of the VkPhysicalDeviceFragmentDensityMapPropertiesEXT structure to the pNext chain of VkPhysicalDeviceProperties2 and query those properties with vkGetPhysicalDeviceProperties2. We will use these properties in *step 4*.

3. The FDM extension is a device extension and its name needs to be passed in during the creation of the VkDevice object: "VK_EXT_fragment_density_map" (or the definition, VK_EXT_FRAGMENT_DENSITY_MAP_EXTENSION_NAME).

4. An FDM's size doesn't map to the framebuffers on a one-to-one ratio. One texel of the map affects an *area* of the render target. This area's size can be queried from VkPhysicalDeviceFragmentDensityMapPropertiesEXT, from the minFragmentDensityTexelSize and maxFragmentDensityTexelSize properties.

In our recipe, we will create an FDM with texels that map to an area that is at least 32 x 32 of the render target, bounded by minFragmentDensityTexelSize:

```
const glm::vec2 mapSize = glm::vec2(
    std::ceilf(
        oxrContext.swapchain(0)
            ->viewport()
            .recommendedImageRectWidth /
        std::max(
            32u,
            vkContext.physicalDevice()
                .fragmentDensityMapProperties()
                .minFragmentDensityTexelSize.width)),
    std::ceilf(
        oxrContext.swapchain(0)
            ->viewport()
            .recommendedImageRectHeight /
        std::max(
            32u,
            vkContext.physicalDevice()
                .fragmentDensityMapProperties()
                .minFragmentDensityTexelSize.height)));
```

5. An FDM is a regular texture with some special usage flags:

```
std::shared_ptr<VulkanCore::Texture> =
    std::make_shared<VulkanCore::Texture>(
        vkContext, VK_IMAGE_TYPE_2D,
        VK_FORMAT_R8G8_UNORM,
        static_cast<VkImageCreateFlags>(0),
        VK_IMAGE_USAGE_FRAGMENT_DENSITY_MAP_BIT_EXT,
```

```
              VkExtent3D{static_cast<uint32_t>(mapSize.x),
                        static_cast<uint32_t>(mapSize.y),
                        1},
              1, 2, VK_MEMORY_PROPERTY_DEVICE_LOCAL_BIT,
              false, VK_SAMPLE_COUNT_1_BIT,
              "fragment density map", true,
              VK_IMAGE_TILING_LINEAR);
```

6. The format of the texture is `VK_FORMAT_R8G8_UNORM`. Each pixel stored in the map specifies the density of fragments to be used for that area of the render target, where 255 means the density should be the highest (or the default: one fragment per render target's pixel; 128 for half the density, and so on). In our recipe, our map is initialized to 128 (half density) and then manipulated to have an area in the center with a radius equal to 2 texels with full density:

```
std::vector<uint8_t> fdmData(mapSize.x *mapSize.y * 2,
                             255);
constexpr uint16_t high_res_radius = 8;
const glm::vec2 center = mapSize / 2.f;
for (uint32_t x = 0; x < mapSize.x; ++x) {
  for (uint32_t y = 0; y < mapSize.y; ++y) {
    const float length =
        glm::length(glm::vec2(x, y) - center);
    if (length < high_res_radius) {
      const uint32_t index =
          (y * mapSize.x * 2) + x * 2;
      fdmData[index] = 255;      // full density
      fdmData[index + 1] = 255; // full density
```

Note that the image has two layers, one for each eye. The data is uploaded to the device twice, once for each layer of the image.

7. Once the data has been uploaded for each layer of the map, the texture's layout needs to be transitioned to the special layout, `VK_IMAGE_LAYOUT_FRAGMENT_DENSITY_MAP_OPTIMAL_EXT`.

8. The FDM needs to be specified and referenced by the render pass in a `VkAttachmentDescription` structure, just like any other attachment used in the render pass:

```
const auto fdmAttachDesc = VkAttachmentDescription{
    .format = VK_FORMAT_R8G8_UNORM,
    .samples = VK_SAMPLE_COUNT_1_BIT,
    .loadOp = VK_ATTACHMENT_LOAD_OP_DONT_CARE,
```

```
        .storeOp = VK_ATTACHMENT_STORE_OP_DONT_CARE,
    .initialLayout =
        VK_IMAGE_LAYOUT_FRAGMENT_DENSITY_MAP_OPTIMAL_EXT,
    .finalLayout =
        VK_IMAGE_LAYOUT_FRAGMENT_DENSITY_MAP_OPTIMAL_EXT,
};
```

9. The FDM must not appear as a color or depth stencil attachment in the `VkSubpassDescription::pColorAttachments` or `VkSubpassDescription::pDepthStencilAttachment` arrays. Instead, it must be referenced in an instance of the special `VkRenderPassFragmentDensityMapCreateInfoEXT` structure:

```
const VkRenderPassFragmentDensityMapCreateInfoEXT
    fdmAttachmentci = {
        .sType =
            VK_STRUCTURE_TYPE_RENDER_PASS_FRAGMENT_DENSITY_MAP_CREATE_INFO_EXT,
        .fragmentDensityMapAttachment =
            {
                .attachment =
                    fragmentDensityAttachmentReference,
                .layout =
                    VK_IMAGE_LAYOUT_FRAGMENT_DENSITY_MAP_OPTIMAL_EXT,
            },
};
```

The `fragmentDensityAttachmentReference` variable in the preceding snippet refers to the *index* of the `VkAttachmentDescription` structure that mentions the FDM in the attachment description array passed to `VkRenderPassCreateInfo::pAttachments`.

> **Bug prevention notice**
>
> The order in which this structure appears in the `VkRenderPassCreateInfo::pAttachments` array must match the index of the `VkImage` array passed to `VkFramebufferCreateInfo::pAttachments`.

10. The instance of the `VkRenderPassFragmentDensityMapCreateInfoEXT` structure needs to be added to the pNext chain property of the `VkRenderPassCreateInfo` structure:

```
const VkRenderPassCreateInfo rpci = {
    .sType = VK_STRUCTURE_TYPE_RENDER_PASS_CREATE_INFO,
    .pNext = &fdmAttachmentci,
    ...
};
```

11. The image view of the FDM needs to be part of the framebuffer as well. Its image view must be added to the `VkFramebufferCreateInfo::pAttachments` array and its index into this array must match that of the `VkAttachmentDescription` structure passed to the creation of the render pass.

This marks the end of our guide on static foveated rendering. In the upcoming sections, we'll expand our exploration into the realm of dynamic foveated rendering.

See also

For more information, check out the extension information at the following links:

- https://registry.khronos.org/vulkan/specs/1.3-extensions/man/html/VK_EXT_fragment_density_map.html
- https://registry.khronos.org/vulkan/specs/1.3-extensions/man/html/VK_QCOM_fragment_density_map_offset.html

Retrieving eye gaze information from OpenXR in your app

The realm of VR has evolved to the extent that some HMDs are now equipped with the capability to track the user's eye gaze. This feature, which identifies the direction in which the user is looking, can be harnessed for a variety of tasks, enhancing the interactivity and immersion of VR experiences. In this recipe, we will guide you through the process of enabling and retrieving eye gaze data from OpenXR in your application. Additionally, we will illustrate how to calculate the focal region—the specific area the user is looking at—in pixel coordinates on the render target used for display.

Getting ready

For this recipe, you will need an HMD that supports eye-tracking features, such as Meta's Quest Pro. You will also need to provide permission to the app to track the user's eye, which can be achieved through the **Settings** menu on most devices.

Also, get acquainted with how spaces and actions are supported and used in OpenXR (see the *Getting started with OpenXR* recipe).

This recipe was authored and tested with Meta's Quest Pro device, so some of the code shown here is specific to that platform. Your implementation might require small tweaks to work on your device.

How to do it...

Adding eye gaze support requires allowing the device to track the user's eyes. This requires executing the following steps:

1. Before using the eye-tracking feature in your app, you need to request permission by adding the following lines to the `AndroidManifest.xml` file of your app:

    ```xml
    <uses-permission android:name="com.oculus.permission.EYE_TRACKING" />
    <uses-permission android:name="oculus.software.eye_tracking" />
    <uses-feature android:name="oculus.software.eye_tracking"/>
    ```

2. Grant permission to your app to track the user's eye with the following:

    ```
    adb shell pm grant com.example.openxrsample com.oculus.permission.EYE_TRACKING
    ```

    Run the preceding command on a terminal on your desktop with your headset connected to it. The command grants permission to the app called `com.example.openxrsample` and you might need to change it to your app's name.

3. Enable the OpenXR extension when creating your OpenXR instance by adding `XR_EXT_EYE_GAZE_INTERACTION_EXTENSION_NAME` to the `XrInstanceCreateInfo::enableExtensionNames` array:

    ```cpp
    const XrApplicationInfo appInfo = {
        .applicationName = "OpenXR Example",
        .applicationVersion = 0,
        .engineName = "OpenXR Example",
        .engineVersion = 0,
        .apiVersion = XR_CURRENT_API_VERSION,
    };

    std::vector<const char *> requestedExtensions = {
        XR_KHR_VULKAN_ENABLE_EXTENSION_NAME,
        XR_FB_SWAPCHAIN_UPDATE_STATE_VULKAN_EXTENSION_NAME,
        XR_EXT_EYE_GAZE_INTERACTION_EXTENSION_NAME,
    };
    const XrInstanceCreateInfo instanceCreateInfo = {
        .type = XR_TYPE_INSTANCE_CREATE_INFO,
        .createFlags = 0,
        .applicationInfo = appInfo,
        .enabledApiLayerCount = 0,
        .enabledApiLayerNames = nullptr,
        .enabledExtensionCount = static_cast<uint32_t>(
            requestedExtensions_.size()),
    ```

```
        .enabledExtensionNames =
            requestedExtensions_.data(),
};
XR_CHECK(xrCreateInstance(&instanceCreateInfo,
                          &instance_));
```

4. We begin by adding a few member variables to the OXR:Context class:

```
XrActionSet eyegazeActionSet_  = XR_NULL_HANDLE;
XrAction eyeGazeAction_        = XR_NULL_HANDLE;
XrSpace gazeActionSpace_       = XR_NULL_HANDLE;
XrSpace localReferenceSpace_   = XR_NULL_HANDLE;
```

5. Eye tracking is considered an input action in OpenXR, so we create an action set to store the eye-tracking action (OXR::Context::eyegazeActionSet_):

```
const XrActionSetCreateInfo actionSetInfo{
    .type = XR_TYPE_ACTION_SET_CREATE_INFO,
    .actionSetName = "gameplay",
    .localizedActionSetName = "Eye Gaze Action Set",
    .priority = 0,
};
XR_CHECK(xrCreateActionSet(instance_, &actionSetInfo,
                           &eyegazeActionSet_));
```

6. We then create an action that represents the eye gaze input:

```
const XrActionCreateInfo actionInfo{
    .type = XR_TYPE_ACTION_CREATE_INFO,
    .actionName = "user_intent",
    .actionType = XR_ACTION_TYPE_POSE_INPUT,
    .localizedActionName = "Eye Gaze Action",
};
XR_CHECK(xrCreateAction(eyegazeActionSet_, &actionInfo,
                        &eyegazeAction_));
```

7. We'll need paths that identify the input action and its pose:

```
XrPath eyeGazeInteractionProfilePath;
XR_CHECK(xrStringToPath(
    instance_,
    "/interaction_profiles/ext/eye_gaze_interaction",
    &eyeGazeInteractionProfilePath));
```

```
XrPath gazePosePath;
XR_CHECK(xrStringToPath(
    instance_, "/user/eyes_ext/input/gaze_ext/pose",
    &gazePosePath));
```

8. The action and its pose need to be bound together using an instance of the `XrActionSuggestedBinding` structure:

```
const XrActionSuggestedBinding bindings{
    .action = eyegazeAction_,
    .binding = gazePosePath,
};
const XrInteractionProfileSuggestedBinding
    suggestedBindings{
        .type =
            XR_TYPE_INTERACTION_PROFILE_SUGGESTED_BINDING,
        .interactionProfile =
            eyeGazeInteractionProfilePath,
        .countSuggestedBindings = 1,
        .suggestedBindings = &bindings,
    };
XR_CHECK(xrSuggestInteractionProfileBindings(
    instance_, &suggestedBindings));
```

9. Actions need to be attached to a session to work, which can be done by calling `xrAttachSessionActionSets` with the action set that stores the eye gaze action:

```
const XrSessionActionSetsAttachInfo attachInfo{
    .type = XR_TYPE_SESSION_ACTION_SETS_ATTACH_INFO,
    .countActionSets = 1,
    .actionSets = &eyegazeActionSet_,
};
XR_CHECK(xrAttachSessionActionSets(session_,
                                    &attachInfo));
```

10. We also need to create an action space for the eye gaze action to define a position and orientation of the new space's origin within a natural reference frame of the pose action:

```
const XrActionSpaceCreateInfo createActionSpaceInfo{
    .type = XR_TYPE_ACTION_SPACE_CREATE_INFO,
    .action = eyegazeAction_,
    .poseInActionSpace = poseIdentity_,
```

```
};
XR_CHECK(xrCreateActionSpace(session_,
                             &createActionSpaceInfo,
                             &gazeActionSpace_));
```

11. The last initialization step is to create a local reference space, which we'll use to base the eye gaze position and orientation. The type of the reference space is XR_REFERENCE_SPACE_TYPE_VIEW as the eye gaze is locked to the eye or headset location and orientation. The eyePoseIdentity variable is initialized with the identity orientation, at a height of 1.8 meters:

```
const XrPosef eyePoseIdentity = {
  .orientation = {.x = 0,
                  .y = 0,
                  .z = 0,
                  .w = 1.f},
  .position = {0, 1.8f, 0},
};
const XrReferenceSpaceCreateInfo
    createReferenceSpaceInfo{
        .type = XR_TYPE_REFERENCE_SPACE_CREATE_INFO,
        .referenceSpaceType =
            XR_REFERENCE_SPACE_TYPE_VIEW,
        .poseInReferenceSpace = eyePoseIdentity,
    };
XR_CHECK(xrCreateReferenceSpace(
    session_, &createReferenceSpaceInfo,
    &localReferenceSpace_));
```

12. In the OXR::Context::beginFrame method, we update the current state of the eye gaze action, but only if the current state of the app is focused. We can then get the action's state pose with xrGetActionStatePose:

```
if (currentState_ == XR_SESSION_STATE_FOCUSED) {
  XrActiveActionSet activeActionSet{
      .actionSet = eyegazeActionSet_,
      .subactionPath = XR_NULL_PATH,
  };
  const XrActionsSyncInfo syncInfo{
      .type = XR_TYPE_ACTIONS_SYNC_INFO,
      .countActiveActionSets = 1,
      .activeActionSets = &activeActionSet,
  };
  XR_CHECK(xrSyncActions(session_, &syncInfo));
```

```
    XrActionStatePose actionStatePose{
        XR_TYPE_ACTION_STATE_POSE};
    const XrActionStateGetInfo getActionStateInfo{
        .type = XR_TYPE_ACTION_STATE_GET_INFO,
        .action = eyegazeAction_,
    };
    XR_CHECK(xrGetActionStatePose(session_,
                                    &getActionStateInfo,
                                    &actionStatePose));
```

13. If `actionStatePose` is `active`, that means we can go ahead and locate the action in `localReferenceSpace` at the predicted time from the frame state queried before:

```
    if (actionStatePose.isActive)
      XrEyeGazeSampleTimeEXT eyeGazeSampleTime{
          XR_TYPE_EYE_GAZE_SAMPLE_TIME_EXT};
      XrSpaceLocation gazeLocation{
          XR_TYPE_SPACE_LOCATION, &eyeGazeSampleTime};
      XR_CHECK(xrLocateSpace(
          gazeActionSpace_, localReferenceSpace_,
          frameState.predictedDisplayTime,
          &gazeLocation));
```

14. If both the gaze's orientation and position are valid, we can use them to calculate where, in pixel coordinates, the user is looking at the image being presented on the device:

```
    const bool orientationValid =
        gazeLocation.locationFlags &
        XR_SPACE_LOCATION_ORIENTATION_VALID_BIT;
    const bool positionValid =
        gazeLocation.locationFlags &
        XR_SPACE_LOCATION_POSITION_VALID_BIT;

    if (orientationValid && positionValid) {
      eyeGazePositionScreen_[0] =
        screenCoordinatesFromEyeGazePose(gazeLocation,
                                          0, 0);
      eyeGazePositionScreen_[1] =
        screenCoordinatesFromEyeGazePose(gazeLocation,
                                          1, 0);
    }
```

15. Calculating the screen coordinates of the user's gaze is simple. The following function performs all the math to convert from an `XrPosef` structure (the eye gaze location) to the coordinates on the screen. It uses the swapchain dimensions to convert the canonical view direction in OpenXR, which points to the -Z direction, to screen space:

```
glm::vec3
Context::screenCoordinatesFromEyeGazePose(
  XrSpaceLocation gazeLocation, int eye,
  float offset) {
  XrVector3f canonicalViewDirection{0, 0, -1.f};
  // Reset the position. We won't need it
  gazeLocation.pose.position = {0, 0, 0};
  XrVector3f transformedViewDirection;
  XrPosef_TransformVector3f(
     &transformedViewDirection, &gazeLocation.pose,
     &canonicalViewDirection);

  XrMatrix4x4f proj;
  XrMatrix4x4f_CreateProjectionFov(
     &proj, GRAPHICS_OPENGL, views_[eye].fov,
     near_, far_);
  const XrVector4f tanAngle = {
    -transformedViewDirection.x /
       transformedViewDirection.z,
    -transformedViewDirection.y /
       transformedViewDirection.z,
    -1.f, 0};

  const auto width = swapchain(0)
                        ->viewport()
                        .recommendedImageRectWidth;
  const auto height =
    swapchain(0)
       ->viewport()
       .recommendedImageRectHeight;

  XrMatrix4x4f scalem;
  XrMatrix4x4f_CreateScale(&scalem, 0.5f, 0.5f,
                                    1.f);
  XrMatrix4x4f biasm;
  XrMatrix4x4f_CreateTranslation(&biasm, 0.5f,
                                  0.5f, 0);
  XrMatrix4x4f rectscalem;
  XrMatrix4x4f_CreateScale(&rectscalem, width,
```

```
                                       height, 1.f);
    XrMatrix4x4f rectbiasm;
    XrMatrix4x4f_CreateTranslation(&rectbiasm, 0, 0,
                                    0);
    XrMatrix4x4f rectfromclipm;
    XrMatrix4x4f_Multiply(&rectfromclipm,
                    &rectbiasm, &rectscalem);
    XrMatrix4x4f_Multiply(&rectfromclipm,
                    &rectfromclipm, &biasm);
    XrMatrix4x4f_Multiply(&rectfromclipm,
                    &rectfromclipm, &scalem);
    XrMatrix4x4f rectfromeyem;
    XrMatrix4x4f_Multiply(&rectfromeyem,
                    &rectfromclipm, &proj);
    rectfromeyem.m[11] = -1.f;
    XrVector4f texCoords;
    XrMatrix4x4f_TransformVector4f(
      &texCoords, &rectfromeyem, &tanAngle);

    return glm::vec3(texCoords.x,
                     height - texCoords.y - offset,
                     texCoords.y);
}
```

The function uses the helper types and functions defined in `xr_linear.h`. The projection matrix is calculated in the function, and not cached at the class level, to allow it to be modified while the app is running.

The sample app in the repository displays a washed-out round cursor, about 10 pixels in radius, for each eye if eye-tracking is supported by the device to help you see how the eye gaze behaves in the final output.

Implementing dynamic foveated rendering using Qualcomm's fragment density map Offset extension

In the *Implementing static foveated rendering with a fragment density map* recipe, we discussed how to render fragments at a lower density than one fragment per pixel using a map that dictates the fragment density for regions of the render target. Although useful, the application of a static map is limited because the user's gaze changes as they look around to inspect the scene displayed on the device. Recomputing and modifying the map for each frame, based on the user's input, may be computationally expensive and tax the CPU with extra work, making the performance gained with the FDM moot.

Implementing dynamic foveated rendering using Qualcomm's fragment density map Offset extension

Another option is to apply an offset to the static FDM and let the GPU perform the heavy lifting of translating the densities from the map to the rendered scene. Thanks to Qualcomm's FDM Offset device extension, this is possible.

In this recipe, we will show you how to use this extension to dynamically translate the FDM based on the user's gaze direction.

Getting ready

For this recipe, you will need an HMD that supports eye-tracking features, such as Meta's Quest Pro. This recipe was authored and tested with Meta's Quest Pro device, so some of the code shown here is specific to that platform. This recipe assumes you have already implemented static foveated rendering using a fragment density map. If not, you might want to refer to our previous guide on that topic to understand the foundational concepts.

How to do it...

This extension simplifies the application code by applying an offset to the FDM at render time, inside the render loop:

1. All attachments used in the render pass where the offset is applied to the FDM must be created with the `VK_IMAGE_CREATE_FRAGMENT_DENSITY_MAP_OFFSET_BIT_QCOM` flag. Since we are rendering directly to swapchain images, the swapchain images need to be created with that flag. Swapchain images are created by OpenXR. Thankfully, Meta devices provide the ability to provide additional Vulkan flags to be used during the creation of swapchain images. For that, create an instance of the `XrVulkanSwapchainCreateInfoMETA` structure and add the flag mentioned before to its `addditionalCreateFlags` property:

```
const XrVulkanSwapchainCreateInfoMETA
  vulkanImageAdditionalFlags{
    .type =
      XR_TYPE_VULKAN_SWAPCHAIN_CREATE_INFO_META,
    .next = nullptr,
    .additionalCreateFlags =
      VK_IMAGE_CREATE_SUBSAMPLED_BIT_EXT |
      VK_IMAGE_CREATE_FRAGMENT_DENSITY_MAP_OFFSET_BIT_QCOM,
};

Const XrSwapchainCreateInfo swapChainCreateInfo = {
  .type = XR_TYPE_SWAPCHAIN_CREATE_INFO,
  .next = &vulkanImageAdditionalFlags,
  ...
};
```

The instance of the `XrVulkanSwapchainCreateInfoMETA` structure must be added to the pNext chain of the `XrSwapchainCreateInfo` structure.

2. Before enabling the FDM Offset feature, it is necessary to check whether the physical device supports it. Doing so requires appending an instance of the `VkPhysicalDeviceFragmentDensityMapOffsetFeaturesQCOM` structure to the pNext chain of `VkPhysicalDeviceFeatures2` passed to the `vkGetPhysicalDeviceFeatures2` function.

   `VkPhysicalDeviceFragmentDensityMapOffsetFeaturesQCOM::fragmentDensityMapOffset` specifies whether the FDM Offset extension is supported.

3. The extension has properties that need to be queried to be used properly. To do that, also include an instance of the `VkPhysicalDeviceFragmentDensityMapOffsetPropertiesQCOM` structure to the pNext chain of `VkPhysicalDeviceProperties2` and query those properties with `vkGetPhysicalDeviceProperties2`. We will use them later.

4. The FDM Offset extension is a device extension and its name needs to be passed in during the creation of the `VkDevice` object: `"VK_QCOM_fragment_density_map_offset"` (or `VK_QCOM_FRAGMENT_DENSITY_MAP_OFFSET_EXTENSION_NAME`).

5. The FDM texture needs to be created with the `VK_IMAGE_CREATE_FRAGMENT_DENSITY_MAP_OFFSET_BIT_QCOM` creation flag.

6. The offsets are applied to the FDM by creating an instance of the `VkSubpassFragmentDensityMapOffsetEndInfoQCOM` structure and adding it to the pNext chain of the `VkSubpassEndInfo` structure. Note that, in this case, you need to call `vkCmdEndRenderPass2`. `vkCmdEndRenderPass` isn't extensible (we'll see how to calculate the offsets in the next step):

```
const std::array<VkOffset2D, 2> offsets = {
  leftEyeOffset,
  rightEyeOffset,
};
const VkSubpassFragmentDensityMapOffsetEndInfoQCOM
  offsetInfo = {
    .sType =
      VK_STRUCTURE_TYPE_SUBPASS_FRAGMENT_DENSITY_MAP_OFFSET_END_INFO_QCOM,
    .fragmentDensityOffsetCount =
      offsets.size(), // 1 for each
                      // layer/multiview view
    .pFragmentDensityOffsets =
      offsets
        .data(), // aligned to
                 // fragmentDensityOffsetGranularity
};
```

```
const VkSubpassEndInfo subpassEndInfo = {
  .sType = VK_STRUCTURE_TYPE_SUBPASS_END_INFO,
  .pNext = &offsetInfo,
};
vkCmdEndRenderPass2KHR(commandBuffer,
                       &subpassEndInfo);
```

7. The `eyeGazeScreenPosLeft` and `eyeGazeScreenPosRight` offsets can be calculated using the previous recipe, *Retrieving eye gaze information from OpenXR in your app*. In the sample app provided in the repository, they can be retrieved from the context with the `OXR::Context::eyeGazeScreenPos(int eye)` function:

```
const glm::vec2 swapchainImageCenter =
  glm::vec2(oxrContext.swapchain(0)
              ->viewport()
              .recommendedImageRectWidth /
          2.f,
         oxrContext.swapchain(0)
              ->viewport()
              .recommendedImageRectHeight /
          2.f);
const glm::vec2 offsetInPixelsLeft =
  glm::vec2(eyeGazeScreenPosLeft) -
  swapchainImageCenter;
const glm::vec2 offsetInPixelsRight =
  glm::vec2(eyeGazeScreenPosRight) -
  swapchainImageCenter;
const glm::vec2 fdmOffsetGranularity = glm::vec2(
  vkContext.physicalDevice()
    .fragmentDensityMapOffsetProperties()
    .fragmentDensityOffsetGranularity.width,
  vkContext.physicalDevice()
    .fragmentDensityMapOffsetProperties()
    .fragmentDensityOffsetGranularity.height);

const VkOffset2D leftEyeOffset{
  offsetInPixelsLeft.x,
  offsetInPixelsLeft.y,
};
const VkOffset2D rightEyeOffset{
  offsetInPixelsRight.x,
  offsetInPixelsRight.y,
};
```

This extension is powerful because it allows static FDM to be used to achieve dynamic foveation without the need to impose an extra CPU load of recalculating the map every frame. *Figure 8.2* shows the result of rendering the bistro scene on a Quest Pro with an FDM plus Qualcomm's FDM Offset extension. The white circle is the cursor used to help visualize the eye gaze direction.

Figure 8.2 – The bistro scene rendered on a Quest Pro with an FDM applied to the eye gaze direction

This concludes our recipe on dynamic foveated rendering. In the next recipe, we will learn how we can reduce memory load since the VR devices have limited GPU memory.

Using half floats to reduce memory load

A **half float**, also known as a **half-precision floating point**, is a binary floating-point format that occupies 16 bits. It plays a crucial role specifically for its application in VR devices and other low-performance hardware. A half-precision floating point has a smaller memory footprint and requires less bandwidth, which can significantly improve the performance and efficiency of such devices. They are ideal for scenarios where the precision of full single-precision floating-point numbers is not necessary, such as storing pixel values in graphics, performing large but simple computations in machine learning models, and certain calculations in 3D graphics. Employing 16 bits not only bolsters throughput but also diminishes register usage, a key determinant of GPU performance. The quantity of shaders that can run concurrently is directly contingent upon the available registers, thus making their efficient usage crucial. In this recipe, we demonstrate how to use half floats in Vulkan and how we can reduce memory consumption by storing vertex data in 16-bit floats instead of 32-bit.

Getting ready

To implement a half float in your application, there are several Vulkan and GLSL features that you need to be aware of. Vulkan supports half floats by enabling the `storageBuffer16BitAccess` and `shaderFloat16` features. The `storageBuffer16BitAccess` feature allows you to use a 16-bit format for storage buffers, which can save memory and bandwidth. The `shaderFloat16` feature enables the use of 16-bit floating-point types in your shaders, which can improve performance by reducing the amount of data that needs to be processed.

On the GLSL side, you would need to enable the `GL_EXT_shader_explicit_arithmetic_types_float16` and `GL_EXT_shader_16bit_storage` extensions. The `GL_EXT_shader_explicit_arithmetic_types_float16` extension allows you to perform arithmetic operations with half-precision floating-point numbers directly in your shaders. Meanwhile, the `GL_EXT_shader_16bit_storage` extension enables you to store half-precision floating-point numbers in your shader storage blocks and interface blocks.

By leveraging these Vulkan and GLSL features, you can effectively incorporate a half float in your application, optimizing performance, especially for low-performance devices.

How to do it…

Follow these steps to effectively implement the 16-bit float, starting with the activation of specific features and then modifying the shader code:

1. Initially, we must activate two specific features: `storageBuffer16BitAccess` (found in `VkPhysicalDeviceVulkan11Features`) and `shaderFloat16` (located in `VkPhysicalDeviceVulkan12Features`). To facilitate this, we have incorporated a function within the `VulkanCore::Context` class:

    ```
    void Context::enable16bitFloatFeature() {
      enable11Features_.storageBuffer16BitAccess = VK_TRUE;
      enable12Features_.shaderFloat16 = VK_TRUE;
    }
    ```

2. Next, we change our shader code and add GLSL extensions to it. This is done inside the `app/src/main/assets/shaders/Common.glsl` file. We also change the vertex structure inside this file to use `float16_t` instead of `float`. We also use `glm::packHalf1x16` to convert a 32-bit float to 16-bit when loading GLB assets:

```
#extension GL_EXT_shader_explicit_arithmetic_types_float16 : require
#extension GL_EXT_shader_16bit_storage : require
struct Vertex {
  float16_t posX;
  float16_t posY;
  float16_t posZ;
  float16_t normalX;
  float16_t normalY;
  float16_t normalZ;
  float16_t tangentX;
  float16_t tangentY;
  float16_t tangentZ;
  float16_t tangentW;
  float16_t uvX;
  float16_t uvY;
  float16_t uvX2;
  float16_t uvY2;
  int material;
};
```

In conclusion, implementing a 16-bit float offers significant improvement in GPU performance, especially in the context of VR and other low-performance devices. By activating the necessary features in Vulkan and making the appropriate adjustments in our GLSL shaders, we can take advantage of the benefits that a 16-bit float has to offer. It's a relatively straightforward process that involves enabling specific features, adjusting shader code, and modifying data structures to accommodate the half-precision format.

In this chapter, you embarked on a journey through the world of OpenXR. You started by grasping the fundamentals and swiftly moved on to mastering advanced techniques. You learned how to implement single pass multiview rendering and how to utilize the fragment density map for static foveated rendering. You also gained the skills to retrieve eye gaze information for your app. Further, you unlocked the secrets of implementing dynamic foveated rendering using Qualcomm's fragment density map Offset extension. Lastly, you discovered the power of using half floats to significantly reduce memory load in your applications.

9
Debugging and Performance Measurement Techniques

Debugging failures and reverse engineering an implementation, as well as measuring the performance of a system once it has been authored, are as important as writing new code. Vulkan is a vast and complicated API and, more than ever, knowing how to debug it is paramount. In this chapter, we will explore several recipes on how to debug and inspect your implementation. We will also demonstrate how to measure the performance of your implementation once you can display an image onscreen. After all, graphics programming is all about extracting the last drop of performance from the hardware and Vulkan was designed to help you do just that.

In this chapter, we're going to cover the following main topics:

- Frame debugging
- Naming Vulkan objects for easy debugging
- Printing values from shaders in Vulkan
- Intercepting validation layer messages
- Retrieving debug information from shaders
- Measuring performance in Vulkan with timestamp queries

Technical requirements

For this chapter, you will need to make sure you have VS 2022 installed along with the Vulkan SDK. Please revisit *Chapter 1, Vulkan Core Concepts*, under the *Technical requirements* section for details on setting up. Additionally, you will need RenderDoc and Tracy for this chapter. The steps to download and install these tools will be provided in the corresponding recipes within this chapter.

Frame debugging

Capturing and replaying a frame is very important for debugging graphics applications. Different than a live capture, in which results are captured and displayed as your application is running, capturing means recording all the commands sent to the GPU along with their data. This includes all the draw calls, shaders, textures, buffers, and other resources used to render the frame. Replaying a frame means executing those recorded commands again. Frame replay is a powerful feature for debugging because it allows developers to closely examine the rendering process, step by step, and see exactly what's happening at each stage. If a bug or graphical glitch occurs, frame replay can help pin down exactly where and why it's happening. There are multiple tools for frame debugging, such as RenderDoc, PIX, NVIDIA's Nsight Graphics, and AMD Radeon GPU Profiler.

In this recipe, we will focus on how to use **RenderDoc** since it is open source, cross-platform, and works on almost all GPUs.

Getting ready

As a first step, you need to download RenderDoc from `https://renderdoc.org/builds`.

RenderDoc's UI contains the following main components:

- **Timeline**: This is typically found on the top row of RenderDoc's user interface. The timeline provides a graphical representation of all the API calls (events) that occurred during the frame you've captured. It's color-coded to indicate different types of events (such as draw calls or compute dispatches), making it easy to get a high-level overview of what's happening in your frame. You can select any event in the timeline to view more detailed information in **Event Browser** (on the left side of the UI) and the various tabs on the right side of the UI.

- **Event Browser**: Located on the left side of the UI, **Event Browser** provides a detailed, hierarchical view of all the events in your frame. It shows the order of the API calls and allows you to navigate through them easily. When you select an event in **Event Browser**, RenderDoc will highlight the corresponding event in the timeline and update the tabs on the right side of the UI with information related to that event.

    - **Tabs (Texture Viewer, Mesh Viewer, Pipeline State**, and so on): These tabs are found on the right side of the UI, and they provide detailed information about the currently selected event. Each tab focuses on a different aspect of the rendering process:

    - **Texture Viewer**: This tab allows you to view all of the textures that are used in your frame. You can inspect each texture's properties, visualize their contents, and see how they are used in your shaders.

    - **Mesh Viewer**: This tab provides a visual and numerical view of the vertex and index buffers used by a draw call. You can inspect the raw buffer data, view the resulting geometry, and see how the vertices are transformed by your vertex shader.

- **Pipeline State**: This tab shows the complete state of the GPU pipeline for the selected event. You can see all the bound resources (such as buffers and textures), inspect the shaders being used, and view the configuration of the various pipeline stages.

Figure 9.1 shows RenderDoc's main UI elements with a captured frame opened for inspection.

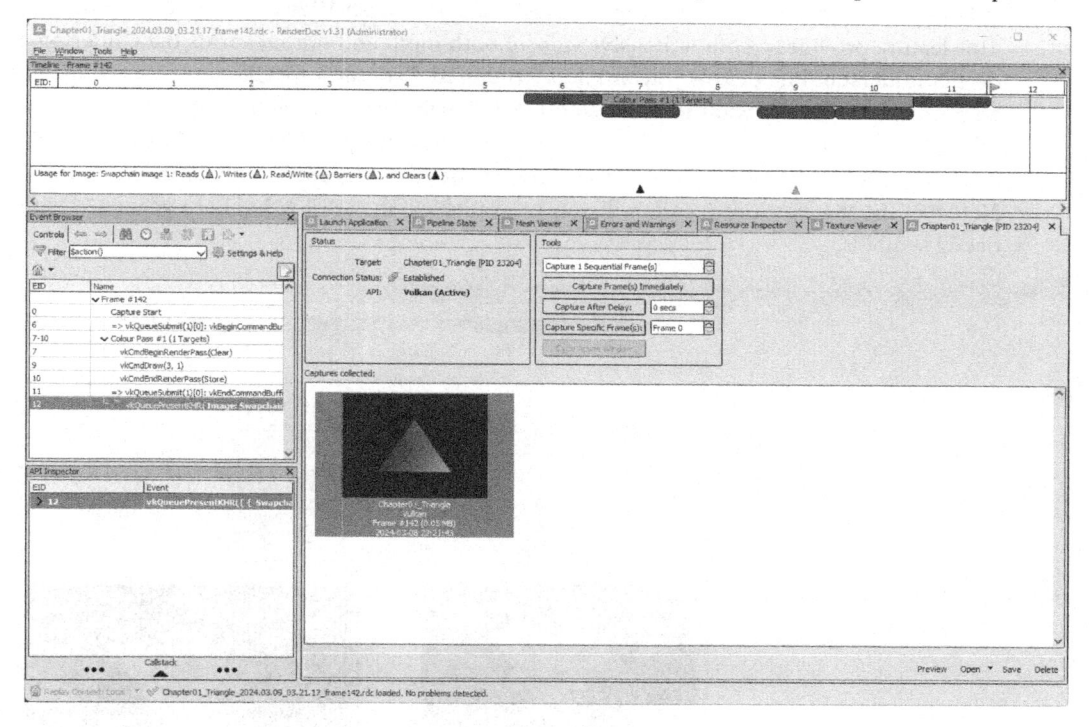

Figure 9.1 – RenderDoc main screen

In the next section, we will demonstrate how to use RenderDoc using executables from *Chapter 1, Vulkan Core Concepts*, and *Chapter 3, Implementing GPU-Driven Rendering*.

How to do it...

Capturing a frame (or frames) with RenderDoc can be done programmatically or interactively, using the user interface. The next steps will explain how to capture frames from your application using RenderDoc's user interface:

1. As a first step, you can launch the application by selecting the application to launch in the **Launch Application** tab. Once the application is launched, click **Capture Frame(s) Immediately**. This will capture the current frame of the application, which we can inspect. Once the frame is captured, double-clicking it will open it for inspection. You can also save the frame on disk to open it later.

304 Debugging and Performance Measurement Techniques

2. After the capture, we can select the draw call in **Event Browser** (on the left of the UI) that we would like to inspect. In this case, that call is vkCmdDraw (EID 7). Once you select it, you will see all the input and output textures used by this draw call in the **Texture Viewer** tab as depicted in *Figure 9.2*.

3. When you're interested in exploring the mesh data, the **Mesh Viewer** tab is your go-to tool. This feature provides a comprehensive view of both input and output vertex data, offering a deeper understanding of how your mesh is structured. Let's say a specific vertex is giving you trouble, or you simply want to understand its behavior better. To achieve this, you need to select the vertex in question. A right-click will then reveal an option named **Debug this vertex**. Selecting this option will lead you to the vertex shader that was used in rendering your mesh. Note that the shader's source code will only be available if the SPIR-V has been generated with debug symbols.

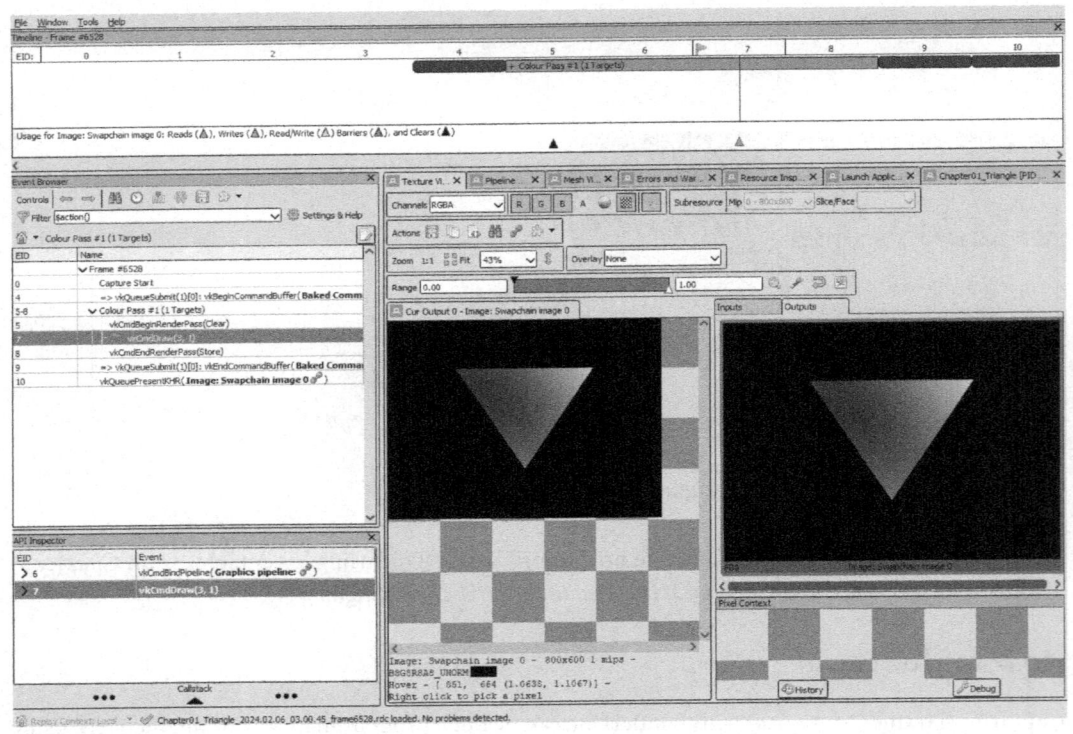

Figure 9.2 – RenderDoc Texture Viewer

4. The **Pipeline State** tab is a crucial component in the RenderDoc UI. It offers an extensive view of the various stages, and their states, involved in the graphics pipeline, serving as a powerful tool for analyzing and debugging your rendering process. In the vertex shader stage, you can inspect the operations applied to each vertex. This includes transformations to position vertices in the correct 3D space, as well as calculations to determine vertex colors or texture coordinates. You can also select **View Shader** to inspect the shader source code used during this draw call. Moving on to the fragment shader stage, the **Pipeline State** tab allows you to scrutinize how each fragment (potential pixel) is processed. This includes operations such as determining its final color based on lighting, texture, and/or other factors. Debugging this stage can help you resolve issues related to color computations, texture mapping, and more.

5. To debug a specific fragment, you'll need to select a pixel in **Texture Viewer**. You can do this by clicking on the pixel you're interested in. The values of this pixel represent the output of the fragment shader for that specific pixel. After selecting a pixel, you can debug the fragment shader that produced it. To do this, right-click on the pixel and select the **Debug** button shown inside the **Pixel Context** window. This will open a new **Shader Viewer** tab, where you can step through the shader code line by line. For each line, you can inspect the values of your variables and see how they change as the shader executes.

The compute shader stage is used for performing general-purpose computations on the GPU. Here, you can inspect and debug the operations that aren't directly related to rendering, such as physics simulations or culling. In the next step, we will demonstrate using the executable from *Chapter 3, Implementing GPU-Driven Rendering*, in the *Frustum culling using compute shaders* recipe.

1. To understand how to debug the compute shader, we will first need to launch `Chapter03_GPU_Culling.exe` from RenderDoc. Once the application is up, we will take a capture. Next, navigate to the **Pipeline State** tab. Now, your focus should be on the `vkCmdDispatch` call. Selecting this call in **Event Browser** will display the associated pipeline used by this call in the **Pipeline State** tab, as demonstrated in *Figure 9.3*:

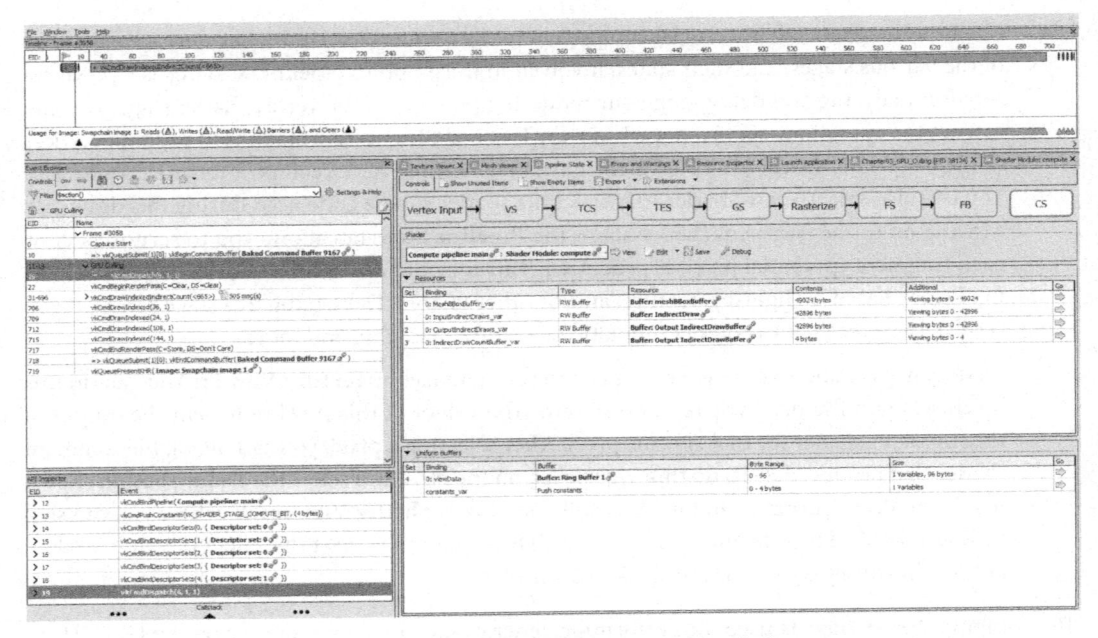

306 Debugging and Performance Measurement Techniques

Figure 9.3 – Compute shader as seen in RenderDoc

2. When it comes to culling, we launch as many threads as there are meshes. Then, on the GPU, we're simply discarding any mesh that isn't visible in the frustum. Let's assume we're interested in understanding why mesh number 5 is outside the frustum. To debug this, click the **Debug** button and specify the thread ID in the **Debug Compute Shader** window. This window allows you to specify either a global thread ID or a thread group and a local thread ID. In our case, to debug mesh number 5, you would enter 5 in the global X dimension (in the **Dispatch Thread ID** section). Once you click the **Debug** button, a new window containing the shader source code will be launched. Here, you can inspect and debug the compute shader, enabling you to understand why a particular mesh was discarded. The process is demonstrated in *Figure 9.4*:

Frame debugging 307

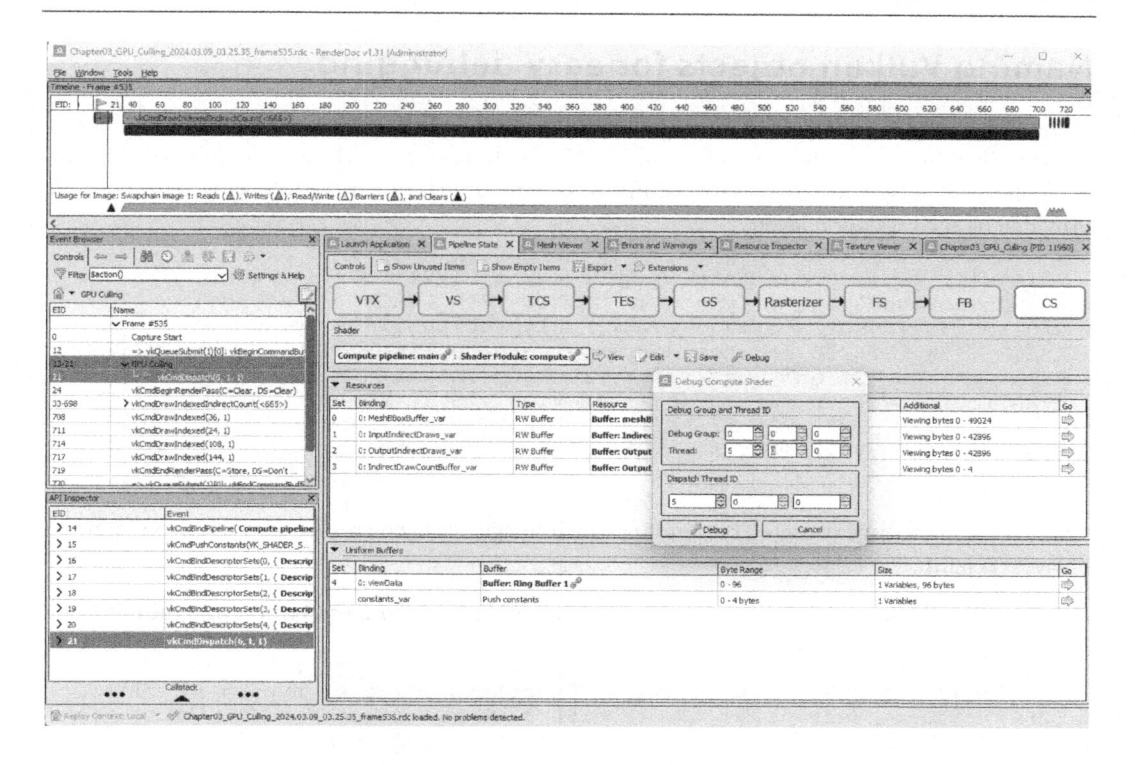

Figure 9.4 – Debugging a compute shader in RenderDoc

This recipe is a very brief introduction to *one* frame debugging tool. Keep in mind other tools exist and operate in different ways.

See also

For a comprehensive understanding of how to utilize RenderDoc, we highly recommend viewing the following video tutorials. These will provide you with detailed insights into its usage:

- `https://youtu.be/7eznPe3TyAY`
- `https://youtu.be/EMFG5wmng-M`
- `https://renderdoc.org/docs/getting_started/quick_start.html`

Naming Vulkan objects for easy debugging

Using Vulkan means you need to create and manage many Vulkan objects. By default, those objects are identified by their handle, a numerical ID. Although numerical IDs are easy to maintain from an application perspective, they are meaningless to humans. Consider the following error message, provided by the validation layer:

```
VUID-VkImageViewCreateInfo-imageViewType-04974 ] Object 0: handle
= 0xcb3ee80000000007, type = VK_OBJECT_TYPE_IMAGE; | MessageID =
0xc120e150 | vkCreateImageView(): Using pCreateInfo->viewType VK_
IMAGE_VIEW_TYPE_2D and the subresourceRange.layerCount VK_REMAINING_
ARRAY_LAYERS=(2) and must 1 (try looking into VK_IMAGE_VIEW_TYPE_*_
ARRAY). The Vulkan spec states: If viewType is VK_IMAGE_VIEW_TYPE_1D,
VK_IMAGE_VIEW_TYPE_2D, or VK_IMAGE_VIEW_TYPE_3D; and subresourceRange.
layerCount is VK_REMAINING_ARRAY_LAYERS, then the remaining number of
layers must be 1
```

The preceding message is useful, but finding which image has been created with the wrong number of layers is hard.

If, on the other hand, we give that image a name, the validation layer message becomes the following:

```
VUID-VkImageViewCreateInfo-imageViewType-04974 ] Object 0: handle =
0xcb3ee80000000007, name = Image: Swapchain image 0, type = VK_OBJECT_
TYPE_IMAGE; | MessageID = 0xc120e150 | vkCreateImageView(): Using
pCreateInfo->viewType VK_IMAGE_VIEW_TYPE_2D and the subresourceRange.
layerCount VK_REMAINING_ARRAY_LAYERS=(2) and must 1 (try looking into
VK_IMAGE_VIEW_TYPE_*_ARRAY). The Vulkan spec states: If viewType
is VK_IMAGE_VIEW_TYPE_1D, VK_IMAGE_VIEW_TYPE_2D, or VK_IMAGE_VIEW_
TYPE_3D; and subresourceRange.layerCount is VK_REMAINING_ARRAY_LAYERS,
then the remaining number of layers must be 1
```

Note that the name of the object is now part of the error message. That makes it much easier to know where to look in your code and fix the error.

In this recipe, you will learn how to use a Vulkan extension to give human-readable or meaningful names to all Vulkan objects.

Getting ready

To be able to assign names to a Vulkan object, you first need to enable the VK_EXT_debug_utils instance extension. This extension's name needs to be provided during the creation of the Vulkan instance as either a string, VK_EXT_debug_utils, or using the VK_EXT_DEBUG_UTILS_EXTENSION_NAME macro. The following code snippet initializes a Vulkan instance with debug utilities enabled:

```
VkInstance instance_ = VK_NULL_HANDLE;
std::vector<const char *> instanceExtensions = {
  VK_EXT_DEBUG_UTILS_EXTENSION_NAME};
const VkInstanceCreateInfo instanceInfo = {
```

```
    .sType = VK_STRUCTURE_TYPE_INSTANCE_CREATE_INFO,
    ...
    .enabledExtensionCount = static_cast<uint32_t>(
      instanceExtensions.size()),
    .ppEnabledExtensionNames =
      instanceExtensions.data(),
};
VK_CHECK(vkCreateInstance(&instanceInfo, nullptr,
                          &instance_));
```

Now you are ready to start naming your Vulkan object. Let's see how in the next section.

How to do it...

Once the extension has been enabled, here are the steps to name your objects:

1. Once the extension has been enabled, you may add a name to any Vulkan object, given its handle, by calling the vkSetDebugUtilsObjectNameEXT function:

   ```
   VkDevice device_; // Valid Vulkan device
   VkObjectType type = VK_OBJECT_TYPE_UNKNOWN;
   std::string name; // human readable name
   const VkDebugUtilsObjectNameInfoEXT
     objectNameInfo = {
       .sType =
         VK_STRUCTURE_TYPE_DEBUG_UTILS_OBJECT_NAME_INFO_EXT,
       .objectType = type,
       .objectHandle =
         reinterpret_cast<uint64_t>(handle),
       .pObjectName = name.c_str(),
   };
   VK_CHECK(vkSetDebugUtilsObjectNameEXT(
     device_, &objectNameInfo));
   ```

   The object type (type) is one of the values of the VkObject enumeration and must match the object's type (VK_OBJECT_TYPE_IMAGE for a Vulkan Image, for example). The handle is the object's handle, which needs to be cast to type uint64_t.

2. This function is only available if the extension is also available, so make sure to guard it in an #ifdef block and check whether the extension has been enabled for the instance.

   In the repository, the VulkanCore::Context:: setVkObjectname method wraps this function in a templated class and does the casting for you. Also, it's worth mentioning that names aren't only displayed on validation error messages. They also appear in frame capture and debugging tools.

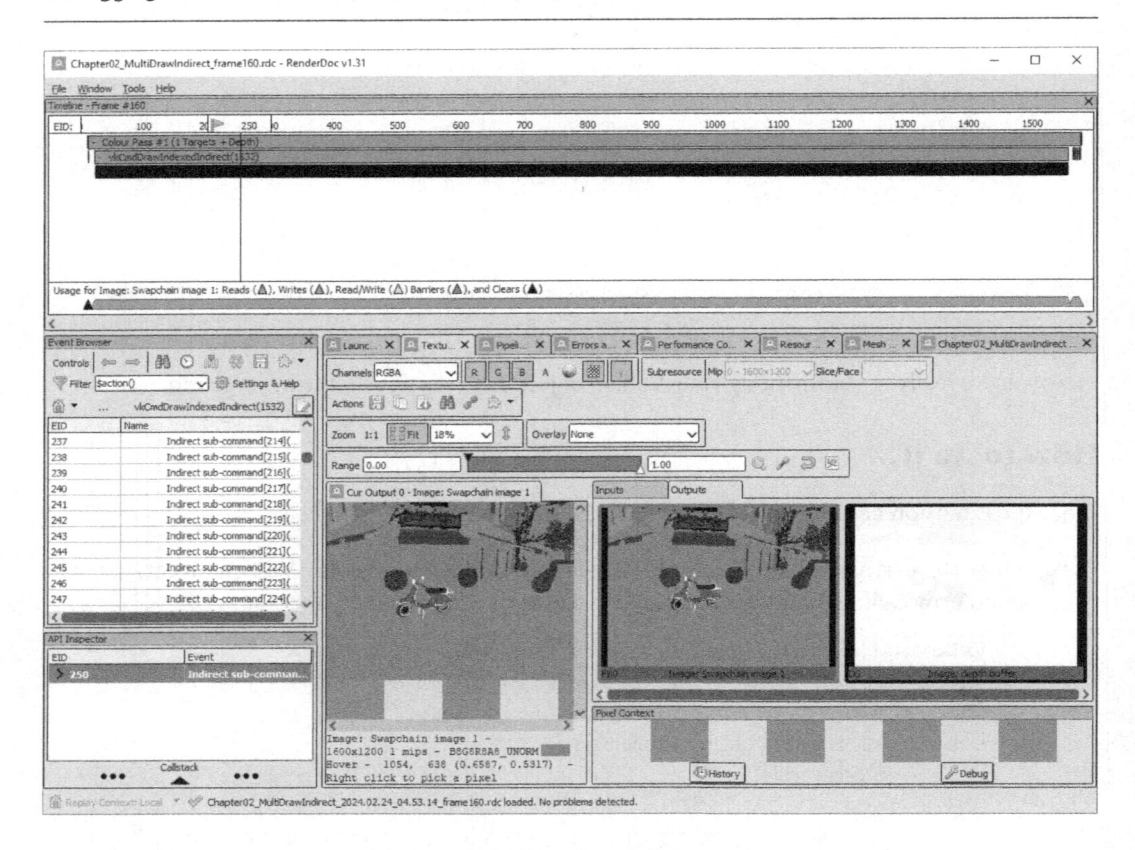

Figure 9.5 - Examples of how object names appear in RenderDoc

Figure 9.5 shows how object names are displayed in RenderDoc. In the screenshot, one of the swapchain images is named **Image: Swapchain image 1**. The depth buffer is named **Image: depth buffer**.

Printing values from shaders in Vulkan

As graphics programmers, we must all agree that debugging shaders is one of the most frustrating aspects of our jobs. Even though some frame capture software provides shader debugging, it may still be difficult to find the exact pixel you would like to debug, or you may need another piece of information about a set of pixels instead of just inspecting them one by one.

Thankfully, Vulkan provides a way to print values directly from shaders. The information can be inspected directly on RenderDoc, for example, or retrieved from the validation error messages (please refer to the *Retrieving debugging information from shaders* recipe for more details on how to do this).

In this recipe, you will learn how to print values from your shader code using a simple function that is like `printf`.

Getting ready

To utilize the functionality of printing values from shaders, it's a prerequisite to enable the VK_KHR_shader_non_semantic_info device extension. This can be achieved by adding either the VK_KHR_shader_non_semantic_info string or the VK_KHR_SHADER_NON_SEMANTIC_INFO_EXTENSION_NAME macro to the VkDeviceCreateInfo structure during the creation of a Vulkan device. This process is demonstrated in the following code snippet:

```
VkPhysicalDevice physicalDevice; // Valid Vulkan
                                 // Physical Device
const std::vector<const char *> deviceExtensions =
  {VK_KHR_SHADER_NON_SEMANTIC_INFO_EXTENSION_NAME};
const VkDeviceCreateInfo dci = {

  .sType = VK_STRUCTURE_TYPE_DEVICE_CREATE_INFO,
  ...
  .enabledExtensionCount = static_cast<uint32_t>(
    deviceExtensions.size()),
  .ppEnabledExtensionNames = deviceExtensions.data(),
};
VK_CHECK(vkCreateDevice(physicalDevice_, &dci,
  nullptr, &device_));
```

Now that the extension has been enabled, let's see what the steps are to print values directly from shaders.

How to do it...

Once the extension has been enabled, you will also need to add a GLSL extension to your shaders:

1. Enable the GL_EXT_debug_printf extension in your shader code:

   ```
   #version 460
   #extension GL_EXT_debug_printf: enable
   ```

2. Call debugPrintfEXT in your shader code whenever you would like to print values. In the following code snippet, we are printing the value of gl_VertexIndex:

   ```
   debugPrintfEXT("gl_VertexIndex = %i", gl_VertexIndex);
   ```

3. The function provides specifiers for vector values as well. Here's an example of a call that prints all components of a vec3 variable:

   ```
   vec3 position;
   debugPrintfEXT("%2.3v3f", position);
   ```

   The preceding function call prints the x, y, and z components of position as a floating-point value with 3 decimals.

Debugging and Performance Measurement Techniques

Here's the abridged version of the vertex shader used in *Chapter 1, Vulkan Core Concepts*, with the added `debugPrintfEXT` call to print the `gl_VertexIndex` value:

```
#version 460
#extension GL_EXT_debug_printf: enable

layout(location = 0) out vec4 outColor;

vec2 positions[3] = vec2[]( ... );
vec3 colors[3] = vec3[]( ... );

void main() {
    gl_Position = vec4(positions[gl_VertexIndex], 0.0, 1.0);
    debugPrintfEXT(«gl_VertexIndex = %i», gl_VertexIndex);
    outColor = vec4(colors[gl_VertexIndex], 1.0);
}
```

Figure 9.6 shows how the printed values can be inspected in RenderDoc:

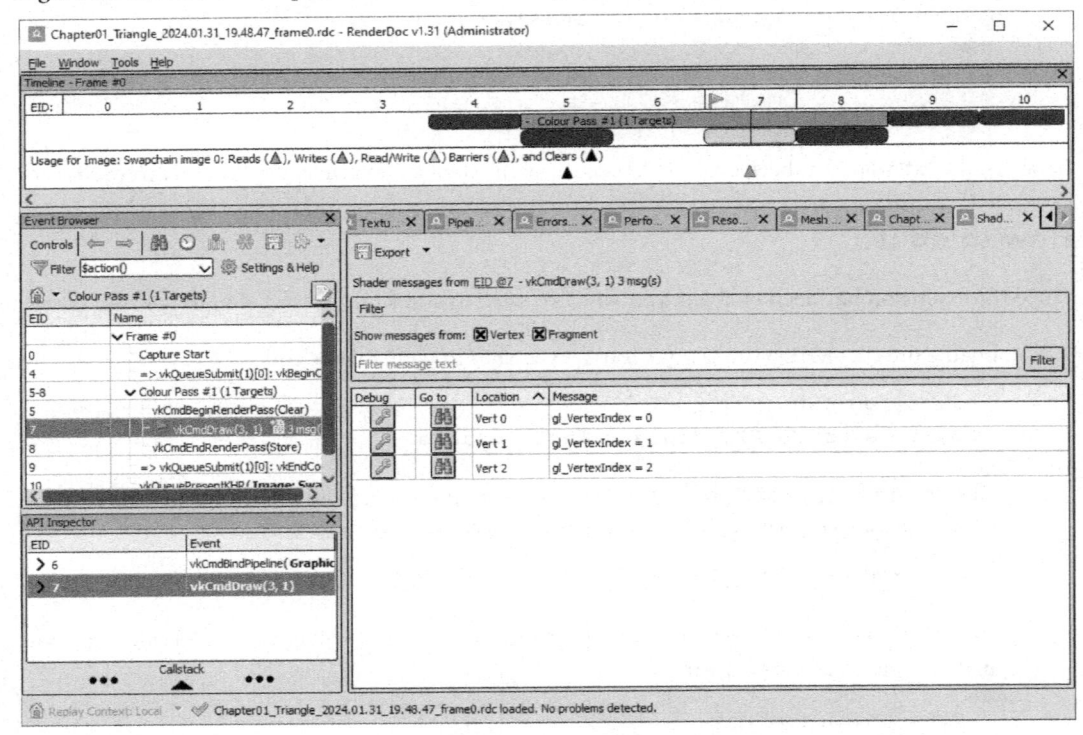

Figure 9.6 – debugPrintfEXT values visible in RenderDoc

Intercepting validation layer messages

In some circumstances, validation errors are so plentiful that it becomes impossible to know where the cause of the problem is. For that reason, it would be ideal to interrupt the execution of your program as soon as an error is detected, especially when debugging your application. The debug utility extension (`VK_EXT_debug_utils`) allows you to install a callback function that is invoked whenever an error is detected.

In this recipe, you will learn how to install a debug callback to intercept error messages emitted by the validation layer and make your debugging sessions more productive.

Getting ready

To be able to set a callback whenever an error occurs, you need to enable the `VK_EXT_debug_utils` extension. Please refer to the *Getting ready* section of the *Naming Vulkan objects for easier debugging* recipe to learn how to enable this extension when creating a Vulkan instance.

How to do it...

Before installing and using the callback, you need to define one. After that, and once the extension has been enabled and a Vulkan instance object has been created, you need to install the callback using a special Vulkan function:

1. Define a callback function with the following signature:

   ```
   typedef VkBool32 (
   VKAPI_PTR
       PFN_vkDebugUtilsMessengerCallbackEXT)(
   VkDebugUtilsMessageSeverityFlagBitsEXT
       messageSeverity,
   VkDebugUtilsMessageTypeFlagsEXT messageTypes,
   const VkDebugUtilsMessengerCallbackDataEXT
       pCallbackData,
   void *pUserData);
   ```

2. Here's the function used as a callback provided in the repository:

   ```
   VkBool32 VKAPI_PTR debugMessengerCallback(
   VkDebugUtilsMessageSeverityFlagBitsEXT
       messageSeverity,
   VkDebugUtilsMessageTypeFlagsEXT messageTypes,
   const VkDebugUtilsMessengerCallbackDataEXT
       pCallbackData,
   void *pUserData) {
   ```

```
            if (
              messageSeverity &
              (VK_DEBUG_UTILS_MESSAGE_SEVERITY_ERROR_BIT_EXT)) {
              LOGE("debugMessengerCallback : MessageCode "
                   "is %s & Message is %s",
                   pCallbackData->pMessageIdName,
                   pCallbackData->pMessage);
#if defined(_WIN32)
              __debugbreak();
#else
              raise(SIGTRAP);
#endif
            } else if (
              messageSeverity &
              (VK_DEBUG_UTILS_MESSAGE_SEVERITY_ERROR_BIT_EXT)) {
              LOGW("debugMessengerCallback : MessageCode "
                   "is %s & Message is %s",
                   pCallbackData->pMessageIdName,
                   pCallbackData->pMessage);
            } else {
              LOGI("debugMessengerCallback : MessageCode "
                   "is %s & Message is %s",
                   pCallbackData->pMessageIdName,
                   pCallbackData->pMessage);
            }

            return VK_FALSE;
        }
```

Your callback can decide how to treat the message, if at all, based on its type (general message, validation message, performance message) or its severity (verbose, info, warning, or error). The `pCallbackData` parameter (of type `VkDebugUtilsMessengerCallbackDataEXT`) provides a plethora of different information you can use, while the `pUserData` parameter may contain your own data, which is provided when installing the callback.

3. Install the callback once you have a valid Vulkan instance by creating an instance of the `VkDebugUtilsMessengerCreateInfoEXT` structure:

```
VkInstance instance; // Valid Vulkan Instance
VkDebugUtilsMessengerEXT messenger =
  VK_NULL_HANDLE;
const VkDebugUtilsMessengerCreateInfoEXT messengerInfo = {
  .sType =
    VK_STRUCTURE_TYPE_DEBUG_UTILS_MESSENGER_CREATE_INFO_EXT,
  .flags = 0,
```

```
    .messageSeverity =
      VK_DEBUG_UTILS_MESSAGE_SEVERITY_VERBOSE_BIT_EXT |
      VK_DEBUG_UTILS_MESSAGE_SEVERITY_INFO_BIT_EXT |
      VK_DEBUG_UTILS_MESSAGE_SEVERITY_WARNING_BIT_EXT |
      VK_DEBUG_UTILS_MESSAGE_SEVERITY_ERROR_BIT_EXT,
    .messageType =
      VK_DEBUG_UTILS_MESSAGE_TYPE_GENERAL_BIT_EXT |
      VK_DEBUG_UTILS_MESSAGE_TYPE_VALIDATION_BIT_EXT,
    .pfnUserCallback = &debugMessengerCallback,
    .pUserData = nullptr,
};
VK_CHECK(vkCreateDebugUtilsMessengerEXT(
    instance, &messengerInfo, nullptr, &messenger));
```

4. Make sure to destroy the messenger once you are done with your Vulkan instance. This is necessary because, in Vulkan, any resources created need to be explicitly destroyed when they're no longer needed to avoid memory leaks and to free up system resources:

```
vkDestroyDebugUtilsMessengerEXT(instance_,
                                messenger_,
                                nullptr);
```

The debug callback is very useful and should always be used. Make sure to have one as soon as possible and know how to use it.

Retrieving debug information from shaders

One of the most difficult tasks in graphics programming is writing tests. Be those smoke, integration, end-to-end, or unit tests, how do you ensure that the output of your engine is really what you would expect? Except for simple tests, screenshot-like types of tests are prone to several problems. One particularly difficult problem is testing shader code – since you don't usually have access to the hardware, testing shader code is very painful.

Thankfully, Vulkan has a mechanism that allows you to capture the value output from shaders with the `debugPrintfEXT` function directly from the validation layer. This mechanism isn't new and could be enabled using the **Vulkan Configurator**. But, introduced with the `Vulkan SDK 1.3.275`, the `VK_EXT_layer_settings` instance extension allows you to enable this mechanism directly from your application without manually having to edit any other configuration.

In this recipe, you will learn how to enable this feature and retrieve the output of `debugPrintfEXT` calls from shaders.

Getting ready

For this recipe, you will need `Vulkan SDK version 1.3.275`. Although all the code in the repository was tested with `SDK version 1.3.265`, the `VK_EXT_layer_settings` extension was only available with `SDK 1.3.275`.

How to do it...

Enabling this feature is easy and requires only a few steps. Let's get to them:

1. The `VK_EXT_layer_settings` extension introduces a way for you to change individual layer settings. Each setting must be set using an instance of the `VkLayerSettingEXT` structure, defined as follows:

   ```
   typedef struct VkLayerSettingEXT {
     const char *pLayerName;
     const char *pSettingName;
     VkLayerSettingTypeEXT type;
     uint32_t valueCount;
     const void *pValues;
   } VkLayerSettingEXT;
   ```

2. To enable the feature that allows you to receive output from shaders, you need to enable a few settings of the `VK_LAYER_KHRONOS_validation` layer. Let's start by creating a constant with the layer name for which we'll change the settings:

   ```
   const std::string layer_name =
     "VK_LAYER_KHRONOS_validation";
   ```

3. Now we create arrays to store the values of the settings we'll use:

   ```
   const std::array<const char *, 1>
     setting_debug_action = {"VK_DBG_LAYER_ACTION_BREAK"};
   const std::array<const char *, 1>
     setting_gpu_based_action = {
       "GPU_BASED_DEBUG_PRINTF"};
   const std::array<VkBool32, 1>
     setting_printf_to_stdout = {VK_TRUE};
   ```

   The `debug_action` setting was changed to `VK_DBG_LAYER_ACTION_BREAK` so that the callback is called whenever there's a new value from `debugPrintfEXT`. The `validate_gpu_based` setting is set to receive the `debugPrintEXT` values (`GPU_BASED_DEBUG_PRINTF`) and the `printf_to_stdout` setting (set to `VK_FALSE`) specifies we don't want those values to go to `stdout`; we want to receive them in the callback.

4. We create instances of the `VkLayerSettingEXT` structure for each setting we would like to change. Here, we are changing the following settings of the `layer_name` layer: `debug_action`, `validate_gpu_based`, and `printf_to_stdout`:

```
const array<VkLayerSettingEXT, 3> settings = {
  VkLayerSettingEXT{
    .pLayerName = layer_name.c_str(),
    .pSettingName = "debug_action",
    .type = VK_LAYER_SETTING_TYPE_STRING_EXT,
    .valueCount = 1,
    .pValues = setting_debug_action.data(),
  },
  VkLayerSettingEXT{
    .pLayerName = layer_name.c_str(),
    .pSettingName = "validate_gpu_based",
    .type = VK_LAYER_SETTING_TYPE_STRING_EXT,
    .valueCount = 1,
    .pValues = setting_gpu_based_action.data(),
  },
  VkLayerSettingEXT{
    .pLayerName = layer_name.c_str(),
    .pSettingName = "printf_to_stdout",
    .type = VK_LAYER_SETTING_TYPE_BOOL32_EXT,
    .valueCount = 1,
    .pValues = setting_printf_to_stdout.data(),
  },
};
```

5. Then we add those settings to an instance of the `VkLayerSettingsCreateInfoEXT` structure:

```
const VkLayerSettingsCreateInfoEXT
  layer_settings_ci = {
    .sType =
      VK_STRUCTURE_TYPE_LAYER_SETTINGS_CREATE_INFO_EXT,
    .pNext = nullptr,
    .settingCount =
      static_cast<uint32_t>(settings.size()),
    .pSettings = settings.data(),
};
```

6. Finally, we add this instance to the `pNext` chain of the `VkInstanceCreateInfo` structure used to create the Vulkan instance:

```
const VkInstanceCreateInfo instanceInfo = {
  .sType = VK_STRUCTURE_TYPE_INSTANCE_CREATE_INFO,
```

```
        .pNext = &layer_settings_ci,
        ...
};
VK_CHECK(vkCreateInstance(&instanceInfo, nullptr,
                          &instance_));
```

When enabled for *Chapter 1, Vulkan Core Concepts,* code in the repository, the message received by the callback looks something like this:

```
Validation Information: [ WARNING-DEBUG-PRINTF ] | MessageID =
0x76589099 | vkQueueSubmit():  gl_VertexIndex = 1
```

It is possible to enable a verbose output, in which case the preceding message would look like this:

```
Validation Information: [ WARNING-DEBUG-PRINTF ] Object 0: handle =
0x26e6bf17bd0, type = VK_OBJECT_TYPE_QUEUE; | MessageID = 0x76589099 |
vkQueueSubmit():  Command buffer (Command buffer:  0)(0x26e6c6613b0).
Draw Index 0. Pipeline (Graphics pipeline: )(0x26e78d000d0). Shader
Module (Shader Module: )(0x26e73b68450). Shader Instruction Index =
92.  gl_VertexIndex = 1 Debug shader printf message generated at line
21.
21:     outColor = vec4(colors[gl_VertexIndex], 1.0);
```

Hopefully, this feature will help you write tests for obscure corners of your code that weren't even possible to test before.

Measuring performance in Vulkan with timestamp queries

Measuring the performance of CPU and GPU workloads side by side is invaluable. The **Tracy profiler** allows you to do just that in a cross-platform way with minimal intrusion. And it's easy to use, all within a small C++ library.

In this recipe, you will learn how to integrate Tracy Profiler into your app and instrument it to collect GPU performance information.

Getting ready

The first thing to do is to download Tracy from `https://github.com/wolfpld/tracy` and include it in your project. You should also download the Tracy client/server to collect and inspect the data.

How to do it…

Instrumenting your code to use with Tracy is easy and requires only a few steps. To be able to collect data about the GPU performance, you will need a Tracy/Vulkan context along with a dedicated command buffer for it to calibrate the timestamps. After that, instrumenting your code is straightforward:

1. First, include the Tracy header file in your application:

    ```
    #include <tracy/Tracy.hpp>
    #include <tracy/TracyVulkan.hpp>
    ```

2. Second, you need a Tracy/Vulkan context that can be created by using a macro provided by the Tracy library. There are two options: one that creates a context with calibrated timestamps and one that creates a context without calibrated timestamps. Vulkan provides ways to correlate the time an operation happened on timelines of different time domains. Without calibration, Tracy can only guess when an operation on the device happened in relation to the ones that took place on the CPU. Here's how you can initialize the context that better suits your needs:

    ```
    VkPhysicalDevice physicalDevice;
    VkDevice device;
    int graphicsQueueIndex;
    VkCommandBuffer commandBuffer;
    #if defined(VK_EXT_calibrated_timestamps)
    TracyVkCtx tracyCtx_ = TracyVkContextCalibrated(
      physicalDevice, device, graphicsQueueIndex,
      commandBuffer,
      vkGetPhysicalDeviceCalibrateableTimeDomainsKHR,
      vkGetCalibratedTimestampsKHR);
    #else
    TracyVkCtx tracyCtx_ = TracyVkContext(
      physicalDevice, device, graphicsQueueIndex,
      commandBuffer);
    #endif
    ```

    The command buffer used here is a dedicated one and it should not be shared with any other operations.

3. Collecting GPU information is now easy. All you must do is use one of the macros provided by Tracy, such as the following:

    ```
    TracyVkZone(tracyCtx_, commandBuffer, "Model upload");
    ```

    Note that the `commandBuffer` variable used in this macro is the command buffer you wish to capture data from, the one being recorded. This command buffer is *different* than the one provided during the construction of the Tracy context.

This macro should be added whenever you would like to instrument your GPU execution. For example, you might want to add this macro to a scope where you issue the draw call (such as `vkCmdDraw`). You will then get information about that command being processed in the GPU. In the repository, you can find examples of how this macro is used.

4. Tracy also provides macros that allow you to identify the zone with a color or name, such as `TracyVkNamedZone`, `TracyVkNamedZoneC`, and so on.

   Occasionally, you need to tell Tracy to collect the timestamps from the command buffer by calling `TracyVkCollect`. This macro can be called at the end of a frame:

   ```
   TracyVkCollect(tracyCtx_, commandBuffer);
   ```

5. After exiting the render loop, and before shutting down your application, you need to destroy the Tracy context by calling `TracyVkDestroy`:

   ```
   TracyVkDestroy(tracyCtx_);
   ```

6. The last step is to build your project with `TRACY_ENABLE` defined. If using CMake, you can do this by adding the following parameters when generating the project's build files:

   ```
   -DTRACY_ENABLE=1
   ```

   Now all you must do is compile your code and run it. Make sure to start the Tracy client beforehand and start a connection. The Tracy client will automatically detect your application and start collecting data once it starts.

   If you instrument your code to collect CPU data using Tracy, which you can do using macros such as `ZoneScoped`, `ZoneScopedC`, and so on, you will see the results side by side after collection. *Figure 9.7* shows the result of capturing one of the executables from *Chapter 2, Working with Modern Vulkan*. Note the CPU and GPU zones in the screenshot.

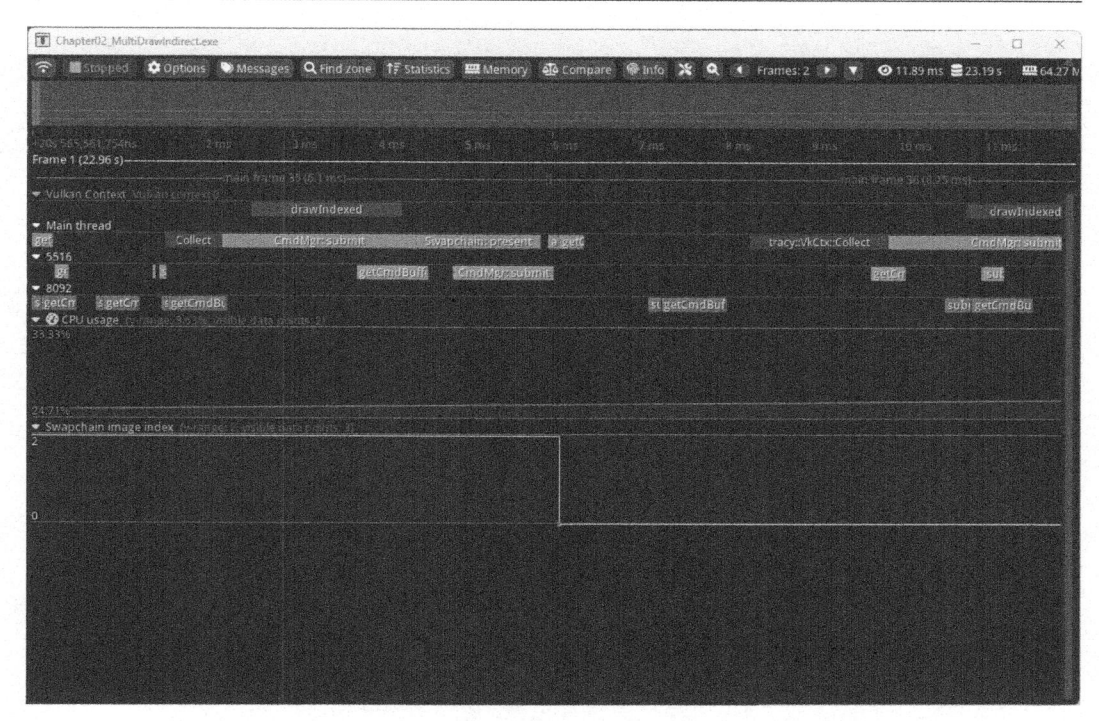

Figure 9.7 – Tracy profiler capture with GPU and CPU information side by side

Tracy is a very simple-to-use library that provides invaluable information about your application. It provides nanosecond resolution along with CPU and GPU performance tracking and is cross-platform. If you don't already have other performance-measuring libraries or facilities in your code base, Tracy can get you up and running in no time.

Index

A

acceleration structure 248
API functions
  calling 26-28
application render loop
  xrBeginFrame 273
  xrEndFrame 273, 281
  xrWaitFrame 273

B

bidirectional reflectance distribution function (BRDF) 244
bottom level acceleration structures (BLASs) 249
bounding volume hierarchy (BVH) 248
buffers
  creating 85-87
  data, uploading to 87-89

C

command buffers 48
  reusing 51-53
command pool
  creating 48, 49

commands
  allocating 49-51
  recording 49-51
  submitting 49-51
compute shaders
  used, for frustum culling 147-154
Cook-Torrance lighting model 177

D

data
  uploading, to buffers 87-89
data races
  avoiding, with ring buffers 90-92
debug information
  retrieving, from shaders 315-318
Deep Learning Super Sampling (DLSS) 215
  applying 237-241
  reference link 242
deferred rendering
  G-buffer, implementing 156-159
Depth-Peeling
  implementing 186-192
descriptor pool
  creating 106, 107
descriptor sets
  allocating 107, 108

specifying, with descriptor set layouts 101-104
updating, with rendering 108-111
Dual Depth-Peeling
implementing 192-201
dynamic foveated rendering
implementing, with Qualcomms fragment density map Offset extension 294-298
dynamic rendering
used, for adding flexibility to rendering pipeline 117, 118
dynamic state 66, 67

E

error checking
with Validation Layer 33, 34
Extended Reality (XR) 269
eye gaze information
retrieving, from OpenXR 287-294

F

Fast Approximate Anti-Aliasing (FXAA) 215
applying 219-229
fences 70
First In First Out (FIFO) 76
foveated rendering 283
fragment density map (FDM) 283
used, for implementing static foveated rendering 283-287
fragment shading rate 269
framebuffers
creating 59, 60

frame debugging 302-307
Frames Per Second (FPS) 269
frustum culling
with compute shaders 147-154

G

geometry buffer (G-buffer)
implementing, for deferred rendering 156-159
ghosting effect 230
glslang library
reference link 63
GPU-driven line rendering
implementing 126-132
GPU ray tracer 248
implementing 244-265
Monte Carlo method 247, 248
shader stages 249, 250
Graphics Library Transmission Format's (glTF) 263
graphics pipeline
creating 68, 69

H

half float 298
using, to reduce memory load 298-300
half floats 269
half-precision floating point 298
Head-Mounted Displays (HMDs) 269
high dynamic range (HDR) 256
hybrid rendering 243
implementing 265-268

I

images
 creating 95-97
 presenting 74
image view
 creating 60, 61, 97, 98
importance sampling 248
instance extensions
 enabling 36, 37
instance layer
 enabling 34-36
irradiance 246

L

Lambert's cosine law 264
lighting pass
 implementing, for illuminating scene 177-184
line-drawing techniques
 expanding, to render textual values from shaders 133-139
Linked-List Order-Independent Transparency
 implementing 201-208

M

Model View Projection (MVP) 167, 232, 283
Monte Carlo method 247, 248
Multi-Draw Indirect (MDI)
 implementing 113-115
Multisample Anti-Aliasing (MSAA) 215

N

Next Generation OpenGL (glNext) 25
normalized device coordinates (NDCs) 135, 168

O

OpenXR 270, 271, 272, 273, 274, 275-279
 eye gaze information, retrieving 287-294
 XrBeginFrame 270
 XrEndFrame 270
 XrInstance 270
 XrSession 270
 XrSpace 270
 XrSwapchain 270
 XrSystemId 270
 XrViewConfigurationType 270
Order-Independent Transparency (OIT) 201

P

Percentage closer filtering (PCF) 169
Peripheral Component Interconnect Express (PCI-E) 83
physical device extensions
 enabling 43, 44
physically based rendering (PBR) 263
pipeline barriers
 setting up 92-95
 types 94
pipeline layout
 creating 105, 106
pipeline state objects (PSOs) 66
Plug and Play (PnP) 34

probability density function (PDF) 248
Programmable Vertex Pulling (PVP) 63
  implementing 113
  using 115, 116
push constants
  updating, with rendering 111
  used, for pushing data to shaders 104, 105

Q

Qualcomms fragment density map Offset extension
  used, for implementing dynamic foveated rendering 294-298
queue families
  properties, caching 41, 42
  reserving 44, 45
  resources, transferring between 118-123
queue object handle
  retrieving 47, 48

R

radiance 246
radiant intensity 246
radiometry 246
  irradiance 246
  radiance 246
  radiant intensity 246
rasterization 244
ray tracing 243
real-time shadows
  shadow maps, implementing 164-170
RenderDoc 302
  reference link 302
rendering equation 246, 247
  reference link 247

rendering pipeline
  flexibility, adding with dynamic rendering 117, 118
render pass
  creating 53-59
resources
  transferring, between queue families 118-123
ring buffers
  used, for avoiding data races 90-92
Russian Roulette 246

S

sampler
  creating 99, 100
scene
  illuminating, by implementing lighting pass 177-184
Schlick's approximation 179
screen space ambient occlusion (SSAO)
  implementing 172-176
  reference link 177
screen space reflection (SSR)
  implementing 159-163
  references link 164
semaphores 70
shader
  behavior, customizing specialization constants 112, 113
shader binding table (SBT) 254
shader data
  descriptor pool, creating 106, 107
  descriptor sets, allocating 107, 108
  descriptor sets, specifying with descriptor set layouts 101-104
  descriptor sets, updating during rendering 108-111

Index

passing, with push constants 104, 105
pipeline layout, creating 105, 106
providing 100, 101
push constants, updating with rendering 111
resources, passing to 111
shaders
  compiling, to SPIR-V 63-66
shader stages
  intersection shader 248
  miss and hit shader 248
  ray generation shader 248
shader storage buffer (SSBO) 100
shadow mapping
  technique, limitations 171
shadow maps
  implementing, for real-time shadows 164-170
Signed Distance Fields (SDF)
  used, for drawing text 139-147
single pass multiview rendering 269
  implementing 281-283
SPIR-V 63
  used, for compiling shaders 63-66
staging buffer
  creating 89, 90
Standard Portable Intermediate Representation V (SPIR-V) 24
static foveated rendering
  implementing, with fragment density map (FDM) 283-287
submission information for presentation
  populating 73
surface
  creating 39, 40
swapchain 69
  synchronization 70-72
synchronization
  in swapchain 70-72

T

Tail Blending 208
Temporal Anti-Aliasing (TAA) 215
  utilizing 229-236
text
  drawing, with SDF 139-147
textual values from shaders
  rendering, to expand line-drawing techniques 133-139
timestamp queries
  used, for measuring Vulkan performance 318-321
top level acceleration structures (TLASs) 249
Tracy profiler 318
transparency techniques
  handling 213
triangle
  rendering 74-80

V

validation layer
  messages, intercepting 313-315
  using, for error checking 33, 34
velocity 230
Virtual Reality (VR) 270
VMA library
  instantiating 84, 85
Volk 30
  reference link 30
  using, to load Vulkan extensions 30, 31
  using, to load Vulkan functions 30, 31
Vulkan API 25
Vulkan Configurator 315
Vulkan device (VkDevice) 29
Vulkan extensions
  loading, with Volk 30, 31

using 31-33
Vulkan functions
  loading, with Volk 30, 31
Vulkan graphics pipeline 61, 63
Vulkan instance
  initializing 38, 39
Vulkan logical device
  creating 46, 47
Vulkan objects
  creating 308-310
  learning 28, 29, 30
Vulkan performance
  measuring, with timestamp queries 318-321
Vulkan physical devices
  enabling 40, 41
Vulkan shaders
  values, printing 310-312
Vulkan's memory model 82-84
  types 83
Vulkans MSAA
  enabling 216-219
  using 216

W

watts per square meter per steradian (W/m^2/sr) 246
watts per square meter (W/m^2) 246
watts per steradian (W/sr) 246
Weighted Order-Independent Transparency (WOIT)
  implementing 208-212
  reference link 213

<packt>

packtpub.com

Subscribe to our online digital library for full access to over 7,000 books and videos, as well as industry leading tools to help you plan your personal development and advance your career. For more information, please visit our website.

Why subscribe?

- Spend less time learning and more time coding with practical eBooks and Videos from over 4,000 industry professionals
- Improve your learning with Skill Plans built especially for you
- Get a free eBook or video every month
- Fully searchable for easy access to vital information
- Copy and paste, print, and bookmark content

Did you know that Packt offers eBook versions of every book published, with PDF and ePub files available? You can upgrade to the eBook version at packtpub.com and as a print book customer, you are entitled to a discount on the eBook copy. Get in touch with us at customercare@packtpub.com for more details.

At www.packtpub.com, you can also read a collection of free technical articles, sign up for a range of free newsletters, and receive exclusive discounts and offers on Packt books and eBooks.

Other Books You May Enjoy

If you enjoyed this book, you may be interested in these other books by Packt:

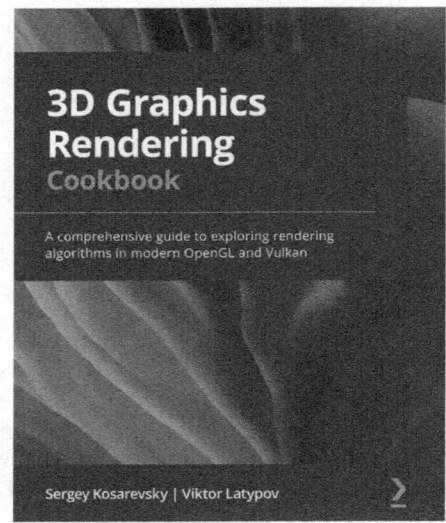

3D Graphics Rendering Cookbook

Sergey Kosarevsky | Viktor Latypov

ISBN: 978-1-83898-619-3

- Improve the performance of legacy OpenGL applications
- Manage a substantial amount of content in real-time 3D rendering engines
- Discover how to debug and profile graphics applications
- Understand how to use the Approaching Zero Driver Overhead (AZDO) philosophy in OpenGL
- Integrate various rendering techniques into a single application
- Find out how to develop Vulkan applications
- Implement a physically based rendering pipeline from scratch
- Integrate a physics library with your rendering engine

Mastering Graphics Programming with Vulkan

Marco Castorina | Gabriel Sassone

ISBN: 78-1-80324-479-2

- Understand resources management and modern bindless techniques
- Get comfortable with how a frame graph works and know its advantages
- Explore how to render efficiently with many light sources
- Discover how to integrate variable rate shading
- Understand the benefits and limitations of temporal anti-aliasing
- Get to grips with how GPU-driven rendering works
- Explore and leverage ray tracing to improve render quality

Packt is searching for authors like you

If you're interested in becoming an author for Packt, please visit `authors.packtpub.com` and apply today. We have worked with thousands of developers and tech professionals, just like you, to help them share their insight with the global tech community. You can make a general application, apply for a specific hot topic that we are recruiting an author for, or submit your own idea.

Share Your Thoughts

Now you've finished *The Modern Vulkan Cookbook*, we'd love to hear your thoughts! Scan the QR code below to go straight to the Amazon review page for this book and share your feedback or leave a review on the site that you purchased it from.

`https://packt.link/r/1-803-23998-0`

Your review is important to us and the tech community and will help us make sure we're delivering excellent quality content.

Download a free PDF copy of this book

Thanks for purchasing this book!

Do you like to read on the go but are unable to carry your print books everywhere?

Is your e-book purchase not compatible with the device of your choice?

Don't worry!, Now with every Packt book, you get a DRM-free PDF version of that book at no cost.

Read anywhere, any place, on any device. Search, copy, and paste code from your favorite technical books directly into your application.

The perks don't stop there, you can get exclusive access to discounts, newsletters, and great free content in your inbox daily

Follow these simple steps to get the benefits:

1. Scan the QR code or visit the following link:

    `https://packt.link/free-ebook/9781803239989`

2. Submit your proof of purchase.
3. That's it! We'll send your free PDF and other benefits to your email directly.

Made in the USA
Coppell, TX
25 August 2024